The Presidency in the Constitutional Order

The Presidency in the Constitutional Order

Edited by JOSEPH M. BESSETTE

and JEFFREY TULIS

LOUISIANA STATE UNIVERSITY PRESS

BATON ROUGE AND LONDON

Design: Albert Crochet
Typeface: VIP Bembo
Composition: G&S Typesetters, Inc.

Second Printing (February, 1982)

LIBRARY OF CONGRESS CATALOGING IN PUBLICATION DATA

Main entry under title:

The Presidency in the constitutional order

Chiefly papers from workshops held at the White Burkett Miller Center, University
of Virginia, 1977–1978.
Includes index.
1. Presidents—United States—Addresses, essays, lectures. I. Bessette, Joseph
M. II. Tulis, Jeffrey. III. White Burkett Miller Center.
JK516.P65   353.03′1   80-14250
ISBN 0-8071-0774-3
ISBN 0-8071-0781-6 pbk.

To the memory of
HERBERT J. STORING (1928–1977)
who worked tirelessly to keep an idea alive:
that the serious study of our constitutional foundation
is indispensable for understanding American politics

Contents

Preface

A recent report to the Ford Foundation on the state of scholarship on the American presidency calls attention to the "strong revival" of the public-law approach, with its emphasis on the constitutional powers and obligations of the president.[1] The collection of new studies presented here aims to contribute to the contemporary debate on the constitutional presidency. Unlike most recent works of this type, however, this book is authored by political scientists, not law professors. Accordingly, it evidences the political scientist's concern with structures as well as powers, with conflict between the branches of government as well as the functional separation, and with political prescription as well as legal analysis. Underlying the entire volume is a persistent attention to the nature of executive power and its particular manifestation in the American system.

In Part One the design and principles of the Constitution are delineated. Joseph Bessette and Jeffrey Tulis begin the volume by identifying the predominant approaches to the study of the presidency. Illustrating how the gap between the "legal" and "political" modes of analysis can be bridged, they suggest that constitutional analysis may be indispensable to an adequate description of political behavior while also serving as the source of standards for evaluating presidential conduct. A factor inhibiting the full development of the constitutional approach to the study of the presidency has been the great number and variety of interpretations of the Constitution since its framing. This has made it easy to assume that the Constitution has no single and enduring meaning. One of the earliest and most famous disagreements over the constitutional presidency was between James Madison and Alexander Hamilton. In their respective essays Ruth and Stephen Grant and Harvey Flaumenhaft articulate Madison's and Hamilton's theories of the Presidency and show how significant disagreement on important points can nevertheless rest on a common foundation of agreement on fundamental principles. The contributions to this volume mirror the character of that earlier debate. Like Madison and Hamilton, the authors here begin with the assumption that the Constitution has an enduring meaning, seek to discern its principles, share a common approach, yet disagree on some specific interpretations.

The six essays in Part Two address prominent issues in the contemporary political and scholarly debate. In the lead essay Robert Scigliano assesses the constitutionality of the War Powers Act of 1973, the high-water mark of Congress' efforts to ensure that American involvement in military hostilities would result from the collective judgment of Congress and the president. Scigliano examines the extent to which this landmark legislation follows the plan of the Constitution in providing pragmatic checks on the exercise of military power by the president, but without so constraining him as to prevent necessary emergency actions. Gary Schmitt follows with a reconsideration of another point of controversy from the Nixon years: the right of a president to withhold information from Congress or the public. Schmitt's analysis reaches conclusions opposed to those of Raoul Berger, whose influential argument holds that executive privilege is a constitutional myth. The third essay of this group, by Murray Dry, deals with an issue which has only recently become a public controversy: Congress' use of the so-called legislative veto to invalidate actions taken by the executive branch. President Carter publicly attacked the propriety and constitutionality of legislative vetoes and threatened to ignore them. Indeed, most recent presidents have opposed at least some forms of the legislative veto. Dry argues, however, that although this device is not specifically sanctioned in the Constitution, it is consistent with the broader principles on which the Constitution rests.

The final three essays address issues which are usually not examined in their broader constitutional context. It is well known, for example, that the modern presidential selection system bears little resemblance to the electoral college scheme devised by the framers of the Constitution in 1787. James Ceaser shows, however, that throughout much of its history the party-based system inaugurated in the Jacksonian era has worked remarkably well in fulfilling the purposes of the original constitutional design. Ceaser suggests that these purposes have been jeopardized by the reforms of the past decade and that this may have deleterious consequences for the American political order. One of the more prominent arguments that undercuts the constitutional approach to the study of the presidency is that the functioning of the executive office is less influenced by its structure and powers than by the personality of its occupant. In his analysis of the leading statement of this view, that presented by James David Barber in *The Presidential Character*, Jeffrey Tulis discusses the limitations of the personality approach and suggests several empirical and normative benefits of constitutional analysis overlooked by personality theorists. In the final essay of the volume Harvey Mansfield, Jr., maintains that much of the contemporary scholarly debate on the presidency reflects disagreement over the meaning of "executive power" in the United States Constitution. He argues that there is an older doctrine that explains both the "weak" and "strong" aspects of executive power. An understanding of this doctrine is necessary to comprehend the nature of the constitutional presidency.

The entire volume is dedicated to Herbert J. Storing, who, at the time of his death, was director of the Program on the Presidency at the White Burkett Miller Center of Public Affairs, University of Virginia. For nearly two decades, Storing taught graduate courses on the presidency and other aspects of American politics at the University of Chicago, where he had an immense influence upon a large number of students. Many of the authors of these essays were his students and the rest were colleagues and friends. It is our hope that this work measures up to the standards set by him.

This volume would not have been possible without the initial support and encouragement of Frederick E. Nolting, who served as the first director of the White Burkett Miller Center of Public

Affairs at the University of Virginia from 1975–1978. His successor, Kenneth W. Thompson, was most helpful in guiding publication of the work. Most of the articles in this volume began as papers delivered at Miller Center workshops during the fall of 1977 and the spring of 1978. The others were specifically commissioned by the center for inclusion in this volume. We thank the center for its generous support throughout the preparation of this work. Part of one study, James Ceaser's "Presidential Selection," originally appeared in the *Journal of Politics*, XL (August, 1978), 708–41. We gratefully acknowledge the permission to reprint it here. Finally, we wish to thank Shirley Kingsbury, secretary at the Miller Center, for her diligence in typing the drafts and her extraordinary patience with authors and editors who seemed to be constantly preparing yet more revisions.

Joseph M. Bessette and Jeffrey Tulis

NOTE TO PREFACE

1. Hugh Heclo, *Studying the Presidency: A Report to the Ford Foundation*, August 1977, pp. 18–19.

PART ONE: *Foundations*

I

The Constitution, Politics, and the Presidency

JOSEPH M. BESSETTE and JEFFREY TULIS

It was not long ago that a large portion of the political and scholarly community proudly shared the view that our government was presidential government. It was widely believed that the dynamics of American politics virtually guaranteed a compatibility between presidential policy and the highest goals of the American regime, that what was good for the presidency was good for the country. The administrations of two strong presidents, Lyndon Johnson and Richard Nixon, however, effectively shattered the consensus on these points. In the wake of sustained public criticism of what appeared to be unfettered executive power, scholarship on the nation's highest office has entered a new period characterized by dissatisfaction with the settled views of the recent past and a renewed attention to the problems posed by executive power for constitutional government.

Although the current reconsideration of the role and purposes of the executive branch is unprecedented in scope, much of the recent literature is in fact a manifestation of a mode of analysis that was given classic expression nearly four decades ago in what was for many years the standard text on the presidency: Edward Corwin's *The President: Office and Powers*. Corwin described his work as "primarily a study in American public law." Its central theme was "the development and contemporary status of presidential power and of the presidential office under the Constitution." The study begins with an analysis of the executive office as established by the Constitutional Convention in 1787, goes on to examine the legal and constitutional development of the office since its inception, and ends with a call for institutional reforms to check "a history of [presidential] aggrandizement." Not sur-

prisingly, much of the study is an examination of the legal doctrines promulgated by the federal courts. In his final edition Corwin cites over 250 judicial decisions. The clear import of his
analysis is that the modern presidency threatens to break free
from constitutional restraints, that this poses a serious danger for
American democracy, and consequently that a regeneration of respect for constitutional principles and norms is called for. However beneficial presidential leadership might be in specific instances, Corwin suggests, an unfettered executive power is the
antithesis of constitutionalism.[1]

Around the time that the last edition of *The President: Office and
Powers* was published (1957), Corwin's work was both substan-
tively and methodologically at odds with far-reaching developments in scholarship on American politics. One of these was the
increasing extent to which political scientists were turning their
attention away from formal rules and procedures to focus instead
on actual political behavior, which, it was argued, was little influenced by laws and constitutions. In the field of presidential studies this new orientation was given its most articulate and influential expression in Richard Neustadt's *Presidential Power: The
Politics of Leadership*. Neustadt's subject was the "power problem"
faced by every president: "From the moment he is sworn the man
confronts a personal problem: how to make those powers work
for *him*. That problem is the subject of this book. My theme is
personal power and its politics: what it is, how to get it, how to
keep it, how to use it." Neustadt emphasized that the formal authorities vested by the Constitution were not the main determinants of effectual presidential power: "*The probabilities of power do
not derive from the literary theory of the Constitution.*" Rather, a president's power "is the product of his vantage points in government,
together with his reputation in the Washington community and
his prestige outside." According to Neustadt some of these "vantage points" derive from the formal authorities vested by the
Constitution, thus "formal power" is indispensable to a president's "personal influence." Although Neustadt conceded this
much, what was truly distinctive about his approach was how
little it had to say about specific constitutional provisions. The
whole thrust of his analysis was to move us away from formal

authority in explaining actual presidential power; for distinctions of the sort employed in constitutional analysis seemed to him to have no effect on presidents: "The things [the president] personally has to do are no respecters of the lines between 'civil' and 'military,' or 'foreign' and 'domestic,' or 'legislative' and 'executive,' or 'administrative' and 'political.' At his desk—and there alone—distinctions of these sorts lose their last shred of meaning."[2]

While Neustadt was rejecting the Constitution as the most important source for understanding the actual exercise of presidential power, other students of American politics were rejecting constitutional analysis for a related but distinct reason: because, in their view, the principles of separation of powers and checks and balances, which lay at the heart of the American constitutional order, made it virtually impossible for American institutions to generate the political leadership necessary to meet contemporary national needs. The foremost proponent of this view was James MacGregor Burns. Reflecting a theme that dates back at least to the writing of Woodrow Wilson, Burns argued that the fear of arbitrary power and of majority tyranny so dominated the minds of the framers that they devised a political system that made any kind of effective political action extremely difficult, if not impossible, at least while constitutional forms were observed. To a large extent "our system was designed for deadlock and inaction."[3] For Burns and a host of other political scientists the way to get around the inherent limitations of the American constitutional system was twofold: to reform the American two-party system in the direction of more programmatic and more highly structured nationally based organizations, and to strengthen the institution of the presidency at the head of the majority party. Consequently, these political scientists recommended a variety of political reforms, some simply requiring voluntary changes on minor matters, some requiring new legislation at the state or national levels, and some mandating amendments to the Constitution. In the last category were proposals for a four-year term for members of the House of Representatives (and perhaps also for senators) synchronized with the presidential term, reform of the electoral college in favor of a more direct

popular election, and a reduction in the numbers of senators necessary to ratify a treaty from two-thirds to a simple majority.
Those who advanced these and other similar reforms implicitly
rejected several principles of the American constitutional order as
the proper standard for guiding American politics in the middle
of the twentieth century.[4]

As a result of the developments reflected in the works of Neustadt, Burns, and others, by the middle of the 1960s the constitutional or public-law approach was well out of the mainstream of
presidential studies. This began to change when Vietnam, Watergate, and other perceived abuses of presidential power led some
scholars to reject the predominant political approaches to the
study of the presidency because of their apparent lack of standards to limit presidential conduct and their implicit encouragement of executive branch aggrandizement. One result of this reaction was the resurgence of the public-law approach in a variety
of studies that attempted to judge presidential action against the
traditional standard of constitutionality.[5] In varying degrees the
authors of these studies turned to the document written in 1787,
to the original intention of its framers, and to the development of
constitutional doctrine throughout American history for a set of
standards against which to judge the legitimacy of presidential
actions and on the basis of which to curb future abuses. Although
these studies have been valuable in reminding us that executive power unconstrained by law is a danger to republican government, they suffer from the same kinds of limitations that
characterized the earlier constitutional approach to the study of
American politics. First, they are of little help in explaining why
political leaders behave the way they do: the connection between
constitutional forms and political practice is largely undeveloped.
Second, they are particularly weak at demonstrating why the
constitutional standards that derive from the document drafted in
1787 should be embraced as a guide for contemporary politics.

It should be noted that most of the contributors to the new
public-law studies have been law professors rather than political
scientists.[6] This is one reason why these studies are not centrally
concerned with explaining political behavior. Moreover, a mode
of analysis which focuses on questions of legality cannot in itself

determine whether greater political benefits will derive from strict adherence to the existing fundamental law or perhaps from its alteration or even rejection. In the post–Watergate period legalists have forcefully argued that our national well-being will be enhanced if we reinvigorate the principles of the American Constitution. Such prescriptions, however, are derived not from legal analysis per se but from political reasoning and political judgment.

Of course political scientists have also contributed to the current reconsideration of presidential power. Several new works have appeared which, like the public-law studies, are highly critical of the earlier "textbooks" on the presidency for emphasizing political effectiveness over public responsibility.[7] They differ from these earlier political studies not so much in method or approach as in their call for a more accountable or democratic presidency. As with the new constitutional studies, their purpose is to establish a set of principles or guidelines that will bring executive power under control. Contrary to the public-law approach, however, these principles are not sought primarily through a reconsideration of the nature of the American constitutional design, but rather derive largely from assessments of recent administrations.

As a result, the constitutional and political approaches are now effectively divorced. The legalists seem unable or unwilling to show how constitutional interpretation is relevant to understanding contemporary political behavior. The political scientists seem susceptible to the charge that it was the emancipation of presidential studies from a concern with legal and constitutional restraints that implicitly encouraged the abuses of executive power that we have recently witnessed, and that newly devised standards for restraining presidents have an unsatisfactory ad hoc quality to them and cannot match the long-term effectiveness of constitutional safeguards.

We contend that contemporary presidential scholarship is ill served by this divergence between the legal and political approaches—a divergence that stems, perhaps, from agreement on one central point. Whether praising the actions of Franklin Roosevelt or castigating those of Richard Nixon, it is generally implied by legalists and political scientists alike that the most interesting aspects of these presidencies lie outside or beyond the constitutional order. That is to say, the explanation of the inner workings or the real "stuff" of recent presidential politics is to be found elsewhere than in the legal or constitutional sphere. While the legalists certainly want to get the presidency back under the Constitution, thereby implying that the Constitution could limit presidential behavior, and while political scientists concede that the Constitution is an indispensable source of actual political power, neither makes a serious attempt to explain how constitutional forms mold political behavior. We can begin to bridge the gap between the legal and political approaches by reconsidering the various ways in which political forms may influence political practice.

THE CONSTITUTION AND POLITICAL BEHAVIOR

No argument poses a greater challenge to the pertinence of constitutional analysis to the study of the contemporary American presidency than the charge that this nearly two-century-old document has little if any impact on present practice, in either the legal or political sphere. As one contemporary observer states:

> The historical Constitution remains an honored relic, preserved intact in the National Archives. It is a symbol of the nation, much like the flag. In a secular society such as the United States, it is a substitute for God. The ancient Document is worshipped, and vested with mystery and authority and seeming power that no parchment could ever have.[8]

Political scientists in particular tend not to attach much explanatory weight to the Constitution in their accounts of American politics—either because they believe that 190 years of social, economic, and technological change have rendered the original arrangements obsolete, or because in their view constitutional forms never have much more than a tenuous relationship to practice. Nonetheless most students of contemporary politics would at least concede that the United States Constitution establishes the parameters for political conflict, or serves as the arena in which that conflict works itself out. In effect the Constitution sets forth the "rules of the game" for the players in American politics, rules that are not comprehensive, unambiguous, or universally adhered to, but rules on which there is such widespread consensus among the American people that their flagrant violation is not readily tolerated (at least outside of national emergency situations). The Watergate controversy illustrates the point well. It is a constitutional rule that a president may be removed from office when a majority of the House of Representatives accuse him of, and two-thirds of the Senate convict him of, "Treason, Bribery, or other high Crimes and Misdemeanors." This rule had lain dormant for a century and serious constitutional scholars had come to judge it a dead letter. Yet Congress resuscitated the relevant twenty-one words of the founding document when circumstances seemed to call for it. A mark of the force of the rule is that there was no serious issue whether Nixon would peaceably step down after possible conviction by the Senate. This seems to have been assumed by all. And certainly this attachment to constitutional principle extended to the civilian and military employees of the executive branch, few of whom, it seems safe to speculate, would have taken orders from the "president" after a conviction vote by the Senate. There *was* some thought that Nixon would refuse to comply with an order of the Supreme Court to turn over incriminating tapes. Especially significant is the fact that even a constitutional rule not explicitly set forth in the document itself and which had been the subject of some controversy earlier in our history—namely that the president must comply with the directives of the Supreme Court respecting the interpretation of his own powers—even this rule was so widely accepted during the Watergate period that many believed that Nixon's refusal to comply would itself be sufficient to ensure conviction and removal from office.

Extraordinary times have a way of bringing constitutional issues to the fore; ordinary times are as much influenced by constitutional rules and procedures, but because that influence is regular and pervasive it is less noticed. For example, the constitutional mandate that members of the House must run for reelection every two years and senators every six years, that membership in the two branches be based on different principles of representation, that the Senate must consent to treaties and appointments, or that every bill passed by Congress must go to the president for a possible veto—these are all part of the "rules of the game" that affect everyday politics. In a wide variety of ways political actors are forced to accommodate their behavior to generally accepted constitutional requirements.

It often happens, however, that the constitutional status of a proposed action, especially one to be taken by the president, is ambiguous. May a president constitutionally refuse to spend all the money appropriated by Congress if massive budget deficits pose a severe inflationary threat? May he constitutionally refuse to fulfill a congressional request for sensitive information related to national security matters? May he constitutionally employ the armed forces without statutory authorization to protect Americans overseas? In cases like these presidents are invariably led to defend their actions as consistent with the principles of the constitutional system. These public explanations or justifications are often dismissed by scholars as mere rhetoric, attempts to give a cover of legitimacy to actions which have their source in political calculations rather than constitutional analysis. What is often overlooked, however, is that the necessity to find some constitutional grounds for questionable political acts may itself influence the selection or character of the actions. Although the influence of explanation on political decision making has not been thematically addressed by students of the American presidency, several congressional scholars have recently argued that voting decisions made by United States congressmen may be influenced by their judgment as to whether these actions can be successfully defended to their constituents.[9] If this is true on ordinary policy matters, it is likely to be true when constitutional issues are at stake. It follows that the written document may mold political behavior by forcing presidents and congressmen to give serious thought to the constitutional propriety of anticipated actions, even if they have no personal constitutional scruples per se.

At times it may even happen that the resolution of a political conflict will be more influenced by constitutional rhetoric, however insincere, than by the policy dispute or personal motive that gave rise to the controversy. For example, it is well known that Nixon had long-standing partisan differences with Congress over the proper distribution of the federal budget. To resist congressional direction, Nixon occasionally resorted to impounding funds, that is, to refusing to spend appropriated monies. He justified his actions not simply by arguing the merits of specific bills (regarding sewage treatment plants, educational programs, highways, etc.), but also by taking a higher road, arguing that the president had a special constitutional responsibility for the well-being of the whole nation and that only his office was properly structured to oversee the entire federal budget. Politically it mattered little whether these reasons were accurate reflections of Nixon's motives or were disingenuously contrived after the policy decision was made. Whichever the case, Congress was forced to respond to them. Although the partisan disputes over who got what, when, and how from each of the controversial bills have since been forgotten, the institution of a more responsible congressional budget process in the Congressional Budget Act of 1974 is indicative of the long-term effect of the constitutional rhetoric.

Of course there is nothing in the nature of constitutional rhetoric that prevents it from being a sincere expression of personal beliefs. We must take seriously the possibility, without belittling alternative explanations, that in some cases political actors may be moved by their own independent judgment of constitutional principle. The Constitution itself requires that all those who serve under it "shall be bound by Oath or Affirmation, to support this Constitution"; and it imposes on the president the special obligation "faithfully [to] execute the office of President of the United States, and . . . [to] preserve, protect and defend the Constitution of the United States." Although these injunctions alone are not sufficient to guarantee fidelity to the Constitution, they do reflect the principle that the successful functioning of the constitutional system requires the firm attachment of the officers of government to the principles of the fundamental law.

The issue then is whether a political actor's independent understanding of the Constitution influences his behavior. Questions of this type are often relegated to studies of the Supreme Court, the thought being that the Court's authority of judicial review frees presidents and congressmen to subordinate constitutional to political considerations. It is important to note that historically this view has not characterized the thinking of many of this country's prominent political leaders. Jefferson, Jackson, and Lincoln all shared the strong belief that presidents and congressmen had an obligation to give full consideration to the constitutional dimensions of their actions, that they were not free simply to pass the buck to the Supreme Court. Jackson put the point clearly in his veto of the bill to recharter the Bank of the United States:

> The Congress, the Executive, and the Court must each for itself be guided by its own opinion of the Constitution. Each public officer who takes an oath to support the Constitution swears that he will support it as he understands it, and not as it is understood by others. It is as much the duty of the House of Representatives, of the Senate, and of the President to decide upon the constitutionality of any bill or resolution which may be presented to them for passage or approval as it is of the supreme judges when it may be brought before them for judicial decision.[10]

Although Jackson went further than Jefferson and Lincoln in suggesting that the president was not obligated to follow the Supreme Court's interpretation of the Constitution, all three agreed that the members of the political branches must engage in constitutional analysis.

Because Americans now have a greater tendency to defer to the Supreme Court on constitutional matters, it may be thought that presidents and congressmen do not bother much with constitutional questions when deliberating on policy issues. Yet in thinking about our recent political history, is it possible to understand fully Congress' reassertion of its authority against the president during the past decade without recognizing this as a conscious effort to recover the proper constitutional status of the legislative body in American politics? Would Congress, for example, have been led to undertake a major reform of the budget process in 1974 (Congressional Budget and Impoundment Control Act) if it had not been clear to Congress that de facto presidential preeminence in setting budgetary priorities and in impounding appropriated funds violated the constitutional distribution of powers? In the equally important reform of the previous year intended to limit the president's war-making powers (War Powers Resolution), Congress explicitly stated its desire to recover the constitutional design in the legislation itself: "It is the purpose of this joint resolution to fulfill the intent of the framers of the Constitution of the United States." And later the legislation sets forth Congress' understanding of the "constitutional powers of the President as Commander in Chief to introduce United States armed forces into hostilities." [11] There may be reasons for questioning the accuracy of Congress' interpretation of the Constitution; but this doesn't belie the very strong evidence that the major participants in Congress were influenced by a constitutional understanding.

Apart from a political actor's conscious effort to act in ways consistent with either his own or the public's understanding of constitutional rules, procedures, or principles, there is another more subtle and perhaps more pervasive way in which the document written nearly two centuries ago continues to influence American politics. This is through the effect that the institutions created by the Constitution have in molding the behavior of those who serve in public office. Investigating the principles that underlie the structure of these institutions may elucidate important aspects of their current functioning. For example, one of the principal fears when the Constitution was drafted was that the nonlegislative institutions of American government would lack the independence necessary to resist encroachments from the body of the people's representatives (a lesson learned from the state experience during the Confederation period). In the case of the presidency the solution was to so construct the office that the occupant would have both the personal incentive and the means to stand up to Congress when the constitutional balance was threatened. This meant structuring the executive office to make it institutionally independent of Congress (by a nonlegislative mode of election and a salary that could not be raised or lowered during the president's term); giving the president the means to block legislation that encroached on his office (qualified veto); and making the office weighty enough to generate personal efforts by its occupant to protect its constitutional status (four-year term, indefinite reeligibility, and significant powers). The extraordinary success of this element of the original design has been largely overlooked, yet the historical record demonstrates that even the so-called "weak presidents," presidents who were unwilling or unable to compete with Congress for the direction of national policy, have vigorously defended the prerogatives of the executive office when thought to be threatened by congressional action.[12] Perhaps the most striking case was the adamant opposition of James Buchanan (usually regarded as among the weakest of the weak presidents and cited by Teddy Roosevelt as the ministerial or messenger-boy president *par excellence*) to what he took to be an improper investigation into the conduct of the executive branch by the House of Representatives in 1860: "Except in [cases of impeachment]," he protested to the House, "the Constitution has invested the House of Representatives with no power, no jurisdiction, no supremacy whatever over the President. In all other respects he is quite as independent of them as they are of him. As a coordinate branch of the Government he is their equal. . . . He will defend [the people] . . . to the last extremity against any unconstitutional attempt, come from what quarter it may, to abridge the constitutional rights of the Executive and render him subservient to any human power except themselves."[13] This hardly reflects the accepted historical assessment, derived from the first Roosevelt, that Buchanan held "the narrowly legalistic view that the President is the servant of Congress rather than of the people."[14]

If the "weak" and "strong" presidents are as one in the desire to preserve the constitutional independence of the executive office, they differ unmistakably in their impact on public policy, a difference which is at least partly attributable to personal inclinations. Some presidents seem clearly to have conceded congressional supremacy in policy making; others have spared little effort to move the country and the Congress in the direction they have thought wise. American political history has been punctuated in an irregular way by presidents of the latter type: Jefferson, Jackson, Polk, and Lincoln in our first century; the two Roosevelts, Wilson, Kennedy, Johnson, and Nixon in the past century. The emergence of such activist presidents appears more the result of accident or chance than the manifestation of systemic factors. A reconsideration of the constitutional design indicates, however, that two particular provisions play a large role in inclining presidents to exercise their powers in a positive way to promote their policy aims.

In the Federalist Papers Alexander Hamilton identified these as the substantial (four-year) term of office and the opportunity a president has to succeed himself. Together these would give the president "the inclination and the resolution to act his part well" and would provide "the community time and leisure to observe the tendency of his measures and thence to form an experimental estimate of their merits." The prospect of reelection would encourage the president to undertake projects in the public interest and the four years between elections would ensure that he had "time enough . . . to make the community sensible of the propriety of the measures he might incline to pursue." Further discussion in *The Federalist* shows that the reelection provision was also intended to encourage even those occupants of the executive office who might lack the wisdom and virtue of the ideal type to act in ways conducive to the public good. "An avaricious man," for example, "who might happen to fill the office" will want to do a creditable enough job to be reelected, even if only to continue to satisfy his avarice. Similarly, an "ambitious man . . . seated on the summit of his country's honors" will want to act in ways to merit reelection in order "to prolong his honors." At the peak of the hierarchy of passions is "the love of fame, the ruling passion of the noblest minds." The institution of the presidency accommodates even this passion by making it possible for the president "to plan and undertake extensive and arduous enterprises for the public benefit, requiring considerable time to mature and perfect." If these projects are successful, the president earns enduring fame from future generations.[15]

As we have seen, not all presidents have striven to promote "extensive and arduous [public] enterprises." Some have been content to carry out a much more limited function in the American governmental system. If, as we have argued, the Constitution has a real molding effect on presidential behavior, how can we explain the obvious differences between a Buchanan and a Lincoln, the first Roosevelt and his successor Taft, or a Hoover and an FDR? One reason for these sharp contrasts is suggested by the above quotations from *The Federalist*: the presidency is by constitutional arrangement such a highly personalized office that it will necessarily reflect the particular virtues (and vices), talents, passions, and goals of its occupant. Consequently, we would expect the functioning of the executive office throughout American history to manifest some of the variety in human types characteristic of those who have served in high political office in the United States. There will not, however, be a simple or direct relationship between personality and the exercise of presidential power. Once he assumes office a new president will be subject to an independent set of influences rooted in the constitutional order. While these influences may have varying impacts on different presidents, for all they will shape the potentialities of executive power in American government. Before this can be more fully elucidated, we must examine in greater detail the nature of executive power under the United States Constitution.

EXECUTIVE POWER AND AMERICAN
CONSTITUTIONALISM

To many contemporary observers the recent history of presidential power has been characterized by the violation of one of the central principles of American constitutionalism: the need to channel and restrain the exercise of executive power through a fabric of law. As Louis Fisher concludes in *The Constitution Between Friends: Congress, the President, and the Law*: "The general drift of authority and responsibility to the President over the past two centuries is understandable. This trend by itself should not be cause for alarm. More threatening is executive authority cut loose from legislative moorings and constitutional restrictions— presidential action no longer tethered by law." [16] On this point most of those who have contributed to the resurgence of the public-law approach to the study of the presidency seem to agree. Whether the issue is the president's control over the military forces, his refusal to provide information to Congress, or his failure to spend money appropriated by the legislative branch, in nearly all cases the conclusion is reached that the president has acted outside the legal framework which was established to govern the exercise of political power in the national government.

Effective legal restraints seem particularly necessary to limit that power of government which is intrinsically least subject to internal checks, that is, to the procedural safeguards of discussion, deliberation, and consensus building which moderate the exercise of judicial and legislative power.

This absence of formal internal checks on the exercise of executive power in American government is no accident. The architects of the presidential office consciously rejected a plural executive or one checked by an executive council in order to ensure that the presidency would possess those capacities which, they believed, characterized every well-constructed executive branch: decision, activity, secrecy, and dispatch.[17] While these qualities enable the holder of the executive power to act with speed and decisiveness when need arises, legal and constitutional restraints on the exercise of power may inhibit the executive's ability to take actions he deems necessary. Consequently, the very qualities which make for an effective executive (and therefore effective government generally) contribute also to the tension between executive power and the law. We are led to the curious conclusion that in the kind of office it created the Constitution itself contributes to the difficulty of constitutionally directing and restraining presidential power.

We can begin to make sense of this fact by realizing that the Constitution not only restrains, it also empowers. It assigns broad responsibility to the executive branch of government—command of the armed forces, pardoning power, nominating the principal officers of government, the veto, and recommending measures to Congress—and then makes these the possession of a single individual so that they might be exercised in a direct and forceful way. Neither a timid grant of power nor internal checks were the means chosen by the framers to prevent abuses and usurpation by the executive branch. This was not because they were unmindful of the dangers of an unchecked executive, but because there was an alternative means of control which less jeopardized governmental effectiveness. This means was twofold. First, as discussed above, the framers designed the executive office so that the occupant would have a positive incentive to act responsibly. Second, they created competing structures of power which would have both the inclination and the means to oppose aggrandizement by any one branch. The institutions of government would be so carefully constructed and the distribution of powers so artfully contrived that as the members of the several branches acted to promote their own interests they would serve, as it were, as "sentinel[s] over the public rights."[18]

Presidential power, for example, would become a threat to popular liberties when the executive overreached his own legitimate sphere of authority. In most cases, however, this would involve an encroachment on the constitutional sphere reserved to Congress or the Supreme Court. Because the members of these branches have a personal stake in the power and status of their institution they could be expected to fight improper presidential designs. This kind of institutionalized conflict would be much more effective in preventing governmental abuse than "parchment barriers," mere constitutional prohibitions of the type that failed to preserve political balance in the state constitutions during the revolutionary period.[19] And equally important, this scheme frees the president to make effective use of the executive power in the first instance, reserving to Congress and the Court the opportunity to act subsequently to restrain the exercise of executive power if they judge it an encroachment on their own spheres. So viewed, the constitutional design positively encourages presidential initiative (balanced by the fact that on many matters Congress or the Court will have final say).

This brief discussion suggests that in neither the structure of the office, the grant of powers, nor the provision for controls is the United States Constitution unfriendly to the exercise of executive power. On the contrary, it is striking how far the framers went to make the fundamental law hospitable to executive power. In this their actions conform to their broader purpose to fashion a Constitution fully adequate to national needs. In *The Federalist* Hamilton argued that the new government "ought to be clothed with all the powers requisite to complete execution of its trust" and that "it is both unwise and dangerous to deny the federal government an unconfined authority in respect to all those objects which are intrusted to its management." The danger of establishing a government incapable of achieving its proper ends is that in any struggle between "parchment provisions" and "public necessity" necessity will invariably win out. When certain actions are demanded by the force of events, political leaders will take them whether or not constitutionally authorized to do so. History proves that:

> Nations pay little regard to rules and maxims calculated in their very nature to run counter to the necessities of society. Wise politicians will be cautious about fettering the government with restrictions that cannot be observed, because they know that every breach of the fundamental laws, though dictated by necessity, impairs that sacred reverence which ought to be maintained in the breast of rulers towards the constitution of a country, and forms a precedent for other breaches where the same plea of necessity does not exist at all, or is less urgent and palpable.

A constitution which is not comprehensive enough to meet the dangers posed by extraordinary circumstances will soon lose, through the precedent of disobedience, much of its restraining force in more ordinary times. A properly framed constitution, then, must embrace two distinct and seemingly conflicting characteristics. On the one hand it must assure that "a power equal to every possible contingency . . . exist[s] somewhere in the government." On the other hand, it must genuinely channel, moderate, and restrain governmental power in normal circumstances.[20]

The adequacy of the constitutional system to meet the demands of necessity is most severely challenged during periods of armed conflict. Military emergencies place great strains on constitutional governments, strains which in the American system are focused particularly on the presidency. The problem is whether that branch of government encharged with "directing and employing the common strength" can be granted the means and flexibility to meet the common danger without subverting the original constitutional balance.[21] In 1866 the United States Supreme Court for the first time addressed the problem of whether and how constitutional restraints should be preserved during periods of military emergency. The issue presented to the Court in *Ex parte Milligan* was whether a civilian citizen of Indiana could be lawfully executed for treasonous activities by order of a military tribunal acting under authority of the president after the cessation of hostilities. In issuing a writ of habeas corpus for Milligan's release from custody, the Court held that "it is the birthright of every American citizen when charged with crime, to be tried and punished according to law" and consequently that military authority could not lawfully supersede civilian authority "where the courts are open and their process unobstructed." To allow otherwise would place in jeopardy "the rights of the whole people" by violating one of the fundamental principles of American constitutionalism:

> The Constitution of the United States is a law for rulers and people, equally in war and in peace, and covers with the shield of its protection all classes of men, at all times, and under all circumstances. No doctrine, involving more pernicious consequences, was ever intended by the wit of man than that any of its provisions can be suspended during any of the great exigencies of government. Such a doctrine leads directly to anarchy or despotism, but the theory of necessity on which it is based is false; for the government, within the Constitution, has all the powers granted to it, which are necessary to preserve its existence; as has been happily proved by the result of the great effort to throw off its just authority.[22]

In holding that the Constitution extends its protection to "all classes of men, at all times, and under all circumstances," the court appears to deny martial law any trace of legitimacy. Yet, later in the same opinion the Court maintains that "there are occasions when martial rule can be properly applied":

> If, in foreign invasion or civil war, the courts are actually closed, and it is impossible to administer criminal justice according to law, *then*, on the theatre of active military operations, where war really prevails, there is a necessity to furnish a substitute for the civil authority, thus overthrown, to preserve the safety of the army and society; and as no power is left but the military, it is allowed to govern by martial rule until the laws can have their free course. As necessity creates the rule, so it limits its duration; for, if this government is continued *after* the courts are reinstated, it is a gross usurpation of power. Martial rule can never exist where the courts are open, and in the proper and unobstructed exercise of their jurisdiction.

The Constitution itself, of course, authorizes the suspension of the privilege of the writ of habeas corpus "when in Cases of Rebellion or Invasion the public Safety may require it." The Court is not fully clear on the distinction between the suspension of the writ of habeas corpus and "martial rule," but the controlling principle seems to be the following: the suspension of the writ of habeas corpus authorizes the limited action of arresting and holding dangerous individuals during periods of rebellion or invasion, even when the civil authority remains unobstructed; martial rule, on the other hand, includes a much wider range of activities—virtually whatever is necessary "to preserve the safety of the army and society"—but may only be instituted when the necessity is "actual and present; the invasion real, such as effectually closes the courts and deposes the civil administration."[23]

Although the Constitution makes explicit provision regarding the writ of habeas corpus, it says nothing about martial law. If the Court's doctrine that none of the provisions of the Constitution "can be suspended during any of the great exigencies of government" is to be maintained, then we must conclude that the institution of martial law in the limited circumstances described by the Court has implicit constitutional sanction. Otherwise, how could it be said that the government under the Constitution "has all the powers . . . necessary to preserve its existence?"

Necessity, then, the Court suggests, can make constitutional actions which would not be legitimate in normal circumstances. This is essentially the justification Lincoln presented for the extraordinary actions he took throughout the Civil War: "I felt that measures, otherwise unconstitutional, might become lawful, by becoming indispensable to the preservation of the Constitution, through the preservation of the nation."[24] Lincoln's point was not that "'the constitution is different in time of insurrection or invasion from what it is in time of peace and public security,'" but rather that "the constitution is different, *in its application* in cases of Rebellion or Invasion, involving the Public Safety, from what it is in times of profound peace and public security."[25] The clearest sign of this is the Habeas Corpus Clause, but Lincoln also recurred to the Commander-in-Chief Clause, the Take Care Clause, and the presidential oath to support the argument that the Constitution itself authorizes the president to take certain actions to meet military necessities which would not be lawful in the absence of a grave danger to the nation.[26] In justifying as constitutional extraordinary actions necessary to the preservation of the nation, both Lincoln and the Court in the Milligan case present a view of American constitutionalism consistent with Alexander Hamilton's description of the new order as fully adequate to meet the demands of necessity. However, if Hamilton, Lincoln, and the Court were fearful of the precedent of going outside the Constitution when the nation's well-being was jeopardized, others have argued that on balance the constitutional order is less threatened when the extraordinary actions demanded by extraordinary circumstances are not given the color of law. The most comprehensive contemporary statement of this view is to be found in one of the leading recent works on the presidency, Arthur Schlesinger, Jr.'s *The Imperial Presidency*.[27]

Schlesinger recognizes that there are times when the president must undertake actions to protect the nation's security which are not authorized during normal circumstances: "The question of necessity cannot be burked. Crises threatening the life of the nation have been happily rare. But, if such a crisis comes, a president must act." Such action, Schlesinger urges, should be clearly identified and recognized for what it is: an extra-constitutional resort to raw political power, necessary but not lawful. To try to defend the exercise of this emergency power on constitutional grounds is to threaten to stretch the Constitution all out of shape and thus to give it a malleability that will undermine the restraints it should regularly place on the exercise of political power. Schlesinger's view, then, shifts the issue from one of constitutional interpretation—does the document written in 1787 authorize the specific actions that appear to be necessary at any particular time to the preservation of the nation—simply to a determination whether a true national emergency exists. If there is "a clear, present and uncontestable danger to the life of the nation," then the Constitution may be temporarily set aside and the requisite actions undertaken. The legitimacy of presidential action appears to depend primarily on the seriousness of the danger. On this criterion, Schlesinger argues, both Lincoln during the Civil War and Franklin Roosevelt before and during the Second World War were justified in undertaking strictly illegal actions, but not Truman in the seizure of the steel mills, or Nixon during the Watergate period.[28]

Schlesinger bases his argument on the theory of executive prerogative presented by John Locke in Chapter 14 of his *Second Treatise of Government*, a work, he notes, with which the founding fathers were well acquainted. Locke's main point is that strict obedience of the law by the executive may at times be harmful to the community and therefore there should be reserved to the executive the "power to act according to discretion, for the public good, without the prescription of the Law, and sometimes even against it." [29] Schlesinger translates this into the American context to mean that "the President . . . [must] be conceded reserve powers to meet authentic emergencies." To assert otherwise would be to hold that it is "better to lose the nation than to break the law." Fully cognizant, however, of the dangers of unfettered executive discretion, Schlesinger maintains that "emergency prerogative cannot properly be invoked on presidential say-so alone but only under stringent conditions, both of threat and of accountability, with the burden of proof resting on the President." In the Epilogue to the 1974 edition of his work Schlesinger summarizes "the criteria that alone warrant presidential resort to emergency prerogative":

1. there must be a clear, present and uncontestable danger to the life of the nation
2. the President must define and explain to Congress and the people the nature of this threat
3. the perception of the emergency, the judgment that the life of the nation is truly at stake, must be broadly shared by Congress and by the people
4. time must be of the essence; waiting for normal legislative action must constitute an unacceptable risk
5. existing statutory authorizations must be inadequate, and Congress must be unwilling or unable to prescribe a national course
6. the problem must be one that can be met in no other way than by presidential action beyond the laws and the Constitution
7. the President must report what he has done to Congress, which will serve as the judge of his action
8. none of the presidential acts can be directed against the political process itself

This list makes clear that the justification for presidential exercise of emergency prerogative depends not simply on the nature of the threat to the nation's well-being, as first appeared, but also on how broadly and accurately that threat is recognized by the body politic. If the danger is not "clear" and "uncontestable," if the "perception of the emergency" is not "broadly shared by Congress and the people," if there is ample time for "normal legislative action" to be undertaken, or if Congress is willing and able "to prescribe a national course" contrary to the president's assessment of the national exigencies—if any of these conditions apply when a president undertakes strictly illegal actions believed by him to be essential to the nation's very survival, then such a president, according to Schlesinger's criteria, acts improperly and without warrant.[30]

The problem with this argument is that it contradicts the essential logic of the justification for prerogative in the first place. Certain actions, though strictly illegal, may occasionally be necessary to preserve the nation; the preservation of the nation is a greater good than perfect fidelity to the letter of the law. In principle what justifies prerogative is simply the factual situation, the nature of the danger, not how clearly that danger is perceived by the citizenry or their representatives in Congress. Certainly it is possible that in a given case the president might have a more accurate perception of the common danger than Congress or the people. Indeed many would say that this was so in the United States in the years just before our entry into the Second World War. Are we to conclude that in this situation a president should forego the actions judged by him to be essential to our survival?

The necessity which justifies prerogative cannot support "stringent conditions" controlling its exercise. This is because, as Locke makes clear, the exercise of prerogative depends finally on the discretion or judgment of the executive: "the good of the Society requires, that several things should be left to the discretion of him, that has the Executive Power." We do not fully understand the issue of prerogative until we recognize the radical nature of the original concession. According to Locke, law *qua* law is intrinsically incapable of fully realizing the public good; consequently, personal discretion—which, of course, the law was designed expressly to replace ("a government of laws and not of men")—must be given leeway to operate. If this discretion by its nature operates outside the sphere of law, how can it be restrained? Or must we simply trust the good intentions of the executive? Locke suggests that the only way to control prerogative, once the principle of the thing is granted, is through a public judgment after the fact, perhaps after a series of measures that create an "inconvenience . . . so great, that the majority feel it, and are weary of it, and find a necessity to have it amended." The executive's accountability to the public for his actions (and the public's ultimate right to revolution) is the only proper check on prerogative. This check, however, is not introduced procedurally in the midst of the action (as Schlesinger's conditions would have it), but operates only when enough time has passed that the consequences of the action can be accurately assessed.[31]

One could say that the United States Constitution effectually institutionalizes a version of this principle by its openness to and even encouragement of presidential initiative balanced by the ability of Congress and the Court to act decisively after the fact to endorse or oppose presidential actions. Opposition can take the form of judicial or legislative mandate, the denial of funds, and finally impeachment and removal from office. The Milligan case discussed above is a pertinent example. With the cessation of hostilities and therefore any possible justification for martial law, the court quite vigorously reasserted the primacy of civil law (and of the federal judicial system) in matters regarding personal rights. Similarly, in its fundamental reforms of 1973 and 1974 in the areas of war powers and impoundments Congress forcefully demonstrated its willingness and ability to reassert its role if it determines that the president has abused the freedom to undertake actions beyond his strict constitutional authority.

The decisive fact is that under the United States Constitution the functioning of the coordinate institutions of American government is not suspended nor is their authority dissolved (as would be the case under a fully consistent theory of prerogative as extra-constitutional) when the president undertakes extraordinary actions. Retaining their constitutional status, Congress and the courts have a voice in determining the scope and duration of the president's special powers. Whether the president will abide by the opinion of these institutions will depend on the degree to which the public regards their activity as legitimate. Because the

Constitution is the source of authority for the actions of Congress and the courts, as well as of the president, this public sense of legitimacy will be more effectively supported by a view, like Lincoln's, which relies on the Constitution to meet emergency needs, than by a view which would have presidents go outside the Constitution; for when presidents adopt and articulate an *extra*-constitutional view of prerogative, they foster a public attitude that the Constitution must be "set aside" during emergencies, thereby undermining the claim of Congress and the courts to moderate presidential power.

All of this is not to say that the Constitution solves the problem of accommodating executive discretion to the rule of law. By its nature the problem is incapable of a full resolution. Although the exercise of emergency prerogative is a rare occurrence, we have tried to show that it most clearly reveals the more general tension between discretion and law. A fabric of law is necessary to control the abuses of power so common to political life; but that same law, if rigidly adhered to, can prevent the actions vital to the welfare of the community. The task which confronts us is to find the best practical answer to this insoluble problem. We suggest that a constitutional arrangement that allows for a substantial degree of executive initiative and discretion within a framework of political checks is more effective and less dangerous than a set of arrangements that so constrains and restricts the executive power that it renders it incapable of carrying out its proper tasks or makes it necessary to set aside the Constitution to do what the good of the community requires. Thus the principles that underlay the particular provisions of the original Constitution may serve as standards for evaluating contemporary practice.

CONCLUSION

Several decades ago when presidential power was held in higher esteem than it now is, most students of the presidency believed that a vigorous and energetic executive branch was essential to this nation's well-being. More recently we have been reminded of the need for limits on the exercise of presidential power. Effectiveness and safety are the poles between which scholarly reflections and public attitudes will continue to oscillate. We have tried to show that these poles were, and continue to be, an intrinsic part of the American constitutional order.

It is often said that the United States Constitution virtually guaranteed an unending conflict or struggle between the political branches of American government. However, this was not simply because the Constitution assigned the political powers to two distinct institutions; for with some small changes in the executive provisions the Constitution could have resulted in a presidency decidedly subordinate to Congress. The abolition of the veto, a reduction in terms of office to one year, and the institution of presidential selection by Congress would surely have been sufficient to deny the occupant of the executive office the will and the means to thwart congressional predominance over American government. And as the specific language of the document written in 1787 has given rise to conflict between the political branches, so has it influenced its nature and its scope. The Constitution's qualified veto, for example, ensures that with rare exceptions Congress must make some accommodation to strongly held policy views of the president. Conversely, other constitutional provisions determine that presidents must generally give serious consideration to senatorial views on treaties and appointments. Although the Constitution does not lack ambiguity, it is clear enough on many specific points to define the arena and fashion the weapons of congressional-presidential conflict. And when the boundaries of power are not clear, legally questionable actions by the president or Congress quickly precipitate a constitutional debate, bringing the focus again to the meaning of the fundamental law. Consequently, much of the "political" conflict between president and Congress occurs within a horizon of law.

This conflict generally sets something like the upper limit to the exercise of executive power in American government. Representatives and senators will not long tolerate what appears to them to be an usurpation of their prerogatives by the president, even when they agree with him on basic policy direction. It is this dynamic that gives the language of the Constitution, its specific distribution of powers between Congress and president, a real weight in influencing the reach of presidential power. And if congressional assertiveness usually puts a ceiling on presidential power, it is *presidential* assertiveness that determines the floor. Both illustrate the Constitution's effectiveness in attaching the interests of the officeholder to the rights and duties of the office. At his least assertive the constitutional chief executive is firmly committed to preserving the independence and integrity of the executive branch, takes his responsibilities seriously as commander-in-chief and as director of our foreign relations, and does not shrink from fashioning and recommending legislative proposals or from vetoing what he judges to be unwise measures passed by Congress.

Although this constitutional floor and ceiling are not unbreachable barriers, they do constitute the range within which presidential power will generally operate. It is remarkable that throughout American history even the "weak" presidents have nearly always measured up to the minimal constitutional standards, while the "strong" presidents have been so well checked that for only a few very brief periods has American government been tantamount to one-branch government. This means, then, that the Constitution eliminates a wide variety of types of executives known to us from the historical record and from contemporary practice in other nations. As long as the Constitution remains effective, the president will not be reduced to the status of a city manager or a mere figurehead, nor will he achieve the power of a despot or tyrant.

We do not mean to deny the importance of political skill, public popularity, or historical circumstance in contributing to the successes or failures of particular presidents at particular times. Each of these will help to explain the functioning of the executive office, but without radical transformation of the system they will not drastically alter the broad probabilities of presidential power. Nor do we mean to suggest that such transformations are impossible, that under no circumstances could an especially skilled and popular president, anxious to promote his own power or some uncompromising view of the public good, undermine the constitutional safeguards and subvert the separation of powers and checks and balances system. The most effectual checks on such a design will come initially from the willingness of representatives, senators, and federal judges to fight to uphold the constitutional balance; but the ultimate check will come from the attachment of the people to constitutional principle. These will be fostered by a presidential scholarship which focuses attention on the constitutional order, which is sensitive to the difference between the Constitution and a strict legal code, and which recognizes the sometimes uneasy blending of effectiveness and safety characteristic of our fundamental law.

NOTES TO CHAPTER I

1. Edward Corwin, *The President: Office and Powers* (4th ed.; New York: New York University Press, 1957, orig. pub. 1940), vii, 307. For a full understanding of Corwin's theory of the presidency one should not overlook the excellent collection of his essays in *Presidential Power and the Constitution*, ed. Richard Loss (Ithaca, N.Y.: Cornell University Press, 1976).

2. Richard Neustadt, *Presidential Power: The Politics of Leadership* (New York: John Wiley & Sons, 1960), Preface, 43, 179, 35, 183. See also the preface to the 1976 edition, "Reflections on Johnson and Nixon."

3. James MacGregor Burns, *The Deadlock of Democracy* (Englewood Cliffs, N.J.: Prentice-Hall, 1963), 6.

4. See, for example, Burns, *Deadlock of Democracy*, 327–32, and Louis Koenig, "More Power to the President" in Robert Hirshfield (ed.), *The Power of the Presidency* (2nd ed.; Chicago: Aldine, 1973), 362.

5. The following are the most important: Raoul Berger, *Executive Privilege: A Constitutional Myth* (Cambridge, Mass.: Harvard University Press, 1974); Raoul Berger, *Impeachment* (Cambridge, Mass.: Harvard University Press, 1973); Louis Fisher, *President and Congress* (New York: Free Press, 1972); Louis Fisher, *The Constitution Between Friends: Congress, the President, and the Law* (New York: St. Martin's Press, 1978); Louis Henkin, *Foreign Affairs and the Constitution* (New York: W. W. Norton, 1972); Phillip Kurland, *Watergate and the Constitution* (Chicago: University of Chicago Press, 1978); Abraham D. Sofaer, *War, Foreign Affairs and the Constitution: The Origins* (Cambridge, Mass.: Ballinger Publishers, 1976).

6. The principal exception is Louis Fisher.

7. See particularly Thomas Cronin, *The State of the Presidency* (Boston: Little, Brown, 1975); Thomas Cronin and Rexford Tugwell, *The Presidency Reappraised* (New York: Praeger, 1977); Erwin Hargrove, *The Power of the Modern Presidency* (Philadelphia: Temple University Press, 1974); and the third edition of Louis Koenig's, *The Chief Executive* (New York: Harcourt Brace Jovanovich, 1975).

8. Arthur S. Miller, *Presidential Power in a Nutshell* (St. Paul, Minn.: West Publishing Co., 1977), 323.

9. John Kingdon, *Congressmen's Voting Decisions* (New York: Harper and Row, 1973), 46–53. Richard Fenno, Jr., *Home Style: House Members in Their Districts* (Boston: Little, Brown, 1978), 136–70.

10. James D. Richardson (ed.), *A Compilation of the Messages and Papers of the Presidents, 1789–1897* (10 vols.; Washington: U.S. Government Printing Office, 1896–1899), II, 582.

11. Public Law 93–148, 87 Statutes at Large 555 (1973).

12. One of the few scholars of the presidency who has noticed this fact is James Mac-Gregor Burns in *Presidential Government* (Sentry Edition; Boston: Houghton Mifflin, 1973, orig. pub. 1965), 108.

13. Richardson (ed.), *Messages and Papers of the Presidents*, V, 615.

14. Theodore Roosevelt, *An Autobiography* (New York: Macmillan, 1913), 395. For a brief discussion of other examples of forcefulness on the part of "weak" presidents see Joseph M. Bessette, "The Presidency," in George J. Graham and Scarlett G. Graham (eds.), *Founding Principles of American Government* (Bloomington, Ind.: Indiana University Press, 1977), 205–207.

15. Alexander Hamilton, James Madison, and John Jay, *The Federalist Papers*, ed. Clinton Rossiter (New York: New American Library, 1961), No. 72, p. 436; No. 71, p. 434; No. 72, pp. 437–38. Instructive on this last point was President Nixon's dramatic effort to improve relations with China and the Soviet Union. Arthur Burns, chairman of the Federal Reserve Board during the Nixon Administration, assessed Nixon's actions this way: "'He's a president now. . . . He has a noble motive in foreign affairs to reshape the world, or at least his motive is to earn the fame that comes from nobly reshaping the world. Who can say what his motive is? But it's moving him in the right direction.'" Quoted in William Safire, *Before the Fall* (New York: Belmont Tower Books, 1975), 524.

16. Fisher, *The Constitution Between Friends*, 247.

17. *Federalist* No. 70, p. 424.

18. *Ibid.*, No. 51, p. 322.

19. Cf. Charles C. Thach, Jr., *The Creation of the Presidency, 1775–1789* (Baltimore: Johns Hopkins Press, 1969; orig. pub. 1923), 25–54.

20. *Federalist*, No. 23, pp. 153–54, 156; No. 25, p. 167; No. 26, p. 170.

21. Quoted *ibid.*, No. 74, p. 447.

22. *Ex parte Milligan*, 4 Wallace 2, 119, 121, 118, 120–21 (1866).

23. *Ibid.*, 127.

24. Letter to Albert G. Hodges, April 4, 1864, in Roy P. Bassler (ed.), *The Collected Works of Abraham Lincoln* (9 vols.; New Brunswick, N.J.: Rutgers University Press, 1953), VII, 281.

25. Letter to Matthew Birchard and others, June 29, 1863, *ibid.*, VI, 302.

26. See, for example, Lincoln's letter to James C. Conkling, August 26, 1863, *ibid.*, VI, 408; Message to Congress in Special Session, July 4, 1861, *ibid.*, IV, 430, 440; and First Inaugural Address, March 4, 1861, *ibid.*, IV, 265, 270.

27. Arthur Schlesinger, Jr., *The Imperial Presidency* (New York: Popular Library, 1974). Prior to the publication of this book Schlesinger was well known as a proponent of a strong presidency. But in his recent rethinking of presidential power, Schlesinger returned quite explicitly to the Constitution and to founding-era documents for standards with which to assess the growing power of the modern presidency. See pages 13–14 and 447.

28. *Ibid.*, 310, 450. A somewhat ambiguous case is Jefferson's actions during the Burr conspiracy. Schlesinger appears at times to defend the extraordinary measures taken by Jefferson (p. 36), but he also recognizes that these actions did not meet the standards he sets down to distinguish proper from improper uses of prerogative. See the discussion below.

29. John Locke, *The Two Treatises of Government*, ed. Peter Laslett (Rev. Ed.; New York: New American Library, 1960). All references are to the standard paragraph numbers of the *Second Treatise*. The quote is at No. 160.

30. Schlesinger, *Imperial Presidency*, 309, 450, 450–51.

31. Locke, *Second Treatise*, No. 159, No. 168.

II

The Madisonian Presidency

RUTH WEISSBOURD GRANT

and STEPHEN GRANT

J ames Madison came to the Constitutional Convention
with a clear understanding of the qualities to be desired in the executive of a republican government, but uncertain as to how
those qualities could best be achieved through a constitutional
framework.[1] He saw in the creation of the presidency an opportunity to provide a partial solution to problems inherent in republican government. Republican government is preeminently a
government of laws and it must rest upon a foundation in a representative assembly.[2] But republican assemblies "give almost as
many proofs as they pass laws of the need of some . . . Assistance."[3] As he said in *The Federalist*, "Complaints are everywhere
heard . . . that our governments are too unstable, that the public
good is disregarded in the conflicts of rival parties, and that measures are too often decided . . . by the superior force of an interested and overbearing majority."[4] Madison's executive is intended to improve the laws and provide a corrective for these
defects, but without supplanting the legislature. In principle,
Madison was a partisan of neither the executive nor the legislature. His practical concern, however, was not that the executive
might be too strong for the legislature, but that in a republican
government, which tends to be dominated by its legislature, he
might not be strong enough. Moreover, the difficulty of creating
a strong republican executive was exacerbated by the fact that the
contemporary model for a strong executive was the monarch.
The problematic character of the presidency thus appears in the
need to create an executive capable of counteracting the worst
tendencies of republican legislatures, but firmly grounded in republican principles. Madison's solution emerges as an element of

31

his more comprehensive search for republican remedies for republican diseases.[5] By the time the Constitution was ratified, Madison had developed a distinctive and coherent conception of the American presidency that is impressive for its depth of understanding of the place of the presidency in the constitutional scheme.

But Madison does not come down to us as one whose writings or example we habitually look to when we wish to think about the presidency. One reason for this is that Madison's performance as president does not seem to exemplify a coherent conception of the proper uses of that office. He is generally considered to have been an ineffectual president, and there are good grounds for this assessment. However, Madison's tenure as president is more revealing of the transformations brought about by the development of political parties than it is of his original understanding of the presidency. By the time Madison was elected, the president was nominated by a party caucus, but Madison had developed his conception of the office as part of his general effort to curtail the influence of parties in republican government. For this reason, the presentation of Madison's understanding of the place of the presidency in the constitutional system will be followed by a brief consideration of that understanding in the light of the permanent introduction of parties into the operations of that system.

THE REPUBLICAN EXECUTIVE

Madison's initial thoughts on the executive occur in the context of his observations of republican legislatures. Both the states' experience with legislative supremacy and the national experience with legislative government under the Articles of Confederation exemplified the difficulty of providing in republican government the liberty, efficiency, and impartiality that are requirements of good government. With their eyes fixed upon a vision of danger from a hereditary monarch, and overconfident in the principle of representation, the people had forgotten that in republics it is the legislature against which they "ought to indulge all their jealousy and exhaust all their precautions."[6] Madison rediscovered the need for a strong executive as a precaution against the legislature.

The failures of legislatures appeared to have a partial corrective in a strengthened separation of powers. The national experience in the Confederation congress had demonstrated the need, in the interests of effective government, for a separation of powers that would place the executive function in the hands of independent personnel.[7] The state experience had demonstrated with equal power the weakness of mere "parchment barriers" in maintaining the separation of powers in practice, particularly against legislative encroachments on the executive. In order to preserve the separation, essential for the preservation of free government, a partial mixture of functions has to be admitted into the constitutional structure so that each branch has a defensive check on the others.[8] In addition, each branch must derive sufficient "weight" from an independent constitutional grant and an independent appointment to office to maintain a balance in the government. Adequate checks and balances maintain the separation of powers, and an adequate separation of powers improves the capacity of republican government for both efficiency and liberty by providing an independent executive. Separation of powers was originally understood as a check on the monarch in the interests of liberty.[9] In Madison's analysis, it becomes a check on the legislature in the interest of good government altogether.

The interferences of legislatures with execution of the laws had combined partiality with incompetence, but what was most egregious, republican legislatures had proved unable to do their proper work, lawmaking, competently and justly. Madison condemned the state legislatures, often dominated by majority factions, for the injustice of state laws.[10] That he was aware as well of the possibility of oppressive majorities in the national government is evident from his concern that a northern majority might sacrifice the southern and western interest in access to the Mississippi.[11] For the executive to serve as a check on such factions or parties he must be independent of and impartial between them.

Madison's executive thus needs a well-braced independence not merely for impartial and competent execution of the laws, but also in order to improve the work of lawmaking. Madison shows the importance of executive independence for both execution and legislation in his comments on the Continental Congress' practice of conducting foreign affairs directly, bypassing

the secretary of foreign affairs, John Jay. The obvious consequence of the practice is that it "seems to condemn their own establishment, to affront the Minister in Office, and to put on him a
label of caution agst. that respect and confidence of Ministers of
foreign powers, which are essential to his usefulness." Madison
added: "I have always conceived the several ministerial departments of Congress, to be provisions for aiding their counsels as
well as executing their resolutions, and that consequently whilst
they retain the right of rejecting the advice which may come
from either of them, they ought not to renounce the opportunity
of mak[ing] use of it." Thus not merely the executive but also the
legislature needs executive independence, for when the legislature interferes with execution it deprives itself of an essential element of its deliberations, executive advice.[12]

On the basis of his appraisal of legislative capacities Madison
concluded that the first requirement for a republican executive
is independence from the legislature in the interest of good government. Madison then had to show that an independent executive strong enough to serve this purpose could be made subject to
republican controls without sacrificing his independence and
strength. The second requirement for a republican executive is
responsibility to popular control.

Republicans may be convinced that their government needs
improvement without at the same time being convinced that a
strong executive is a safe improvement. Madison addresses his
argument to republican fears when he asks whether the need for
stable and energetic government, which requires duration and
unity in office, can be made compatible with liberty, which according to jealous republicans requires frequent elections and a
numerous representation.[13] This is a special problem for the executive, who is the institutional culmination of stability and energy in the government and also a favorite object of republican
jealousy. Such jealousy inspired various constitutional proposals
for a plural executive, for a short term, or for executive weakness
to the point of dependence on the legislature.[14] Republicans become jealous on behalf of their liberties when they come to fear
that their representatives will be unfaithful to them. Madison undertakes to relax their jealousy by showing that a strong execu-

tive can be matched by the people's capacity to judge and thus control their government.[15] The people can deliberate adequately in elections, and they can do so because they are sufficiently capable of both appreciating what they need and judging what they get. Madison shows the possibility of transcending republican jealousy and thus justifies republican government by showing how it can simultaneously be made to fit the people's deliberative capabilities and include a strong executive.

Jealous republicans think that they control government best by keeping it close to themselves, so they compel their representatives to return frequently to them, and they multiply their representation in order to make it more like themselves. Their thought is that if representatives are made frequently responsible or accountable to the people in elections, they will behave faithfully (we would say "responsibly") in office, and that if their representation is expanded to include popular elements it will be prevented from becoming oligarchic. They think the natural tendency of representation is to oligarchy rather than incapacity; but their typical corrections of the supposed tendency increase both incapacity and the possibility of oligarchy in government. The shorter the term, "the greater the proportion of new members and the less the information of the bulk of the members," and "the larger the number, the greater will be the proportion of members of limited information and weak capacities." At close quarters, representatives as politically inexperienced and impressionable as the people they represent are exposed to being too easily led and misled by a small number of talented men who have made themselves "masters of the public business." Laws may then be made and decisions engineered by a few, to be voted up by the others as their own. This is oligarchy under democratic cover and shows that when republican principle is shaped by republican jealousy, as in a numerous and frequently changed representation, it can easily yield consent without control. A numerous representation comes to be similar in this respect to the ancient democratic assemblies. Democratization leads to oligarchy at the point at which the people enter government, as they do in effect when their representatives merely mirror their vulnerabilities and as they do literally in direct democracy. When the people try to rule directly, they are in fact ruled by others; democracy is strictly speaking impossible. Representation appears in a new light when one sees that the people are incapable of ruling: "the total exclusion of the people in their collective capacity" from government through representation, which Madison calls the true distinction between republics and democracies, excludes the people from being excessively implicated in rule, in effect from uncontrolled rule by others. Popular politics can only be a politics of control and not of rule because the people's only political capacity is a capacity for control.[16]

Paradoxically, the causes of popular control and energetic government have more in common than jealous republicans think. The people in fact control government best when they stand at a respectable distance from government. This is because the people judge best not in the event but when the results of a measure or policy have become clearly visible. Those things they try to judge immediately are either long-term measures, which cannot be judged well because the final result of such measures is not yet visible, or they are measures that are accessible because they have singly "an immediate, detached, and palpable operation" but for the same reason contribute least to the "collective and permanent welfare." In the best case, the people elect capable men who are sufficiently informed to judge future possibilities; they are themselves informed by visible results and can judge government well enough on the basis of this information. But when the people deprive themselves of this information, the capacity of representatives for good or ill may not be matched by the people's best capacity for judgment. The people may then be misled by measures more brilliant than lasting, if not worse.[17]

This analysis of the people's deliberative capacities makes clear that both popular control and official energy are improved by duration of the executive in office, as well as by executive unity. Madison deepens the understanding of responsibility by asking what it is for, and answers that it is for the successful completion of necessary tasks as well as for honesty. A single executive serves responsibility by making the executive himself visible, so the people know whom to blame. But they will not know what to blame him for if the results of a necessarily gradual "chain of measures" are not visible.[18] In this way, duration in office completes or perfects executive responsibility.

The institutional arrangements for executive energy do not threaten, indeed they improve, executive responsibility. Responsibility to popular control provides some security against the sacrifice of the general good to the private interest of the executive. This is the danger that was most prominent in the minds of republicans who saw in a strong executive a reflection of monarchy, and it is the characteristic danger of monarchy. But a more serious problem for the executive in a republic arises from the characteristic danger of republican government, that one part of the society may sacrifice the rights and interests of another.

Madison poses the problem by comparing the two extremes of the interested majority and the self-interested monarch in the context of his general concern with securing impartial government.[19] Good government must be impartial in two respects. It must be neutral between contending parties of legitimate interests in the society, and it must prevent self-interested men in government or factions of such men from pursuing their own interests to the detriment of the general good. The monarchic danger is mitigated in hereditary monarchy by the ruler's personal stake in the nation. The republican danger is less prominent in monarchies because the monarch is independent of any partial interest in society and has sufficient "weight" from a "settled preeminence" to check a legislative faction or party.[20] The problem is how best to achieve these advantages in a republican, and hence elective, executive. The republican mechanism for responsibility, election, may threaten the capacity of the executive to check factions or parties. If the election of the executive should establish a connection between the executive and a party in the legislature or among the people, his usefulness as a check would be destroyed. Nonpartisanship, the third requirement for a republican executive, can be secured only if the election of the executive can be kept nonpartisan.

But if the executive is too powerful or too controversial, he may become the object of party contests in a way reminiscent of elective monarchy.[21] Madison accepted the common understanding that elective monarchy was the "worst kind" of monarchy,

because the prize was so great and so much rested upon the outcome that monarchic elections tended inevitably to be occasions
for "tumults" or even civil war.[22] "The powers should be confined and defined—if large we shall have the evils of elective
Monarchies."[23] The executive cannot be given the powers of war
and peace entire, for example, not merely because that would be
unsafe but because the executive must be elective. But limiting
the powers of the executive proves to be an insufficient solution.
Madison leads one to wonder whether the executive's powers can
be diminished sufficiently to avoid exciting envy without making
the executive too weak to serve his purpose, since he describes
both elective monarchy and the presidency in the same terms:
"*Elective Monarchies* turbulent and unhappy—Men unwilling to
admit so decided a superiority of merit in an individual as to ac-
cede to his appointment to so preeminent a station—"; "*The Executive Magistrate* would be envied and assailed by disappointed
competitors: His firmness therefore would need support."[24] Apparently an elective executive will in some measure suffer from
the vicissitudes of elective monarchy.

The necessity to diminish the threat that competition between
republican politicians poses to a nonpartisan election eventually
compelled Madison to conclude that the election of the executive
must be made by the people at large. In the Constitutional Convention he had originally suggested that the executive be elected
by the national legislature for a long term, and that he be ineligible to be reelected. The first provision apparently was due to the
desire to secure "National Supremacy in the Executive department," or to the desire to "refine" the choice, or to both. Given
legislative election, the latter two provisions followed as requi-
sites of independence. From the convention debates it appears
that Madison became convinced by James Wilson and Gouverneur Morris that an election by the legislature, *i.e.*, by the politicians, would produce a partisan executive who would not act independently even if he were not reeligible, and that an election by
a diverse and dispersed people would be nonpartisan and inaccessible to any decisive influence by the politicians. Popular election also adds to executive strength in office since it permits the
reeligibility that legislative election forbids and that gives a mo-

tive both to "faithful administration" and to "beneficial undertakings which require perseverance and system."[25]

But popular election, which is intended to prevent the choice of the executive from being made or decisively influenced by parties among the politicians, poses a problem of its own. Should the executive's election become the occasion for a plebiscite or referendum of "great national questions," partisan schisms between the politicians would reenter the process by combining themselves with a divided and susceptible people. Madison did not address this possibility directly, but he analyzed its essential elements when he considered whether constitutional disputes between the branches might be appealed for decision to a convention elected by the people. The "appeal to the people" described in *Federalist* 49–50 is similar to a plebiscitary election, and both are similar to an elective monarchy in this respect: the people *tout court* decide the future direction of government *tout court*. Moreover, the concluding paragraph of *Federalist* 50 contains what is in effect a beforehand description of the flooding of the electoral college by party. Madison supposes—what the constitutional provision for electors in fact requires—that "all persons . . . concerned with the government" might be excluded from the convention called to "revise the preceding administration of the government." But this would not obviate the difficulty: those elected would probably be men of "inferior capacities" who, while "not immediately agents in the measures to be examined," "would probably have been involved in the parties connected with these measures and have been elected under their auspices."[26] The issue would then be decided not in the convention itself but in the elections to it, just as the election of electors today determines the election of the president. The convention as little as the electoral college is an obstacle to a partisan decision when parties form over fundamental issues and the conflict comes to a head.

In a letter written less than a month before *Federalist* 49 appeared in print, Madison made an argument against a second constitutional convention that anticipated the argument of *Federalist* 49, but in considerably sharper terms: In the absence of a "fortunate coincidence of leading opinions," "the very attempt at a second Convention . . . by opposing influence to influence, would in a manner destroy an effectual confidence in either [Convention] and would give a loose to human opinions; which must be as various and irreconcilable concerning theories of Government, as doctrines of Religion; and give opportunities to designing men which it might be impossible to counteract." [27] Political opinions cannot be excluded from political controversy like religious opinions, nor are they reconcilable like interests. Moreover, there is an opinion or prejudice of veneration for the government that provides the stability within which lesser differences of opinion may be settled, but that veneration may be destroyed when differences of opinion are settled by an appeal to the people.

An appeal to the people is especially conducive to a rhetoric of jealousy, a rhetoric to which the executive is especially vulnerable. Such an appeal sets the people and their liberty (readily identified with the "legislative party") against goverment (readily identified with the executive), implicates the people in the governmental parties, and tends to obscure the question of the needs of good government in favor of the question of invasions of rights. It thereby offers a dangerous opportunity to demagogues whose rhetoric can be made perfectly to fit, and therefore conceal, their motive, which is not jealousy of liberty but envy of power. [28] Questions of "real nicety" between the branches of government, which may or may not go to fundamental questions, may then be transformed by the effect of an appeal to the people, or the rhetoric of that appeal, into a question as to the soundness of the government altogether. When partisan policies are forwarded by constitutional encroachments, the two issues will be appealed together, and the constitutional issues will be interpreted in the distorting light of the policy issues. [29] The appeal to the people is an extra-institutional solution that has a tendency to undermine the legitimacy of the institutions from which the appeal is made: the "abuse" of power given is called "usurpation"; the distinction between the question whether a policy is authorized and whether it is good is collapsed; and not merely the rascals but the institution or its jurisdiction is thrown out with the policy. [30] Madison described in *Federalist* 49 what he believed to be a characteristic perversion of the issues in republican debate when politicians compete with each other by directly competing for public support. The "ordinary diversity of political opinions" cannot be managed, nor the venerating opinion secured, without managing the politicians, the "leading characters" whose opinions are the "leading opinions."[31]

The analogy between the appeal to the people and presidential elections is not meant to suggest that presidential elections can or ought to be bereft of issues. It is meant rather to suggest the dangers when those elections are made into referenda of fundamental issues and the people are unable to "concur amicably, or differ with moderation, in the elective designation of the chief magistrate."[32] "Slight or . . . transient" differences may readily be settled or soon disappear, and ordinarily coalitions of opinion on each side of an issue will shift with the issue. But deep and lasting differences produce "fixed and violent" partisanship and rigid opposition on each side of every issue.[33] It is these differences and this partisanship that radically threaten the executive's nonpartisanship and the government's stability.[34]

It may be said that to concede that differences may be deep and lasting is to concede that the executive's election cannot be successfully insulated from such differences. From Madison's analysis, one learns that the president's election must ordinarily be insulated as far as possible from them, and even more from artificially created or intensified differences or from differences raised in premature or distorted form. Institutions must be arranged with a view to preventing, rather than permitting or inviting, the formation of "pernicious factions that might not otherwise come into existence."[35] They ought not to provide an unnecessary "focus" for the "flame" of partisanship; they ought rather to inhibit and diffuse it.[36] An ad hoc appeal to the people does the former. The separation of powers, together with fixed terms and staggered elections, does the latter, and in so doing helps distinguish between genuinely and spuriously fundamental issues. When issues force themselves upon us in spite of institutional obstacles, it is a sign that they are genuine.

The shift from the rejected solution of "great national questions" described in *Federalist* 49 to the separation of powers solution described in *Federalist* 51 requires an accompanying shift

from the rhetoric of an "appeal to the people" to a rhetoric between the branches of the government. Government cannot be
simply purified of either rhetoric or jealousy, but the more informed and less impressionable audience of an intragovernmental
rhetoric renders questions more easily resolvable on their merits.
And the separation of powers is itself a moderating influence:
"Neither party being able to consummate its will without the
concurrence of the other, there is a necessity on both to consult
and to accommodate." The constitutional system thus helps to
teach "the policy which harmonizes jealous interests" by enforcing that policy. To the extent that issues can be settled in government that would otherwise be appealed to the people in elections,
the president's election will provide less occasion for the distorting effects of partisanship. Viewed in the light of its rejected alternative, the separation of powers appears as a device for managing the politicians. Jealousy is brought into government; each
branch, jealous of its own rights against the others, is in effect
jealous on behalf of the people. In the best case, jealousy can be
transformed by being brought into government: it can become
jealousy not on behalf of popular rights against government but
on behalf of good government. For when the executive defends
his constitutional rights, he defends his right to independently
execute his office, which includes the general duty of "maintaining the government in its proper functions" against the irrespon-
sible willfulness of the House of Representatives. By such a defense, which is a rhetoric of deeds or results, the executive can
attract popular support, and he can do so for the reason that the
people know what good government is and appreciate its effects.
It would be perfectly consonant with Madison's purpose if,
through this more wholesome example of jealousy of rights, republican jealousy could at least partially satisfy itself without
being aroused.[37]

Madison thus finds several supports for the nonpartisan election of the executive. The executive's powers are initially limited in an attempt to obviate the evils of elective monarchy. Election by the people, whether directly or indirectly through the
election of electors, decreases the influence of politicians in the
election process.[38] And the operations of the system of separated

powers diminishes the possibility that the election of the executive will become the occasion for a popular referendum on great national questions.

The requirements of separation of powers and republicanism for an independent, responsible, and nonpartisan executive are joined in a coherent view of the presidency that is distinctively Madisonian in character. Madison conceives of the president as a constitutional officer. The president's independent constitutional grant, a requirement of separation of powers, is his commission charging him with the faithful discharge of a set of duties attached to the office, and he takes an oath to "faithfully execute the Office." The president does not simply follow legislative instructions but is authorized to act by his independent constitutional grant. He thus has a status coequal with the legislature.

The expectation that George Washington would be the first to hold the office and could serve as a model for it indicates some of the flavor of the meaning of the president as "officer." A certain degree of veneration attaches to the presidency as a symbol of the respect due to the Constitution and the laws rather than as an agent of the legislature or representative of the people. Through the president's pride of place in holding the office he acquires the personal motive to perform his duties faithfully that is a republican substitution for a monarch's identification with his realm.

The conception of the president as constitutional officer is an entirely appropriate one for a republican government. Unlike the British king, who "can do no wrong," the president is directly responsible through reeligibility and impeachment for his performance in office.[39] He derives his authority in the constitutional system of checks and balances from his office and personal merit rather than from hereditary privilege in a mixed government where authority is based on the representation of social orders. However the president, in Madison's view, is not a republican executive in the sense of a representative executive. Madison does not understand the election of the president to confer upon him a "representative" character. It is a means of appointing a qualified man to a constitutional office. The consent of the people authorizes the appointment and ensures responsibility.[40] And this responsibility characterizes the presidency as republican.

When the meaning of *officer* is counterpoised with that of *representative*, the distinction resembles the common connotations of the distinction between *government* and *politics*. The president, as the only truly national officer, stands above or outside of the arena of partisan politics and consequently can serve to unify and conciliate political divisions. Madison encouraged Washington to remain in office for a second term by arguing that only he could provide this service. Each of the possible candidates to succeed him, Adams, Jay, and Jefferson, was too clearly identified with partisan disputes.[41]

The presidency, then, cannot be characterized either as an extension of republican representation or as a moderated version of a monarch. Because the presidency is not the former, it can improve republicanism, and because it is not the latter, it can do so within the limits of republicanism. The conception of the president as constitutional officer, responsible but neither representative nor partisan and empowered by an independent constitutional grant, is the result of the search for a distinctively republican executive.

THE POWERS OF THE OFFICE

The doctrine of separation of powers requires that the president be empowered by a constitutional grant. In determining the content of that grant, the powers and duties attached to the office had to be justified as properly placed in executive hands and as appropriate to a republican executive. Once granted, the proper extent of presidential powers became a subject of constitutional interpretation.

The content of the president's grant is determined in the first instance by the doctrine of separation of powers itself. While Madison recognized that the tripartite division of governmental functions could not be precisely defined in detail, the general content of powers "in their nature executive" is clear: "to carry into effect the national laws, to appoint to offices in cases not otherwise provided for, and to execute such other powers . . . as may from time to time be delegated by the national legislature . . . the whole perhaps being included in the first member of the proposition." The executive presupposes law and is circumscribed by it. He implements and enforces the law, exercising discretion in applications of the law to particular circumstances. These are functions best entrusted to a single man who can act with decision and easily be held responsible for his actions.[42]

While the executive is thus subordinate to law, he must not be subordinate to the legislature. With the addition of the veto power as a defense of executive rights against the legislature, the minimum requirements of separation of powers are satisfied, and the skeleton of the Madisonian presidency is in place: an effective administrator operating from an independent institutional position. Separation of powers as the sole founding principle yields a president who is institutionally strong and functionally weak— absolute within a narrow sphere.

But as a result of his analysis of republicanism, Madison advocated an expansion of presidential functions in order to introduce qualities into republican government that would counteract the worst tendencies of popular assemblies. The veto power, which on one level is the simple defense of the executive, has an additional object: to "prevent popular or factious injustice."[43] For the veto power to be effective, the president must be given sufficient "weight" to balance the legislature. To supply additional institutional support, Madison proposed including members of the judiciary in the exercise of the veto power in a council of revision.[44] The president is expected to contribute qualities similar to those of the judiciary, *e.g.*, stability and impartiality, and for that reason his function is expanded beyond that of mere administrator to include a positive political effect in the legislative process. In this respect Madison's understanding of the council of revision, the presidency proper, and the Senate are similar. They are the several conclusions of a single search for institutional devices that might correct the specific defects of a republican representation.

The functions of the president are further expanded on the basis of qualities that he alone possesses. The executive office is held by a single man who operates continuously in office. Consequently, the executive has capacities essential to effective administration of the laws that are equally essential to the conduct of foreign affairs. For this reason, negotiation of treaties and command of the military, functions not simply executive in their nature, are placed in his hands.[45]

On the basis of this understanding of presidential powers in foreign affairs, Madison's narrow interpretation of those powers in his *Helvidius Papers* is not inconsistent with his assertion during the Removal Debates that the "vesting clause" is a positive grant.[46] That clause implies that the president possesses *executive* powers, those powers necessary to effectively carry out the laws. Article II then proceeds to enumerate executive powers that are to be qualified, powers that are arguably executive and ought to be made explicitly so, and powers that are not themselves executive but are granted to the Executive by the Constitution.

Article II thus provides three major areas of presidential power: administration, legislation, and foreign affairs. Although each of these functions is given to the president for a distinct set of reasons, the Madisonian president does not simply play three "roles." The conception of the president as constitutional officer unifies Madison's interpretation of the president's functions. The president's powers in legislation and foreign affairs enlarge his sphere beyond the administrative duties given by the separation of powers doctrine, but they are not unlimited powers. They resemble prerogatives of the British crown and therefore require a reinterpretation appropriate to a republican executive and compatible with the limitations of the constitutional separation of powers.[47] Madison's interpretation maintains those limits and provides a common ground for the understanding of all three presidential functions. Because the interpretation is based on the separation of powers doctrine, the president's functions in legislation and foreign affairs are circumscribed within an expanded conception of the meaning of executive administration, the primary executive function as defined by that doctrine.

While the constitutional provisions for a power to veto and a duty to suggest legislation give the president a positive role in the legislative process, that role is limited by the need to keep the branches separate. The veto power minimally construed is a means of preventing legislative encroachments on the executive sphere. It maintains the separation of powers in the interest of political liberty and executive efficiency. Executive interference with legislative deliberations similarly violates the separation of powers, and the president's legislative role is not intended to involve him in the management of legislative factions. The British practice of corruption and influence is clearly rejected.[48] Instead, as Madison's council of revision proposal indicates, the president's role resembles that of a judge or an umpire, and the veto also serves as a means of preventing partisan legislation.

The president's duty to suggest legislation broadens his legislative role, but without assimilating his function to that of a representative. Rather, the conception of the president as administrator is expanded to include an interest in bringing administrative expertise and a nonpartisan political perspective to bear in the formation of just and stable laws. The president's duty to "take care that the laws be faithfully executed" is of a piece with his interest in securing a respectable and stable system of laws. In 1785 Madison thought he had discovered a better "security against fluctuating and indigested laws" than the veto power. "It is that a standing committee composed of a few select and skilful [*sic*] individuals should be appointed to prepare bills on all subjects which *they* may judge proper to be submitted to the Legislature at their meetings."[49] The work of this institution, in effect a third branch of the legislature,[50] is eventually given to the executive. The worst evil of mutable and badly made laws is the loss of public respect for the laws and the government.[51] Attachment of the people to their government and veneration for the laws result from a good administration. And here *administration* is a term encompassing the operations of the government in general.[52]

The peculiar expertise and duty of the head of the executive administration is an essential element of his legislative role. And this is in turn broadened beyond the use of the veto power in the interest of a judge-like impartiality, into the advocacy and defense of good government. The articulation of the executive's legislative role thus parallels the progress of Madison's argument in *The Federalist*, which moves from the minimal condition of justice, the impartial protection of rights from invasion, to the higher and more comprehensive justice of good government.[53]

Madison's interpretation of the proper scope of the constitutional powers of the president in foreign affairs and administration developed after the new government was established under the Constitution. For this reason, his arguments shifted to constitutional interpretation applying the doctrine of separation of powers to particular clauses defining the distribution of powers between the executive and the legislature. Because the doctrine of separation of powers supports both an interpretation of the executive function as circumscribed by law and an interpretation of the institutional position of the executive as an independent and coequal branch of government, Madison's arguments in defense of his understanding of the president's powers in foreign affairs and administration cannot be consistently characterized as advocating either a "weak" or "strong" presidency. That his understanding includes elements of both of these current positions is evident in the comparison between his position in the *Helvidius Papers* and the Removal Debates and within his interpretation of the president's proper role during the Jay Treaty controversy.

Madison wrote the *Helvidius Papers* reluctantly, and he wrote them primarily to combat the interpretation of executive power offered by Hamilton in the *Pacificus Papers* in defense of the Neutrality Proclamation. He conceded that a similar proclamation might be justified on narrower grounds. Hamilton had argued that the foreign affairs powers of the government are in their nature executive and vested in the president by the "vesting clause" of Article II of the Constitution. The legislature's power to declare war and the Senate's participation in treaty ratification are exceptions to the general grant and therefore are to be strictly construed. According to Madison, the only possible source of Hamilton's assertion that foreign affairs powers are executive in nature was the prerogatives of the British crown.[54]

Madison's response to Hamilton's argument offers a reinterpretation of powers formerly understood to be monarchical prerogatives in a manner appropriate to the republican executive of the American Constitution. That reinterpretation is based on an American version of separation of powers that provides new criteria for the interpretation of the distribution of powers in government. In determining whether or not the powers to make treaties and to declare war are executive in character, one must look to both "the quality and operation of the powers" and to the principle that the Constitution could not place any legislative power wholly in the executive or any executive power wholly in the legislature without violating the separation of powers.[55]

With respect to the first criterion, Madison argues that a treaty operates as law and that a declaration of war is a deliberate act altering the state of domestic laws and not itself presupposing a law to be executed. Consequently, neither is an executive function. By interpreting presidential powers in foreign affairs on the basis of the doctrine of separation of powers, Madison continues to maintain that the essence of executive authority is "to see the laws faithfully executed."[56] Just as in general the executive "executes" where the legislature has "enacted," in foreign affairs the executive "conducts" war and negotiations where the legislature "authorizes" or "legitimates" either by declaration of war or by treaty ratification. In the Constitutional Convention Madison recognized the necessity for the presidential power to repel sudden attacks,[57] but in general the executive function depends upon legislative authorization.

With respect to the second criterion, Madison argues that if the declaration of war is an executive power, the Constitution could not have placed that power entirely in the legislative branch. It is therefore not an executive power. Madison argues further that the executive interpretation of treaties cannot in any case include a right to judge whether or not the nation is obligated to go to war under a treaty. Such a right is inseparable from the power to declare war, and as such is a usurpation of a power given to the legislature and a violation of separation of powers.[58]

It would be particularly dangerous for the president to have this power because the executive is prone to war, and so "the separation of the power of declaring war from that of conducting it, is wisely contrived to exclude the danger of its being declared for the sake of its being conducted."[59] Both war itself and the apprehension of war increase the discretionary powers given to the executive. His expanded function is coupled with an enhanced institutional position: his influence and patronage grow; his desire for preeminence is nourished; and he gains control of the nation's military force.[60] If the president's foreign-affairs functions are not properly circumscribed, a republican executive may be transformed through this process into a monarch or a dictator.

Madison's analysis yields the following general interpretation: "Although the executive may be a convenient organ of preliminary communications with foreign governments on the subjects of treaty or war; and the proper agent for carrying into execution the final determinations of the competent authority; yet it can have no pretensions, from the nature of the executive trust, to that essential agency which gives validity to such determinations." Unlike the British king, who represents the nation in foreign affairs, the president is nowhere authorized to exercise legitimating consent on behalf of the people.[61]

Madison's argument in the *Helvidius Papers* is thus consonant with his conception of the president as constitutional officer. Again, the president is not a representative. And, while the foreign-affairs powers of the president expand his role beyond that of mere administrator, the quality of those powers is interpreted as an elaboration of the basic distinction between executive administration and legislative deliberation and authorization.

Just as the president's powers in interpreting a treaty stop short of preempting legislative deliberation, the treaty power altogether cannot preempt the legislative powers of the House. The Jay Treaty controversy raised the question "whether the general power of making Treaties supersedes the powers of the House of Representatives, particularly specified in the Constitution, so as to take to the Executive all deliberate will and leave the House only an executive and ministerial instrumental agency?" Madison argued that the House had no obligation to pass laws necessary to implement a treaty if the treaty "embraced Legislative subjects, submitted by the Constitution to the power of the House." The treaty-making power and the power of congressional legislation must be understood as cooperative powers. Neither constitutional grant takes precedence over the other; powers are distributed between coequal branches; and the limitations of the checks thus established must be preserved.[62]

On the same grounds that Madison defended the limits on the president's foreign-affairs functions, he also went considerably further than his colleagues in defending the institutional rights of the office. When the House requested presidential papers relating to the Jay Treaty, Madison moved for an amendment acknowledging the right of the president to withhold any papers that would be, in his judgment, dangerous to the national interest to disclose. It was the earliest full statement of the doctrine of executive privilege. Madison maintained that each branch, as equal and coordinate with the others, is the proper judge of its objects and functions. The president may not judge the right of the House to request information, and the House may not judge the right of the president to refuse it.[63]

Like Madison's argument for executive privilege, his argument in the Removal Debates finds a constitutional implication of executive strength on the basis of the separation of powers. Again, the issue was one of the president's control within his proper sphere, and on issues of this sort Madison was uncompromising. On the question where the Constitution placed the power of removal of executive officers, the Constitution itself was "silent" but not, Madison thought, "undecided." The power resides in the president alone, as a discretionary power uncontrollable except insofar as the president is broadly responsible to the people at election or to the legislature through impeachment. Madison's position on this point was all but absolute, since he admitted legislative control of executive officers only in the creation of offices, in participation in appointments, and in determination of salaries.[64]

The Constitution's silence, and the importance of removal for the "genius and character of the whole government," meant that a "permanent exposition" of the point, with "everything like ambiguity expunged," had to be established. The rule of construction and the interpretation thus established cannot be separated from the broader institutional reasoning that supports them. Madison gives their relation: "What arguments were brought forward respecting the convenience or inconvenience of such a disposition of the power, were intended only to throw light upon what was meant by the compilers of the Constitution." There is a constitutional level of policy, and such policy arguments are not meant to confuse the issue or to give spurious clarity to an obscure text, but to illuminate a text which embodies them. Madison's opponents argued for responsibility in the executive and on the basis of the separation of powers and concluded that the Constitution required the participation of the Senate in removal. Madison had to argue a different case for responsibility, and he had to make, in a decisive sense, a different separation of powers argument. By taking a constitutional ground, he also opposed a second opinion in his own majority, according to which removal was a question in the legislature's discretion to decide, rather than one decided by the Constitution, because that opinion in effect places the Legislature "at the head of the Executive Branch of the Government."[65]

While Madison's opponents argued for "short leash" responsibility to prevent the possibility of abuse, and made a separation of powers argument in the name of liberty alone, Madison argued for a "remote control" responsibility to permit the possibility of effective execution, and made a separation of powers argument in the name of efficiency as well as liberty. In the Removal Debates, the proper rule of interpretation for implied powers was a point of controversy; and whether the removal power was per se executive, or whether it was even broadly implied in the Take Care Clause, was still more so.[66] Madison's showing that removal must be exercised by the executive alone, and that it was per se an executive power, ultimately rests upon a particular understanding of the executive function and of what that function requires. Even the conclusion that the vesting clause is substantive does not settle *what* it vests. According to Madison, the responsibility of the executive would be destroyed if it were divided between the Senate and the president, and senatorial participation in removal would permanently expose the nonpartisanship of the executive to the intrusions of a senatorial party or parties. Moreover, destroying executive unity does not merely destroy responsibility; dividing the power destroys executive "will," "defeating the very purposes for which a unity in the Executive was instituted."[67] The executive "chain of dependence," culminating in the president and eventually in the people, serves execution as well as responsibility. Ultimately, the most powerful argument for the conclusion that the Take Care Clause, or the executive function, requires removal rather than suspension, for example, is the argument that the function of the chief executive is not merely to oversee execution with a view to checking official misfeasance, but to see to it that the laws are in fact executed promptly and steadily. A *"personal* and *political* harmony with the President" is necessary if the "Executive machinery" is not to be fouled by party, "thus arresting the march of the government altogether." [68] Madison's separation-of-powers argument is directed toward securing in the presidency the qualities of a constitutional officer, fully responsible for the effective and impartial performance of executive duties.

Madison adhered to his uncompromising view of presidential removal power even when, in Andrew Jackson's presidency, the power was abused. The "odium" of the abuse would lead to its correction, but a Senate "veto" of removals, while at all times "worse than inconvenient," "in party times might, by throwing the Executive machinery out of gear, produce a calamitous interregnum." [69] It is precisely in "party times" that the dangers of partisan execution of the laws must be hazarded, because it is especially in such times that there is a serious threat that the laws will not be executed at all.

To the importance of constancy of execution must be added the importance to Madison of an "indefinite" tenure in executive offices, a tenure that is safe on the basis of exclusive presidential responsibility for official conduct and that serves the "salutary permanency of the laws." [70] We are thus reminded of the "stability and energy" Madison as framer intended to secure in good part by separating the executive from the legislature and giving it an independent constitutional grant of power.

Madison did not fear the strength of the president within his sphere as long as that sphere was properly contained. But the executive function of administration has the potential for a dangerous expansion under certain conditions. The executive function is circumscribed by law, but it also supplies the defects of law within those bounds by applying a general rule to particular circumstances. Its discretionary character in the ordinary conduct of executive business is not easily distinguishable in kind from expanded executive discretion under conditions where the variety, number, irregularity, or pressing character of the particulars render them ungovernable by a general rule.

The problem of maintaining limitations on executive power where the law is not adequate to the circumstances is generally addressed with reference to a unique and temporary crisis in which the president would seem to have the greatest claim to stretch his authority beyond or against the limits of law to meet the claims of necessity in the interest of the general good. The problem in this particular form is the clearest case of the problem of prerogative, and it applies with greatest force to the executive. Madison takes a broader view of both the problem and its application. The possibility of a conflict between law and necessity is not confined to the executive, but may also arise with respect to legislative power in a government limited by a written constitution or fundamental law.[71] And with respect to the executive, Madison is primarily concerned with the situation in which the expansion of presidential power to supply the defects of law is less temporary, remains formally within the law, and is coupled with an enhancement of the president's institutional position, a combination that can lead to the transformation of a republican executive into a monarch.

Madison's analysis is presented in the context of the issue of federalism and the Republican attack on Federalist usurpations. His opposition to the broad construction of the powers of the national legislature includes a concern with executive aggrandizement. Expansion of the powers of the national government altogether can enhance the powers of the executive and destroy the balance between the executive and the legislature within the national government. "In proportion as the objects of the legislative care might be multiplied, would the time allowed for each be diminished, and the difficulty of providing uniform and particular regulations be increased. From these sources would necessarily ensue a greater latitude to the agency of that department which is always in existence, and which could best mould regulations of a general nature so as to suit them to the diversity of particular situations. And it is in this latitude, as a supplement to the deficiency of the laws, that the degree of Executive prerogative materially consists."[72] Consolidation, destroying the limits of the federal structure, creates a condition in which the law must apply to so many particular instances that the legislature is compelled to delegate broad authority to the executive. The Alien Act, according to Madison, was just such a delegation. The standards of the law were so general that the president, in enforcing the law, would have to make legislative determinations as well as executive and, in this case, judicial ones. The act was consequently an unconstitutional violation of the separation of powers.[73] (The argument and the problem are familiar in administrative law and in the current terminology of "quasi-legislative" and "quasi-judicial" functions of executive agencies.)

In addition to the expansion of executive discretion that results from consolidation, the number of administrative officers under the president, and consequently his influence, grows to dangerous proportions. "This disproportionate increase of prerogative and patronage must, evidently, either enable the Chief Magistrate of the Union, by quiet means, to secure his re-election from time to time, and finally to regulate the succession as he might please; or, by giving so transcendent an importance to the office, would render the elections to it so violent and corrupt, that the public voice itself might call for an hereditary in place of an elective succession. Whichever of these events might follow, the transformation of the republican system of the United States into a monarch . . . would be equally accomplished."[74] The process described here, recalling the dangers of elective monarchy, is similar to Madison's description, discussed above, of the effects of war or the constant threat of war on the executive.

Madison's defense of the limits of presidential powers permits his advocacy of a strong position for the president in relation to the legislature. Both aspects of Madison's argument are supported by the separation of powers doctrine. The way in which Madison uses that doctrine provides an interpretation of presidential powers in legislation, foreign affairs, and administration that reinforces the conception of the president as a constitutional officer. Both the strengths and limitations of the president are ascertained with a view to securing the qualities required in an effective republican executive.

PARTY AND PRESIDENCY

Madison defended an interpretation of the president's place in the constitutional scheme that would ensure his independence, responsibility, and nonpartisanship. But his own tenure as president cannot be taken as a model for the practical expression of that interpretation. One of the reasons for the disparities between Madison's conception and his practice as president can be found in the effects of party development on the presidency. In general, the development of the relation between party and the presidency exposes the weaknesses of his original solution to the problem of the republican executive.

Madison was not a "weak" president, if that is taken to mean passive. Particularly in foreign affairs, he recognized and attempted to utilize the potential for presidential leadership implicit in the constitutional grant.[75] And in a few instances, he upheld the institutional rights of the office in a manner that might have been expected of him.[76] But Madison was unable to effectively direct his administration and his generals and similarly unable to secure from the Congress the enactment of his policies.

The most striking disparity between Madison's conception and his performance in office is to be found in his failure to maintain firm control of an executive administration independent of the legislature. Madison was prevented by a senatorial faction of his own party from transferring Secretary of the Treasury Gallatin to the Department of State and, to pacify that faction, accepted a completely incompetent secretary of state in Robert Smith.[77] Gallatin was eventually forced out of the cabinet altogether.[78] Cabinet members maintained close ties with legislative factions and hardly exhibited the essential "*personal* and *political* harmony" with the president that Madison consistently advocated.[79]

Madison's relations with the legislature were also disturbed by legislative factionalism. By the end of Jefferson's administration executive control of the congressional party and the unity of the party had collapsed.[80] With the Eleventh Congress, Madison was faced with a variety of factions whose conflicts impeded the pursuit of any clear policy, including the enactment of Madison's suggested legislation.[81] The strength of Madison's position to persuade the legislature on the merits of a policy question was undermined by the fact that factional rivalries reached into the administration. Opposition to presidential initiatives was thus increased by factional concerns. The situation was reminiscent of the fears that Madison had expressed concerning the effects of legislative election on competition among politicians and on the independence of the executive administration.

Madison's situation resulted in part from the unexpected development of the relationship between party and presidency. Madison had hoped that the constitutional provisions for the presidency would maintain a nonpartisan president. Paradoxically, they encouraged, and to a certain extent shaped, the development of a partisan presidency on two levels: first in relation to the legislature, and then in relation to the people in the election process.

Madison advocated a positive role for the president in the legislative process through the powers to veto and to recommend legislation, but that role was to be bounded by the necessity of maintaining a distance between the president and legislative factions. The difficulty of maintaining that boundary became apparent with Hamilton's funding system. Madison's understanding of the president's legislative function included a recognition of the administration's role, and particularly the Treasury Department's, in preparing plans for the consideration of the House.[82] Formal control of the secretary of the treasury was firmly in the hands of the president in accordance with Madison's position in the Removal Debates. Hamilton utilized the power inherent in his position to achieve the success of his funding proposals in the legislature. The opponents of Madison's position on the removal question had feared precisely this result, the introduction into the House of what they understood to be a Treasury ministry on the British model.[83] Madison saw Hamilton's actions leading to the creation of an "artificial party"[84] and seriously exacerbating the divisions that had already begun to appear in the House. Important measures were passed by bare majorities, free and fair deliberation was suppressed, and representatives were further polarized along geographical lines.[85] A system intended to provide a check on legislative partisanship was producing the opposite result. The parties that developed went beyond the anticipated factions of interest and personal ambition to divide both senators and representatives into pro-administration and anti-administration groups with each group united on a variety of issues and principles in both domestic and foreign policy.

The attempt to rid the government of what eventually came to be seen as a monarchical faction, identified as the administration party, and to regain control of government policy involved capturing the presidency for the Republican party because the president had been given both important functions in domestic and foreign policy and a position of institutional independence. The presidency had become the prize of party conflict, and when Jefferson became president, it was as party leader. As such, he exercised considerable influence in Congress during most of his tenure in office. With Madison's presidency, the institutional positions were reversed, with the congressional factions of the Republican party asserting their influence. Neither the nonpartisan character nor the independence of the Madisonian presidency remained intact.

These transformations were soon to be followed by another. With Jackson's election and the developments in party organization that followed, the presidency took on an increasingly representative aspect. The mode of presidential election made it possible for a candidate to make a direct appeal to the people and to develop the rhetoric of a popular mandate. It is not possible to maintain the distinction in practice between representation and responsibility to popular control when the mechanism for ensuring that responsibility is reeligibility in a popular election. And a representative presidency cannot be simply nonpartisan.

Madison had recognized that the natural weakness of a republican executive necessitated a means of providing additional "weight" to balance the legislature. He sought that support within the government through the connection between the president and the judiciary in the council of revision or through the president's connection with the Senate, and extra-institutionally through the national reputation and personal merit of the president. He did not anticipate that it might be supplied by a president's connection to a popular political base through party organization. Madison's response to proposals for reform of the electoral college indicate that his perspective had not altered. He continued to seek in the presidential election process a means for selecting the best man and for diminishing the influence of parties in the process.[86]

Madison understood that republican government could be good government only if partisanship could be controlled. He had intended that the "various and interfering interests" in society be brought into the government, but confined to the legislature, there to be moderated and harmonized partly through the efforts of an independent executive.[87] But the executive's role in shaping policy both encouraged the formation of pro and anti-administration parties and made the presidency an important prize of party contest once those parties had formed. From then on, the impartiality of the presidency would have to be achieved by a president more in the midst of, than free from, the complex of legislative partisanships.

CONCLUSION

The presidency today is, of course, both far more representative and far more partisan that Madison had hoped it would be. But the decentralized and loosely disciplined character of American parties permits, and the nature of the president's office encourages, a degree of presidential nonpartisanship.[88] A newly elected president is not held to his party platform and in office tends to broaden his views not simply in order to broaden his political base. Moreover, for the same reason that American parties permit the president to independently execute his office, they do not automatically guarantee party support for every presidential initiative. In this way they also permit the adversarial relationship between president and Congress to continue despite the role of the president as party leader, or as is often the case, as titular party leader. They therefore do not merely offer him an opportunity for a Madisonian use of his office; they also render him especially dependent upon a persuasive case for his initiatives and a capable defense of his actions. In contests with the Congress, the president must ultimately rely on his constitutional authority and a reasoned defense of his policies, as well as on his popular support. The president retains characteristics of a constitutional officer. He is still shaped, supported, and limited by his office.

Madison's understanding of that office provides a complex alternative to the extremes of a "weak" or "strong" presidency: an independent executive capable of improving the law and checking the legislature without going beyond the law or superseding the legislature. Madison, in attempting to recognize the claims of both branches, reminds us of the ends to be kept in view and adds a cautionary note: "The Constitution of the U.S. may doubtless disclose from time to time faults which call for the pruning or the ingrafting hand. But remedies ought to be applied not in the paroxysms of party and popular excitements: but with the more leisure and reflection, as the Great Departments of Power according to experience may be successively and alternately in, and out of public favour; and as changes hastily accommodated to these vicissitudes would destroy the symmetry and the stability aimed at in our political system." [89]

NOTES TO CHAPTER II

1. Max Farrand (ed.), *The Records of the Federal Convention of 1787* (4 vols.; New Haven: Yale University Press, 1966), I, 21, 70, 74 (hereinafter cited as *Records*); James Madison to Edmund Randolph, April 8, 1787, in Gaillard Hunt (ed.), *The Writings of James Madison* (9 vols.; New York: G. P. Putnam's Sons, 1906), II, 339–40 (hereinafter cited as *Writings*); James Madison to George Washington, April 16, 1787, in *Writings*, II, 348; Notes on Speech on Proposed Amendment to Constitution of Virginia, June 1784, in *Writings*, II, 54n. By the time the convention opened, Madison had decided on a unitary executive, independent and strong in relation to the legislature. For a contrary view, see Charles C. Thach, Jr., *The Creation of the Presidency: 1775–1789* (Baltimore: Johns Hopkins Press, 1923), 81, 83–84. See also note 11 below. Thach argues that Madison's views were vague and that he favored a plural executive. But Thach misreads the Virginia Plan's silence; the plan left undetermined the number of the executive as a politic accommodation to Randolph and Mason, who did oppose a unitary executive.

2. Farrand (ed.), *Records*, I, 49–50, 57.

3. Madison to Caleb Wallace, August 23, 1785, in *Writings*, II, 169.

4. Alexander Hamilton, James Madison, and John Jay, *The Federalist Papers*, ed. Clinton Rossiter (New York: New American Library, 1961), No. 10, p. 77.

5. *Ibid.*, No. 10, p. 84.

6. *Ibid.*, No. 48, p. 309. See Thach, *Creation*, 27; Gordon S. Wood, *The Creation of the American Republic 1776–1787* (New York: W. W. Norton, 1972), 139, 163.

7. Madison to Jefferson, March 19[18], 1787, in *Writings*, II, 327–28.

8. Madison to Caleb Wallace, August 23, 1785, in *Writings*, II, 169; Farrand (ed.), *Records*, II, 77; *Federalist*, Nos. 47, 48, 51. See Thach, *Creation*, 30–54.

9. See M. J. C. Vile, *Constitutionalism and the Separation of Powers* (Oxford: Clarendon Press, 1967), 39–43.

10. "Vices of the Political System of the United States," April, 1787, in *Writings*, II, 365–68.

11. Madison to Jefferson, March 19, 1787, in *Writings*, II, 329; Madison to E. Randolph, April 15, 1787, in *Writings*, II, 343–44; Madison to Jefferson, April 23, 1787, in *Writings*, II, 359–60. Contrary to Thach's opinion, Madison took his lessons equally from the state and national experiences. Moreover, the conclusion he drew from the national experience was not an executive more separate from than equal to the legislature. Thach misreads Madison's mollifying intervention in the convention debates to define "executive power" as if it were a final statement of powers to be vested in the executive and concludes that Madison proposed an "executive essentially subordinate to the legislature." See Thach, *Creation*, 74–75, 84.

12. Madison to J. Monroe, March 21, 1785, in *Writings*, II, 127; see Hamilton's almost identical remarks, *Federalist*, No. 75, p. 452; Madison to J. Monroe, March 21, 1785, in *Writings*, II, 128; Joseph Gales, Sr. (comp.), *The Debates and Proceedings in the Congress of the United States* (Washington: Gales and Seaton, 1834), I, 604–605 (hereinafter cited as *Annals*); see also Thach, *Creation*, 67–70.

13. *Federalist*, No. 37, pp. 226–27, No. 58, p. 357.

14. *Ibid.*, No. 49, p. 316; Farrand, *Records*, I, 65–68, 71–74, 86–88, 99–103, 112–114.

15. Madison had to answer the argument that republican jealousy is identical to the republican "genius" (or character), and that "genius" is "fixed genius." Compare *Federalist*, No. 48, p. 309, No. 55, pp. 345–46, and No. 63, pp. 387, 389, with No. 37, p. 277, No. 39, p. 240, No. 57, p. 353, No. 63, p. 385, and Farrand (ed.), *Records*, I, 66, 71, 72, 88, 90 (Randolph's speeches).

16. *Federalist*, No. 53, p. 335, No. 58, p. 360; No. 53, p. 335; No. 48, p. 309, No. 53, p. 335, No. 58, pp. 360–61, No. 63, p. 386; No. 63, p. 387. See Harvey C. Mansfield Jr.'s analysis of Burke's point (in principle an argument against cabinet government) that the Commons' implication in ministerial actions prevents their controlling the ministers: Harvey C. Mansfield, Jr., *Statesmanship and Party Government* (Chicago: University of Chicago Press, 1965), 142–44. Madison's analysis could be used to support an argument for executive independence in the interest of executive responsibility to the legislature.

17. *Federalist*, No. 63, pp. 383–84; see V. O. Key, Jr., *The Responsible Electorate: Rationality in Presidential Voting, 1936–1960* (New York: Random House, 1966), 51–52, 61–62, 76–77.

18. *Federalist*, No. 63, p. 383.

19. Madison to Jefferson, October 24, 1787, in *Writings*, V, 32; "Vices of the Political System of the United States," April, 1787, *Writings*, II, 368; "Majority Governments," in *Writings*, IX, 520; *Federalist*, No. 51, pp. 323–24.

20. Farrand (ed.), *Records*, I, 138.

21. "Consolidation," *National Gazette*, December 5, 1791, in *Writings*, VI, 67–68.

22. Farrand (ed.), *Records*, I, 65, 70, 72, 290–91. Elective monarchy is a special case of "elections of every kind" that combines the greatest theoretical clarity with the greatest practical danger: Sir William Blackstone, *Commentaries on the Law of England*, ed. James Stewart (London: Stevens and Norton, 1854), Bk. I, Ch. 3, p. 193.

23. Farrand (ed.), *Records*, I, 70.

24. *Ibid.*, I, 72, 138 (emphasis added). Jefferson was for this reason willing to render the office "uninteresting" by making the executive ineligible to be reelected: Jefferson to Madison, Dec. 20, 1787, in Robert A. Rutland *et al.* (eds.), *The Papers of James Madison* (10 vols.; Chicago: University of Chicago Press, 1977), X, 337 (hereinafter cited as *Papers*).

25. Farrand (ed.), *Records*, I, 21, 70, 71; *Records*, I, 50 and Madison to Washington, April 16, 1787, in *Writings*, II, 347; *Records*, II, 29–32, 52–54, 56–57, 109–111; "Observations on the Draught of a Constitution for Virginia," in *Writings*, V, 289.

26. *Federalist*, No. 50, p. 320.

27. Madison to Edmund Randolph, January 10, 1788, in *Papers*, X, 355–56. This immediately preceded the appearances of *Federalist*, Nos. 37 and 38 on January 11 and 12. *Federalist* No. 49 appeared on February 2. Compare *Federalist*, No. 37, p. 231, No. 38, pp. 237–39, and No. 49, pp. 314–15.

28. *Federalist*, No. 49, pp. 316–17.

29. *Ibid.*, No. 48, p. 310; Madison to Henry Lee, June 25, 1824, in *Writings*, IX, 190–91; Madison to John M. Patton, March 24, 1834, in *Writings*, IX, 536.

30. Madison to Jefferson, June 27, 1823, in *Writings*, IX, 141–43; Madison to Edward Coles, August 29, 1834, in *Writings*, IX, 538. Madison's remarks were made in response to attacks on Jackson's removal of the bank deposits and on the Marshall Court's interpretations of federalism questions.

31. *Federalist*, No. 49, pp. 314–17.

32. "Consolidation," in *Writings*, VI, 68.

33. Madison to Monroe, May 18, 1822, in *Writings*, IX, 97; *Federalist*, No. 50, p. 319.

34. Does Madison in effect give an analysis of elements of "critical elections" that he feared as well as an analysis of the "'politics as usual'" he intended? See Walter Dean Burnham, *Critical Elections and the Mainsprings of American Politics* (New York: W. W. Norton, 1970), 6–7, 9–10, 176–81; V. O. Key, Jr., "A Theory of Critical Elections," *Journal of Politics*, XVII (1955), 3–19.

35. Madison to Jefferson, February 4, 1790, in *Writings*, V, 437n, 438–39.

36. Madison to Turbeville, November 2, 1788, in *Writings*, V, 299.

37. Madison to Jefferson, June 27, 1823, in *Writings*, IX, 141; see also *Federalist*, No. 49, p. 314, No. 51, pp. 320–22, and Gales (comp.), *Annals*, I, 500–501; Madison to Henry Lee, June 25, 1824, in *Writings*, IX, 191; *Federalist*, No. 58, pp. 359–60; *Federalist*, No. 37, p. 227; see also Madison to Jefferson, Dec. 9, 1787, in *Papers*, X, 313.

38. Farrand (ed.), *Records*, I, 110–11.

39. Blackstone, *Commentaries*, Bk. I, Ch. 7, p. 247. See "Report on the Resolutions," in *Writings*, VI, 388, where Madison indicates that "hereditary" and "responsible" are opposites.

40. Compare with Wilson, Morris, and Mercer: Farrand (ed.), *Records*, II, 30, 52–53, 285.

41. Farrand (ed.), *Records*, II, 81; "Substance of a Conversation with the President," May 5, 1792, in *Writings*, VI, 108–109.

42. Farrand (ed.), *Records*, I, 67, and *Federalist*, No. 37, p. 228; see Gales (comp.), *Annals*, I, 499.

43. Farrand, (ed.), *Records*, II, 587.

44. See Madison to J. Hillhouse, May, 1830, *Writings*, IX, 368; Farrand (ed.), *Records*, I, 138.

45. Farrand (ed.), *Records*, II, 318, 392.

46. See p. 52 herein. Abraham D. Sofaer says, without showing, that Madison was inconsistent: Abraham D. Sofaer, *War, Foreign Affairs and Constitutional Power* (Cambridge: Ballinger, 1976), 114.

47. See Vile, *Constitutionalism*, 142–43.

48. Farrand (ed.), *Records*, I, 379–82, 386–89, 392.

49. Madison to Caleb Wallace, August 23, 1785, in *Writings*, II, 168–69 (emphasis added). In the same spirit Morris moved, in the Constitutional Convention, to change *may* to *shall* (recommend legislation) "in order to make it the *duty* of the President to recommend, and thence prevent umbrage or cavil at his doing it." Farrand (ed.), *Records*, II, 405.

50. Madison to Caleb Wallace, August 23, 1785, in *Writings*, II, 169. Madison would have made its members "incapable of holding any other office Legislative, Executive or Judiciary," in order not merely to remove "the danger of their acquiring an improper influence" but also as an "antidote" to "jealousy," *i.e.*, to increase their proper influence.

51. *Federalist*, No. 62, pp. 380–82.

52. *Ibid.*, No. 46, p. 295.

53. Compare *Federalist*, No. 10 with No. 37, pp. 226–27 and Nos. 62 and 63, where "good government" is explained at length. What Madison says about the Senate applies *a fortiori* to the president. *Federalist*, No. 37, p. 227, and No. 58, pp. 259–60.

54. Madison to Jefferson, July 18, 22, 30, 1793, in *Writings*, VI, 135, 136–38, 138n.1; "Letters of Helvidius," August–September, 1793, in *Writings*, VI, 181–82, and Madison to Jefferson, June 13, 1793, in *Writings*, VI, 131; "Pacificus No. 1," June 1793, in Harold Syrett (ed.), *The Papers of Alexander Hamilton* (26 vols.; New York: Columbia University Press, 1969), XV, 38–40; "Helvidius," in *Writings*, VI, 150.

55. "Helvidius," in *Writings*, VI, 144, 143, 147; see also *Federalist*, No. 47, pp. 304–305.

56. "Helvidius," in *Writings*, VI, 145, 149.

57. Farrand (ed.), *Records*, II, 318.

58. "Helvidius," in *Writings*, VI, 147, 152–56, 188.

59. James Madison, "Political Observations," April 20, 1795, *American Political Pamphlets Before 1800* (Aldine Collection), I, 12; see Farrand (ed.), *Records*, II, 540.

60. Farrand (ed.), *Records*, I, 465; "Helvidius," in *Writings*, VI, 174–75; James Madison, "Political Observations," *American Political Pamphlets*, I, 9–10.

61. "Helvidius," in *Writings*, VI, 146; Blackstone, *Commentaries*, Bk. I, Ch. 7, pp. 257–58, 261; Madison to Jefferson, June 13, 1793, in *Writings*, VI, 131.

62. *Annals*, V, 437–38, 774, 488*ff*; Madison to Roane, May 6, 1821, *Writings*, IX, 62.

63. Gales (comp.), *Annals*, V, 438, 773.

64. *Ibid.*, I, 461–62, 576, 577, 582; Madison to E. Pendleton, June 21, 1789, in *Writings*, V, 406. Much later, in response to a law setting a four-year term for a host of executive branch offices, Madison wrote that such a limitation of the tenure of office was unconstitutional, being in effect a power of removal: Madison to Monroe, December 29, 1820, in *Writings*, IX, 43; Madison to J. Patton, March 24, 1834, in *Writings*, IX, 534–35. He also said that the attempt to remove an officer by repealing the law establishing his office "would be a virtual infringement" of the president's removal power: Madison to Monroe, December 29, 1820, in *Writings*, IX, 44.

65. Gales (comp.), *Annals*, I, 495, 578, 464, 500, 547.

66. *Ibid.*, 496.

67. *Ibid.*, 499.

68. Madison to John Patton, March 24, 1834, in *Writings*, IX, 535 (emphasis added). See also Madison to Randolph, May 31, 1789, in *Writings*, V, 373. Compare *Myers v. U.S.*, 272 U.S. 52, [at] 247, 293 (1926) (Brandeis, J.).

69. Madison to E. Coles, August 29, 1834, in *Writings*, IX, 539–40; Madison to Charles F. Adams, October 12, 1835, in *Writings*, IX, 564.

70. Gales (comp.), *Annals*, I, 546, 576.

71. *Federalist*, No. 20, pp. 136–37, No. 38, p. 240; "Report on the Resolutions," in *Writings*, VI, 386–87.

72. "Report on the Resolutions," in *Writings*, VI, 358.

73. *Ibid.*, 369–71.

74. *Ibid.*, 358; Madison to John Jackson, December 27, 1821, in *Writings*, IX, 75; Madison to Charles Adams, October 12, 1835, in *Writings*, IX, 565–66; "Consolidation," in *Writings*, VI, 67.

75. Irving Brant, *The Fourth President: A Life of James Madison* (Indianapolis: Bobbs-Merrill Co., 1970), 409–416, 539; James D. Richardson (ed.), *A Compilation of Messages and Papers of the Presidents: 1789–1897* (10 vols.; Washington: Government Printing Office, 1896), I, 480–81, 488, 562–69, 573–80.

76. See, for example, "To the Senate of the United States," in *Writings*, VIII, 250–51.

77. Irving Brant, *James Madison: The President, 1809–1812* (Indianapolis: Bobbs-Merrill Co., 1956), 25.

78. Madison to Gallatin, August 2, 1813, in *Writings*, VIII, 252–56.

79. Madison to John Patton, March 24, 1834, in *Writings*, IX, 535; Madison to J. Hillhouse, May, 1830, in *Writings*, IX, 368–69; "Memorandum as to Robert Smith," April, 1811, in *Writings*, VIII, 144; Ralph Volney Harlow, *The History of Legislative Methods in the Period Before 1825* (New Haven: Yale University Press, 1917), 198; James Sterling Young, *The Washington Community: 1800–1828* (New York: Columbia University Press, 1966), 234. The existence of a party nominating caucus encouraged these ties in ambitious cabinet members during James Monroe's administration in particular. See Leonard D. White, *The Jeffersonians: A Study in Administrative History, 1801–1829* (New York: Macmillan Co., 1951), 54. Young, *Washington Community*, 235–36.

80. Harlow, *History of Legislative Methods*, 194–95.

81. Brant, *James Madison*, 269; Harlow, *History of Legislative Methods*, 196–97; Young, *Washington Community*, 182–83.

82. Gales (comp.), *Annals*, I, 604–605; see Freeman W. Meyer, "A Note on the Origins of the 'Hamiltonian System,'" *The William and Mary Quarterly*, XXI (1964), 579–88.

83. Gales (comp.), *Annals*, I, 592, 594–95, 600, 604–606; II, 1425, 1449–50.

84. "Parties," January 23, 1792, in *Writings*, VI, 86.

85. For discussions of developing party divisions in the First Congress, see Rudolph Bell, *Party and Faction in American Politics: The House of Representatives, 1789–1800* (Westport: Greenwood Press, 1973), and Kenneth R. Bowling, "Politics in the First Congress, 1789–1791," Ph.D. dissertation, Univ. of Wisconsin, 1968. For Madison's opinion see Gales (comp.), *Annals*, I, 857, II, 1534, and Madison to H. Lee, April 13, 1790, in *Writings*, VI, 10*n*.

86. Madison to George Hay, August 23, 1823, in *Writings*, IX, 147–55; Madison to George McDuffie, January 3, 1824, in *Writings*, IX, 147*n*; Madison to Robert Taylor, January 30, 1826, in *Writings*, IX, 149*n*; Madison to Jefferson, January 14, 1824, in *Writings*, IX, 174.

87. *Federalist*, No. 10, p. 79.

88. See for example Edward C. Banfield, "In Defense of the American Party System," in Robert Goldwin (ed.), *Political Parties, U.S.A.* (Chicago: Rand McNally, 1964), 29–30; Morton Grodzins, "Party and Government in the United States," in Goldwin (ed.), *Political Parties, U.S.A.*, 102–106, 119–20, 126–30, 132–34; Arthur N. Holcombe, "Presidential Leadership and the Party System," *Yale Review*, XLIII (March, 1954), 321–25; Theodore J. Lowi, "Party, Policy, and Constitution in America," in W. Nisbet Chambers and Walter Dean Burnham (eds.), *The American Party Systems* (New York: Oxford University Press, 1967), 263, 276. In 1824, Madison suggested that the "spirit of party" might be diminished even within an environment of "party distinctions": Madison to H. Lee, June 25, 1824, in *Writings*, IX, 190–91. See also Madison to Monroe, May 18, 1822, in *Writings*, IX, 97.

89. Madison to J. Patton, March 24, 1834, in *Writings*, IX, 536.

III

Hamilton's Administrative Republic and the American Presidency

HARVEY FLAUMENHAFT

At Washington, if anywhere, are to be found those men who preside over the fortunes of free government in our day. The form of government that has its home there is distinguished among free governments by the name "presidential" government. Presiding over its birth and its first days was that monumental man named Washington; indeed, without the splendid solidity of Washington's character there would have been no such government to speak of. But that character would have lost efficacy without the brilliant operation of the mind of another man, Alexander Hamilton, who spoke of Washington as "an Aegis very essential to me." The exploits for which that aegis was essential were informed by the master writings from which Hamilton learned that "the science of politics . . . has received great improvement. . . . in modern times." According to Montesquieu, who taught Hamilton much of the reborn political science, "In the birth of societies, it is the chiefs of republics who make the institution; and it is afterward the institution which forms the chiefs of republics." Unlike Hamilton, we are not among the chiefs who have instituted republics; our republic was made by our predecessors. Those who made it formed those who modified it, and we in turn have been formed by this institutional inheritance; we cannot be fully free unless we inform ourselves about the minds of its original makers. Hamilton was among those who laid the foundation of the constitutional edifice within which we dwell, subject to constraint yet able to be free; but Hamilton was not merely one among many. He was the chief minister of the first chief magistrate of the American republic, as well as the chief proponent in America of chiefdom in a republic.

65

To understand the institution of the American presidency, to understand ourselves as the posterity for whom it was to have a central place in securing the blessings of liberty, we must rethink the thoughts of Alexander Hamilton.[1]

POPULAR REPRESENTATION

The want of safety against the power of their governors first led men to popular government, said Hamilton. The interests of the people required government intimately connected with the people. The first crude attempts at institutionalizing this connection identified government for the people with government by the people. The enlightened foundation of modern government on the equal right of every man to secure his safety and prosperity resurrected the ancient prejudice against establishing power far from the hands of the people who are to be affected by the exercise of that power. The modern doctrine of equality had, however, also generated a modern improvement which permitted government to be popular yet free from the defects of government by the collective body of the people: the principle of popular representation, said Hamilton, gave the decisive advantage to modern republics over ancient republics.

The animating principle of the ancient body politic was animosity. The true condition of the people in the ancient republics was that of a nation of soldiers; in those barbarous times war was the principal business of man. Antiquity was a time of sweat and blood, of poverty and ferocity, of unimproved spades and dominating swords. In the classical republics, those wretched nurseries of unceasing discord, the citizens were inflated with glory. Their virtue was valor; but their valiant displays were vicious. The assembled people, jealous of authority, were an ungovernable mob; when not fighting against other peoples, they clashed tumultuously among themselves. Domestic carnage filled up the intervals of foreign wars. Among themselves, they alternated between anarchy and despotism; with others, between despotism and servitude.

But, said Hamilton, the ferocious maxims of antiquity were replaced by the humane innovations of later times according to the pronouncements of enlightened reason. It came to be acknowledged that profitable business, not heroic display, is the business of government.

The industrious habits of a modern people, absorbed in gainful pursuits and devoted to productive improvements, are incompatible with the condition of a nation of soldiers, where civic life centers on an assembly of warriors whose delight is to dominate. The industrious habits of a modern people are incompatible with the condition of a nation of citizens in the fullest sense; for if merely the power of appointing officers of government were ordinarily exercised by the people at large, said Hamilton, they would not have time for anything else. If those who might otherwise be industrious and enterprising at business were busy where the action is, the citizenry would be impoverished—unless the action were that collective piracy which supported the armed splendor of antiquity. But modern humanity discountenances fierce rapacity; modern enlightenment looks not to dominion and plunder, but to commerce and production. The common good, the good common to common men, requires that participation in government be uncommon. Government by the people cannot secure popular safety and prosperity. The liberty of a people is not a stage or arena for displaying popular action, but rather a protective fence properly erected by popular fear and desire, which, prudently managed by wise and energetic leadership, may become a productive force: liberty is that moral security for life and property provided by checks and controls on government. Political society is a means of coping with men's insecurity, an insecurity preceding political society, though political society may complicate that insecurity. It is not a heightened manner of living, but machinery for the organization of swords and purses: swords, to protect the lives of vulnerable men exposed to the violence of other men; and purses, to energize the spades of needy men laboring to ease their lives by transforming nature's rawness. Fear and desire are the governing beginnings of government: its ends are safety and prosperity. The contest of swords and words for which the ancient republic provided a stage or arena is to be replaced by reliable machinery for cooperation.

We must, said Hamilton, prefer our own governments to those of the ancient republics, because every power with us is exercised by representation, not in tumultuary assemblies of the collective body of the people, where the art or impudence of the orator or tribune, rather than the utility or justice of the measure, could seldom fail to govern. We must prefer our own governments not because they are our own, but because they are preferable. But that which leads us to prefer them requires us to perfect them if we can. Those who estimate the value of institutions, not from the prejudices of the moment but from experience and reason, Hamilton went on, must be persuaded that jealousy of power has prevented our reaping all the advantages from the example of other nations which we ought to have done, and has rendered the constitutions of the American governments in many respects feeble and imperfect. The apportioning of governmental power among several depositories of power, justifiable as an auxiliary precaution against abuse of power, was the means for completing the innovation made in government by the principle of popular representation.[2]

The end of government is to secure the safety and prosperity of the people, who are its source. Government by the collective body of the people endangers and impoverishes the people. Popular representation secures the people against government, as it secures the people against themselves by removing government from the hands of the collective body of the people. The body of representatives is different from the body of the people. The representative body is superior to the people in its ability to serve the people's interests. The interests of the representatives are not superior to the people's interests, but the representatives might come to think they are. Safety requires, therefore, that the members of the representative assembly be many in number and frequently elected. But while representation is at the foundation of good government, representation is not the whole of it. As government without popular representatives is an unchecked danger to the people, so also an unchecked representative body is a danger to the people.[3]

In a nation of states, the state governments may contribute to safety against the government of the whole by their multiplying the depositories of power; from one point of view, the state governments are *the* parts of the whole. But there is something problematic in a multiplicity of depositories of power that are wholes of a sort similar to the whole of which they are parts. The government of such a whole verges on being a mere league of governments or a government over governments, that is, no government at all. If the whole is not to be an anarchy, the parts must lose their similarity to the whole, thus leaving the government of the whole a great mass of power deposited in a single representative body. However urgent the question of the partition of power among the component parts of a compound republic, the central question is the question of the partition of power among the several departments in a single government.[4]

Government flowing from the people must be divided to work for the people. The propriety of this partition resides in the fact that some partition of governmental power is essential to free government: the very definition of despotism is "a government, in which all power is concentered in a single body." Its most obvious form is absolute monarchy. Absolute monarchy, however, is not the only form contrary to free government. No single body, not even a representative assembly, is a safe depository of ample unchecked power. Practically speaking, government must have both purse and sword, but purse and sword must not both be in the same hands.[5]

There is a sense in which good government is thoroughly representative; under the proposed constitution, said Hamilton, the president of the United States would be himself a representative of the people who would act to protect the people against an unfaithful Congress. Nonetheless, the most proper name of one of the branches is "The House of Representatives," for that assembly is the representative body. By means of representation, the people obtain public servants, whom the people hire to free themselves for business other than the public business, and whom they can fire for acting as if they themselves were free to neglect their tie to the people. The ends of representative government are served by government conducted according to law: legislation is the most manifestly public of acts. And legislation by a numerous assembly most represents the multitudinous people.

The legislature seems to represent the immediate being of the society. There is no question that free government requires a freely elected popular assembly: the question is what else it needs.[6]

The principle of representative government is perfected by the partitioning of governmental power. But it is more difficult to hold to such partition than to representation. Insofar as the parts do not approach being whole governments themselves, the parts must be differentiated organs. But one of them, the popular legislative assembly, the part most properly called representative, tends to primacy and even hegemony; and when the part becomes the partitioner, the partitioning of governmental power in its sovereign sense is destroyed. The partitioning of power, and even the intermixture of the powers of the parts, have a general explanation in the need for checks upon power and in the need for balance to preserve the system of checks. The general explanation, however, explains only partly. The whole explanation must show partitions of power as differentiations of power, each with its peculiar property.[7]

Government flowing from the people must be divided to work for the people. As has been said, partition is a means to prevent bad deeds by multiplying the number of agencies whose cooperation is necessary for action. But, it needs to be said, partition is also a means to promote good deeds by differentiating agencies so that different sorts of work are done. The device to decrease danger can be employed against inefficacy; government can be energized by the very safeguard against governmental oppression. A modern "Publius" can hope to popularize unpopular truths by building upon popular acceptance of the rule which teaches the propriety of a partition among the various branches of power.

EFFICACIOUS ADMINISTRATION

Popular representation freed the populace from continual contention, and for productive industry, while safeguarding them against their governors. Americans had accepted this governing principle, but imperfectly, Hamilton thought. Only replacing the vestiges of democratic participation by an efficacious administrative system could supply the energy to protect them against turmoil and invasion and the energy to manage their prosperity. The people had to choose: government by the people, affecting democratic workings—or government from and for the people, effecting popular works. The partition of power understood as a differentiation of parts enables government to effect its works. Government flowing from the people must be divided to work *for the people*; if the government is to *work* for the people, the division must be a differentiation. The proper end of government is popular, as is its source. Popular representation is the fundamental reliance for keeping the ends of government popular. According to Hamilton, as we have seen, the chief executive is in one sense a representative, but the representatives in the most precise signification are the officials who are most numerous and have the shortest duration in office of all the men elected to public office. On the other hand, as we shall see, Hamilton also thought that although the administration of government, the actual business of governing, is in one sense the work of all the parts of the government, the administration of government in the most precise signification is the work of the executive part; the "democratical" part of government, the numerous assembly of representatives with short duration in office, cannot itself do the actual work of governing. Popular representation avails little without efficacious administration. Although the beginning and the end of good government is the people, between the source and the outcome operates that organization of means which is administration. The double meaning of *administration* is as significant for the projector of the modern republic as is the multiple meaning of *politeia* for the contemplator of the classical polis.

Practically speaking, the classical political aspiration was shown by Thucydides when he depicted Pericles reminding his fellow citizens that they would leave behind in everlasting remembrance the splendor of their domineering. The persuasion of a Pericles could concentrate and stabilize a multitude of such imperious wills; his leadership of the polis sometimes required the suspension of even the appearance of politics. But, unfortunately, Periclean leadership requires that fortune supply a Pericles; the deficiency of institutionalized authority must be supplied by extraordinary personal persuasiveness. Pericles' mind and the esteem in which he was held enabled him to hold down the multitude, says Thucydides, leading them rather than being led by them, speaking harsh things rather than sweet things—and so, though in word a democracy, in work it was rule by the first man; whereas those who came after, being equal among themselves and straining to be first, gave in on practical affairs to what pleased the people. The polis depicted by Thucydides was spoken of as an arrangement in which the assembled people's power prevailed, but at its peak it was in effect an arrangement in which a chief subjected affairs to his initiative: the mind of one headman prevailed over the valiant he-men because he knew how to speak to them. Hence the first *technologia*, the first know-how set out in speech among the Greeks, was the art that spoke about artful public speech. The term *technologia* was borrowed by the Romans to designate a systematic treatment of language.[8]

With the coming of modernity, politic men were taught to seek what is useful even if not resplendent: the effectual or factual truth. They were taught to look not to the fact of doing but to its effect; for the vulgar, who fill the world, are taken with outcomes, with what eventuates from doing. They were taught that the multitude desires liberty not for commanding but for living securely, that is, for living under government that keeps the laws unbroken.[9] So taught, politic men reassessed the inherited wisdom. The ancients were puerile: prompt to prattle, but unable to generate. Their teachings were fine words barren of works. The classical wise men were adolescents, they were ostentatious and pugnacious, like the classical citizens—they merely substituted disputation for slaughter, the word for the sword. Rhetoric was the substance of ancient wisdom.[10] Under cover of bold privacy, bold genius resolutely overturned public things by turning men's minds from the contemplation of the looks of things to methodical operation.[11] In the governing of men, pacification by the spirit of modern technology was to replace the polemic art of ancient rhetoric. According to Hobbes, democracy is the worst form of government: though the right of sovereignty be in the assembly, which is virtually the whole body, yet a democracy in effect is no more than an aristocracy of orators, interrupted sometimes with the temporary monarchy of one orator. Men favor popular over monarchical government, supposing that not to participate in public business is to all men grievous, since the desire of praise, which is natural to humans, is most delightfully satisfied when they can show their wisdom, knowledge, and eloquence in deliberating matters of the greatest difficulty and moment. But, says Hobbes, this loss of an opportunity for vainglory is a grievance only if it is a grievance to men to be restrained for fighting, though the valiant may delight in it; only the desire for applause would lead a man to mind the public rather than his own business—as, of old, Coriolanus from his actions of war had only the delight of pleasing his mother by winning applause. Moreover, large assemblies are inconvenient for deliberations. Few men are skilled in public affairs; the display of alluring eloquence, which seeks victory, replaces the informing effort which seeks truth; faction arises, leading to sedition and civil war, or to instability in the laws; and secrets cannot be kept from the enemy. Hence, Hobbes concludes, aristocracy is good to the extent that it is like monarchy, and bad to the extent that it is like popular government; and democracy would be good, like monarchy, to the extent that the people in a democracy would bestow on one or a few the power of deliberating, being content with the naming of magistrates and public ministers, that is, with the authority without the "ministration." [12] Subsequently, the work of the modern republican spirit, in which the polemic polity of spiritedness gave way to the productive spirit of political economy, was promoted by the publication of Montesquieu's *De l'Esprit des Lois*. In it, Montesquieu discussed the need to separate the legislative, executive, and judicial powers, in the chapter on the constitution of England, in the book on the laws that form political liberty in its relation with the constitution. There he wrote that political liberty in a citizen is that tranquility of mind which proceeds from the opinion each person has of his security; and to have this liberty requires a government such that one citizen not fear another citizen. But since in a free state every man who is counted as having a free soul ought to be governed by himself, the people as a body need to have the legislative power, something that is impossible in large states and is subject to many inconveniences in small ones; hence the people need to do by their representatives what they cannot do by themselves. It was a great vice in most of the ancient republics, says Montesquieu, that the people had a right to take active resolutions which require some execution; the people, however, ought not to enter into the government but for choosing its representatives. And the representative body, Montesquieu also says, ought not to be chosen for taking any active resolution, but for making laws, or for seeing if those which it has made have been well executed.[13]

Spiritedness, to be sure, continued to play a part in modern civil society, as may be seen from Adam Smith's discussion, in *The Wealth of Nations*, of the sources of the quarrel that developed from taxation without representation.[14] But bad conscience overwhelmed the display of spiritedness. The poetry of antagonism gave way to the prose of cooperation. To use the words of Hume, "the prudent views of modern politics," which seek not glory but security, are to be contrasted with "the ancient Greek spirit of jealous emulation."[15] From the point of view of modern prudence, being businesslike seemed better than being rhetorical. Concomitant with the downgrading of rhetoric came a change in vocabulary. To judge from the earliest listing of *energy* in the *Oxford English Dictionary*, the word entered English "with reference to speech or writing," having the meaning of "force or vigour of expression"—as in Sidney's *Defense of Poesie* (1581): "That same forcibleness or Energeia (as the Greeks call it) of the writer." According to the OED, "This sense (found in Late Latin and in Romanic) is originally derived from an imperfect understanding of Aristotle's use of *energeia* (*Rhet*. III. xi. 2) for the species of metaphor which calls up a mental picture of something 'acting' or moving." With the progress of modernity, *energy* outgrew its primary rhetorical meaning. When Hamilton spoke of "energy," he did not have in mind display: he meant business. The rejection of classical politics culminates in the politics of administration.

Hamilton sought to move his fellow Americans with forceful words depicting what they needed in order to have a government capable of doing the work they needed done.[16] Good intents do not suffice for securing good effects, he said, and the tendency to produce good outcomes is essential to good government. To good intentions, America owed her independence; the outcome of the struggle, insofar as it was not an immediate gift of fortune, was the product of a fortunate inspiration of enthusiasm. There is a certain enthusiasm in liberty that makes human nature rise above itself in acts of bravery or heroism. The enthusiasm inspired by the transition from slavery to liberty may possibly be a substitute for the energy of a good administration, and be the spring of great exertions, but the ebullitions of enthusiasm must ever be a precarious reliance. Reliance for good government on the good intentions of the people had its source in an excessive distrust. The noble enthusiasm of liberty is too apt to be infected with a spirit of narrow and illiberal distrust of governmental power, even though the vigor of government is essential to the security of liberty. The zeal for liberty was too often more ardent than enlightened. A glorious struggle had been conducted in a disastrous manner; and "notwithstanding we have by the blessing of providence so far happily escaped the complicated dangers of such a situation. . . . It would be unwise to hazard a repetition of the same dangers . . . or to continue this extensive empire under a government unequal to its protection and prosperity." But it was hardly to be expected that in a popular revolution the minds of men should stop at that salutary mean between power and privilege which combines the energy of government with the security of private rights. Too little regard for the rights and liberties in defense of which the people fought and suffered was not the American error, which was rather that through excess of caution and impracticable zeal the public counsels were devoid of consistency and stability. A new improved organization of power was needed. This meant strengthening nation against state and executive against legislature.[17]

Americans suffered many evils because they confused popular government with governmental popularity. Government, however, is more truly popular when the people like the long-run and long-lasting outcomes of government than when the immediately effective source of governmental outcomes is like the people or tends to what is immediately popular. A principle like this was hard to make immediately clear to the people; and many leaders of the people took the way more immediately pleasant to themselves of immediately pleasing the people, that is, they became flattering demagogues—instead of leading the people, they misled the people by flattering the people's prejudices. In the American practice of taxation and public finance Hamilton found many examples of this pernicious popularity. The little politicians who lack the capacity to govern but are consummate in the paltry science of courting and winning popular favor, he said, stigmatize an enlightened zeal for the energy and efficacy of government as the offspring of a temper fond of despotic power and hostile to the principles of liberty. Yet a dangerous ambition more often lurks behind the specious mask of zeal for the rights of the people than under the forbidding aspect of zeal for the firmness and efficacy of government. Hamilton, after helping to found the new government, sought to have it operate in a manner opposed to the feeble and contracted views of those who lacked the wisdom to plan and the spirit to adopt energetic measures. In every community, natural resistance to government results from the human passions, but the people need to submit to present displeasures to avoid the more oppressive future burdens with which necessity will afflict those who, lacking foresight and fortitude, live under the delusion that they are free from necessity. Popular safety and prosperity require efficacious administration; but efficacious administration requires what is not immediately popular. Popular prejudice against being governed, when it is formed into political opinion, operates under the name of republican jealousy: to grant power is to concentrate the capacity to harm the people, and thus to contribute to the erection of monarchy on the ruin of the republic. To Hamilton, the confusion between good government and popularity was exemplified in the leadership of Jefferson, who wrote to Madison: "I am not a friend to very energetic government. It is always oppressive." Jefferson, not a friend to Hamilton, called the movement led by Hamilton "the *monocratic* party." There is a certain aptness in the term *monocrat: E pluribus unum* might be taken as Hamilton's motto in more ways than one. But the term, used in contradistinction to *republican*, was devised as a weapon of revolutionary war: the popular prejudice against being governed was being enlisted by faction in a war of principles, thought Hamilton. In an election address the year after his allies lost the great battle of that war,

Hamilton explained why the leaders he opposed could be called hostile to our national constitution:

> They have openly avowed their attachment to the excessive principles of the French Revolution, and to leading features in the crude forms of government which have appeared only to disappear; utterly inconsistent with the sober maxims upon which our federal edifice was reared, and with essential parts in its structure. . . . The contest between us is indeed a war of principles—a war between tyranny and liberty, but not between monarchy and republicanism. It is a contest between the tyranny of Jacobinism, which confounds and levels every thing, and the mild reign of rational liberty, which rests on the basis of an efficient and well-balanced government.

According to Jefferson, the culmination of the struggle was a revolution. Though it was "not effected . . . by the sword . . . but by the rational and peaceable instrument of reform, the suffrage of the people," he said, "the Revolution of 1800 was as real a revolution in the principles of our government as that of 1776 was in its form." [18] According to Madison, who was Hamilton's great collaborator in the effort to constitute a new government and his first great opponent in its operation, the prime source of this great party struggle was Hamilton's straining of *administration*.[19]

Hamilton would not trust to fortune for splendid feats of virtue that would bless and keep the republic. He deemed it wiser to secure energetic administrative machinery that would operate reliably throughout an extended territory during a protracted time to produce one general interest from many most common interests. Good government, that is, protection and prosperity through a system of liberty, requires concentration of power and constancy in policy. Those who are dominated by apprehension of being dominated, when they think of security from government, think mostly of how to secure the endangered people against government, and little of how to secure popular ends by means of government. Safety from government means keeping government from doing bad things. The fear that leads to precautions against government's doing bad things may lead to arrangements that keep government from doing much of anything, good or bad. This is, literally, anarchy. The precaution against government's doing bad things is the separating of the powers to do anything, on the presumption that the several depositories of power will have difficulty in coming together, and in staying together, in order to do bad things, but will be able to come together, and to stay together, in order to do good things. However, in a government amply arranged for safety against government, adequately arranging for energy of government is a problem. The problem is twofold: to concentrate power sufficiently to cause many wills to act as one at one time, and to stabilize policy sufficiently to concert many actions during a long time for constant purposes. Unless the powers of government are apportioned to promote administrative efficacy, those who take part in the multitudinous affairs of the multitudes of men massed in political society will be uncooperative and improvident. The work of a founder is to lead men to agree to arrangements that will foster, among the leading men who will follow, the energetic wisdom that is leadership. There cannot be energetic wisdom without the two ingredients of efficacious administration: unity and duration.

UNITY

The most urgent though not most central work of unification in America was the "federalist" work that the words *E pluribus unum* first call to mind: from the point of view of urgency, *the* problem of unity was the problem of the Union, the need to form a more perfect union. But the single-minded attention to security against concentrated power is most concentrated in the fear of monarchy, the arrangement that most facilitates authoritative action by authorizing action to proceed from one mind without requiring the concurrence of other minds. The single-minded attention to security from abuse of power does not attend with due care to the mischiefs that may be occasioned when the public business cannot go forward at critical seasons. When unanimity or something approaching it is required in public bodies, security is the intent, but the effect (besides increased danger of foreign corruption) is always weakness, sometimes bordering on anarchy:

> When concurrence of a large number is required by the constitution to the doing of any national act, we are apt to rest satisfied that all is safe, because nothing improper will be likely *to be done*; but we forget

how much good may be prevented, and how much ill may be produced, by the power of hindering the doing what may be necessary, and of keeping affairs in the same unfavorable posture in which they may happen to stand at particular periods.

Whenever two or more persons are engaged in any common enterprise, there is always danger of difference of opinion, and there is peculiar danger of personal emulation and even animosity if it be a public trust or office in which they are clothed with equal dignity and authority. Men often oppose a thing merely because they have had no agency in planning it, or because it may have been planned by those whom they dislike, or because they had once been consulted and happened to disapprove. The principles of a free government require submitting to the inconveniences of dissension in the formation of the legislature. There, moreover, prompt decision is more often bad than good; there, deliberation and moderation are often promoted by the differences of opinion and the jarring of parties that may sometimes obstruct salutary plans. But in the executive department, dissensions do no good that counterbalances the harm they do to the vigor and expedition that should characterize it.[20]

Hamilton early argued that the Continental Congress should arrange for administration by a single man in each department of affairs, and he went on to complete the argument as a warm advocate on behalf of the executive power vested by the Constitution of the United States in a single man.

In 1780 he presented to a member of the Congress his thoughts on the defects of the system and the changes necessary to save the Americans from ruin. Listed right after the fundamental defect, which is a want of power in Congress vis-à-vis the states (that is, the imperfection of the Union), the very next defect is want of method and energy in the administration, which, though it partly results from the other defect, results in a great degree from prejudice and the want of a proper executive. It is impossible, says Hamilton, for such a body as Congress, numerous and constantly fluctuating, to act with sufficient decision or with system. Congress, convinced at last of these inconveniences, acknowledged that administration by a large assembly is a bad arrangement—by going into appointing boards. But this practice lately adopted by Congress is bad, for boards partake of the inconveniences of larger assemblies; greatly preferable would be the plan of vesting the great executive departments in the hands of individuals—a single man in each department of the administration.

Hamilton characterizes boards in contrast to an administration by single men: Their decisions are slower. Their decisions, one might say, are less decisive, for they react instead of being active, that is, their energy is less. Their responsibility is more diffuse. Whatever else is bad about this characteristic last mentioned, it seems to be responsible for another bad characteristic: boards will not have the same abilities and knowledge as an administration by single men—less ability, since men of the first pretensions will not so readily engage in them, because they will have less opportunity of distinguishing themselves; and less knowledge, since those who do become members of boards will take fewer pains to inform themselves and arrive to eminence, because they have fewer motives to do so. Since administration by single men in each department would give America a chance of more knowledge, more activity, more responsibility, and more zeal and attention, while of course these men will be at all times under the direction of Congress, we shall by this arrangement "blend the advantages of a monarchy and republic in our constitution."

The heart of the difficulty seems to be the love of honor. The question has been asked whether single men could be found to undertake these offices. Hamilton remarks that he thinks they could, because there would then be everything to excite the ambition of candidates, but Congress must by their manner of appointing them and by the duties marked out show that they are in earnest in making these offices of real trust and importance. This appeal to love of honor, however, seems to frustrate the love of honor of those who would have to make the appeal. Hamilton fears that a little vanity has stood in the way of these arrangements, as though they would lessen the importance of Congress and leave them nothing to do. But happily the frustration is imaginary. Freed from vain imaginings, the members of Congress would have the same rights and powers as before, happily disencumbered of the detail; they would have to inspect the conduct of their ministers, deliberate upon their plans, originate others for the public good—the difference only being their observing the rule that they ought to consult their ministers and get from them all the information and advice they could before entering into any new measures or making changes in the old. Further on in the letter, when Hamilton says what offices ought to be established, and with what powers and duties, it becomes clear that his mention of the advantages of monarchy in connection with administration by single men is not a mere matter of terminology, for his express model is French administration under the *ancien régime*.[21]

Later, urging adoption of the proposed constitution, Hamilton declared in favor of a numerous legislature, as best adapted to deliberation and wisdom, and best calculated to conciliate the confidence of the people and to secure their privileges and interests—and in favor of a single executive, because the proceedings of one man are most eminently characterized by decision, activity, secrecy, and dispatch. The persons to whose immediate management are committed those matters that constitute the administration of government properly understood ought to be considered as the assistants or deputies of the chief magistrate.[22]

In one sense, the executive is but a part of the government. The First Congress under the new Constitution was warned by Madison that for the meaning of terms used in the laws and Constitution of the United States, they ought not to look to other countries, whose situation and government are different from that of the United States: in monarchies, both absolute and limited, the residence of the monarch is the seat of government, but in such a government as ours the seat of government cannot be at a place other than where Congress sits, for the government comprehends Congress as well as the executive; and "so the term Administration, which in other countries is specially appropriated to the Executive branch of Government, is used here for both the Executive and Legislative branches." However, those to whom the new Constitution had been proposed for ratification were told by Hamilton that "the administration of government, in its largest sense, comprehends all the operations of the body politic, whether legislative, executive or judiciary, but in its most usual and perhaps its most precise signification, it is limited to executive details, and falls peculiarly within the province of the executive department." Hamilton presented a list of the sorts of "executive details" that constitute what seems to be most properly understood by the administration of government: "the actual conduct of foreign negotiations, the preparatory plans of finance, the application and disbursement of the public monies, in conformity to the general appropriations of the legislature, the arrangement of the army and navy, the direction of the operations of war; these and other matters of a like nature."[23]

Central for Hamilton were the preparation of plans for getting money, and the spending of money following general appropriations. He spoke emphatically of the need, in preparing plans of finance, for the unity characteristic of executive power. It is impossible that the business of finance could be ably conducted by a body of men, however well-composed or well-intentioned. Although it is necessary to accommodate the diversity and crudity of the opinions and the passions and interests of the parties which cause the public deliberations on matters of finance to be distracted between jarring and incoherent projects, accommodation is not submission; there is need for a rallying point.[24] Hamilton was equally emphatic about the need to recognize that the business of administration cannot be as fully subordinated to rule as some would wish; the machinery cannot work without latitude in interpreting the rules for the expenditure of public money.[25]

First and last on Hamilton's list are matters which cannot be simply prescribed by a general rule because what a government must do in respect to them must take into account the actions of men not subject to the authority of that government's laws. These matters are the actual conduct of foreign negotiations, and the arrangement of armed forces and the direction of their operations in war.

In the management of foreign negotiations the executive is the most fit agent, having the indispensable qualities of secrecy and dispatch, which come from unity. But a magistrate elected for a scant few years, not having the personal stake in the government possessed by a hereditary monarch, is in too much danger of being corrupted by foreign powers to be trusted alone to conclude treaties. And there is a peculiar propriety in vesting this power in an executive-legislative union. On the one hand, treaties are products that operate more like the products peculiarly legislative than like those peculiarly executive, since a treaty once made operates as law. Hence it is unsafe to trust treaty making to an agency without legislative participation. A treaty, however, is not a law in the strict sense. On the other hand, treaty making calls for the operating qualities found in the executive, rather than in the legislature. Hence it is inefficacious to empower a legislative body to negotiate treaties. Making a treaty, however, is not an instance of the activities of executive power most strictly defined; it is not executing laws or employing the common strength for law enforcement or for the common defense. Thus the heart of the argument against vesting the power to make treaties in the chief magistrate alone, without any requirement of legislative concurrence, is that while one can do it more efficaciously, this would be unsafe in a republic. In treaty making, the making is executive, while what is legislative is the concurring; and even the legislative share does not belong to the more representative branch, which is less fit.[26]

Finally, it is the direction of war which of all governmental concerns most peculiarly demands those qualities which distinguish the exercise of power by a single hand. It is of the nature of war to increase the executive at the expense of the legislative authority. Americans recognize this, for even those state constitutions which have in other respects coupled the chief magistrate with a council have for the most part concentered the military authority in him alone. And while with republican caution the Constitution of the United States does not place in a single hand the power of generating either the condition of war or the forces to fight war, it does designate as commander-in-chief the chief executive, placing in a single hand the power to employ in a war already begun forces provided by a body of men. Moreover, the energy of the unitary executive is an ingredient of good government not only in the conduct of the operations of war, but also with a view to being able to anticipate distant danger and prepare to meet the gathering storm. As Demosthenes said, a wise politician should be like a general, who marches at the head of his troops; the statesman should march at the head of affairs, not awaiting the event to know what measures to take, but taking measures which produce the event. While avoiding the exercise of authority only doubtfully constitutional, and being as accommodating toward foreign powers as honor and interest permit, the executive ought to be energetic as well as prudent; in times of crisis the executive ought to have a well-digested plan before Congress meets, and ought to cooperate in getting it adopted. Energy is not, however, merely a necessary supplement to wisdom, energy at times *is* wisdom.[27]

The apportionment of power into several depositories is not an item-by-item distribution guided only by the wish to prevent abuse by equilibrating the capacity for abuse. There are sorts of work into which the various powers of government have a natural tendency to be sorted. The executive power has an inherent nature; it is not a mere convention produced by the Constitutional Convention. What our Constitution did was to vest the executive power, with certain expressed exceptions and qualifications, in an official called the president; the executive powers it enumerates are not exhaustive of the president's powers. There is unanimous agreement that the vesting of the executive power in the president ought to be interpreted in conformity to other parts of the Constitution which express exceptions and qualifications. There is also unanimous agreement that it ought to be interpreted in conformity to the principles of free government. But about the meaning of the latter there is antagonistic disagreement. According to Hamilton, free government must not only be free, it must also be government; and free government need not simply be popular but may also be monarchical.[28]

The idea that a vigorous executive is inconsistent with the genius of republican government is, to say the least, not without its advocates. Some of them are therefore not unfriendly to monarchy—but these are not those whom Hamilton seeks to persuade that the proposed constitution ought to be adopted. Rather, he seeks to persuade those who were unfriendly to the proposed constitution out of belief that a vigorous executive is inconsistent with the genius of republican government. Those unfriendly to the proposed constitution because its executive is energetic are placed in a dilemma: they must choose between government that is republican but bad, and government that is good but non-republican. Opposition to the energetic executive must be abandoned by enlightened well-wishers to republican government, for energy in the executive is a leading character in the definition of good government. Energy in the executive is essential to the protection of the community against foreign attacks, and is not less essential internally. Internally, it is essential to the steady administration of the laws; it is essential to the protection of property against those irregular combinations which sometimes interrupt the ordinary course of justice, and to the security of liberty against the enterprises and assaults of ambition, faction, and anarchy. Whatever our theory about the preferability of republican over monarchical government, practice shows the necessity of an energetic executive.

Hamilton's problem is to persuade enthusiastic defenders of republicanism that a due dependence on the people, and a due responsibility, the two circumstances which constitute safety in the republican sense, can consist with an executive attacked as monarchical because of its energy. At the root of the monarchical problem is the unity of the executive; the chief or central difficulty with which Hamilton must contend is the fear that concentrating governmental power in one man, the chief executive, is not safe. In America Hamilton finds ample concern for republican safety; the difficulty is in sufficiently providing the unity of power and stability of policy necessary for energetic government. The Americans' habits and opinions in the situation impede the effort to protect their rights and promote their interests; they resist being governed, because they fear to be oppressed.[29]

It is often best in a monarchy for the prince to relinquish a part of an excessive prerogative to establish a more moderate government, better adapted to the happiness or temper of his people. A government characterized by the absolutely unqualified monarchical principle is less truly energetic than its antithesis, free government. But, though freedom has this tendency to energize government through the extensive feelings that identify public and private, it also has a tendency to enfeeble government, through the fear, and through the envy manipulating fear, which resist the concentration of power in men elevated above their fellows to exercise public authority. Freedom is not identical with energy; freedom energizes when the requirements of energy are not ignored. A country, like Great Britain, in which the principle of freedom has been joined to the monarchical principle, may have governmental energy and popular enthusiasm.[30]

The opinions that led many Americans to desire an executive weaker than should be desired by an enlightened and reasonable people account for the arrangement of Hamilton's most extensive discussion of the executive, the discussion in *The Federalist*. The part of *The Federalist* which treats the constitution of the executive department of the proposed government is the only part which begins with a long discussion of the slanders against the proposal. Number 67, the first paper in the discussion, presents the proposed executive as having been so outrageously opposed that it is difficult to maintain the attitude appropriate to civil argument.[31] The second paper on the executive, Number 68, pairs with the first, which gave an instance of something that the outrageous opposition has misrepresented (an alleged power of appointment by the president which was not in fact proposed), by setting over against it an instance of something that even the opposition has somewhat approved (the mode of appointment of the president which came to be called the "Electoral College"). What the most plausible opponents deign to admit is that the mode of appointment of the chief magistrate is pretty well guarded; their concern is safety. Hamilton does not hesitate to venture somewhat further: the manner of it is at least excellent, uniting in an eminent degree all the advantages to be desired. Putting aside a consideration of what might not be perfect in it, Hamilton lists five advantages happily combined in the plan. The consideration treated first and the two considerations treated last might be called "popular"; they initiate and conclude a discussion which contains two other considerations, of central concern to Hamilton, which might be called "nonpopular."

In the *first* place, the sense of the people should operate in the choice of the person to whom so important a trust is to be confided by the people. It is equally desirable, in the *second* place, to consider the superior efficacy in operation of men who are select and act in circumstances that are suitable for doing the work. But it is also desirable to prevent what is dreadful. While it is not dangerous that there be a magistrate with so important an agency in the administration of the government as the president of the United States, the process of electing him could be very dangerous. In the election of such a magistrate, tumult and disorder are to be dreaded; in the *third* place, therefore, it is desirable to afford as little opportunity as possible to this evil. Effectual security against it is provided in part by an arrangement that has already commended itself as most effectual for obtaining a man who may not be immediately popular but has qualities adapted to the station: the people are to be not the immediate source but rather the source of the source of the choice. Their making a preliminary choice of several will be much less apt to generate any extraordinary or violent movements than would their final choice of one. With the object of choice more diffuse, because of the number of men immediately chosen, and the final object more distant, because of the number of operations in the mediated process of choice, the popular emotions will be less concentrated and hence less likely to convulse the community with commotion as it moves to concenter power in one man. Further precautions are needed, however, just because there is an intermediate body of electors. The elite elected by the people to make the final election is itself susceptible to heats and ferments which might from them inflame the people. Hence the several persons chosen in the first of several operations are to meet not in one but in several bodies. Thus, the process is made less intense by its beginning with a choice of more than one man, is protracted by its containing more than one step, and is extended by its having the central step taken simultaneously in more than one place.

It is desirable, however, not only to take precautions against the people's being inflamed by the elite they select but also to set up obstacles against the people's being betrayed by those selected; in the *fourth* place, therefore, every practicable obstacle should be opposed to cabal, intrigue, and corruption—these most deadly adversaries of republican government. The danger is chiefly to be expected from the desire in foreign powers to gain an improper ascendant in our councils by raising a creature of their own to the chief magistracy. The guard against this danger is that there are to be no preexisting bodies of men to be tampered with, since the choosing begins with an act of the people and the immediate outcome of that beginning is the temporary appointment of persons for the single purpose of appointing a president. But the danger of corruption is not only that the electors of the president might serve foreign powers; the electors might also be subservient to the president already in office. All officials of the United States, including members of either branch of Congress, are excluded from eligibility as electors, so that the people will not be betrayed because the electors of the next president lack independence from the president in office. This arrangement also secures another desideratum that is no less important, the *last* on Hamilton's list: that the people not be betrayed because the president in office, eager for reelection, himself lacks independence from the body of electors. This is another reason for giving the appointment of the president to persons temporarily appointed for that single purpose; the electors of the president are the elected officers furthest from having a considerable duration.

In Hamilton's list of five considerations, only the first desideratum might be called "popular" simply; the fourth and fifth desiderata with which Hamilton concludes his list might also be called "popular," but they are consequences of the second and third desiderata, which are "non-popular." The concluding considerations of popular safety arise from central considerations of what is requisite for governmental efficacy. While popular safety first requires that the sense of the people should operate at bottom, the people should not have an immediate operation on the outcome. Operating intermediately between the sense of the people and the final choice should be those selected by the people because they are particularly capable of supplying the requisite information and discernment; this small number of men is to act under circumstances favorable to deliberation and to a judicious combination of considerations proper to govern choice.

After listing the advantages of the mode of appointing the president, Hamilton in Number 68 finds it no inconsiderable recommendation of the proposed constitution that, because the process of election affords a moral certainty that the office of president will seldom fall to the lot of any man who is not eminently qualified, the office will therefore probably be filled by characters preeminent for ability and virtue. He finds this a considerable recommendation because he is one of those able to estimate the share which the executive in every government must necessarily have in its good or ill administration.

> Though we cannot acquiesce in the political heresy of the poet who says—
> "For forms of government let fools contest—
> That which is best administered is best."
> —yet we may safely pronounce, that the true test of a good government is its aptitude and tendency to produce a good administration.

The poet was right to emphasize a good administration, but he was wrong to dismiss as an occupation of fools the contest for forms of government: forms of government differ in their aptitude and tendency to produce a good administration. It is not foolishness to take part in contentions to produce a form of government which has the aptitude and tendency to produce a good administration, which is productive of good works. It is the work of statesmen to establish and foster forms of government in which there will flourish administrative energy, rather than talents for low intrigue and the little arts of popularity.[32]

Hamilton introduces, in Number 70,[33] his presentation of the executive in itself with a brief statement that executive energy is essential to good government, however much it may be thought non-republican, and he devotes the rest of the 70th paper to unity, the first ingredient of executive energy. The argument that executive authority lacking unity would be exercised with a spirit habitually feeble and dilatory applies with principal weight to one of the two methods of destroying the unity of the executive: the arrangement in which there is a plurality of magistrates of equal dignity and authority. This feeble arrangement is also unsafe, owing to the danger of differences that might split the community into the most violent and irreconcilable factions. Its advocates are not likely to be numerous. More numerous are the advocates of the second method of destroying the unity of the executive; in this method, executive power is vested ostensibly in one who is wholly or partly subject to the control and cooperation of others who are the members of his council. For an example of the first method, Hamilton recurs to ancient history, adducing the two consuls of Rome; for the second method, however, examples are found more recent and closer to home, in the constitutions of several of the states. This is the more popular method of destroying executive unity in America.

To this arrangement that makes a council's concurrence constitutionally necessary to the operations of the ostensible executive, the argument that a plural executive is an executive without energy does not apply with equal weight; but it does apply with a weight that is considerable. The argument for an executive council is turned against itself by Hamilton's argument: this method not only makes for an executive which, though not as feeble as in that other plan found in the classical republic, is still quite feeble—this method of a council is, in addition, equally subject to the objection that it makes for an executive which is unsafe. The method of an executive council, as much as the other method for plurality in the executive, tends to conceal faults and destroy responsibility, thus depriving the people of their securities against infidelity in elected officials. These are the removal and punishment of wrongdoers, and, even more important in an elective government because more commonly required, the censure of public opinion.

The implicit argument for a council would seem to be something like this: since *even* a monarchy like England's annexes to the executive a constitutional council who may be responsible to the nation for the advice they give, therefore *a fortiori* a republic like America's should do so. Hamilton's reply is that such a council is needed in England *only because* it is a monarchy. Without a council, the British government would not be free, for without a council the British executive would have no responsibility whatever; the council in the monarchy increases responsibility—from no responsibility whatever, to responsibility in some degree (though only in some degree, for the English monarch is not bound to do as they say). But with a council the American executive would be less responsible, and hence with a council the American executive would be more dangerous to republican liberty. The maxim of republican jealousy has been applied where it is inapplicable because not even a little consideration has been given to the proper combination of unity and multiplicity in human affairs. To recognize that many cannot exercise executive authority well but to stop short of vesting that authority in one is to reduce the security against infidelity to the people. A few may combine more easily than many, but are harder to watch than one. The state government of Hamilton's immediate audience has no council except for the single purpose of appointing to offices. The republican fear of unity in the executive seems to make its last stand on the ground of appointments: even if there is only one chief magistrate, there must be many other magistrates. And to allow him to name them all alone would make him a lone magistrate, followed by his friends and servants.[34]

The discussion of the executive beginning with Number 67 is immediately preceded by the papers on the ultimate legislative check on what is most properly called administration: removal of the men who administer the government. What is discussed in the papers that precede these immediately preceding papers is discussed again in the concluding papers on the executive, the papers on executive powers: legislative participation in the executive powers of making treaties and appointing officials.[35] As the reader approached the discussion of the executive, so he departs it: noting how the executive is subject to the control of a branch of the legislative body.

The executive is subject to control by legislators: the legislators themselves are not to be the holders of executive office; they are not to constitute the administration. For a good administration, the right men are needed to fill the offices. But the right sort of arrangement is better calculated to promote a choice of the right men than is some other sort of arrangement. What is the right sort of arrangement? If the power of appointment is to be reposed in a body of men, that body must be, not the people at large, but a select body of a moderate number. But, though the people collectively are too numerous and too dispersed to be regulated in their movements by a systematic spirit of cabal and intrigue, this spirit does regulate the movements of men in a select assembly of a moderate number. This systematic spirit of cabal and intrigue is the chief objection against reposing the power of appointment in a body of men. The resolutions of a collective body are frequently distracted and warped by diversity of views, feelings, and interests, and nothing is so apt to agitate men's passions as personal considerations, whether relating to themselves or to others whom they are to choose or prefer. Hence, the process of appointing to office when an assembly of men exercises the power will be a display of attachments and animosities the result of which will be a choice not for merit but for what gives to one party a victory or to many parties a bargain. One man, by contrast, will have fewer personal attachments to gratify than a body of men each of whom may be supposed to have an equal number. Moreover, a single man with the sole and undivided responsibility will have a livelier sense of duty and a more exact regard for reputation. He will be led by the concentration of obligation and interest to investigate with care what qualities merit appointment, and to prefer with impartiality men who have those qualities. Hence, to analyze and to estimate the peculiar qualities adapted to particular offices, one man of discernment is better fitted than a body of men of equal or perhaps even of superior discernment. (Not necessarily any one man, but one man of discernment; in the case of the president, though, the mode of his own appointment is such that there would always be great probability of having the place filled by a man of abilities at least respectable.)

However, to reduce the danger of evils from one man's uncontrolled agency in appointments, it would be well to restrain him by making it dangerous to his reputation or even to his political existence for him to play favorites or to follow popularity. An efficacious check would be to require the Senate's cooperation for appointment to office. Such a check would not impair executive energy, because the Senate restrains only by the power to concur or not; the president retains the initiative.[36]

DURATION

For governmental efficacy, not only must one will be composed out of many wills in time to do what needs to be done for the public safety and prosperity; also, one will must not decompose into many wills through time. Brief efficacy is little efficacy: the efficacy derived from unity must be protracted. Unity at an instant in time must be combined with duration through a long interval of time. For energetic government, power must be concentrated for action that is soon enough; for wise government, policy must be kept constant for action that lasts long enough. Men are feeble (though many) if they cannot consist; if they cannot persist, they fall into folly. Hence, the other great enterprise in Hamilton's project of an administrative republic is the establishment of stability. Republican governments are endangered by their natural liability to change, which tends to their destruction; vibrations of power are of the genius of our government.[37] Governmental complexity promotes steadiness of measures and helps make constitutions lasting. Partly it does this merely by having several parts that must concur to undo old measures as well as to pass new ones.[38] However, stability requires not only that there be several independent parts in the governmental whole, but that the several parents be diverse as well. It has been sufficiently emphasized that safety against government, which requires that government be representative, requires also that the power of representative government be partitioned among several depositories: bad works are impeded when separated depositories of power share the exercise of power. But it has not been sufficiently explained how efficacy of government requires that the organs of government be diversified. We have examined the theme of unity, the organization of power so that its operation will lead the multitudinous wills of an extensive country to consist with each other in time to meet present urgencies; we need now to examine the theme of duration, the organization of power so that its operation will lead the short-sighted wills of a mutable populace to persist through time in making provision for a long future. The chief departments of power, which differ in the number of officials who compose them, differ as well in the duration of their office holding. To diversify the duration of office holding in a complex representative government is to prolong the terms of those who are not members of the body most strictly called representative; this helps to fortify general and remote considerations against momentary passions and immediate interests.

The president's duration in office is longer than that of the representatives. A short period of office for the executive is believed by many to give greater security against the evil designs of ambition and of avarice. The time during which a man holds the office of president may be prolonged without limit by multiplying the number of his terms of limited length; the reasons against prohibiting such reeligibility suggest reasons for each term itself to be long.[39]

One advantage supposed to result from prohibiting reeligibility is greater security to the people; but popular security would not be increased by the exclusion. The people, attached to a favorite, and disgusted by what they might be induced to consider an odious and unjustifiable restraint, might sacrifice their permanent interest in constitutional liberty to their temporary inclination to perpetuate their favorite in office. The executive himself would be tempted by the exclusion to sordid views, to peculation, and in some instances to usurpation. Consider a man in office with the prospect of inevitable exclusion at the end of his term. If a man were avaricious, he would feel a propensity to use his opportunity while it lasted, by corrupt expedients making the harvest as abundant as it was transitory. But, with a different prospect, he might be content to enjoy the regular perquisites of his station, and might be unwilling to risk the consequences of abusing his station; thus his avarice might guard against his avarice. If a man were vain or ambitious as well as avaricious, his avarice would be likely to overcome his caution and his vanity or ambition—but, with the expectation that good conduct would prolong his honors, he might hesitate to lose honors for the sake of gain; thus one appetite might guard against the other. If a man were simply ambitious, he would be much more violently tempted to embrace at every personal hazard a favorable conjunction for attempting to prolong his power than if he could probably achieve the same end by doing his duty. And consider the situation, not of one man who is still in office with the prospect of his inevitable descent from eminence, but of a number of men who, having had credit enough to ascend to the supreme magistracy, had descended from office, but yearn for a forbidden reascent. The mandatory rotation in office would disturb the peace of the community, and would even threaten the stability of the government.[40]

Another advantage supposed to result from prohibiting re-eligibility is greater independence in the magistrate. But the prohibition would be no more likely to render the magistrate more independent than to render the people more secure. It is to be doubted that there would be greater independence in the magistrate if the exclusion were only temporary. It is even to be doubted if the exclusion were perpetual—for the magistrate will have friends for whom he might sacrifice his independence, and he would be less willing to make enemies when he must see himself, in the time fast approaching, their equal, or perhaps their inferior, exposed to their resentments. It is not to be doubted, however, that greater independence in the magistrate is an advantage. This is so if only for the sake of safety, since the abuse of governmental power cannot be checked internally unless the several depositories of power that are balanced against each other are independent of each other; but Hamilton's concern for executive independence, while taking into account the situation of the executive when the legislature is outraging its constituents, chiefly considers another situation.[41]

Prior to discussing reeligibility, Hamilton discusses the prior decision for a term of some fixed limit; in arguing that the executive should have a considerable time before the end of his limited term, Hamilton says that to regard as the executive's best recommendation his servile pliancy to a prevailing current in the legislature or even in the community at large one must entertain very crude notions both of the ends for which government was instituted and of the true means by which the public happiness may be promoted. Hamilton, who rejects notions that are "very crude" as well as ideas in which there is an "excess of refinement," then goes on to interpret, not to question, the republican principle. The republican principle seems to reveal the ends for which government was instituted or the fundamental equality of men: the interests of the people are to be served by those to whom they entrust the management of their affairs. But intention is not effect; it is the proper interpretation of the republican principle that reveals the means by which the means to effect those ends are made operative. Those who would move the public business forward must do it by looking far ahead. Leadership is necessary to place impediments in the way of sudden passions, temporary delusions, and persistent prejudices, so that right reasoning may prevail in the choice of means. The people have the dangerous prejudice, which is flattered by would-be tyrants, that the institutionalization of leadership is dangerous and even tyrannical. Republican leadership is government that is itself governed by the deliberate sense of the community; but to be governed by the *deliberate* sense of the community is *not* to be governed by transient popular impulses excited by the flattering arts and deceptive artifices of cowardly or mean-spirited men who prefer to rule by manipulating popular inclinations, rather than by insisting upon arrangements that give the people time and opportunity for more sedate reflection. To avoid temporarily attractive but eventually fatal courses, the people must be led. The reward of leadership is the pleasure of receiving, at last, lasting monuments of popular gratitude for serving with courage and with magnanimity the lasting interests of the people; the price of leadership is the pain of suffering, in the meantime, the immediate perils of popular displeasure for withstanding the people's temporary inclinations toward means that do not promote their interests.[42]

The longer the duration in office of the executive magistrate, the more probable is his personal firmness in the employment of his constitutional powers. A man will be more attached to what he enjoys by a durable or certain title than by one that is momentary or uncertain; he is apt to take less interest in an advantage he holds precariously. For what he holds by a tenure more firm, a man will more firmly take risks and endure pains; a short-lived advantage affords him little inducement to expose himself, on account of it, to any considerable hazard or even inconvenience. Hence, an executive with a short duration in office will be feeble and irresolute: a man acting as chief magistrate, under the consciousness that in a very short time he must lay down his office, will be apt to feel too little interested in it to hazard any material censure or perplexity from exerting his powers independently, or from encountering the ill-humors which may happen to prevail, however transiently, in a considerable part of the society itself, or even only in a predominant faction in the legislative body; and if the case should be, not that he must lay it down at the end of his term but only that he must lay it down if not continued by a new choice, then the tendency would be still more powerful for his wishes, conspiring with his fears, to corrupt his integrity or debase his fortitude.

Though it cannot be affirmed that any limited duration would completely answer the end proposed, still, a duration of four years, while not long enough to endanger the public liberty, would be long enough to make a very valuable contribution to the firmness of the executive. During the interval between the commencement and termination of such a period, the prospect of annihilation would be remote enough to have no improper effect upon the conduct of a man imbued with a tolerable portion of fortitude, for it would be remote enough to have the effect of making the community sensible of the propriety of the measures he might incline to pursue. And as the moment approached when the public were by a new election to signify their sense of his conduct, though his firmness would probably decline, yet it would still derive support from the opportunities he had had, from his previous continuance in office, of getting the esteem and good will of his constituents by giving proofs of his wisdom and integrity.[43]

The people must be led; hence some of the people must be led to undertake the task of being leaders. Men need inducements to become leaders. Their courage and magnanimity must be activated. Virtue may be its own reward, but exertion of virtue on behalf of multitudes requires the prospect of another reward. Even the noblest minds will hesitate to exert themselves in ruling if their ruling passion, the love of fame, cannot hope to be rewarded. Virtue practically takes the form of excellence; only the desire to excel will sufficiently prompt the exertions of self on behalf of countless others; political excellence is that laudable ambition which takes gratification from popular gratitude for promoting vast projects of public benefit. Few officials will last in the struggle to do their duty if they cannot hope to last in office; few officials will engage themselves in long-lasting effort to plan and undertake vast enterprises unless they can hope to have their merit acknowledged by lasting monuments, and this requires lasting in office long enough to have something to show for the effort. Arrangements must be such that officials will be induced by their own passions and interests not only to resist firmly the transient errors of others, but also to persist arduously in their provident long-term projects.[44]

The longer his duration in office, the more probable it is that an executive with a merely tolerable portion of fortitude will resist the transient errors of others; but so long as the duration in office is limited, reeligibility is necessary to counter what deters the generality of men in such a situation from planning and undertaking ambitious projects requiring for their completion persistence through a long time. The passionate regard for reputation which distinguishes noble minds acts as an inducement to such public enterprise only in situations where the initiators can hope for the reward of the fame which follows upon the work's completion. Arrangements must be made not with a view to what a few men might do but with a view to what is to be expected from the generality of men. To make mankind's interest coincide with their duty is to rely on the best security for mankind's fidelity. Arrangements must provide incentives to be provident; even if a very few of the best minds might rise even above the ruling passion of the noblest minds, it is more rewarding for the public to base political hopes on one of the strongest incentives of human conduct, the desire of reward. A long enough term of office diminishes the incentives to collaborate with public enemies or to become oneself a public enemy; exclusion from office after a limited term would diminish the inducements to become a public benefactor. If the public is prevented from following the maxim of looking at the end in judging the means adopted by their leaders, the public will prevent the governors of the republic from being governed by the maxim of looking to the end in choosing the means. Lacking incentives to provide for ends a long time off, the governors will improvise means that merely look good in the meantime. They will choose specious means to the general good.[45]

Duration in office as requisite to the energy of the executive authority, writes Hamilton at the beginning of the first of two *Federalist* papers on the subject, relates to two objects: the personal firmness of the executive magistrate in the employment of his constitutional powers, discussed in Number 71 in connection with the need for a term of considerable extent; and the stability of the system of administration which may have been adopted under his auspices, discussed in Number 72 in connection with the need for reeligibility. The two objects of executive duration are firmness and stability. Arrangements for the executive must consider the relation between time and incentives—incentives that encourage (or enfeeble) resistance against transient impulses toward harmful measures, and incentives that inspirit (or deter) persistence in great projects for long-term benefit. In both cases, the longer a time the executive can count on his holding the office, the longer a time that will count in his handling of the office. The intention of increasing safety by decreasing the duration of the executive, like the intention of increasing safety by increasing the number of the executive, would have the ill effect of decreasing safety. Executive responsibility to the people is essential to republican safety, but a short-sighted attention to the requisite responsibility for short-term effects loses sight of the requisite responsibility for effects that are long-term.[46]

Because the administration of government is most properly located within the executive department, the duration of the executive magistrate in office is intimately connected with the stability of the system of administration. It is not generally to be expected that men will vary and measures remain uniform. A man new to an office wishes to prove his capacity; and he wishes, in addition, to assure those upon whom he depends for his position that he is a man after their own heart. To undo what a predecessor has done is very often considered by a successor the best proof he can give of his own capacity; and, if the successor was substituted for his predecessor by public choice, he supposes that his predecessor was dismissed because his measures were disliked, and hence that the successor will be the more liked by his constituents the less he resembles his predecessor. Moreover, a new chief executive's propensity to change measures from these considerations will join with a propensity to place those who depend upon him personally for position; and these propensities together will give him a propensity to change men in subordinate positions, thus multiplying the mutability of measures. Excluding men from reeligibility for the presidency would therefore have the ill effect of operating as a constitutional interdiction of stability in the administration. By necessitating a change of men in the first office of the nation, it would necessitate a mutability of measures. There will be little enough stability when popular constancy is permitted; to interdict it constitutionally would be fatal. In particular situations of crisis, replacing an experienced man by an inexperienced man even of equal merit would dangerously unsettle the train of the administration; and even in ordinary times, there is need for permanence in a wise system of administration, but experience is the parent of wisdom, and experience comes with time.[47]

It is in suggesting the intimate connection between the duration of the executive magistrate in office and the stability of the system of administration, that Hamilton says that the person having immediate management of those matters constituting the administration of government most properly understood ought to be considered the assistants or deputies of the chief magistrate. On this account, he says, they ought to derive their offices from his appointment or at least from his nomination, and ought, Hamilton also says, to be subject to his superintendence. Hamilton does not say what might be expected—that they ought to be subject to removal by him or at least to superintendence by him. A few papers later, in discussing the mode of appointing the officers of the United States, Hamilton says that to require the cooperation of the Senate, besides being an excellent check upon a spirit of favoritism or of popularity in the president, will in addition be an efficacious source of stability in the administration; he begins the next paper by recalling having mentioned this contribution to administrative stability that is to be expected from the Senate's cooperation in the business of appointments, and he goes on to add that the consent of the Senate will be necessary not only to appoint but to displace as well. If the chief magistrate were the sole disposer of offices, then a change of the chief magistrate would occasion a more violent and more general revolution in the officers of the government; but administration will be made steadier by the provision that connects the official existence of public men to the approbation and disapprobation of the part of the government most permanent in its composition and hence in all probability least subject to inconstancy. The consequence is that where a man in any station had given satisfactory evidence of his fitness for it, a new president would be restrained from attempting a change in favor of a man more agreeable to himself, by the apprehension that the Senate's discountenance might frustrate his attempt and discredit him.[48]

Because of certain statements made by Hamilton in the first "Pacificus" paper, it has been contended that Hamilton changed his mind on the residence of the power of removal. In that paper, Hamilton says that the appointing power is an executive power in itself, but that by the Constitution it is a power specifically excepted from the executive power vested in the president alone, and is vested instead in the president with the consent of two-thirds of the Senate. He does not say, however, that the removal power is an incident to the appointing power. What he does say is that the power of removal from office is an important instance of recognition by Congress of the true construction of the clause vesting executive power in the president, the construction according to which the president has all executive power that the Constitution does not specially except or qualify. Two of these exceptions or qualifications, Hamilton reminds his readers, he had noticed earlier in the paper—the Senate's participation in the appointment of officers and in the making of treaties; he now mentions as a third the legislature's right to declare war and grant letters of marque and reprisal. Otherwise, he says, the executive power of the Union is completely lodged in the president, as Congress recognized when, in formal act upon full consideration, it allowed that the president alone might remove officers even though the power to appoint is vested in the president with the Senate's consent.[49] Perhaps rather than changing his mind about the power of removal, Hamilton thought that the question of the power of removal was a matter relatively minor compared to the recognition by Congress of an important general doctrine for construing the Constitution with respect to executive power, so that he was willing to accept a more questionable interpretation of a less important point to confirm a principle of the utmost importance. Perhaps Hamilton had earlier adopted an interpretation to which he was not firmly committed but which was the interpretation most likely to seem plausible to those whose consent was needed to ratify the proposed constitution and whose dominating concern was republican safety—an interpretation which was moreover capable of being put to use in promoting the unpopular cause of administrative stability.[50]

In any case, discussing the removal power in *The Federalist*, Hamilton does speak of the Senate as that body which, from the greater permanency of its own composition, will in all probability be less subject to inconstancy than any other member of the government; and he says elsewhere that stability is a principle even more essential to the Senate than to the president.[51] As the president is the incarnation of unity, so the Senate is the embodiment of duration. A full examination of governmental constancy would require a consideration of the Senate;[52] but we must move on, and consider briefly our two themes as the two aspects of Hamilton's one problem: to give efficacy to the American constitution of republican liberty.

REPUBLICAN CONSTITUTION

It was not simply to get things done that Hamilton was a proponent of constitutional arrangements for energizing and stabilizing the exercise of governmental power. Things may get done, soon and so as to last a long time, even when a constitution makes for fragmented and mutable government. If the constitutionally provided machinery of government lacks efficacy, an extra-governmental political machine unknown to the constitution may be improvised to do the job. Effective decisions can be made and enforced by a boss sitting in the back room, then sent up front for dignified promulgation by those who formally preside; or the man who presides up front with a popular air of republican humility may himself do the effective work, operating his own machine in the back room. But constitutional arrangements that necessitate such extra-constitutional arrangements so that the public business may in some way go forward are dangerous and demeaning.

Hamilton repeatedly declared himself "*affectionately* attached to the Republican theory." He said that he had "strong hopes of the success of that theory," but in candor ought to add that he was "far from being without doubts": "I consider its success as yet a problem," he said. As yet, successful republican government is not an accomplished fact but a project to be accomplished, for "it is yet to be determined by experience whether it be consistent with that *stability* and *order* in Government which are essential to public strength & private security and happiness."[53] In the circumstances, he said, republican theory ought to govern governmental practice. "In the abstract," or neglecting the circumstances here and now, the non-republican theory may seem to be better. "Permanent or hereditary distinctions" of political rights are an essential part of the British constitution, a constitution that is good as well as the best that has yet been. Experience thus shows that the *non*-republican theory *can* be successful in practice. Experience, moreover, gives cause to *doubt* whether the *republican* theory can be successful in practice. But "every good man" ought to have "good wishes" for the republican theory's essential "idea of a perfect equality of political rights among the citizens"; the republican theory has a more desirable constitutive principle than does the non-republican theory. The non-republican theory would seem to be better only because the republican theory would seem to be less practicable. The republican theory merits "the best efforts to give success to it in practice." It has "hitherto from an incompetent structure of the Government . . . not had a fair trial, and . . . the endeavour ought then to be to secure to it a better chance of success by a government more capable of energy and order." Hamilton "declared in strong terms that the republican theory ought to be adhered to in this Country as long as there was any chance of its success."[54] The republican problem could be solved only by the development of what we might call an "administrative" republic—a republican form of government not lacking the aptitude and tendency to produce a good administration. If such a form were not developed, warned Hamilton, if popular prejudices against being governed were flattered to the point of inciting those popular propensities which bring on the self-destruction of popular government, then monarchy would after all prevail.[55] Proclaiming long and loudly the merits of the Brit-

ish constitution, Hamilton tried to teach emphatically what he
thought Americans needed most to learn—that government cannot be good unless it joins to private safety public strength. In
rejecting the hereditary principle in government, a British inheritance from less enlightened times, Americans had not cast off
their unenlightened parochial prejudice against executive energy.
But the necessity of executive energy was rooted in the nature of
things: in some way or other it would return; and if refused a
stately republican admission, it would break violently through
the front door—or enter by stealth through the back. In some
way or other, Hamilton thought, the public business would go
forward, or the republic would cease to be. His wish was that the
public business might go forward in a way not fatal to liberty and
to honor. Monarchy under the free British constitution produced
a good administration, but the independent Americans did not
have the materials for a constitution of the British sort; their
failure to solve the republican problem would produce a tyrant or
a boss.

  In his last word on the subject, Hamilton said that he hoped for
"the experiment of republican government" to be "as complete,
as satisfactory, and as decisive as could be wished"; "I sincerely
hope, that it may not hereafter be discovered," he said, that the
experiment has been inadequate "even in this country." Until this
American attempt, republican government was a failure; in the
full knowledge of previous failure, Americans made another attempt. We find it hard to keep in mind how hard it must have
been to take a leading part in this attempt; the act appears less
questionable in comfortable retrospect. To a good man considering with care the prospects then there might at times have come
such thoughts as these: As the failure of previous attempts did not
deter the American attempt, so, since hope springs eternal in the
human breast, the failure of the American attempt will not deter
subsequent attempts, but repetition of the attempts will only
multiply human misery, for republican government cannot succeed. However, the only way to prove this, and thus to deter subsequent attempts, is by an experiment in which trial is made of a
government that is republican but is so constructed as to have all
the energy and stability reconcilable with the principles of the re-

publican theory. Patriotism would recoil from making such an experiment if it could be avoided, but Americans will "endure nothing but a republican government," so a senseless repetition of previous experience is the only alternative to the experiment. Hence philanthropy supplies inducements to what patriotism does not forbid—a true test of the republican theory. If republican government fails despite its being so constructed, succeeding generations of mankind will be spared the miserable consequences of attempts at republican government.

But this is not a line of thought to lift the spirit; there is a more encouraging point of view, from which we easily can imagine that the man we are considering had thoughts much more like these: While the failure of the American attempt may not deter some thoughtless subsequent attempts, the effect of which can only be to multiply republican failures, thus further confirming the bad reputation of republican government, it is likely that subsequent attempts will rarely if ever be made, for the failure of the American attempt will be taken as proof that republican government must be a failure. But the experiment might prove no more than what previous experience had already shown about the republican theory—that republican government fails when it is not "so constructed as to have all the energy and stability reconcilable with the principles of that theory." Now republican government might succeed if so constructed, and not only will Americans endure nothing but a republican government, but "in the actual situation of the country" it is "in itself right and proper that the republican theory should have a fair and full trial." Hence the inducements of philanthropy will join those of patriotism to make all considerate and good Americans wish for a true test of the republican theory in America, and therefore advocate republican institutions of the greatest possible energy and stability.[56]

All good men must rejoice if the outcome of the American experiment at Philadelphia proves that the republican theory need not fail in practice, said Hamilton, and he did all that he could to make it succeed; but he did not regard republican government as something for immediate export to all mankind. Writing to the same man whom he told of his hopes for an adequate experiment of republican government in this counry, Hamilton on another occasion said: "No regular system of Liberty will at present suit St. Domingo. The Government if independent must be military—partaking of the feodal system." [57] Moreover, of the country by which Santo Domingo had been dominated, Hamilton a month earlier wrote to another correspondent: "The suspension of the King and the massacre of September . . . cured me of my good will for the French Revolution. I have never been able to believe that France can make a republic and I believe that the attempt while it continues can only produce misfortunes." "I hold with *Montesquieu*," he said, "that a government must be fitted to a nation as much as a Coat to the Individual, and consequently that what may be good at Philadelphia may be bad at Paris and ridiculous at Petersburgh." [58]

Hamilton resisted efforts at Philadelphia, capital of the government of the young American nation of that day, to hurry through a redefinition of treason which would punish American partisans of the menacing disorder that had its capital at Paris: "Let us not establish a tyranny," he said. "Energy is a very different thing from violence." [59] As this remark suggests, we must bear in mind Hamilton's constitutional purpose when we read his administrative arguments, such as the argument on behalf of executive energy: "A feeble executive implies a feeble execution of the government. A feeble execution is but another phrase for a bad execution: And a government ill executed, whatever it may be in theory, must be in practice a bad government." [60] Hamilton does not say that a government is good if only its executive is not feeble; he says only that a government is not good if its executive is feeble. Very ill-executed government, whatever it is theoretically, may be practically anarchy, which is an ill condition not to be endured; but we must bear this in mind: government that is practically tyranny or despotism, whatever it may be theoretically, is also an ill condition, which may unfortunately have to be endured. In such a case, ill-executed despotism or despotism tempered by anarchy may be not so ill a condition as efficacious despotism or despotism well executed.

At Petersburgh, in Hamilton's day, was to be found the capital of that government about which a Russian writer of that day said, "The good fortune of Russia is in the bad execution of bad laws."

Next to this quotation in a chapter on the "Strong Boss" system of the Russians, Hedrick Smith reports another: "Thank God we are not Germans," says a Russian writer of the present day. "If we were it would be intolerable."[61] He is speaking about that government which rules over the enduring Russian nation as successor to the government at Petersburgh.

NOTES TO CHAPTER III

1. To spare the reader I shall avoid using many quotation marks and shall conflate and compress phrases and sentences from Hamilton without constantly repeating "Hamilton says"—so I may in this essay sometimes appear to be commenting when I am trying to report. The quotations in this paragraph are from: Letter to Tobias Lear, January 2, 1800, in Harold C. Syrett (ed.), *The Papers of Alexander Hamilton* (New York: Columbia University Press, 1969–79), XXIV, 155 (hereinafter cited as *Papers*); Alexander Hamilton, James Madison, John Jay, *The Federalist*, ed. Jacob E. Cooke (Middletown, Conn.: Wesleyan University Press, 1961), No. 9, p. 51 (hereinafter cited as *Federalist*); Montesquieu, *Considérations sur les Causes de la Grandeur des Romains et de leur Décadence*, Ch. 1.

2. Sources for this and the four previous paragraphs may be found in my article "Alexander Hamilton on the Foundation of Good Government," in the Bicentennial Issue of *The Political Science Reviewer*, VI (Fall, 1976), 143–214, from which I have borrowed for this essay.

3. Titus Manlius, "The Stand No. 1," March 10, 1798, in Henry Cabot Lodge (ed.), *Works of Alexander Hamilton* (8 vols.; New York, 1885), V, 396 (hereinafter cited as *Works*); *Federalist*, No. 76, p. 510; To the Electors of the State of New York, April 7, 1789, in *Papers*, V, 322–24; *Federalist*, No. 84, p. 584; Constitutional Convention, September 8, 1787, in *Papers*, IV, 244; New York Ratifying Convention, June 21, 1788, in *Papers*, V, 38, and June 27, 1788, in *Papers*, V, 96–97.

4. *Federalist*, No. 26, pp. 168–69; No. 28, pp. 178–80; No. 60, p. 404; No. 61, pp. 412–13; No. 82, pp. 555–56; No. 84, pp. 581–83; New York Ratifying Convention, June 21, 1788, in *Papers*, V, 38, 43–44; New York Assembly, February 15, 1787, in *Papers*, IV, 81–82.

5. *Federalist*, No. 71, p. 483; New York Ratifying Convention, June 20, 1788, in *Papers*, V, 20, 43; June 27, 1788, in *Papers*, V, 94–97, 104; Remarks on the Quebec Bill, Part One, June 15, 1775, in *Papers*, I, 166–69; Unsubmitted Resolution, July 1783, in *Papers*, III, 420–21; *Federalist*, No. 84, p. 584; *Federalist*, No. 73, p. 498; *Federalist*, No. 78, pp. 528, 530; Letter to Robert Livingston, April 25, 1785, in *Papers*, III, 609.

6. New York Ratifying Convention, June 21, 1788, in *Papers*, V, 38; *Federalist*, No. 70, p. 472; No. 71, pp. 481–83; No. 74, p. 501; No. 65, pp. 440–41; No. 60, pp. 404–405.

7. *Federalist*, No. 71, pp. 483–86; New York Ratifying Convention, June 21, 1788, in *Papers*, V, 54–55; *Federalist*, No. 73, pp. 493–98; Letter to Washington, May 5, 1789, in *Papers*, V, 335; Constitutional Convention, September 12, 1787, in *Papers*, IV, 248; *Federalist*, No. 65, pp. 439–44; No. 66, pp. 445–47; No. 75, p. 504.

8. Thucydides, *The Peloponnesian War*, II, 64–65, and II, 22; Aristotle, *Rhetoric* 1354b17, 26, and 1356all; Liddell and Scott, *A Greek-English Lexicon* (9th ed.; Oxford, 1940), 1785; *Cf.* Friedrich Nietzsche, *Götzen-Dämmerung*, "Was ich den Alten verdanke," 3.

9. Niccolo Machiavelli, *Il Principe*, Chapters 15 and 18; Machiavelli, *Discorsi*, I, 9; III, 35; I, 13.

10. Francis Bacon, *Novum Organum*, Aphorism LXXI.

11. René Descartes, *Regulae ad Directionem Ingenii*; *Discours de la Méthode*; *La Géométrie*.

12. Thomas Hobbes, *The Elements of Law*, Tonnies edition (New York: Barnes & Noble, 1969), Part 2, Chap. 2, ¶ 5, pp. 120–21; Hobbes, *The Citizen*, X, 9–15 and 19.
13. Montesquieu, *De l'Esprit des Lois*, Bk. 11, Ch. 6.
14. Adam Smith, *The Wealth of Nations* (New York: Modern Library, 1965), Bk. 4, Ch. 7, Part 3, pp. 586–88.
15. David Hume, *Essays*, "Of the Balance of Power."
16. It was "excusable" for Americans to err at the beginning, when "good intentions, rather than great skill, were to have been expected from us":

> We began this revolution with very vague and confined notions of the practical business of government. To the greater part of us it was a novelty: Of those, who under the former constitution had the opportunities of acquiring experience, a large proportion adhered to the opposite side, and the remainder can only be supposed to have possessed ideas adapted to the narrow colonial sphere, in which they had been accustomed to move, not of that enlarged kind suited to the government of an INDEPENDENT NATION. There were no doubt exceptions . . . but . . . their influence was too commonly borne down by the prevailing torrent of ignorance and prejudice.

But to persist in error despite time for reflection and experience becomes "disgraceful and even criminal." "Continentalist No. 1," July 12, 1781, in *Papers*, II, 649–50.
17. Letter to Washington, May 3, 1799, in *Works*, VI, 167; *Federalist*, No. 70, p. 472; *The Farmer Refuted*, February 23, 1775, in *Papers*, I, 155–56; Letter to Washington, September 15, 1790, in *Papers*, VII, 51; "The Continentalist No. 1," July 12, 1781, in *Papers*, II, 649–50, 661–62; "The Continentalist No. 3," August 9, 1781, in *Papers*, II, 663; Letter to Robert Morris, September 28, 1782, in *Papers*, III, 170; Letter to Robert Morris, April 30, 1781, in *Papers*, II, 621; *Federalist*, No. 26, p. 164; *Federalist*, No. 1, p. 5; Unsubmitted Resolution, July, 1783, in *Papers*, III, 425–26; Letter to Washington, March 17, 1783, in *Papers*, III, 292; Letter to Washington, August 18, 1792, in *Works*, II, 267–71; New York Ratifying Convention, June 21, 1788, in *Papers*, V, 44–45; Catullus to Aristides No. 3, September 29, 1792, in *Works*, VI, 355. One might expect the Americans to be a people more likely to fall prey to false alarms of tyranny than to submit with ease to a tyrant's depredations— they were, after all, a people who "descrying Tyranny at a distance, before they had yet felt the scourge of oppression, could nobly hazard all in defence of their rights." Lucius Crassus No. 17, March 20, 1802, in *Papers*, XXV, 576.
18. Lansing or Burr, 1804, *Works*, VII, 325; Letter to Theodore Sedgwick, July 10, 1804, in *Works*, VIII, 616; New York Ratifying Convention, June 21, 1788, in *Papers*, V, 39–40; New York Ratifying Convention, June 27, 1788, in *Papers*, V, 94; "Defence of the Funding System," July 1795, in *Papers*, XIX, 36; "The Continentalist No. 6," July 4, 1782, in *Papers*, III, 102–104; New York Assembly, January 19, 1787, in *Papers*, IV, 11–12; New York Assembly, February 17, 1787, in *Papers*, IV, 94–96; Letter to Robert Morris, August 13, 1782, in *Papers*, III, 135–37; Letter from Robert Morris, August 28, 1782, in *Papers*, III, 154; Letter to John Jay, July 25, 1783, in *Papers*, III, 416–17; *Federalist*, No. 1, pp. 5–6; Letter to Rufus King, January 5, 1800, in *Works*, VIII, 540; "Lucius Crassus No. 18," April 8, 1802, in *Works*, VII, 322. Letter to Richard Harrison, January 5, 1793, in *Works*, VIII, 292. "Camillus No. 5," 1795, in *Works*, IV, 414–15; Constitutional Convention, September 17, 1787, in *Papers*, IV, 253; "Defence of the Funding System," in *Works*, VII, 416–17, 420; Letter to George Clinton, February 24, 1783, in *Papers*, III, 272–73; Letter to Washington, July 3, 1787, in *Papers*, IV, 223–25; "Lucius Crassus No. 1," December 17, 1801, in *Works*, VII, 200–201; "Lucius Crassus No. 9," January 18, 1802, in *Works*, VII, 244–46; "Lucius Crassus No. 18," April 8, 1802, in *Works*, VII, 314, 322; Letter to Rufus King, January 5, 1800, in *Works*, VIII, 540; Letter to Rufus King, January 3, 1802, in *Works*, VIII, 600, 602; Letter to C. C. Pinckney, December 29, 1802, in *Works*, VIII, 605–606; Letter to Washington, March 25, 1783, in *Papers*, III, 306; *Federalist*, No. 6, pp. 34–35; *Federalist*, No. 12, pp. 75–77; *Federalist*, No. 30, p. 193; *Federalist*, No. 36, pp. 229–30; Letter to Edward Carrington, May 26, 1792, in *Works*, VIII, 248, 262; Address to the Electors of the State of New York, 1801, in *Works*, VII, 184–86, 199–200; Jefferson to Madison, December 20, 1787, in Paul Ford (ed.), *The Writings of Thomas Jefferson* (10 vols.; New York:

Putnam, 1892), IV, 473; Jefferson to William B. Giles, December 31, 1795, in *Writings of Jefferson*, VII, 41; Jefferson to Spencer Roane, September 6, 1819, in *Writings of Jefferson*, X, 140.

19. Madison, quoted in Memoranda by N. P. Trist, September 27, 1834, reprinted in Max Farrand (ed.), *Records of the Federal Convention of 1787* (4 vols.; New Haven: Yale University Press, 1966), III, 534:

> Mr. M., ". . . I deserted Colonel Hamilton, or rather Colonel H. deserted me; in a word, the divergence between us took place—from his wishing to *administration*, or rather to administer the Government (these were Mr. M's very words), into what he thought it ought to be; while, on my part, I endeavored to make it conform to the Constitution as understood by the Convention that produced and recommended it, and particularly by the State conventions that *adopted* it."

20. *Federalist*, No. 22, pp. 140–42; No. 70, pp. 474–78.

21. Letter to James Duane, September 3, 1780, in *Papers*, VI, 400–401, 404–406, 408–409; *Cf.* Unsubmitted Resolution, July 1783, in *Papers*, III, 420–21. See also: Letter to Unknown Addressee, between December, 1779, and March, 1780, in *Papers*, II, 246–47; Letter to Isaac Sears, October 12, 1780, in *Papers*, II, 472.

22. *Federalist*, No. 70, p. 472; No. 72, p. 486. See also: Pay Book of the State Company of Artillery, 1777, in *Papers*, I, 397. *Federalist*, No. 70, pp. 473–74.

23. *Federalist*, No. 72, p. 486; Madison, Speech on the location of the capital, September 18, 1789, in Gaillard Hunt (ed.), *The Writings of James Madison* (New York: Putnam, 1906), V, 423 (I am obliged to Murray Dry for drawing my attention to this remark of Madison); *Federalist*, No. 72, pp. 486–87; *cf.* New York Assembly, February 15, 1787, in *Papers*, IV, 75.

24. Finance: Letter to Robert Morris, April 30, 1781, in *Papers*, II, 604–606; Letter to Washington, August 18, 1792, in *Works*, II, 246–47; "Defense of the Funding System," July, 1795, in *Papers*, XIX, 3–6, 41–42; "Continentalist No. 4," August 30, 1781, in *Papers*, II, 673.

25. Spending: Explanation, November 11, 1795, in *Works*, VII, 81, 87, 110; Letter to McHenry, November 12, 1799, in *Works*, VI, 257–59; Letter to McHenry, March 21, 1800, in *Works*, VI, 288–91; Letter to McHenry, May 5, 1800, in *Works*, VI, 293–94; Letter to Caleb Swann, May 26, 1800, in *Works*, VI, 302–304; "Lucius Crassus No. 11," February 3, 1802, in *Works*, VII, 256–62. And in *Works*, VI, 139, note that among the "measures to be taken without delay," in the list of "Measures of Defence" compiled by Hamilton in 1799 during the crisis with France, is this item VII: "It is essential that the Executive should have half a million of secret-service money. If the measure cannot be carried without it, the expenditure may be with the approbation of three members of each House of Congress."

26. Foreign relations: *Federalist*, No. 75, pp. 504–509; No. 64 (Jay, referred to in No. 75, p. 505), pp. 434–36; No. 69, pp. 467–68; No. 84, pp. 585–86; No. 22, pp. 139–43; Letter to Washington, March 7, 1796, in *Papers*, XX, 68–69; Letter to Washington, March 24, 1796, in *Papers*, XX, 82–85; Letter to Washington, March 29, 1796, in *Papers*, XX, 85–102; Letter to Washington, April 2, 1796, in *Papers*, XX, 106–107; Letter to William Loughton Smith, March 10, 1796, in *Papers*, XX, 72–73; Letter to Rufus King, March 16, 1796, in *Papers*, XX, 76–77.

27. War: "Continentalist No. 3," August 9, 1781, in *Papers*, II, 663; *Federalist*, No. 74, p. 500; No. 70, p. 476; No. 6, p. 46; No. 69, p. 465; Pay Book of the State Company of Artillery, 1777, in *Papers*, I, 390; *Federalist*, No. 25, p. 161; Letter to George Clinton, June 1, 1783, in *Papers*, III, 368–69; Letter to Rufus King, February 15, 1797, in *Works*, VIII, 448; Letter to Oliver Wolcott, February 17, 1797, in *Works*, VIII, 448–49; Letter to Timothy Pickering, March 22, 1797, in *Works*, VIII, 454; Titus Manlius, "The Stand No. 6," April 19, 1798, in *Works*, V, 437, 439; No. 4, April 12, 1798, in *Works*, V, 421; No. 1, March 10, 1798, *Works*, V, 399–400; Letter to McHenry, May 3, 1799, in *Works*, VI, 168–69; Letter to McHenry, May 17, 1798, in *Works*, VIII, 481; Letter to McHenry, June 27, 1799, in *Works*, VI, 185–86; Letter to Oliver Wolcott, March 30, 1797, in *Works*, VIII,

455–56; Letter to Rufus King, April 8, 1797, in *Works*, VIII, 461; Letter to C. C. Pinckney, December 29, 1802, in *Works*, VIII, 606; Letter to Oliver Wolcott, Jr., June 5, 1798, in *Papers*, XXI, 487.

28. "Pacificus No. 1," June 29, 1793, in *Papers*, XV, 33–43. At *Federalist*, No. 69, p. 468, referring to the exclusive possession by the Union of that part of the sovereign power which relates to treaties, Hamilton delicately raises the question whether, if the confederacy were to be dissolved, that delicate and important prerogative of the British sovereign would not vest *solely in the executives* of the several states.

29. *Federalist*, No. 70, pp. 471–72; No. 85, p. 590.

30. Pay Book of the State Company of Artillery, 1777, in *Papers*, I, 396; Notes taken in the Federal Convention, June 1, 1787, in *Papers*, IV, 163; Letter to James Duane, September 3, 1780, in *Papers*, II, 413; "The Continentalist No. 3," August 9, 1781, in *Papers*, II, 663.

31. *Federalist*, No. 67, pp. 452–57. Compare *Federalist*, No. 67 with No. 52 (House of Representatives), No. 62 (Senate), and No. 78 (Judiciary).

32. *Federalist*, No. 68, pp. 457–62. It should be noted that "moral certainty" is not "absolute certainty"; "seldom" is not "never" and "probably" is not "certainly." Hamilton finds in the mode of electing the president "no inconsiderable recommendation of the constitution"; he does not say that the mode of election is such a guaranty of ability and virtue in the president as to render checks on him dispensable.

33. Having devoted the first of the papers on the executive to a most blamable misrepresentation of the plan by the opposition, and the second of the papers to a most praiseworthy feature of the plan acceptable to the opposition, Hamilton in the third paper, Number 69, traces the real characters of the proposed executive in order to place in a strong light the unfairness of the representations which have been made in regard to it.

34. *Federalist*, No. 70, pp. 471–80.

35. All that remains to the discussion of executive power after this is the discussion of those remaining powers of the executive to which no objection has been made—except some cavils not worth discussing.

36. See *Federalist*, Nos. 65–66; No. 64, pp. 432–38; No. 65, p. 439; No. 76, pp. 509–513; No. 77, pp. 516–19; No. 66, pp. 448–50; No. 69, pp. 468–69; No. 77, pp. 519–20.

37. New York Assembly: First Speech, January 19, 1787, in *Papers*, IV, 12; Second Speech, January 19, 1787, in *Papers*, IV, 16; Letter to Rufus King, June 3, 1802, in *Works*, VIII, 601; Letter to James Duane, September 3, 1780, in *Papers*, II, 404–405, 409–411; "The Continentalist No. 6," July 4, 1782, in *Papers*, III, 103.

38. This consequence of departmentalizing governmental power was discussed by Hamilton in connection with his great official project, to render the credit of the United States solid and enduring: "The Continentalist No. 4," August 30, 1781, in *Papers*, II, 670–71; Second Report on the Further Provision Necessary for Establishing Public Credit (Report on a National Bank), December 13, 1790, in *Papers*, VII, 331–33, 326–29; Report on the Public Credit, January 16, 1795, in *Works*, III, 5–8, 40–41; Letter to Washington, June 1, 1796, in *Works*, VIII, 402; Letter to William Short, September 1, 1790, in *Papers*, VII, 11 (copy enclosed in Report on Foreign Loans, February 13, 1793); Address to the Public Creditors, September 1, 1790, in *Papers*, VII, 2; Report on a Plan for the Further Support of Public Credit, January 16, 1795, in *Papers*, XVIII, 94–95; Defense of the Funding System, July 1795, in *Papers*, XIX, 61; *Federalist*, No. 6, p. 31; No. 73, pp. 495–97.

39. *Federalist*, No. 71, p. 484; No. 72, pp. 487–88, 491.

40. *Ibid.*, No. 72, pp. 491–92, 488–89.

41. *Ibid.*, No. 72, p. 491.

42. *Ibid.*, No. 71, pp. 481–83; No. 72, pp. 487, 492.

43. *Ibid.*, No. 71, pp. 481–82, 484–85.

44. *Ibid.*, No. 71, pp. 482–83. *Cf.* Letter to William Hamilton, May 2, 1797, in *Papers*, XXI, 78. Recommending Hamilton for high military position in 1798, Washington wrote to the president about the "abilities and integrity" of this man who had been "the principal

and most confidential aid of the Commander in Chief": "By some he is considered an ambitious man, and therefore a dangerous one. That he is ambitious I shall readily grant, but it is of that laudable kind which prompts a man to excell in whatever he takes in hand." John Fitzpatrick (ed.), *The Writings of George Washington* (39 vols.; Washington: Government Printing Office, 1931), XXXVI, 460*ff.*

45. *Federalist*, No. 72, p. 488.

46. *Ibid.*, No. 71, p. 481; No. 72, pp. 487–88.

47. *Ibid.*, No. 72, pp. 486–91.

48. *Ibid.*, No. 72, p. 487; No. 76, pp. 513, 515–16.

49. "Pacificus No. 1," June 29, 1793, in *Papers*, XV, 39–40. When Hamilton was approached by Hopkins, who was to republish *The Federalist* in 1802, Hamilton "hesitated his consent to republication"; he gave Hopkins the impression that "he did not regard the work with much partiality"; the hesitant Hamilton apparently had formed the purpose of writing a treatise on government, and told Hopkins that "*Heretofore* I have given the people *milk*; *hereafter* I will give them *meat*." "But nevertheless," said Hopkins, Hamilton "consented to the republication" of the collected *Federalist* papers, insisting however that the edition include the *Pacificus* letters. "He remarked to me," said Hopkins, that "some of his friends had pronounced them to be his best performance": John C. Hamilton (ed.), *The Federalist* (Philadelphia: J. B. Lippincott & Co., 1877), I, xcii, ciii. Madison was indignant at Hamilton's thus making use of *The Federalist* (in the writing of which Madison had, at Hamilton's request, collaborated) to support *Pacificus* (which Madison had, at Jefferson's request, opposed in print).

50. Later on, Hamilton did take for granted the president's power of removal. Alleging that President John Adams through vanity refrained from counseling with his constitutional advisers, Hamilton said that it must be Adams' own fault if he be not surrounded by men who, for ability and integrity, deserve his confidence, as the president nominates his ministers, and may displace them if he pleases. (The Public Conduct and Character of John Adams, Esq., President of the United States, 1800, in *Works*, VI, 419.)

51. *Federalist*, No. 77, pp. 515–16; "Catullus No. 4," October 17, 1792, in *Works*, VI, 357.

52. The Senate is that part of government the very root of whose name suggests its connection with lasting a long time. With respect to number, the few senators are more than one but less than many; with respect to number, the Senate and the House of Representatives differ from each other only in degree, while both differ in kind from the president—bodies of men are more or less numerous, but unity is not numerous at all. With respect in number, the Senate differs from the president in kind, but from the House only in degree. The Senate is distinguished by duration: the Senate is a continuing body, for at no time can its membership entirely, or even mostly, change, and its members remain in office longer than any other officials elected in the republic.

53. Letter to Edward Carrington, May 26, 1792, in *Papers*, XI, 426–29, 442–44.

54. Washington to Hamilton, July 29, 1792, in *Papers*, XII, 129–33; Letter to Washington, August 18, 1792, in *Papers*, XII, 228–29; Letter to Washington, Enclosure: "Objections and Answers respecting the Administration of the Government," August 18, 1792, in *Papers*, XII, 251–54, esp. 253. See also, for example, "Catullus No. 3," September 29, 1792, in *Papers*, XII, 505, where Hamilton says of himself:

> Among the sources of the regret, which his language and conduct have testified, at the overdriven maxims and doctrines that too long withstood the establishment of firm government in the United States, and now embarrass the execution of the government which has been established, a *principal one* has . . . been their tendency to counteract a *fair trial* of the theory, to which he is represented to be adverse.

55. "Unquestionably," he said, "the only path to a subversion of the republican system of the Country is by flattering the prejudices of the people, and exciting their jealousies and apprehensions, to throw affairs into confusion, and to bring on civil commo-

tion. Tired at length of anarchy, or want of government, they may take shelter in the arms of monarchy for repose and security." Letter to Washington, Enclosure: "Objections . . ." August 18, 1792, in *Papers*, XII, 252.

56. Letter to Timothy Pickering, September 18, 1803, in *Works*, VIII, 607–608. (See also *Federalist*, No. 1, p. 3.)

57. Letter to Timothy Pickering, February 21, 1799, in *Papers*, XXII, 492–93, in reply to: From Timothy Pickering to Hamilton, February 6, 1799, in *Papers*, XXII, 473–74.

58. Letter to Marquis de Lafayette, April 28, 1798, in *Papers*, XXI, 450–51; From Marquis de Lafayette to Hamilton, August 12, 1798, in *Papers*, XXII, 73–76; Letter to Marquis de Lafayette, January 6, 1799, in *Papers*, XXII, 404; Montesquieu, *De l'Esprit des Lois*, Bk. I, Chap. 3. See also: "The Farmer Refuted," February 23, 1775, in *Papers*, I, 104, 121–22, 164–65; Second Letter from Phocion, April, 1784, in *Papers*, III, 557; Letter to Marquis de Lafayette, October 6, 1789, in *Papers*, V, 425.

59. Letter to Oliver Wolcott, Jr., June 29, 1798, in *Papers*, XXI, 522.

60. *Federalist*, No. 70, pp. 471–72—right after an example from Roman history, showing "how often that republic was obliged to take refuge in the absolute power of a single man, under the formidable title of dictator."

61. Hedrick Smith, *The Russians* (New York: Quadrangle, 1976), 272.

PART TWO: *Contemporary Issues*

IV

The War Powers Resolution and the War Powers

ROBERT SCIGLIANO

It would be correct, though insufficient, to say that the War Powers Resolution, enacted on November 7, 1973, over President Nixon's veto,[1] was a belated reaction by Congress to the Vietnam War and an effort to prevent future Vietnams. Although growing opposition to American participation in that war was the impetus to the legislation, it is by no means clear that the resolution of itself will make it appreciably more difficult for the United States to enter foreign war again or that it would have had that effect on entry into the Vietnam War. But the resolution would have had a significant impact on the way American foreign affairs were conducted after the Second World War, and perhaps on their substance, for it implicitly repudiates the claims of executive authority upon which important parts of that policy were based. The resolution goes further yet than this, according to its leading sponsors in Congress, for it does nothing less than repudiate an accretion of precedents going back to the very beginning of this nation's life under the Constitution. "The doctrine of executive war powers," Jacob Javits, the main sponsor of the resolution in the Senate, said in debate, "has been erected for nearly two hundred years. We are breaking the thread of our history." And, according to Clement J. Zablocki, its main House sponsor, the resolution says "in effect, that this power [to declare war] is not inherent in Presidents—despite the fact that they have assumed it even from the time of Washington."[2] The War Powers Resolution has then the radical objective of taking us back to first principles: "to fulfill the intent of the Framers of the Constitution of the United States," as it announces in its statement of purpose (sec. 2[c]). In doing so, it rejects the opinions of those who have

115

said that the Constitution grants the president authority to do whatever he thinks is in the national interest, or that it would have given him the authority had its framers been able to see beyond the conditions of the eighteenth century, or that it left the power vague thereby inviting whoever could to exercise it.

It is my purpose to study the War Powers Resolution in its relationship to the Constitution. My plan is, first, to take up the resolution, considering its most important features (for our purposes, anyway) and the nation's brief experience under it; next we shall turn to the resolution's source, the Constitution, using evidence from the founding period as guides to its meaning and the views of Locke and Montesquieu as guides to the meaning of the founders; and, finally, we shall return to the resolution in order to judge its constitutional understanding by our own.

THE RESOLUTION

What the War Powers Resolution does is to assign to the president the war-making authority intended for him by the Constitution and to exercise some of that which Congress claimed for itself. The presidential allotment was made in the following terms:

> The constitutional powers of the President as Commander in Chief to introduce United States armed forces into hostilities, or into situations where imminent involvement in hostilities is clearly indicated by the circumstances, are exercised only pursuant to (1) a declaration of war, (2) specific statutory authorization, or (3) a national emergency created by attack upon the United States, its territories or possessions, or its armed forces (sec. 2[c]).

Hostilities are not necessarily marked by armed conflict, according to the House committee's gloss on the resolution, but include confrontations where no shots have been fired; and authorization, according to the resolution itself, is not to be inferred from treaties unless implemented by legislation or from appropriations unless clearly specified (sec. 8[a]).

Congress defined its own war powers by implication: everything not assigned to the president belongs to it. In fact, the Senate committee reported to its chamber that "the residual legislative authority over the entire domain of foreign policy—not just the war power—was placed in Congress by the Constitution."[3] The scope of congressional authority can be glimpsed in the restraints the resolution places on the president's actions. He must consult with Congress "in every possible instance" before introducing the armed forces into hostilities or hostile situations (sec. 3). He must, in the absence of declared war, report to its presiding officers in writing within forty-eight hours of having taken these and certain other actions (which we shall not take time to consider) and to report at least every six months thereafter (sec. 4). He must, again in the absence of declared war, terminate his introductions of the armed forces within sixty days, or ninety days if their safe removal imposes "unavoidable military necessity" (sec. 5[b]). Last, in the absence of declared or authorized war, he must remove the armed forces from hostilities conducted outside of American territory if Congress so directs by concurrent resolution (sec. 5[c])—a legislative action not requiring executive approval.

In reminding the president of his constitutional powers in war making, the War Powers Resolution does not prohibit him from exercising others. Congress placed the description of his powers in the "Purpose and Policy" section of the resolution (sec. 2) where it lacks legal effect, rather than in the body of the legislation. This seeming paradox, contrived in conference committee, reveals congressional ambivalence with respect to staking down the executive. Both the Senate and House of Representatives were agreed that Congress should be empowered to control the president after he had engaged American forces in hostilities, but the Senate had wanted to limit the purposes for which he could engage them as well, whereas the House wanted to be silent on this subject. The House was, its leaders told their Senate counterparts, "adamantly opposed" to testing the constitutional authority of the president and, as they said within their own chamber, unwilling to "shackle" him.[4] The two chambers compromised their differences by incorporating their distinct approaches into the resolution: the Senate got the president's constitutional authority defined and the House kept the definition from having the force of law.

Where does this leave the president? According to Congressman Zablocki, the resolution merely conveys "a sort of sense of Congress" with respect to his authority. One of the resolution's leading Senate sponsors, Thomas F. Eagleton, agreed with him (and abandoned the resolution for this reason); and the executive, once the legislation had surmounted its veto, took a similar position, observing that the definition of presidential authority was "at most a declaratory statement of policy" which "neither requires nor prohibits any particular action." However, Senator Javits insisted that the compromise effected only a "minor" change in the Senate version of the legislation and that the president gained no power from it. Both sides could be right. The restrictive provision expresses an opinion of the president's war powers, and thus it leaves the president free to act upon a different opinion; but it expresses an opinion of what the Constitution commands and so, if its opinion is correct or is accepted as correct, the president may ignore it at his peril. He might justify going beyond his assigned constitutional powers by a plea of public necessity, but such a plea is based on an emergency and the only "national emergency" referred to by the War Powers Resolution is that created by an attack on the territory or armed forces of the United States. The resolution appears to assume that the constitution is adequate to every contingency, and yet it seems to recognize emergencies beyond a "national emergency" in not giving legal effect to its definition of presidential powers. That this was the intention of Zablocki, who led the fight against the Senate's approach, is made clear in his comment to the House that "when the President assumes authority he doesn't have, this Resolution permits him to proceed for a limited time."[5]

The War Powers Resolution stakes its control of the president's war making on its assertion of congressional authority rather than on its opinion of his authority. The legislative restraints placed in the resolution "are not dependent upon" that opinion, as the report of the Senate-House conference committee notes, and so they apply to the president's actions whatever may be his view of them.[6] As members of Congress expressed it, the resolution relies on a "performance test" and not an "authority text" of these actions. But this seems to mean that the president's constitutional powers are dependent upon those of Congress and thus may be restrained in their exercise by the consulting, reporting, and terminating provisions of the resolution. Assuming that Congress may control presidential war making in these ways when the president exceeds his authority, may it do so when he acts within it? And, if not, are we not still faced with the question: what is the scope of the president's war powers?

Far from regarding its war powers as being independent of the president's, the Senate was inclined to believe they were inclusive of them, except perhaps for the power to meet attacks on American territory. As Senator Javits put the matter, "A President is commander in chief, period." [7] This opinion underlay arguments for permitting congressional termination of most presidentially initiated hostilities by concurrent resolution, and it entered into the discussion of the president's constitutional powers themselves. Should the executive be empowered to forestall attacks on American territory? on the armed forces? be empowered to retaliate for such attacks? to rescue Americans from foreign danger? These and similar questions were discussed in terms of expediency as well as constitutionality, and the Senate-enacted legislation, which allowed him to do all these things except retaliate for attacks on the armed forces, withheld the latter because of the fear that the president might abuse it. [8] (The House resolution, it will be recalled, did not attempt to define the president's constitutional authority.) All of these grants of authority were deleted in conference committee. In explaining why the committee had eliminated one of them, the power of rescue, Senator Javits said it was decided the power was "neither desirable nor necessary" for the president to have. [9] But if the War Powers Resolution delegates most of the president's war powers to him, how can it describe those powers as having been given him by the Constitution? And if the Resolution betrays indecision respecting the president's powers, may it have omitted powers from its definition? We are led to a further question: what is the constitutional basis for the broad powers the resolution assumes for Congress?

Congress evidently believed that the Constitution's "necessary and proper" clause furnished authority for its legislative restraints on the president, for the Senate-House conference committee report states that the clause, which is quoted in paraphrase in the resolution (sec. 2[b]), "provides the basis for congressional action in this area," that is, in controlling the president.[10] But it is one thing to enact laws "for carrying into execution . . . powers vested by the Constitution in the President," as the clause authorizes, and quite another to enact laws which limit and override the powers vested in the president. The "necessary and proper" clause in fact leaves Congress's enumerated powers unchanged or, at most, allows Congress "the free use of means which might otherwise have been implied" when it carries its powers and those vested elsewhere in the government into execution.[11] The only relevant express power of Congress mentioned in the resolution is that of declaring war. This may sustain the resolution's reference to war authorized by specific statute, as an implied power of Congress, and the legislative branch may well possess, in addition, powers which are "a result from the whole mass of the powers of the government and from the nature of political society."[12] But the president is equally endowed by the Constitution with implied and resulting powers, and so the War Powers Resolution leaves us with the question it seeks to settle: what are the war powers of the president and Congress?

Has experience under the War Powers Resolution helped resolve the constitutional issues that the resolution leaves uncertain? The resolution has, as of early 1980, been in existence nearly seven years and in this period the president and Congress have had several occasions to interpret their war-making powers under it and the Constitution. We may start our inquiry into their views by sketching the six or arguably seven times that American forces have entered into hostilities or hostile situations since November, 1973. All but one of the actions occurred during the administration of President Ford; all were without congressional authorization, were for the limited purpose of rescuing civilians from danger, and were brief in duration, lasting from a few hours to about a week.[13] Most of the actions were connected with the fall of Indochina to the Communists in the spring of 1975. In the early part of April of that year, American ships evacuated some Americans and a great number of Vietnamese from central Vietnam to temporary safety to the south. As that action was being completed, helicopters, protected by a marine force and fighter aircraft, evacuated Americans and Cambodians from Pnom Penh; and at the end of the month a similar evacuation, on a much larger scale, was made of Americans and Vietnamese from Saigon. Finally, about the middle of May, American forces recovered a merchant vessel, the *Mayaguez*, from its Cambodian Communist captors and compelled the return of the vessel's crew.

Two of the non-Indochinese incidents went almost unnoticed both in the United States and in the country where they occurred: only a small number of the Americans and other foreigners in Lebanon in 1976 accepted offers of the American government, made in June and again in July, to be evacuated from that country, during a heightening of its prolonged civil strife. The arguable incident concerns an American and British helicopter evacuation from Cyprus, in late July, 1974, of several hundred Americans and others caught in fighting between Greek Cypriot and Turkish military forces on the island.[14] The Nixon Administration stated that the American aircraft had not entered a hostile situation here inasmuch as the place of rescue, a British base on Cyprus, was not itself a "hostile area."[15] American forces engaged in fighting only in the Saigon evacuation, where they returned antiaircraft and small-arms fire, and in the *Mayaguez* affair, where they attacked patrol boats, oil depots, and an airfield of the new Communist regime in Cambodia and invaded one of its offshore islands. It was these incidents which drew the greatest attention from Congress and the public and stimulated the greatest—almost the only—discussion of the president's powers under the War Powers Resolution and the Constitution.

In acting as he did, President Ford neither concurred in nor considered himself bound by the War Powers Resolution's definition of his constitutional authority. He believed the Constitution empowered him to rescue endangered Americans, though he did ask Congress on April 10, 1975, to "clarify" his authority with respect to evacuating Americans from Vietnam, as well as to grant him authority to evacuate those Vietnamese for whose safety the United States had incurred an obligation.[16] His position was complicated by several acts of legislation based squarely on Congress's appropriation power which prohibited the spending of funds for combat activities in Indochina. And yet the administration had already carried out its central Vietnamese and Pnom Penh evacuations at this time, and the Saigon evacuation was executed while the Senate and House were trying to agree upon authorizing legislation. Not only that, but in the reports he submitted on the Indochina incidents (he made no formal reports on the others), the president stated that he had acted pursuant to his "constitutional authority as Commander in Chief and Chief Executive." [17] Thus he seems to have acted on the understanding that his constitutional authority extended not only beyond the War Powers Resolution's notion of a "national emergency" (in the case of rescuing Americans) but allowed him to exercise powers he did not believe he possessed (in the case of rescuing foreign nationals). [18] Further, he made clear that his reports were submitted not because he thought himself commanded by the resolution but "in accordance with my desire to keep the Congress fully informed." [19] And he did not "consult" with Congress prior to any of his actions, though he did inform some of its members after he had reached his decision. As Mr. Ford made clear after leaving the presidency, he had not believed himself bound to observe the reporting or consulting or, for that matter, any of the restraints which the resolution attaches to the executive's war-making powers. [20] Although the Carter Administration has not yet been put to the test (as of early 1980), it too has expressed reservations regarding the War Powers Resolution's constitutionality, while more or less assuring Congress of its intention to observe its provisions. [21]

Most members of Congress who addressed the issue of presidential power to rescue American civilians agreed with the president. Senator Eagleton, for example, said after the Vietnamese and Cambodian evacuations that the executive "possesses an inherent right to rescue endangered Americans," and the Senate Foreign Relations Committee, with apparent unanimity, gave its "support [to] the President in the exercise of his constitutional powers" in the *Mayaguez* affair, with Senator Javits remarking that the deletion of the removal power in conference had been "regrettable." [22] We should not, however, read too much into this concession by Congress. For one thing, it extends to a single power among a number in possible dispute between the two branches. Congress did not acknowledge the president's power to rescue foreign nationals but merely acquiesced in what President Ford had done; nor did it, or President Ford for that matter, believe that the president could reenter the Vietnam War when the North Vietnamese launched their offensive at the beginning of 1975, despite President Nixon's written pledge to the South Vietnamese government that the United States would respond with force if North Vietnam violated the agreements which brought fighting to a halt in January, 1973. Moreover, Congress considered the consulting and reporting provisions of the War Powers Resolution to be binding on the president and much of its discussion of the *Mayaguez* affair was directed to the question of whether President Ford had conducted meaningful consultation with its members.[23]

We should not even conclude that Congress, or others, have accepted the president's opinion that he has the right to rescue Americans in distress or that the War Powers Resolution's definition of his constitutional powers is without legal effect. There were members of Congress who maintained that the president had acted unconstitutionally in the *Mayaguez* incident and some of them argued that he had acted illegally as well; and press stories at the time assumed the president's emergency powers to be limited to those assigned him by the resolution.[24] It should be emphasized that all of President Ford's actions were quickly and successfully carried out and that serious fighting occurred only in the *Mayaguez* rescue. How would Congress as a whole (and the public) have reacted, if, say, the *Mayaguez* operation had miscarried? If, for example, the captured American seamen had not been given over and perhaps had been killed by the Cambodians in retaliation for American attacks on their people and sovereignty? Or if the other operations had resulted in armed clashes? Or if American forces had been drawn into protracted fighting in the *Mayaguez* or any of the other incidents? Would Congress have ignored or excused the fact that the president had assumed powers it had instructed him he did not possess under the Constitution? Or might it have ordered the president to cease fighting, perhaps have censured him before the nation, perhaps even have found grounds for impeaching and removing him from office?

And so the constitutional issues raised by the War Powers Resolution remain. They are not resolved by the resolution or by practice since its enactment; nor could they be, for the resolution, in testing all precedents by the intention of the Constitution's framers, rejects all which are inconsistent with that intent. Thus it calls upon us to test recent precedents, including that of the resolution itself, by this standard.

THE CONSTITUTION

Our understanding of the Constitution, early authority tells us, is to be had from the fair meaning of the text, keeping in mind its purposes as stated in the document. We may look to contemporaneous interpretation of the Constitution in order to illustrate, confirm, or explain doubtful phrases of the text, but the credit to be given any interpretation depends on how widely it was shared and the abilities of those who held it, keeping in mind that no interpretation can change the text.[25] With this preface, we turn to relevant provisions of the Constitution.

The Constitution expressly divides the war powers as follows. It gives Congress power "to declare war, grant letters of marque and reprisal, and make rules concerning captures on land and water," and it makes the president "commander-in-chief of the army and navy of the United States; and of the militia of the several States when called into the actual service of the United States." This can only mean, as Jefferson once expressed it, that it belongs "exclusively to Congress to declare whether the nation, from a state of peace, shall go into that of war." According to the records of the Constitutional Convention, we might note, a solitary delegate, Pierce Butler, spoke in favor of vesting the power of declaring war in the executive, and he may have changed his mind by the end of the convention.[26]

May Congress put the country into war by means other than a declaration? If not, then all but one of the wars which this nation made upon other nations in its early years were unconstitutional, for only the War of 1812 with Great Britain was "declared." But the others were undeclared only in the sense that they were not formally declared, for in each instance Congress authorized the waging of war: against the Western Indians (in Ohio), in several acts from 1789; various Barbary states, in 1802, 1804, and 1815; and France, in several acts during 1798 and 1799. The difference between a war which is formally declared and one which is authorized corresponds to the difference, well understood in the eighteenth century, between general (or "perfect") war and partial (or "imperfect") war, between war that "destroys the national peace and tranquillity" and war that "interrupts it only in some particulars." [27] It would make little sense to say that Congress may allow full-scale war to be unleashed but not limited war, and Jefferson's opinion seems incontrovertible: "The Constitution has authorized the ordinary legislature alone to declare war against any foreign nation. If they may enact a perfect, they may a qualified war, as was done against France. In this state of things they may modify the acts of war, and appropriate the proceeds of it." [28] And if early practice is a reliable guide, Congress may authorize war, or declare it, contingently. In 1804, it permitted the president to extend the limited war then being waged against Tripoli "to any other of the Barbary powers which may commit hostilities against the United States." [29] And in 1811, it permitted him to occupy Spanish East Florida if any other foreign power attempted its occupation. May war be authorized contingently by treaty? It would appear not, since *Congress* authorizes war and the *Senate* consents to treaties. How could the Senate, elected by the state legislatures to represent the states in their equal corporate capacities, be deemed competent to act for the House of Representatives? In the great disputes that arose over implementing two of the nation's earliest treaties, nobody doubted the need for legislative action. In the French Treaty of 1778, the United States undertook to protect that country's possessions in North America in the event of war between France and any other power; and in the Jay Treaty of 1795, it agreed to establish special commissions in order, among other purposes, to settle private claims. When France and Great Britain went to war in 1793, Americans were sharply divided as to whether the president could determine that the United States would not be obligated to become France's partner in the war should she invoke the treaty guaranty; but partisans on both sides of the issue, including Hamilton and Madison in opposition, assumed that legislation was required to put the guaranty into effect. The issue in the dispute over the Jay Treaty's execution, again with Hamilton and Madison on opposing sides, was whether Congress had to appropriate the necessary funds and not whether legislative action was required. Hamilton's opinion, incidentally, won out, and by the 1820s it was "universally held, whatever doubts may have once existed, that Congress is bound to provide for carrying a treaty into effect," and so Congress's power to implement treaties obligating the country to war seems to be little more than a formality.[30]

The Constitution does not require the president to obtain congressional consent whenever he engages in hostilities, since the president may call the militia into service "to execute the laws of the Union, suppress insurrections, and repel invasions," once Congress has provided for calling them forth. Congressional legislation dates from 1789, in a limited militia act empowering the executive to use the militia "as he may judge necessary for . . . the purpose of protecting the inhabitants of the frontiers of the United States from the hostile incursions of the Indians." This and subsequent legislation, which broadened the president's authority to all three purposes mentioned in the Constitution, was used a number of times by President Washington and his early successors without recourse to Congress. Now if the president may use the militia for these purposes, it follows that he may use the army and navy as well, once they have been provided for, as it would seem absurd to interpret the Constitution as allowing the executive to call forth the militia of the states, say, to repel an invasion by a foreign power but not to call forth the armed might of the nation. Support for this interpretation can be found in the Constitutional Convention's concern with "leaving to the executive the power to repel sudden attacks" and making him "able to repel . . . war." Moreover, the president, it appears, does not have to await the launching of an insurrection or invasion, for the Constitution could not intend him to be less equipped than the states, to whom it gives the power to "engage in war" without congressional consent when "actually invaded, or in such imminent danger as will not admit of delay." Otherwise, the states possess *no* constitutional authority in respect to war or foreign affairs.[31]

Little that we have said so far calls seriously into question the War Powers Resolution's distribution of the war-making powers, in which Congress is required to declare war or authorize hostilities and the president is allowed to meet attacks on the United States or its armed forces. Our understanding of the Constitution only adds to, or clarifies, the resolution in one respect: like the state governments, the president, it appears, may engage in preemptive war (what the Senate bill called "forestalling attacks"). But now we must enter upon disputed ground, where supporters of presidential claims contest the boundaries marked out by the resolution and where the resolution seems uncertain of its own claims. Is the executive constitutionally limited to defensive measures only in meeting attacks or may he carry hostilities to the attacker? Does the Constitution allow him to engage the armed forces in hostilities for other purposes than defending the country and its armed forces, for example, in order to rescue Americans or to protect them where they are on the high seas or in foreign lands? To answer these questions satisfactorily, we must deal first with a more basic one: what is the *nature* of the war powers? The Constitution gives certain of these powers to the executive and certain of them to the legislature, but whose powers are shared with whom? The underlying assumption of the War Powers Resolution, as we have seen, is that the war powers are mostly or perhaps entirely legislative in character. Is this correct?

Two eminent founders, Hamilton and Madison, have addressed the question of the nature of the war powers in remarkable essays, and we might profitably begin our inquiry by considering their arguments. The occasion of their writing was President Washington's proclamation of April, 1793, declaring it to be "the duty and interest" and the "disposition" of the country to be impartial in the war which had broken out in Europe between France, on one side, and Great Britain and its allies on the other, and warning American citizens not to "contravene such disposition." Indirectly, the proclamation let it be known that, in the president's judgment, the United States was not obligated under its 1778 treaty with France to enter the war on the side of that nation. Hamilton justified the proclamation on constitutional and prudential grounds in newspaper essays under the name of "Pacificus," and Madison, as "Helvidius," answered him saying little about the proclamation but a great deal about the constitutional argument by which Hamilton justified it.[32]

Hamilton's argument runs as follows. The Constitution, in Article II, conveys a "general grant" of executive authority to the president in establishing that "the executive power" shall be vested in him. This grant is made with certain exceptions: the power to declare war is given to Congress and the powers to consent to treaties and appointments are given to the Senate. Otherwise, the grant is complete. The enumeration of executive powers which follows the general grant, except insofar as they are intended to restrict the president, as above, serve to specify the "principal articles" implied in the "more comprehensive grant"; examples are the commander-in-chief power and the duties to receive ambassadors and to take care that the laws be faithfully executed. It would have been difficult for the document to have contained a "complete and perfect specification of all cases of executive authority," and so it left the rest "to flow" from the general grant. This understanding is confirmed by the different expressions by which the Constitution conveys authority to the president and Congress. Whereas it vests "the executive power" in the one, it vests "all legislative powers herein granted" in the other. As exceptions to the president's general power, the powers to declare war and to consent to treaties and appointments should be strictly construed and "extended no further than is essential to their execution." Thus, while only Congress can "actually transfer the nation from a state of peace to a state of war," the president can "do whatever else the laws of nations, co-operating with the treaties of the country, enjoin in the intercourse of the United States with foreign powers."[33]

And Madison's answer: the power to declare war, like the power to make treaties, cannot be properly called executive. "The natural province of the executive is to execute laws, as that of the legislature is to make laws," and treaties and declarations of war are neither executions of laws nor do they presuppose the existence of laws. Although the president may be "a convenient organ of preliminary communications" on questions of war or treaties, and the proper person to execute Congress' determinations, he can have no part in giving "validity to such determinations." Further, even if these two powers are not "purely legislative" in nature, they are so much more so than they are anything else that Congress has an unrivaled claim to them. And since they are "substantially" legislative, executive "pretensions" to sharing in them must be strictly interpreted. The Constitution itself considers the power to declare war to be legislative in character, for it vests the power in Congress along with "every other" legislative grant. Although the treaty power is given jointly to the president and Senate, the two-thirds vote required for treaties, in contrast to the majority vote required "in all other cases," is a "substitute or compensation" for participation by the House of Representatives; and, more importantly, the Constitution gives treaties "the force and operation of laws." Pacificus has borrowed his doctrine of executive power from the British government, where the power of declaring war and making treaties are royal prerogatives and, accordingly, regarded as executive prerogatives by British commentators.[34]

Because Hamilton and Madison disagree as to the nature of the war powers, it does not mean that the question is insoluble on the basis of the Constitution. Indeed, they have assisted our own inquiry by illumining the question and by presenting arguments and evidence that can be weighed against each other. Moreover, not everything of importance is in dispute between them. Madison no less than Hamilton (and the founders generally) believed that the "vesting clause" of Article II conveys a general grant of executive power to the president, but he differs from him in limiting that power to the execution of the laws, broadly understood: that is, as Madison makes clear elsewhere, it includes the appointment, supervision, and removal of subordinate officers. He does not, however, claim the powers of war and management of foreign affairs to be legislative in nature but only those of *declaring war* and *making treaties*; indeed, he goes no further than to say that these two specific powers are "substantially of a legislative, not an executive character." Moreover, he infers only a moderate amount of additional power from them, most importantly, the rights to judge the causes of war and to unmake, or suspend, treaties. But how can the same power be both legislative and executive in character, and how are we to account for the large amount of governmental activity not embraced by Madison's conception of them? What of the power to recognize foreign governments (assigned by Hamilton to the executive)? Madison says only that the question is not given to the executive for decision. What of the power to conduct relations with other countries (Hamilton's "organ of intercourse")? Madison says the executive "may be a convenient organ of preliminary communications" with them "on the subjects of treaty or war," but he is silent about other subjects and the relation of this convenience to the powers of government. What of meeting attacks, protecting citizens in foreign danger, and doing a number of other things involving the use of military and naval force which Hamilton would allow "to flow" from the executive power? Again, Madison is silent.[35]

The reasons Madison offers for considering the powers of treaty and declaring war to be legislative in nature are rather puzzling. With respect to the first power, there is no evidence, in the Convention proceedings or in the Constitution itself, suggesting that the two-thirds vote by which the Senate must consent to treaties was intended as a "substitute or compensation" for House action. The document requires a two-thirds vote for a number of decisions and not, as Madison says, solely in the case of treaties: for overriding vetoes, proposing constitutional amendments, convicting on impeachment charges, and expelling members; and it does so because it regards each of these decisions to be of special importance. In the second place, treaties seem not to be laws, which the framers understood as rules for governing society, but to be contracts with other nations. They have the force of laws in the Constitution because the document gives them that force. In England, where treaties were (and are) made exclusively by the executive, they needed parliamentary implementation in order to have the status of law. Madison might have attached more importance than he did to the fact that the Constitution uses basically the same form in the appointment and treaty clauses; if the first power is executive in character, as Madison concedes, it may be inferred that the document regards the second to be executive as well. As for the power to declare war, Madison meets Hamilton's argument that the power is an executive one given over to Congress, with the "fundamental principle" that power belonging to one branch cannot be placed "entirely" in another branch. Hamilton would not have disagreed and might have asked Madison, had he replied to his Helvidius essays, whether the principle did not also prevent the major part of a power belonging to one branch, that of *making* treaties, from being placed in another branch. But Hamilton does not consider the power of declaring war to be a power whole in itself but rather part of the "more comprehensive grant" of executive power, which is hardly an unusual view since Madison himself regards the veto power, a legislative power delegated to the president, to be part of a more comprehensive legislative power.[36]

If Madison's argument is puzzling, Hamilton's justifies concern, for he ascribes broad authority to the executive without defining its limits. Article II of the Constitution only enumerates particular cases of the president's powers in war and foreign affairs, according to him, leaving their full range to be discovered by interpreting the general grant "in conformity to other parts of the Constitution and to the principles of free government." Madison does not like what Hamilton has already discovered in the grant and is alarmed by what may come in the future, since Hamilton's doctrine, in removing "the landmarks of power," has implications dangerous to peace and to liberty itself. But Madison's charge that Hamilton's doctrine was borrowed from the "executive prerogatives" of the British crown is too indefinite, for royal prerogatives were considered to include the powers of sending and receiving ambassadors, making appointments, and commanding the army and navy, in addition to declaring war and making treaties. Rather than look to "British commentators" in general for the source of Hamilton's ideas on the powers of government, we should direct our attention to those two writers, Locke and his French counterpart Montesquieu, who above all others seem to have influenced his thinking on the subject.[37]

Locke calls executive that power which encompasses "the execution of the municipal [internal] laws of the society" and legislative that power which enacts those laws, and treats judicial power as part of executive power. There is a third power of government for Locke, which he terms "federative": "the power of war and peace, leagues and alliances, and all the transactions with all persons and communities without the commonwealth." Inasmuch as this power operates on foreigners and not one's own people, it is much less capable than the executive power of being directed by laws. Locke does not explain why he calls this power as he does and, in fact, is "indifferent as to the name"; but the apparent reason is instructive and serves to clarify Locke's doctrine of executive power in relation to the other powers of government. When men form civil societies, they agree to give over to a common sovereign the powers each has exercised for himself in the state of nature: to *execute* the law of nature by *judging* transgressions of it. Thus were established the legislative power to replace the unwritten natural law with positive law and the executive power to enforce it, the two powers in all "well-framed governments" being placed "in distinct hands." But civil societies, lacking a common sovereign over them, exist in a state of nature in relation to each other: each constitutes a single body which judges the law of nature (now called the law of nations) for itself and executes its own judgments. The power to do so is federative because it corresponds to the power established when several political bodies confederate for the purpose of providing for their external security (as Americans did in forming the Articles of Confederation and the Federal Union). Although the federative power is distinct from the executive power in Locke's doctrine, not having to do with the execution of "municipal laws" but with "the management of the security and interest of the public without," the two powers "are hardly to be separated and placed at the same time in the hands of distinct persons."[38]

It is easy to move from calling these two powers "executive" and "federative" to speak simply of two kinds of executive power, one relating to municipal and one relating to external concerns, as Montesquieu in fact does. Montesquieu also separates judging from the executive power and indicates in much more detail than Locke the objects to which the "foreign" executive power extends: disposing of the public moneys, arbitrating the affairs of allies, deciding on war and peace, fixing the number of troops, assigning the command of provinces and armies and naming successors, receiving and sending embassies, establishing security, and preventing invasions.[39] Only one more step was needed to collapse Locke's distinction between the executive and federative powers entirely, which Hamilton took in his Pacificus essay.

Madison-Helvidius warns us not to be guided by Locke and Montesquieu; they wrote, he says, before the powers of government had been illuminated and they were, besides, warped by their regard for the government of England. We should look instead to the "nature and operation" of these powers and to the American Constitution. It is, of course, precisely the nature and operation of governmental powers that Locke and Montesquieu purport to explain, based on their reflections on the natural condition of men and the reasons they enter into civil society; moreover, Madison himself accepts their theory in its essentials and, in fact, describes Montesquieu in *The Federalist* as "the oracle who is always consulted and cited" on the question of the distribution of governmental powers. Upon what theoretical grounds then does he regard the powers of government to be "naturally" limited to making laws and executing them? We do not know for sure, but it may be that the republican Madison had not accommodated executive power to his preferred form of government. "I have scarcely ventured as yet," he had written Washington on the eve of the Constitutional Convention, "to form my own opinion either of the manner in which [a national executive] ought to be constituted or the authorities with which it ought to be clothed."[40]

But it is the founders generally who command our attention and not Hamilton and Madison only. What view of executive power did they hold and act upon? Did they agree with Locke and Montesquieu, and Hamilton, that the powers of war and foreign transactions were executive (-federative)? We begin with the Constitutional Convention, for the issue arose practically at the threshold of its deliberations. On June 1 Charles Pinckney questioned the eighth Virginia Resolution's provision for a plural executive "to possess the executive powers of [the Continental] Congress" (there being no executive branch in the Confederal government). He was, he said, "afraid that the executive powers of [the existing] Congress might extend to peace & war &c." James Wilson then made his famous motion: "that the executive consist of a single person," upon which John Rutledge returned to Pinckney's fear: "he was for vesting the executive power in a single person, tho' he was not for giving him the power of war and peace." The strain was eased when Madison, seconded by Wilson, moved an amendment to the resolution which, as adopted, stipulated that the yet unformed executive would have "power to carry into effect the national laws [and] to appoint to offices in cases not otherwise provided for." Madison defined these powers as "in their nature executive," and Wilson defined them as "strictly executive." And yet we do not know how the convention as a whole regarded them, since it decided merely on the powers which the executive would possess under the new Constitution. We do know that Pinckney and Rutledge feared that the executive powers might be construed to include "peace & war &c," and Madison's motion is evidence that others shared their concern. Indeed, we cannot say from the convention's records of this date what Madison and Wilson thought was the nature of the powers of war and foreign affairs, but only that Madison considered war and peace not to be executive and that Wilson considered "peace & war &c" to be neither legislative nor, "strictly" speaking, executive. Could Wilson, or both men, have thought them to be "federative"? At any rate, when the Committee of Detail had finished with Madison's motion, the presidency appeared before the convention, on August 6, fully armed with authority and with the declaration that "the Executive Power of the United States shall be vested in a single person."[41]

From this point, the evidence supports Hamilton's conception of the executive power and Hamilton's presidency. With respect to the treaty powers and the management of foreign affairs generally, the evidence seems overwhelming. The Committee of Detail's report would have required the Senate to keep and publish a record of its proceedings only when "acting in a legislative capacity." Elbridge Gerry moved, on August 10, that it be required to publish them when "exercising its peculiar authorities" (others called them "additional authorities"). It is obvious that these "authorities" were the powers to make treaties and appoint ambassadors, both of which the committee had assigned exclusively to the Senate. John Mercer on August 11 spoke in opposition to "other powers than legislative" being given to the Senate and a few days later argued explicitly that the treaty power belonged to the executive. William Davie, one of the North Carolina delegates, explained the whole treaty business to his state's ratifying convention as follows: "The power of making treaties," he said, "has in all countries and governments been placed in the executive departments," but the Philadelphia Convention had withheld the whole power from the president because of "that jealousy of executive power which has shown itself so strongly in all the American governments." And where were Madison and Wilson in all this? Madison cosponsored a motion which would have exempted the Senate from publishing its proceedings "when not acting in its legislative capacity," that is, when acting on treaties and appointments, and Wilson opposed making the Senate a court of impeachment and partially vesting the treaty and appointment powers in it, on the ground that by these accretions to its regular authority "the legislative, executive & judiciary powers are all blended in one branch of the government." It is possible that some framers, in referring to the treaty power as nonlegislative, did not think of it as being specifically executive, and Hamilton himself states in *The Federalist* that it seems "to form a distinct department" of power. Locke's federative power appears not to have made its complete passage into the executive power at the time of the convention, although nearly so, and as soon as the Senate organized itself it established an "Executive Journal" for its proceedings respecting treaties and appointments.[42]

It is clear that the founders did not think of the treaty power as being different in nature from the general power of managing foreign affairs. Consider, for example, the legislation enacted in 1789 by the First Congress establishing the departments of Foreign Affairs and the Treasury and shortly after broadening the sphere of the first department and changing its name to the Department of State. The secretary of foreign affairs was informed by law that he would "perform and execute such duties as shall, from time to time, be enjoined on or entrusted to him by the President," but the relevant laws specified the duties of the secretaries of the Treasury and State, insofar as the latter's domestic responsibilities were concerned.[43] In these ways did Congress indicate its belief that executive duties in the realm of foreign affairs derived from the constitutional powers of the president and in domestic affairs from those possessed by Congress. Should more evidence be needed to settle the question, or to instruct us as to the scope of the president's authority in foreign affairs, the need is admirably met by the following opinion which Jefferson, as secretary of state, prepared for President Washington in April, 1790:

> It [the Constitution] has declared that the executive powers shall be vested in the President, submitting specific articles of it to a negative by the Senate, and it has vested the judiciary power in the courts of justice, with certain exceptions also in favor of the Senate.
> The transaction of business with foreign nations is executive altogether. It belongs, then, to the head of that department, except as to such portions of it as are specially submitted to the Senate. Exceptions are to be construed strictly.[44]

It is, of course, the war power and not the foreign affairs power which is directly at issue in this inquiry, although it is hard to see how one can be detached from its Lockeian connection to the other. But perhaps the founders did separate the two; after all, some of them expressed alarm at the idea that the power of war might be carried to the executive from the old constitution. Did other founders than Hamilton state or suggest that Congress' power to declare war was drawn from the executive power? And was Hamilton always of the same mind? It is said that Hamilton-Publius had a narrower view of the president's war power than Hamilton-Pacificus, since in *The Federalist*, No. 69 he stated that the president's authority as commander-in-chief "would amount to nothing more than the supreme command and direction of the military and naval forces." But we must know what Hamilton meant by "supreme command and direction" before we can say what scope he gave to the Commander-in-Chief Clause. In the

Pacificus essay we have examined, he joined it to a general power of war, and in the "Plan of Government" that he presented to the Constitutional Convention he made clear that it entailed "the direction of war when authorized or begun"—begun, that is by another nation. We might point out that the First Congress, in establishing the War Department, described its secretary's powers in terms identical to those used for the secretary of foreign affairs: in short, his powers, too, came from the constitutional authority of the president. And Jefferson once more takes his place alongside Hamilton, in this remark to Madison in 1789: "We have already given, in example, one effectual check to the dog of war, by transferring the power of declaring war from the executive to the legislative body, from those who are to spend, to those who are to pay." Jefferson's emphasis is on restraining the president, but the restraint is achieved by a constitutional transfer of part of the executive power, that of declaring war, to Congress. Finally, when the delegates to the Constitutional Convention discussed giving war-making power to Congress, they seemed to assume that whatever wasn't given to the legislature would lie with the president, even without express constitutional language to that effect. On August 17 they took up the Committee of Detail's proposal that Congress shall have power "to make war." Madison and Elbridge Gerry "moved to insert 'declare,' striking out 'make' war," and, according to the convention records, the delegates "debated the difference between a power to declare war, and to make war—amended by substituting declare." Rufus King observed that "'make' war might be understood to 'conduct' it, which was an executive function"; however, other delegates considered "make" in the related sense of "enter into," as in the power to make treaties. But it doesn't matter to our present inquiry which meaning the convention's members attached to "make war"; what is important is that they acted on the assumption that this expression gave broader power to Congress than "declare war," that is, that it drew more power from a reservoir of executive power. For example, Madison and Gerry thought that congressional power to "declare war" would have the effect of "*leaving* to the Executive the power to repel sudden attacks," whereas, their comment implies, power to "make war" would leave him without it. On the other hand, Roger Sherman thought that "declare war" enabled the president to repel war, but that "make war," by *narrowing* the power [of Congress] too much," would enable him "to commence war." [45]

Where does Congress' power to declare war leave the president's power to make it? If Sherman meant by "commence war" that the president could make war when the United States is at peace, he must have been mistaken: for that would take away Congress' check on the "dog of war." If by "repel sudden attacks," Madison and Gerry meant that the president would be confined to strict self-defense when a foreign nation began war on the United States, they must have been mistaken also: for that would take away from his power to make, or conduct, war. It is Congress' right to declare war, that is, as we quoted Jefferson earlier, "to declare whether the nation, from a state of peace, shall go into that of war." "But when a foreign nation declares or openly and avowedly makes war upon the United States," to shift to Hamilton, "they are then by the very fact already at war, and any declaration on the part of Congress is nugatory; it is at least unnecessary." [46] It seems fitting to join Jefferson and Hamilton in this way since, as by now should be clear, the two men held closely similar views on the nature of executive power and on the powers which the Constitution gave the American president.

Jefferson a Hamiltonian? How could this be when advocates of the War Powers Resolution turned to him perhaps more often than to any other founder as authority for their opinion that the president's war power was limited to meeting attacks? Well might we be asked to examine Jefferson's presidential message to Congress of December, 1801, in which he reported on a sea fight that occurred in the Mediterranean in early August of that year between the American naval schooner *Enterprise* and a Tripolitan cruiser. Tripoli had shortly before declared war on the United States, Jefferson reported, and the cruiser, searching for American merchant ships, had "fallen in with, and engaged," the *Enterprise* "and was captured, after a heavy slaughter of her men." And then: "Unauthorized by the Constitution, without the sanction of Congress, to go beyond the line of defense, the vessel being disabled from committing further hostilities, was liberated with its crew." [47] This is Jefferson's report, but this is what happened: first, the American ship, as Jefferson knew, had been the attacker; and, second, it had acted pursuant to instructions issued by the secretary of the navy after cabinet approval. The *Enterprise* was part of a squadron of ships sent to the Mediterranean in May, 1801, in order to be "in a situation to chastise" Algiers or Tripoli "in case of their declaring war or committing hostilities" on American merchant shipping, and prisoners were to be released because "this mode will be humane and will shew that we have no sort of fear, what such men can do—It will also tend to bring those powers back to a sense of justice, which they owe us." [48] Madison, incidentally, agreed with the cabinet decision that "the captains may be authorized, if war exists, to search for and destroy the enemy's vessels wherever they can find them," except that he thought they could enter the enemy's harbors only in pursuit. [49] As for Jefferson, we can only speculate as to why he misled Congress and the nation as he did: fearing the energetic executive, equipped as it was with broad powers, and yet believing that this is what the Constitution had established, he sought—and this would not be the only occasion—to reform the presidency in order to render it safe for republican government. [50]

Thus the president may engage the armed forces in war when Congress places the country in that condition or when a foreign nation "openly and avowedly" does so. He may, moreover, engage them in a number of other ways, since not every use of the army and navy constitutes war. Foreign war, as an opinion of the Supreme Court in 1800, in the case of *Bas* v. *Tingy*, defines it, is a "contention by force between two nations, in external matters, under the authority of their respective governments." [51] The president does not make war when, as their commander-in-chief, he disposes the armed forces within American territory and waters or when he sends them into other nations at their invitation or into international waters. Nor does he make war when he engages in hostilities against groups without government, such as pirates or "unorganized societies" (both were numerous at the founding and for some time after) for the purpose, say, of protecting Americans and their property. Nor do all hostile acts of a foreign power constitute war: not, for example, French seizures of American merchant ships in the late 1790s.[52] And when they do not, the president's authority is limited accordingly. It is then his right "to repel force by force (but not to capture), and to repress hostilities within our own waters." This was Hamilton's advice to the secretary of the navy in 1798, which he supported with this reason: "In so delicate a case, in one which involves so important a consequence as that of war—my opinion is that no doubtful authority ought to be exercised by the President."[53] It would seem within Congress' power to ensure presidential adherence to Hamilton's advice, for if the president can protect the nation and its citizens by measures short of war, surely the legislature can keep him from venturing too close to its borders.

We may summarize to this point as follows. The Constitution's comprehensive grant of executive power to the president embraces what Locke calls the "federative power" and Montesquieu the "executive power of things which relate to the law of nations"; that is, it embraces the powers of war and the conduct of foreign affairs. The Constitution allows legislative participation in some of this power: Congress has the right to declare war and the Senate has the right to consent to treaties. To be sure, these are not the only means Congress has for acting upon war and foreign affairs generally, as it possesses impressive legislative powers as well: most notably, its powers to regulate commerce and to provide for the common defense, for an army and navy, and for calling forth the militia. Congress could, for example, compel the president to terminate hostilities by the "disagreeable mode of negativing supplies for the war," or it could allow him to engage in hostilities in voting him supplies so long as its intention was made clear in the legislation. Otherwise a military appropriation expresses no authority to make war: members of Congress may have supported it in order to keep up the armed forces, from the necessity of supplying forces already engaged in combat, or for other reasons. Thus the president employs the force of the community but the legislature directs how the force shall be used; he possesses the sword but it selects the weapon and provides for its readiness. And behind its several powers, legislative and executive, stands that final arbiter of contests with the president: the power to impeach and remove him from office.[54]

There is another power in Locke's scheme of government which he calls prerogative, "the power of doing public good without a rule." Prerogative differs from the federative power in that it is exercised domestically whereas the federative power is exercised in relation to foreigners; but, like the federative power, it is possessed by the person who has the executive power in his hands and it operates where human affairs are uncertain and variable. Prerogative, no less than the federative power, is evidence of the insufficiency of the rule of positive law or, put another way, of the inability of men to transcend the state of nature: the distinction which Locke makes between executive and federative power, and thus between domestic and foreign affairs, is weakened with the introduction of prerogative.[55]

Prerogative may be exercised "where the law [is] silent," that is, in the "many cases" for which legislators have not provided or cannot provide, and in "some cases" "against the direct letter of the law." Modern scholars usually understand Locke to mean that the executive may violate or, to use the earlier expression, suspend or dispense with the laws, but Locke himself may mean no more than that he may pardon those who have violated them, for example, and this is the only one he gives: those who may have pulled down an innocent man's home in order to prevent the spread of fire. Why else should he speak of the people having set limits to prerogative when dissatisfied with its exercise, if prerogative may freely set aside those limits? Or why say that the king has no more right than a constable to exceed the bounds of his authority? We might note in this regard that Blackstone, after introducing the pardoning power among specific prerogatives of the British crown, proceeds to render Locke's definition of prerogative as the power of acting "where the positive laws are silent."[56]

Whatever Locke's meaning, early American statesmen understood "prerogative" in the way we have suggested: the president may act where the laws are silent but not in derogation of them.[57] For example, if Congress had not specified the means by which the Non-intercourse Act of 1799 was to be enforced, he might have been justified, according to the Supreme Court in *Little* v. *Barreme*, in ordering the seizure of all American ships engaged in prohibited commerce with France. That law was not, however, silent, in the Court's opinion, for in authorizing the seizure of American ships when traveling *to* French ports it had precluded their seizure when bound *from* such ports; and so President Adams' more general instructions to naval commanders were illegal.[58] It is not only statutes that speak to the president but also the Constitution, since that too is positive law; thus the law is less often silent in the United States than it is in governments contemplated by Locke. An American president may not exercise his prerogative, that is, his discretionary authority, say, to purchase military supplies when "accidents and necessities" render legislated funds insufficient, since the document stipulates that "no money shall be drawn from the treasury, but in consequence of appropriations made by law" (Art. I, sec. 9[6]). What then is a president, or subordinate official, to do when the public good seems to demand that he act in a way that statute or Constitution does not allow? He acts, as Presidents Washington and Jefferson did in making military purchases when the threat of war suddenly loomed in 1793 (with France) and in 1807 (with Great Britain); and he justifies himself before Congress and sometimes before a court of law.[59] It is for Congress to decide whether his action was in fact justified and, if so, to immunize him from civil suit or reimburse him from adverse judgments already rendered. The sequence to Captain Little's illegal capture of an American ship, though made pursuant to presidential instructions and not pursuant to an emergency, illustrates our point: Barreme was awarded damages in a civil suit and Congress reimbursed Little for the amount.

When the president suspends or dispenses with the prescriptions of law in special situations, we may say that he exercises emergency power so long as we understand that the source of this power is not, strictly speaking, the Constitution or statutory law but the "law of necessity."[60] We qualify this statement because the need for the president to act in emergencies seems also to be acknowledged by the Constitution, in the oath which it requires him, and him alone, to take, to "preserve, protect, and defend the Constitution of the United States" (Art. II, sec. 1[8]). Easily overlooked in ordinary times, this provision suggests the crucial part which the energetic executive plays in the American form of republican government.

With these remarks we complete our inquiry into the Constitution's allocation of the war powers and return to the War Powers Resolution to apply some of what we have learned.

THE RESOLUTION AND THE CONSTITUTION

The War Powers Resolution is correct in its opinion that the president needs congressional approval, by declaration or authorization, before he can take the country into war. Thus President Truman was mistaken in believing he had authority as commander-in-chief to commit American forces to the Korean conflict in June, 1950, and he worried unnecessarily that by going to Congress for consent he would have impaired the powers of his office. President Kennedy was similarly mistaken in September, 1962, in regard to his authority to act against Cuba, before the situation there became a crisis, and in thinking it would be merely "useful" for members of Congress to "express their view" on the situation. Likewise President Lyndon Johnson in insisting, in August, 1967, that in conducting hostilities in Vietnam "we did not think the [Southeast Asia] Resolution was necessary to do what we did and what we are doing. We think we are well within the grounds of our constitutional authority." [61] The War Powers Resolution is correct, too, in denying that treaties and appropriations in themselves furnish a basis for presidential war making, and the Johnson Administration placed false confidence in the Southeast Asia Collective Defense Treaty and in military appropriations as authority for the Vietnam War. [62] But Presidents Kennedy and Johnson did receive statutory authority to act against Cuba and in Vietnam, in joint resolutions enacted in September, 1962, and August, 1964, respectively. The latter legislation, repealed in January, 1971, declared the United States to be "prepared, as the President determines, to take all necessary steps, including the use of armed force, to assist any protocol or member state of the Southeast Asia Collective Defense Treaty [including Vietnam] requesting assistance in defense of its freedom." [63] It is ironic that the war in Vietnam, criticized as having been undeclared and hence as unauthorized, and cited "time and time again" in congressional debate as evidence of the need for war powers legislation, should be constitutionally vindicated by the product of that debate.[64]

In acknowledging the president's authority to introduce the armed forces into hostilities when American territory or armed forces have been attacked, the War Powers Resolution is in agreement with the Constitution in not limiting him to defensive measures. When attacks on this nation or its forces clearly mark the start of war, as Japan's attack on Pearl Harbor in December, 1941, did, the executive may do what is necessary to wage war. However, these are not the "only" circumstances in which the armed forces may be used in hostilities. In the first place, war may be made upon the United States in ways other than those mentioned in the resolution: Tripoli, for example, made it against American commerce in 1801. Moreover, the power to defend against attack implies the power, contained in the Senate bill, of forestalling attack or, to use the harsher expression, of conducting preemptive strikes, which the conference committee deleted from the final legislation.

Finally, the War Powers Resolution does not recognize the president's right under the Constitution to use the armed forces in hostilities short of war or in situations marked by armed confrontation (according to the House Committee's explanation of "hostilities"). The resolution would, if followed, impair a president's ability to take forceful measures to protect or rescue American citizens abroad when their lives are endangered, or even to deploy American power in the service of American diplomacy. It was argued in the Senate that President Nixon would not have been prevented from sending naval units into the eastern Mediterranean in a show of force on behalf of Jordan in September, 1970, when invasion threatened that country, or on behalf of Israel in October, 1973, during the Yom Kippur War.[65] But would not his deployments have been empty gestures if the president, as the senators assumed, could not have backed his moves with the threat that naval power might actually be used? Indeed, does not the resolution, if it is to be obeyed, submit the president's ability to deploy the armed forces to the veto of foreign nations? How could he "introduce" the navy into the eastern Mediterranean if the Soviet Union should warn him of dangerous consequences? Could he even place the navy into waters off the American coasts or the army along the country's frontiers in the face of threatened hostilities or perhaps nothing more than the threat of "armed confrontation"? Because of the harm to American security that could result from presidential obedience to the "authority" part of the War Powers Resolution, it is a good thing that it issues only an opinion to the president and it would be unfortunate if that opinion were to be converted by interpretation into a command.

This brings us to the president's true emergency power. It is not, as the War Powers Resolution assumes, a power exerted when the United States or its armed forces are attacked but, to give the most fell example of it, a power to engage the country in war or at least in acts of war. The resolution reflects a tendency of recent decades to bring emergency action within the scope of the executive power. Until the late 1960s, the tendency usually produced inflated claims on behalf of the president: that he could, without recourse to Congress, fight a limited naval war in the Atlantic and land wars on a large scale in Korea and Indochina and impose a naval blockade around Cuba. Since then a contracted view of his power, such as we find in the War Powers Resolution, has gained strength, but the view persists that the president's emergency actions are part of his executive power. The Executive Article could undergo new expansion as presidents find it necessary to act beyond their constitutional grants and as they, and their supporters, think it necessary to justify extraordinary actions in terms of regular authority. We need therefore to be reminded of what early statesmen clearly grasped: that "circumstances . . . sometimes occur which make it a duty in officers of high trust to assume authorities beyond the law." [66] In a curious way the War Powers Resolution embodies this prudential understanding in not prohibiting the president from exercising power beyond what it says the Constitution allots him. As Congressman Zablocki's remarks at the time of the resolution's passage indicate, it seemed to be the intention of the House conferees on the legislation to preserve a measure of presidential freedom in the service of public necessity. Rather than limit the president's ability to act, they wished to provide means whereby Congress could judge the propriety of his actions, a purpose both constitutional and appropriate in its principle. President Ford was not prevented by the resolution from forcibly recovering the *Mayaguez* and its crew, that is, from engaging in a "contention by force" with the government of Cambodia, but in so doing he exercised a power confided by the Constitution to the legislative branch.

Let us turn from the War Powers Resolution's assignment of presidential authority to its assertion of that of Congress. Congress' power to declare war and to enact laws necessary and proper for carrying out this power seem to furnish the basis for the legislative restraints in the resolution. It is difficult to see how these powers can support certain of the restraints. Prudence if not comity should induce the president to comply with the provision that he consult with Congress "in every possible instance" before committing American forces to combat. Perhaps he can be legally obligated to do so when he engages in an unauthorized act of war, as in the case of the *Mayaguez* (although a president should be able to offer a number of plausible reasons why consultation was not possible), but how can he be compelled to consult when he acts within his executive powers? To be sure, the Constitution requires the president to obtain the Senate's advice in making treaties and appointments; however, these requirements are exceptions to his executive authority and cannot be extended to his other actions. If the president were required by law to consult with Congress before exercising his constitutional power of pardon, the restriction, in all likelihood, would be considered an encroachment on his authority. How can a similar restriction be justified in the case of his constitutional war making? Do not "decision, activity, secrecy, and despatch," qualities which *The Federalist* ascribes to presidential proceedings in general, have a special application to his engagement in hostilities?[67] As for the resolution's reporting requirement, I merely remark that Congress has a right to seek information from the president and he has a right to decline to furnish it, and I refer the reader elsewhere to a full consideration of the constitutional issues.[68] Again, comity and prudence should lead the president into cooperation, except as to those matters which it would be imprudent to reveal at the time and except as to the resolution's time limit (within forty-eight hours of having engaged American forces in hostilities) when the president has more pressing business at hand.

There is some constitutional basis for the War Powers Resolution's stipulation that the president must terminate his use of the armed forces in hostilities within sixty (or ninety) days unless Congress has declared war or extended his time. (We shall not consider the prudence of the stipulation: whether, for example, it would encourage intransigence on the part of an enemy in the hope that Congress would not prolong hostilities or drive a president to the use of extreme measures in the fear that it would not.) The resolution does not delegate authority to the president to go to war, that is, to go from peace into war. Rather it limits the duration of presidential war making regardless of whether the president has exercised power he does not have: to engage in offensive war (for example, to aid an attacked ally), or has exercised power he does have: to engage in defensive war (that is, war launched upon the United States). Now Congress need not authorize defensive war, as Hamilton tells us, and yet it may and has done so (for instance, after the Japanese attack on Pearl Harbor), and it has reason to act when it wishes to confine the scope of war. Limited war, to recur to the Supreme Court's decision in *Bas* v. *Tingy*, confines hostilities "in place, in objects, and in time." [69] If Congress may limit the duration of war by specific laws, the argument can be made that Congress may do so by a general law. As applied to presidential hostilities short of war, the resolution's time limit might be sustained on the argument that when such actions last as long as sixty days they have taken a shape requiring legislative consent for their continuation.

It is not so easy to understand how the resolution can require the president to remove the armed forces from hostilities conducted abroad whenever Congress so directs by concurrent resolution. This procedure was justified in congressional discussions on the principle that the legislative branch may make conditional what it delegates to the executive from its own authority; and it was observed that other laws, most commonly ones authorizing the reorganization of executive agencies, have reserved Congress' right to "veto" particular executive actions and that some laws, for example, the Southeast Asia Resolution, have reserved Congress' right to repeal the laws themselves. We need not examine the principle of conditional delegation, although we have constitutional doubts about it, since we do not find the War Powers Resolution to have delegated anything to the president.[70] All that the resolution does with respect to his powers is to recognize a constitutional right on his part to engage in hostilities in some circumstances and not in others; certainly, Congress' refusal to give this part of the resolution legal effect cannot be construed as delegating to him war-making power beyond what it thought was the scope of his constitutional authority. Indeed, it would be an improper transfer of authority for Congress to allow the president to engage in war without any specification of the enemy or the circumstances.

CONCLUSION

The War Powers Resolution does not disclose its full meaning at once. Our first impression in reading it is of extensive legislative and restrained executive power in war making; then the possibility of larger executive authority emerges as we realize that the resolution's prescription of the president's powers is but an opinion; and, finally, there comes to view the president's emergency power, the discretion to act in cases not provided for by law. In reluctantly yielding its meaning about the scope of presidential war making, the resolution reminds us of the Constitution, with the Legislative Article commanding our attention by its precedence to the Executive Article in the document and by its much greater length; with the conveyance of broad executive power indicated by a slight variance in the wording of the vesting clauses of the two articles; and with emergency power obliquely suggested in the presidential oath. The Constitution itself seems to imitate the caution of that true founding document of modern republican government, Locke's *Second Treatise of Government.* There the legislative is presented as the "supreme power of the commonwealth," "that which has a right to direct how the force of the commonwealth shall be employed," and the executive as that "which should see to the execution of the laws." Then comes the federative power, "hardly to be separated" from the executive power and "much less capable to be directed by antecedent, standing, positive laws than the executive"; it "must necessarily be left to the prudence and wisdom of those whose hands it is in." We are assured that the legislative power is still supreme, with "all other powers . . . derived from and subordinate to it"; however, Locke proceeds to instruct us, the legislative *body* is not superior to the executive when the latter consists of a single person vested with the executive power and a share of the legislative power (the veto). And though the superiority of the legislative *power* to the executive and federative *powers* is reaffirmed, this is not Locke's final word, since there is yet prerogative, encompassing in part, at least, what we have called emergency power.[71]

It seems more than coincidence that the full meaning of the president's power should be veiled in the War Powers Resolution, the Constitution, and Locke's *Second Treatise*, for the power contains a difficulty for representative government. It is a dangerous power because, in the hands of a single person, it is energetic and the energetic executive consorts uneasily with the deliberative legislature. At the same time, energy in the executive is essential to the ends of representative government: the securing of citizens in their rights. It is the energetic executive who protects these rights from foreign and also domestic danger. To be sure, security is also provided by the extensive republic, but the extensive republic itself requires the energetic executive for the steady administration of its laws. What the founders contrived, following Locke's general scheme and Montesquieu's elaboration upon it, was, as they liked to quote Montesquieu, "a kind of constitution that has all the internal advantages of a republican, together with the external force of a monarchical, government." It is well for republicans not to give too much prominence to the monarchical feature of their government.[72]

NOTES TO CHAPTER IV

1. Public Law 93–148, 87 Stat. 555 (1973).
2. U.S. Congress, House of Representatives, Committee on International Relations, Subcommittee on International Security and Scientific Affairs, *The War Powers: A Test of Compliance Relative to the Danang Sealift, the Evacuation of Pnom Penh, the Evacuation of Saigon, and the Mayaguez Incident, Hearings, May 7 and June 4, 1975*, 94th Cong., 1st Sess., 93; *Congressional Record*, 93rd Cong., 1st Sess., 33550.
3. *Senate Reports*, 93d Cong., 1st Sess., No. 220, p. 13.
4. See Javits' report to the Senate on the House position, *Congressional Record*, 93d

Cong., 1st Sess., 33557, and Zablocki's earlier remarks to the House at 14215 and 21209.

5. Clement J. Zablocki, House, International Relations Committee, *War Powers: Test of Compliance, Hearings*, 32; Thomas F. Eagleton, *Congressional Record*, 93d Cong., 1st Sess., 33556, and Thomas F. Eagleton, *War and Presidential Power: A Chronicle of Congressional Surrender* (New York: Liveright, 1974), 206–25; *Congressional Record*, 93d Cong., 1st Sess., 40023, 33557, 33860.

6. *House Reports*, 93d Cong., 1st Sess., No. 547, p. 8.

7. *Congressional Record*, 93d Cong., 1st Sess., 33550.

8. *Senate Reports*, 93d Cong., 1st Sess., No. 220, pp. 22–23.

9. *Congressional Record*, 93d Cong., 1st Sess., 36189.

10. *House Reports*, 93d Cong., 1st Sess., No. 547, p. 7.

11. *McCulloch* v. *Maryland*, 4 Wheaton 316, pp. 419–20 (1819).

12. Alexander Hamilton, "An Opinion on the Constitutionality of an Act to Establish a Bank," in Harold C. Syrett *et al.* (eds.), *The Papers of Alexander Hamilton*, (26 vols.; New York: Columbia University Press, 1961–79), III, 100. I have modernized spelling, capitalization, and punctuation in using quotations from early writings.

13. The incidents are recounted in Pat M. Holt, *The War Powers Resolution: The Role of Congress in U.S. Armed Intervention* (Washington, D.C.: American Enterprise Institute for Public Policy Research, 1978), 11–20; Committee on International Relations, *The War Powers Resolution: Relevant Documents, Correspondence, Reports*, Committee Print, 94th Cong., 2d Sess.; and House, International Relations Committee, *War Powers: Test of Compliance, Hearings*.

14. *Congressional Record*, 93d Cong., 2d Sess., 25915–17.

15. In an opinion given to Eagleton: see Senate, *Congressional Record*, 93d Cong., 2d Sess., 26560.

16. Gerald R. Ford "State of the World Address to Congress," April 10, 1975, *ibid.*; House, 94th Cong., 1st Sess., 10006.

17. See House, International Relations Committee, *War Powers Resolution: Relevant Documents*, 40–45. Although Mr. Ford later said he had reported on the four Indochinese and two Lebanese operations ("The War Powers Resolution," in Senate Committee on Foreign Relations. *War Powers Resolution*, Hearings, July 13, 14, and 15, 1977, 95th Cong., 1st Sess., 327), it appears that reports as required by the resolution were not made with respect to Lebanon (see Holt, *War Powers Resolution*, 11).

18. It was the opinion of the State Department's legal adviser, but not necessarily that of President Ford, that the president has the authority to evacuate foreign nationals when they are so "intermixed" with Americans that the most effective and safest way of rescuing the latter is by rescuing the former, too (House, International Relations Committee, *War Powers: Test of Compliance, Hearings*, 7, 11, 15).

19. House, Committee on International Relations, Subcommittee on International Security and Scientific Affairs, *Background Information on the Use of U.S. Armed Forces in Foreign Countries*, 94th Cong., 1st Sess., 76–80.

20. Ford, "War Powers Speech," 327.

21. See Senator George S. McGovern, "The Administration's Position on the War Powers Resolution," in Senate, Foreign Relations Committee, *War Powers Resolution, Hearings*, 322–23.

22. Thomas F. Eagleton, "Congress's 'Inaction' on War," New York *Times*, May 6, 1975, p. 39; the committee's action is reported in Michael F. Kelley, "The Constitutional Implications of the *Mayaguez* Incident," *Hastings Constitutional Law Quarterly*, III (Winter, 1976), 333; Javits, in House, International Relations Committee, *War Powers: Test of Compliance, Hearings*, 70. Senator McGovern, a member of the Foreign Relations Committee, stated that he had not been consulted on the committee's resolution of support (Kelley, "Constitutional Implications," 336*n*).

23. House, Committee on International Relations, Subcommittee on International Political and Military Affairs, *Seizure of the Mayaguez, Hearings, Part 1, May 14 and 15, 1975; Part 2, June 19 and 25, July 25, 1975*, 94th Cong., 1st Sess.

24. See, for example, House, *Congressional Record*, 94th Cong., 1st Sess., 14497 and 15070–71; House International Relations Committee, *Seizure of the Mayaguez, Hearings*, Pt. 1, p. 173; New York *Times*, May 13, 1975, pp. 1, 19 and May 21, 1975, p. 43. Even the State Department's legal adviser was under the impression, until enlightened by Zablocki, that the resolution's opinion was a statutory command (House, International Relations Committee, *War Powers: Test of Compliance, Hearings*, 29, 32–33).

25. Joseph Story, *Commentaries on the Constitution of the United States*, ed. Melville M. Bigelow (2 vols.; Boston: Little, Brown and Co., 1891), I, 294–337 (esp. rules 1 and 2).

26. Paul L. Ford (ed.), *The Works of Thomas Jefferson* (12 vols.; New York: G. P. Putnam's Sons, 1904–1905), VII, 354*n*; see also Hamilton, "The Examination," in Syrett (ed.), *Papers*, XXV, 455–56; Max Farrand (ed.), *The Records of the Federal Convention of 1787* (4 vols.; New Haven: Yale University Press, 1937), II, 318, 541. Unless otherwise specified, references to the last source are to Madison's notes.

27. *Case of the Resolution*, 2 Dallas 12, 20 (1781). See also *Bas* v. *Tingy*, 4 Dallas 37, 43 (1800) and *Talbot* v. *Seeman*, 1 Cranch 1, 28 (1801).

28. Jefferson, Memorandum to the Secretary of State, July 15, 1801, in *Works*, IX, 277.

29. Act of March 26, 1804, *Annals of Congress*, 8th Cong., 1st Sess., Appendix, XIII, 1301–1302.

30. *Eakin* v. *Raub*, 12 Sergeant and Rawle (Pa. Supreme Court) 330 (1825), Justice Gibson, 351.

31. Act of September 29, 1789, *Annals of Congress*, 1st Cong., 1st Sess., Appendix, II, 2200; Farrand, *Records*, II, 318. See also Alexander Hamilton, John Jay, and James Madison, *The Federalist* (New York: Modern Library, 1937), Nos. 28 and 29, pp. 171, 176. See, however, Act of March 3, 1807, *Annals of Congress*, 9th Cong., 2d Sess., Appendix, XVI, 1286, authorizing the president to employ the army and navy to suppress insurrections where it is lawful for him to call forth the militia. In view of early practice and our understanding of the Constitution, the act seems to be supererogatory.

32. "A Proclamation," April 22, 1793, in James D. Richardson (ed.), *A Compilation of the Messages and Papers of the Presidents, 1789–1897* (10 vols.; Washington: Government Printing Office, 1896–1899), I, 156–57; Pacificus essays (seven essays, published between June 29 and July 27, 1793), in Hamilton, *Papers*, XV, 33–43, 55–63, 65–69, 82–86, 90–95, 100–106, 130–35; Helvidius essays (five essays, published between August 24 and September 18, 1793), in Gaillard Hunt (ed.), *The Writings of James Madison* (9 vols.; New York: G. P. Putnam's Sons, 1900–1910), VI, 138–88.

33. "Pacificus No. 1," Hamilton, *Papers*, XV, 33–43. Subsequent references are to this number.

34. "Helvidius No. 1," Madison, *Writings*, VI, 138–51. Unless otherwise noted, subsequent references are to this number.

35. House, *Annals of Congress*, 1st Cong., 1st Sess., June 16, 1789, I, 463; "Helvidius No. 2," Madison, *Writings*, VI, 151–60 and No. 4, p. 174; "Helvidius No. 3," pp. 165, 164.

36. "Helvidius No. 2," p. 155.

37. "Helvidius No. 4," p. 172; Blackstone, *Commentaries on the Laws of England*, ed. Thomas M. Cooley (2 vols.; Chicago: Callaghan and Co., 1884), Vol. I, Bk. 1, pp. 252–53, 257, 262, 271. For example compare Hamilton in *Federalist* No. 78: "The execution of the laws, and the employment of the common strength, either for this purpose or for the common defense, seem to comprise all the functions of the executive magistrate" (p. 486) with Locke's reference to the power "of employing the force of the community in the execution of such laws, and in the defense of the commonwealth from foreign injury." John Locke, *Two Treatises of Government*, ed. Peter Laslett (Cambridge: University Press, 1967), Second Treatise, 1:3 (references to this work are to chapter and standard paragraph number).

38. Locke, *Second Treatise*, 12:147; 12:146; 2:7–8 and 9:127–30; 14:159; 12:145; 12:147–48.

39. Montesquieu, *L'Esprit des Lois*, ed. Gonzaque Truc (2 vols.; Paris: Librarie Garnier Frères, [n.d.]), Vol. I, Bk. XI, Ch. 6, pp. 163–64; Ch. 17, p. 186.

40. *Federalist*, No. 47, p. 313; letter to Washington, April 10, 1787, in Madison, *Writings*, II, 348.

41. Farrand (ed.), *Records*, I, 64–67; II, 185.

42. *Ibid.*, II, 180, 255–56, 259, 297; III, Appendix A, 348; II, 359, 522–23; *Federalist*, No. 75, p. 486.

43. Acts of July 27, September 2, and September 15, 1789, *Annals of Congress*, 1st Cong., 2d & 3d Sess., Appendix, II, 2187, 2231–35. See also the argument of Marbury's counsel in *Marbury* v. *Madison*, 1 Cranch 137, 139–41 (1803).

44. "Opinion on the Question whether the Senate has the Right to Negative the Grade of Persons Appointed by the Executive to Fill Foreign Missions," in Andrew A. Lipscomb and Albert E. Bergh (eds.), *The Writings of Thomas Jefferson* (20 vols.; Washington: Thomas Jefferson Memorial Assn., 1904–1905), III, 16.

45. *Federalist*, No. 69, p. 448; Hamilton, *Papers*, IV, 208. See also Hamilton's "Draft of a Constitution," in which "the Senate shall exclusively possess the power of declaring war," and the president "shall have the direction of war when commenced" (*Papers*, IV, 258, 263). Act of August 7, 1789, *Annals of Congress*, 1st Cong., 2d & 3d Sess., Appendix, II, 2214–15; Jefferson, *Writings*, VII, 461; Farrand (ed.), *Records*, II, 182, 318–19, 320 (McHenry's notes).

46. "The Examination, No. 1," in Hamilton, *Papers*, XXV, 456.

47. Richardson (ed.), *Messages and Papers*, Jefferson's First Annual Message to Congress, December 8, 1801, I, 326–27.

48. Lt. Andrew Sterrett to Capt. Richard Dale, August 6, 1801, in U.S., Navy Department, Office of Naval Records and Library, *Naval Documents Related to the United States Wars with the Barbary Powers* (6 vols.; Washington: Government Printing Office, 1944), I, 537 (see also the *National Intelligencer & Gazette*, November 18, 1801, *ibid.*, 538–39); acting Sec. of Navy Samuel Smith to Dale, May 20, 1801, *ibid.*, 465–68.

49. Franklin B. Sawvel (ed.), *The Complete Anas of Thomas Jefferson* (New York: Round Table Press, 1903), Cabinet meeting, May 15, 1801, p. 213.

50. The success of Jefferson's "precedent" is demonstrated by the frequency with which it has been cited by scholars and others. See, for example, Edward S. Corwin, *The President's Control of Foreign Relations* (Princeton: Princeton University Press, 1917), 131–33; Quincy Wright, *The Control of American Foreign Relations* (New York: Macmillan Co., 1922), 286–87; "Congress, the President and the Power to Commit Forces to Combat," *Harvard Law Review*, LXXXI (June, 1968), 1779. To our knowledge, the first published scrutiny of the events behind Jefferson's explanation of them was made by Jacob K. Javits and Don Kellerman in *Who Makes War?* (New York: William Morrow & Co., 1973), 43–44, 49–51, but their account is garbled and incomplete. Much better is that furnished by Abraham D. Sofaer, in "The Presidency, War, and Foreign Affairs: Practice under the Framers," *Law and Contemporary Problems*, II (Spring, 1976), 26–27.

51. *Bas* v. *Tingy*, Justice Washington, 40.

52. In an Act of May 28, 1798, after France had been seizing American merchantmen for some time, Congress authorized the president to call troops into service *in the event* a foreign power declared, made, or threatened war on the United States (*Annals of Congress*, 5th Cong., 3d Sess., Appendix, IX, 3729).

53. Letter to James McHenry, May 17, 1798, in Hamilton, *Papers, XXI*, 461–62. Jefferson's opinion was similar; see cabinet meeting, July 28, 1807, in Jefferson, *Anas*, 260.

54. Farrand (ed.), *Records*, II, 548; *cf.* Story, *Commentaries on the Constitution*, I, 372.

55. Locke, *Second Treatise*, 14:166; 12:147; 13:156, 158; 14:159.

56. *Ibid.*, 14:164, 159; 14:159, 162–64; 18:202; Blackstone, *Commentaries*, Vol. I, Bk. 1, pp. 251–52 (see also 141, 237).

57. *Cf.* James Wilson, Speech Delivered in the Convention for the Province of Pennsylvania, January, 1775, in Wilson, *Works*, ed. Robert G. McCloskey (2 vols.; Cambridge: Harvard University Press, 1967), I, 754–56; Lucius Wilmerding, Jr., "The President and the Law," *Political Science Quarterly*, LXVII (September, 1952), 321–38.

58. *Little* v. *Barreme*, 2 Cranch 170, 177–78 (1804).

59. See cabinet meeting, July 15, 1793, in Jefferson, *Anas*, 145; Jefferson, Seventh Annual Message to Congress, October 27, 1807, in Richardson (ed.), *Messages and Papers*, I, 416.

60. See letter to J. B. Colvin, September 20, 1810, in Jefferson, *Writings*, XII, 418.

61. John W. Bricker, *Congressional Record*, 82d Cong., 1st Sess., 1719–20, and Dean Acheson, *Present at the Creation: My Years at the State Department* (New York: W. W. Norton Co., 1969), 414–15; presidential press conference, September 13, 1962, printed in *Congressional Record*, 87th Cong., 2d Sess., 19537, 19539; presidential press conference, *Congressional Record*, 90th Cong., 1st Sess., 23393.

62. Leonard C. Meeker, State Department Legal Adviser, "The Legality of United States Participation in the Defense of Vietnam," *Department of State Bulletin*, March 28, 1966, pp. 485, 487.

63. Southeast Asia (Tonkin Gulf) Resolution, Public Law 88–408, printed in House, International Relations Committee, *Background Information*, 71.

64. Jack F. Kemp, House, *Congressional Record*, 93d Cong., 1st Sess., 33556. See also Gale W. McGee, *ibid.*, 36192.

65. Senate, Foreign Relations Committee, *War Powers, Report*, 25; Javits, *Congressional Record*, 93d Cong., 1st Sess., 36187, and Eagleton and Javits at 36177 and 36188.

66. Jefferson, *Writings*, XII, 418.

67. *Federalist*, No. 70, p. 455.

68. See Gary J. Schmitt, "Executive Privilege," in this volume.

69. *Bas* v. *Tingy*, Justice Chase, 43.

70. See the exchange between Zablocki and Monroe Leigh, State Department Legal Adviser, House, International Relations Committee, *War Powers: Test of Compliance, Hearings*, 94, 96–97.

71. Locke, *Second Treatise*, 11:134 and 12:143; 12:144; 12:147, 148; 13:150; 13:151–52.

72. *Federalist*, No. 37, pp. 227–28; No. 70, p. 454; No. 9, p. 50.

V

Executive Privilege: Presidential Power to Withhold Information from Congress

GARY J. SCHMITT

> There is an idea, which is not without its advocates, that a
> vigorous Executive is inconsistent with the genius of
> republican government. The enlightened well-wishers to this
> species of government must at least hope that the supposition
> is destitute of foundation.
>
> —PUBLIUS

It is now common to describe the Nixon presidency as
having been imperial. It is also common to view his use of executive privilege as an essential ingredient of that phenomenon. Secrecy, so we came to understand, turned the White House into a
palace. Executive privilege and the abuses of power revealed by
the events of those years seem inextricably tied to each other. It
was only natural then that in the heat of the effort to remove
Nixon from office there was also an attempt to deny succeeding
presidents the prerogatives he invoked. Future abuses could be
avoided if the oval office was denied that tool which seemed to
make it immune to congressional or popular accountability.
Open presidencies would be safe presidencies.

Yet, with the events of the Nixon years consigned now to history, it is possible to reexamine the question of whether or not
executive privilege does in fact transform the executive office
into a palace of intriguing guards. It is too readily assumed today
that an administration's inclination for secrecy is traceable to con-
spiratorial motives. This ignores the fact that there are often good
reasons for executive secrecy. For instance, secrecy provided
Nixon with the necessary condition for successful completion of
his initiative with China and, more recently, it provided Carter

with the same in the Mid-East talks held at Camp David. Moreover, the record of the two presidencies since Nixon suggests that secrecy and executive privilege are not implicitly tools of would-be monarchs. Both Presidents Ford and Carter have invoked this prerogative and surely neither administration is usually considered imperial. Executive privilege appears then to be as necessary for administrations that strive to be "as good as the American people" as for those that do not. Imperial or imperiled presidencies may come and go, but the need for executive privilege seems to remain.

Of course, the fact that presidents have found it necessary to claim this prerogative is not a demonstration that its invocation is constitutional. The need for privilege may at times seem clear, but not everything which is necessary is in fact lawful; nor is privilege simply legitimized by past and continued use. As the Constitution indicates, implied powers must not only be "necessary" but also "proper."

The most extensive and influential scholarly examination of the issue of executive privilege is Raoul Berger's *Executive Privilege: A Constitutional Myth*. Berger holds that executive privilege is in fact constitutionally improper. The heart of Berger's argument is that the office of the president was never meant to be so independent of Congress as to justify the implied power of executive privilege. Berger maintains that the framers created a weak and congressionally dependent executive, and that the president's traditional roles of director of foreign affairs, commander-in-chief, and chief executive were meant to be "severely limited" and "designedly subordinate to Congress." Thus, the president who invokes executive privilege and withholds information from Congress has no constitutional leg on which to stand. For Berger, Madison's statement that "in a republican form of government the legislative authority necessarily predominates" is the rule by which we are to judge.[1]

It is Berger's whiggish view of the American presidency and its rejection of the constitutional propriety of executive privilege that this essay will challenge. The argument is in three parts. The essay begins with an analysis of specific constitutional language. As is well known, executive privilege is not mentioned in the

Constitution. However, it is Berger's contention that at least three passages can be understood to be implicit prohibitions of executive secrecy. This essay will critically examine his readings of those passages. The second part of the essay will review Berger's analysis of the scope of the president's powers as director of foreign affairs, commander-in-chief, and chief executive. In reviewing basically the evidence Berger himself presents, it will be shown that his understanding of the intended constitutional design of those roles is incorrect and that each does in fact legitimately support the principle of executive privilege. The final section will examine the proper limits to the exercise of executive privilege in a government of separate but co-equal institutions. In short, it will be argued that executive privilege, far from being a constitutional myth, is when properly understood a critical element in maintaining the intended constitutional independence of the president in a republican form of government where the legislature does *not* necessarily predominate.[2]

CONSTITUTIONAL TEXT

Certainly an analysis of the constitutional propriety of executive privilege must begin with a consideration of the text of the Constitution itself. However, executive privilege is neither explicitly granted nor denied anywhere in that document. Berger maintains, nonetheless, that the Constitution is not simply silent on the issue of executive privilege. While he does not rely solely or even substantially on any one clause, Berger does refer us to three constitutional passages that he thinks indicate the framers' desire to deny the president the right to keep information from Congress.

Berger cites Article Two, Section Four in his effort to deny any constitutional status to executive privilege. Section Four reads:

> The President . . . shall be removed from Office on Impeachment for, and Conviction of Treason, Bribery, or other high Crimes and Misdemeanors.

Berger argues that the power of inquiry that follows implicitly from the power of impeachment cannot be abridged by claims of executive privilege. Surely the framers did not intend to grant the president the power to refuse to supply information requested by Congress as part of an impeachment investigation. As was "cheerfully admitted" by President Polk, the power of impeachment allows "all the archives and papers of the Executive Departments, public or private" to be "subject to the inspection and control" of the House.[3]

However, the question I wish to raise and which was also raised by Polk in that same statement is whether short of impeachment proceedings Congress has such unlimited power over the archives and papers of the executive branch. Berger would reply by suggesting that there is no constitutional area "short of impeachment." The impeachment power is interpreted by Berger as the touchstone of a constitutional system where congressional supremacy is the norm. It follows then, he argues, that the power of inquiry which accompanies impeachment is of such a sweeping scope that claims of executive privilege are at all times groundless.[4]

The core to this argument appears to be Berger's contention that Congress was "patently modeled" on the British Parliament and that Parliament's practice serves as an "index of the scope" of the congressional power of impeachment and inquiry. Berger claims in fact that the parliamentary power to inquire was plenary. "On what ground, then," he asks, "can it be concluded that American [executive] officers now enjoy an immunity [through privilege] to which no member of the English ministries laid claim?" The power to impeach, according to Berger, was intended to ensure that the president would be "accountable to Congress"—accountable not in some exceptional way but as the British ministers normally were to Parliament. Like Parliament, Congress is supreme; and, as such, its power of inquiry is limitless. Therefore, like Parliament, Congress forms the "grand inquest of the Nation."[5]

The above, however, is dubious, since Berger's assumption that parliamentary practice provides ruling precedents for our own Congress is open to question. Certainly equating Parliament's power of inquiry and impeachment with our own is made problematic by the manifest fact that the two systems of government are not the same since one rejects and the other accepts the principle of separation of powers. We may reasonably conclude that the framers intended to implement separation of powers actually to help foreclose the possibility of legislative supremacy and that such an intent would be reflected in a more limited conception of the impeachment power.[6] This is confirmed, ironically, by Berger himself. In an earlier work, *Impeachment: The Constitutional Problems*, Berger asks whether or not the power to impeach is indeed "illimitable?" His answer: "Parliament, it is true, asserted virtually unlimited power; but the Framers had no intention of conferring such power upon Congress."[7]

Yet even if we accept Berger's contention in *Executive Privilege* that British practice is generally instructive for understanding our own government, Berger has not depicted the relevant British precedents correctly. According to legal historian Abraham Sofaer, the "executive exercised control of information . . . during most of the two centuries preceding 1787. Information was frequently withheld from voluntary transmittals to Parliament and even from transmittals in response to legislative requests. Just as Parliament claimed the right to ask for information, the Crown, through its ministers, claimed the right to withhold material in its discretion."[8]

The second provision Berger cites is found in Article Two, Section Three. It reads:

> He shall from time to time give to the Congress information of the state of the Union, and recommend to their consideration such measures as he shall judge necessary and expedient.

Berger uses this constitutional provision in an effort to repudiate executive privilege by interpreting it as the "reciprocal" to Congress' power to inquire.[9] In effect, Berger transforms what has traditionally been thought of as a presidential power into a congressional one. To substantiate the propriety of this metamorphosis Berger "de-majestizes" these clauses by noting that initially the provision read that it was the president's "duty to inform the Legislature of the condition of the U.S. so far as may respect his Department."[10] Berger interprets this earlier formulation as placing the president under an unqualified duty to inform Congress about matters within the executive office. Having rid the provision of its imperial language by tracing it to its origin, he concludes that in its final form this constitutional stipulation is only a "broadened and stylistically improved articulation" of substantially the same unqualified duty suggested by the original clause.[11] Next, Berger removes the apparent discretionary element in the first clause of Section Three by construing the phrase "from time to time" as equivalent to "upon demand of Congress." Berger argues that under the first clause the president is to have no discretion in determining what information is to be supplied to Congress.

In assessing Berger's interpretation we must begin by considering whether the changes made to the original provision in the Constitutional Convention are indeed no more than a refined reiteration. The natural presumption in a case such as this would seem to be that a change in language reflects a change in substance. And, in fact, that is the case here. The deletion and the addition to the first proposal reflects the substantial alteration that the presidency underwent during the time between the initial and final formulation of this provision of Article Two. Berger is incorrect when he cites the earlier proposal as reflective of the final intention of the architects of the Constitution, since the provision precedes both the "independent possession by the executive department of its powers" and "election by a source independent of the legislature." The provision at this time exemplified a presidency which was to some degree, although not simply, subordinate to Congress. As that fact changed, so fittingly did the language of the provision. The claim that the first proposal manifests the true spirit of this segment of the Constitution is dubious. The "majesterial" character of the passage seems, to the contrary, not only intentional but also truly to reflect the substantial and independent character of the presidency.[12]

Moreover, a common-sense reading of the first clause contradicts Berger's somewhat creative interpretation. The president's duty to provide information "from time to time" concerning the "state of the Union" clearly suggests that he has the discretion both in determining what he shall say and when he shall say it. Otherwise we are forced to read the phrases "from time to time" and "state of the Union" in a manner that belies their ordinary and manifest meanings.[13]

Finally, Berger's interpretation may be objected to on the

grounds that it does not appear to reflect the early understanding of the clause. For example, in 1808 a resolution arose in Congress which requested the president to lay before that body information concerning the "military establishment." Yet even among those who favored the resolution it was understood that they had "no power to coerce information" and that their "power is limited to the request." And, more to the issue at hand, it was pointed out that the "Constitution has said, that the President shall from time to time, communicate such information as he deems proper; and has thus made him the judge of what is proper for communication."[14]

The third provision cited to deny the legitimacy of executive privilege is Congress' constitutional grant to keep parts of its proceedings from public view. Article One, Section Five, clause three provides:

> Each House shall keep a Journal of its Proceedings, and from time to time publish the same, excepting such Parts as may in their Judgement require secrecy.

Only Congress is explicitly given discretion to keep its deliberation secret. On the basis of this, Berger argues that the failure to find a similar provision in Article Two indicates an intention by the framers to withhold this discretion from the president. Berger would interpret the single positive grant as a denial of like power to the other branches.[15]

On its face, this interpretation is not unpersuasive. However, upon further investigation Berger's reading of the passage is far from conclusive. Another equally plausible interpretation would suggest that the secrecy provision in Article One be read as an exception to the normal mode of exercising the legislative task and, therefore, in need of a specific grant. And conversely, since secrecy might be understood to be natural in the exercise of either the judicial or executive power, these branches were in no need of explicit grants. Such an understanding is exhibited, for instance, in *Federalist*, Number 64, where "the secrecy of the President" is simply assumed.

This interpretation is supported by the convention's deliberations on this clause. Until August 10 the provision regarding the publication of the journal contained no prerogative for secrecy. At this time, the clause read:

> The House of Representatives, and the Senate, when it shall be acting in a legislative capacity, shall keep a journal of their proceedings; and shall, from time to time publish them.[16]

Then, on the tenth, "Gerry moved to strike out the words 'when it shall be acting in its legislative capacity' in order to extend the provision to the Senate when exercising its peculiar authorities, and to insert 'except such parts thereof as in their judgment require secrecy' after the words 'publish them.'" Gerry seemed to be referring to the Senate's power to ratify treaties. The convention rejected his proposal; yet it was apparently rejected not on its merits but postponed for later consideration.[17] However, on the next day, Madison and Rutledge reintroduced the issue by moving that the clause be amended to allow the Senate to keep secret its deliberations "when acting not in its Legislative capacity." This suggestion was overwhelmingly voted down, but again, not strictly on its merits.[18]

The debate continued that day and centered on the apparent desire of most simply to drop the "objectionable" clause and the fear of others that such an action, elimination of a journal, would "make a conclave of the legislature." Many wanted no journal at all and thus were unwilling to concede the existence of a journal by allowing exceptions to it. However, once the majority determined that there should be journals, they then accepted the motion to include after the words "publish them" the phrase "except such parts thereof as may in their judgment require secrecy."

This ended debate over this passage until September 14, when Mason and Gerry proposed to limit the exception to the Senate alone. They desired publication of the House's entire proceedings. This proposal, however, was rejected on the ground that on some occasions secrecy would be needed by both houses. Specifically mentioned were "measures preparatory to a declaration of war." The objection having been met, the provision reached its final form that day.

A review of the debate reveals, for our purposes, one important fact: the framers' desire to give Congress the discretion to keep certain topics out of the public view, specifically issues related to war and foreign affairs. Yet these are, as this paper will indicate, two areas in which the president was meant to have a particularly important role. Indeed it could be said that the need for congressional secrecy was required to the degree Congress shared in essentially executive powers.[19] This argument undermines Berger's claim that the specific grant of discretion in Section Five of Article One indicates an intention by the framers to withhold a like discretion from the president. Indeed the rationale for the provision would, instead of denying the president that discretion, sustain the logic of executive privilege.

To conclude, then, it appears that none of the three passages to which Berger refers us is an implicit prohibition of executive privilege. In fact, just the opposite appears to be true with the last two provisions. When properly understood, these constitutional passages do "support" the presidential prerogative of executive privilege.

POWERS

We have seen that the exact letter of the fundamental law is not conclusive as to the constitutionality of executive privilege. However, an examination of the spirit that animated the actual adoption of the above provisions opens up the possibility that the framers did not intend, as Berger suggests, to create such a weak and congressionally dependent executive that use of executive privilege could never be justified. To determine whether this is true or not we turn now to examination of Berger's analysis of the president's powers as director of foreign affairs, commander-in-chief, and chief executive.

Director of Foreign Affairs. In his review of the president's role as director of our foreign relations, Berger's goal is to exhibit the erroneous character of the "sources of presidential claims to non-monopolistic control of foreign relations." Berger suggests that if such assertions are groundless then a presidential monopoly over the papers of state is not justifiable. We find, therefore, Berger only indirectly challenging the legitimacy of executive privilege.

Rather, his real concern is to minimize the president's role in foreign affairs from which claims for executive privilege are derived.[20]

According to Berger's analysis, presidential dominance in foreign affairs has manifested itself most dramatically in two specific activities: the acceptance and expanding use of executive agreements and the exclusion of the Senate from participation in the negotiation of treaties.[21] He argues that an investigation of the framers' intention reveals that neither of these activities is constitutional. By these means the presidency has illegitimately come to dominate in the area of foreign affairs.

Berger's interest in executive agreements is understandable since its growing use seems to parallel that of executive privilege. He begins by indicating that, like executive privilege, executive agreements are inventions of "recent vintage."[22] Both prerogatives have evolved as vital elements of what Berger sees as the gradual usurpation by the modern presidency of the prerogative of Congress in foreign affairs. Apparently, these executive powers are the stuff of which "imperial" presidencies are made.

At first glance the use of executive agreements does suggest that presidential power has broken loose from its constitutional moorings. The rise in the number of executive agreements during the past thirty years has indeed been enormous. Yet such numbers are misleading. Two facts make this clear. First, while there has been a growth in the total number of executive agreements (not unexpectedly, since the fairly recent emergence of the United States as a world power), the number of agreements based upon presidential authority alone has remained small. Agreements "sometimes characterized as 'pure' or 'sole' executive agreements" constitute "no more than two or three percent of the total." And second, the number of executive agreements during the nation's first fifty years was far from insubstantial. Between the years 1789 and 1839, during which sixty treaties were ratified, twenty-seven executive agreements were also concluded. Almost one-third of our foreign obligations were in the form of what Berger suggests are inventions of "recent" origin. Although such figures are small in comparison with the percentage that executive agreements make of the whole today, they do indicate that in the early years of the Republic executive agreements were deemed to be a significant constitutional tool.[23]

What is important about this fact is that it suggests the founding generation did recognize the president to be in some situations, at least, the "sole organ" of our foreign relations. Ignoring such evidence, Berger denies that the Constitution's architects ever intended the president to be the "sole organ" of our foreign relations. Instead, he maintains that this title, bestowed on the president by Justice Sutherland in *United States* v. *Curtiss-Wright Export Corporation*, is the result of an "uncritical repetition of a statement torn from its context [and] raised to the level of dogma." [24]

Berger's argument is that these words, first uttered by the then Congressman John Marshall, when placed within their context, reveal that "far from excluding Congress from this 'sole organ' area . . . Marshall regarded the exercise of even this power as subject to Congressional control." However, Berger's own statement of what Marshall truly meant is itself dubious. While Berger may in fact be correct in criticizing Sutherland's attempt to build out of Marshall's words an office with unlimited power, Berger is no more correct when he reads into that speech an analysis of the presidency that would relegate it to being a mere "instrument of communication," an agent for policy made elsewhere in the government.[25]

Marshall does not deny that Congress could, if it so wishes, play a significant role in the issue that the House was debating.[26] Yet that role appears confined to the particular issue that was at hand—the domestic execution of an extradition. Marshall suggests nowhere that Congress' part may be expanded. Instead, we find Marshall arguing that even this possible part is inappropriate since the president "is entrusted with the whole foreign intercourse of the nation, and with the negotiation of all its treaties" and finally that Congress' possible role is circumscribed by the fact that the "political discretion" involved "rests alone with the Executive Department." [27] Between the extreme positions of Berger's president-as-clerk and Sutherland's president-as-sovereign Marshall charts an executive office which, while not simply beyond congressional influence or control, is to an extensive degree dominant in the area of foreign affairs. Berger's protests not withstanding, Marshall does present the president as singularly responsible for the nation's diplomatic policy.

Marshall's view of the president's power was not peculiar to him. Indeed, the debate in the First Congress over the formation of the department of foreign affairs suggests that Marshall's conception of the presidency was the rule rather than the exception.[28] As one member of that Congress succinctly said, "The Departments of Foreign Affairs and War are peculiarly within the powers of the President." [29] This view was given substance by the language used to create the department of foreign affairs. The terms of the act clearly indicate that Congress recognized the president's preeminence in foreign affairs. The secretary of the new department was

> [To] perform and execute such duties as shall from time to time be enjoined on or intrusted to him by the President of the United States, agreeable to the Constitution, relative to correspondences, commissions or instructions to or with public ministers or consuls from the United States, or to negotiations with public ministers from foreign states or princes, or to memorials or other applications from foreign public ministers or other foreigners, or to such other matters respecting foreign affairs as the President . . . shall assign to the said department; and furthermore, that the said principal officer shall conduct the business of the said department in such manner as the President of the United States shall from time to time order or instruct.[30]

The bill's authors formulated the act to ensure that the power of Congress to create the department did not expand into a control of that same department. The purpose of that bill was to effectuate not the legislative but the executive will.[31] According to historian Charles Thach, the "whole question of the secretary's powers was left to the president. . . . Congress would indicate the field of the secretary's activities, but it would go no further. . . . Correspondence, instructions, in short, the transaction of foreign business, was thus recognized as a purely executive function. . . . On every side care was taken to emphasize the exclusively executive quality of the whole field." [32] Furthermore, and most significant for our purposes, the act which actually appropriated funds for the diplomatic service did so by allocating a sum of money and then requiring the president to account specifically only for those expenditures which "in his judgment may be made public." [33] These acts of the First Congress give substance to Marshall's depiction of the president as director of the nation's foreign affairs. Despite Berger's claim, it appears that many of the founding generation assumed that the president was significantly independent in this area. And consistent with that independence it was recognized that in certain situations the public interest may require the president to withhold information from Congress.

The question arises, however, as to whether a claim of privilege may legitimately stand against a request for information by the Senate specifically related to the Senate's constitutional duty to give its "advice and consent" in the making of treaties. Here we turn to Berger's second major objection in his chapter on the presidential powers in foreign relations: the current exclusion of the Senate from an active role in the negotiation of treaties. Such exclusion Berger considers to be a critical and symptomatic example of presidential dominance in foreign affairs. It is his argument that the Senate was originally intended to have an expansive role in the formation of treaties and that, therefore, the president has no constitutional right to withhold from the Senate material in regard to existing or proposed treaty obligations.

Berger, quite appropriately, begins his argument by directing our attention to the text of the Constitution: "If the Constitution provides for Senate participation in treaty making, the Senate cannot now be barred. . . . Accordingly, the focus of discussion . . . the starting place of course must be the constitutional text itself." [34] Repeating an argument made by Senator Henry Cabot Lodge, Berger claims that since the pertinent provision in Article Two, Section Two—"He shall have power, by and with the advice and consent of the Senate, to make Treaties"—does not distinguish between the negotiation of a treaty and its ratification, the Senate has the right to participate fully in the negotiation or formation of all treaties. To further support this claim Berger argues that the phrase "advice and consent" was intentionally borrowed by the framers from the enactment clause found at the beginning of every British statute and is "descriptive of participation in lawmaking." Berger infers from this fact that the Constitution's architects wished to ensure by the use of this phrase the Senate's "full participation in the *making* of a treaty." [35] Indeed, upon inspection of events in the Constitutional Convention, Berger concludes that the power to make treaties is essentially the Senate's, for "it was the President . . . who was finally made a participant in the treaty-making process, which had been initially lodged . . . in the Senate alone." [36] Finally, Berger notes that according to *Federalist*, Number 75, the president and Senate have, for reasons of greater security, "joint possession" of the power to make treaties. Berger takes this to mean that the Senate is constitutionally mandated to be a full partner in the formation of treaties in particular and in the conduct of foreign affairs generally. Consequently, executive privilege is in this area constitutionally groundless.

In assessing Berger's argument we should begin, like him, with the constitutional text. While it is true that the pertinent clause in the Constitution does not distinguish between the actual negotiation and the ratification of a treaty, it need not necessarily follow that the Senate has a right to participate in negotiations. This argument rests largely on a comparison of the treaty clause with the clause vesting the power of appointing the officers of government, which follows immediately in the text of the Constitution. There a distinction is drawn between the nomination of a candidate and his formal appointment; the Senate's "advice and consent" is restricted to the latter. Because no similar distinction is drawn between proposing and ratifying treaties, it has been argued that this failure to so distinguish the two stages can be reasonably interpreted as a positive grant to the Senate to participate in the initiating processes of a treaty's formation, that is, in negotiations.

A comparison of the treaty and appointment clauses, however, can also cut the other way. When the Senate gives its "advice and consent" to a nomination, its task is, after all, effectively only that of sanctioning the appointment. Here the Senate's "advice and consent" is only a yea or nea. A consistent reading of the text of the Constitution would seemingly require then that the phrase "advice and consent" not be given as expansive a reading as Berger has done in the treaty clause. This interpretation is not contradicted by the fact the phrase itself is borrowed from the enactment clause of British statutes. "Advice and consent" might have been taken to mean only that a legislative body has consented to a proposal and has then enacted it as law—in the case of treaties, the supreme law.[37] The point is that if the use of the phrase is as Berger suggests "descriptive of participation in lawmaking," it need not follow that it is descriptive of a Senate right to "full participation in the making of a treaty"; for making a treaty law is only one element in making a treaty.

Finally, we note that Berger ignores the most obvious textual consideration: the location of the treaty-making power in the Second and not the First Article. This fact alone suggests that in the end the framers conceived of the treaty power as essentially executive in nature and that senatorial participation was an exception which might be and was narrowly interpreted.[38] As Jefferson said, "the transaction of business with foreign nations is executive altogether; it belongs, then to the head of that department, except as to such portions of it are specifically submitted to the Senate. Exceptions are to be construed strictly." [39] For these reasons we conclude that Berger's textual argument is far from conclusive.

Berger's interpretation of the text of the Constitution, however, is not his last word, for, as noted above, Berger draws support from Publius' statement in *Federalist*, No. 75, that the power of making treaties is in the "joint possession" of the Senate and president. Although Berger deduces from this that the Senate should share in all aspects of treaty making, on its face the phrase "joint possession" does not indicate how or even how much of that power is shared. Furthermore, it is quite evident from the rest of *Federalist*, No. 75, that a principled distinction can be made between the respective roles of each branch. Publius divides the process of making treaties into two tasks and then implies that each might be reserved to the branch best suited to complete that function:

> The qualities elsewhere detailed as indispensable in the management of foreign negotiations point out the Executive as the most fit agent in those transactions; while the vast importance of the trust, and the operation of treaties as laws, plead strongly for the participa-

tion of the whole or a portion of the legislative body in the office of making them. . . .

To have intrusted the power of making treaties to the Senate alone, would have been to relinquish the constitutional agency of the President in the conduct of foreign negotiations.[40]

The functional distinction made by Publius indicates that the Senate's share of the treaty-making power was not thought to be essentially concerned with the process of negotiations. Rather, it is the president's duty to provide these "qualities elsewhere detailed as indispensable in the management of foreign negotiations." And what are those indispensable qualities? According to Publius in an earlier paper one such quality is the single executive's capacity to keep sensitive matters secret:

It seldom happens in the negotiation of treaties . . . but that perfect *secrecy* [is] requisite [and] there doubtless are many [apprehensive agents] who would rely on the secrecy of the President, but who would not confide in that of the Senate, and still less in that of a large popular Assembly. The convention have done well, therefore, in so disposing of the power of making treaties, although the president must, in forming them, act by the advice and consent of the Senate, yet he will be able to manage the business of intelligence in such a manner as prudence may suggest.[41]

The conduct of foreign policy requires prudential attention to incessantly changing circumstances. In a realm where laws do not rule, the executive capacity to act with decision, dispatch, and secrecy was thought by the framers to be truly necessary. As a Senate report in 1816 stated:

If it be true that the success of negotiations is greatly influenced by time and accidental circumstances, the importance to the negotiative authority of acquiring regular and secret intelligence cannot be doubted. The Senate does not possess the means of acquiring such intelligence. It does not manage the correspondence with our ministers abroad nor with foreign ministers here. . . . The President . . . manages our concerns with foreign nations and must necessarily be most competent to determine when, how and upon what subjects negotiation may be urged with the greatest prospect of success.[42]

The unavoidable fact is that the successful use of the power to make treaties requires that a certain degree of discretion be reserved to the president in determining what matters should remain confidential. The framers thought such discretion in general was indispensable to the effective conduct of foreign affairs. We may conclude then that executive privilege is a constitutionally appropriate prerogative that follows from the distinctive institutional capacities of the executive. It is those capacities that the founders wished to draw upon to ensure among other things that in the negotiations of treaties the new government would not have to suffer as it "heretofore suffered from the want of secrecy."[43]

This conclusion, combined with Marshall's statement, the early and extensive use of executive agreements, and the character of the acts creating and funding the department of foreign affairs, suggests that the presidential role in foreign affairs was not intended to be "severely limited" and "designedly subordinate to Congress." On the contrary, the president was expected to assume a unique and possibly dominant position in foreign affairs, and in order to ensure his effectiveness he was understood to have, and so acted as having, the prerogative of withholding information from Congress.[44]

Commander-in-chief. Related to the president's general power in the area of foreign affairs is his specific constitutional role as commander-in-chief, a source of authority also used to justify the withholding of information from Congress. Berger argues, however, that the president's power as commander-in-chief is so "exceedingly narrow" that it cannot support presidential invocations of executive privilege.[45] Unfortunately, much of Berger's argument is not quite to the point. Berger spends a considerable amount of time explaining that the president as commander-in-chief does not have the constitutional power to begin a war.[46] That point, while important, is not strictly pertinent to the issue of whether or not a president has the prerogative to withhold information from Congress while acting as commander-in-chief. The fact that a President may not have the power to begin a war does not clarify the amount of discretion that a president has in conducting a war.

Berger does however make a substantive argument concerning the president as commander-in-chief that bears on the issue of executive privilege. His contention is that the commander-in-chief position was meant to be limited and congressionally subordinate: "How narrowly the function was conceived may be gathered from the fact that in appointing George Washington Commander-in-Chief, the Continental Congress made sure, as Professor Rostow remarked, that he was to be 'its creature . . . in every respect.'" For Berger the essence of the war powers of the president was accurately described by Publius' statement that the role of commander-in-chief amounts to nothing more than a "first General." [47]

Berger borrows this phrase from *Federalist*, Number 69, to indicate what he believes to be the severely limited power of the president as commander-in-chief. However, a close reading of the essay reveals that the president's power as "first General" was not designated to be simply circumscribed by Congress. Publius' analysis concentrates on the ways in which the president's power as commander-in-chief is not equivalent to or as broad as the British monarch's corresponding power. Specifically, the president, unlike the king, does not have the power to declare war or to raise and regulate the armed forces. The powers are given to Congress. Yet the analysis leaves one power which presumably is not shared with Congress—the actual direction of war. It is reasonable to conclude that Publius meant for us to deduce then that in the actual direction of any war effort the president's power as commander-in-chief will be equivalent to the British monarch's and that like the king's it should be unilaterally exercised. [48]

While the argument in *Federalist*, Number 69, is only implied, Publius makes it explicit in No. 74. There he claims that:

> Of all the cares or concerns of government, the direction of war most peculiarly demands those qualities which distinguish the exercise of power by a single hand. The direction of war implies the direction of common strength; and the power of directing and employing the common strength, forms a usual and essential part in the definition of the executive authority.

Publius' use of the expansive phrase—"direction of war" and "direction of the common strength"—and his pointed reference to the nature of the executive suggest a conception of the role of the president as commander-in-chief which is neither slight nor Congress' "creature . . . in every respect." [49]

This interpretation is supported by the events of the founding period. According to Louis Fisher, during the Revolutionary War General Washington "experienced on a daily basis the inability of Congress to organize itself for a war effort." The Revolutionary experience led the framers to understand the necessity of creating in the new Constitution an executive capable of conducting war effectively. In the Articles of Confederation, Congress had been given the power of "directing" the operations of the armed forces. In contrast, the Constitutional Convention had trimmed Congress' power to "make" war to "declare" and thus ensured, among other things, that Congress' war power would not be understood to include the power to "conduct." The animating spirit behind this change in the letter of the law is further exemplified by the fact that in the First Congress "nothing significant was done or said . . . to create any evidence to support a limited view of the president's authority as commander-in-chief." [50]

The strongest evidence for Berger's thesis of a restricted and congressionally subordinate commander-in-chief is derived not from the history of the founding period but from the actual text of the Constitution. As is often noted, there is a scarcity of references to presidential "war powers" in the Constitution. Berger points out that the "over-towering balance" of the enumerated powers concerning military affairs are found in Article One. He concludes that the "vast bulk of the war powers was conferred on Congress" and therefore that the president's role as commander-in-chief is a "very meager" one. [51]

Yet might not the opposite be true? Might not the actual lack of an enumeration indicate an intent on the part of the framers to grant a substantial amount of discretion? Certainly, the broad drawing of powers in Article Two is consistent with the framers' recognition of the need to avoid burdening government with detailed enumerations. Since the realm of war, as with foreign affairs, is one ruled by necessity and prudence and not law, it is understandable why that branch most directly concerned with the war's direction should not be labored with numerous parchment strictures. Meagerness of text does not necessarily imply a paucity of power. [52]

Both the writings of the best political thinkers of their time and the experience of the Revolutionary War had taught the framers that the direction of war demanded the prudence and dispatch that only a single executive could offer.[53] A legislative assembly could not provide the speed or focus of strength required in war. The likelihood of successful direction of a war was proportional to the degree that the direction went unshared. Thus, to the extent that executive privilege aids in maintaining the desired independence of the president it is consistent with the deepest intentions of the framers. Executive privilege, then, was implied in that constitutional spirit which moved them to create a role whose source was not Congress but the Constitution. Reflecting that understanding, Washington, during his first administration, established in principle his right as commander-in-chief to withhold information from Congress.[54] Washington, unlike Berger, apparently did not consider the president's role as commander-in-chief as so "exceedingly narrow" that it could never support claims for executive privilege.

The Executive. Finally, we must consider the support given the doctrine of executive privilege by the president as the chief executive. Here again Berger maintains that this function was to be restricted and congressionally dominated. Fear of executive tyranny, according to Berger, moved the Constitution's architects to curtail severely the power of the executive. He suggests that the spirit animating the constitutional design was "the prevalent belief . . . 'that the executive magistracy was the natural enemy, the legislative assembly the natural friend of liberty.'" As a result, Berger argues that the framers created an executive whose powers "extended little beyond the execution of the laws." Quoting Roger Sherman, Berger holds that they "considered [the executive office] 'as nothing more than an institution for carrying the will of the Legislature into effect.'"[55]

An examination of the founding material reveals, however, that while the framers were not unconcerned about the abuses that might result from the executive sphere, they feared more the encroachments of an overweening legislature. The unrestrained conduct of the state assemblies during the years before the meeting of the Constitutional Convention had generated in many a "distrust of the legislature" and had in turn led many to "discredit the whole idea of the sovereignty of the legislature." Madison gave voice to that sentiment in the convention: "Experience in all the States had evinced a powerful tendency in the Legislature to absorb all power into its vortex. This was the real source of danger to the American Constitution." [56]

In fact, an "accumulation of legislative abuses on the state level, combined with a demonstration of legislative incompetence on the national, had created . . . a new outlook toward the executive power." The framers, far from wholeheartedly distrusting executive power, envisioned it as the major means of remedying the excesses experienced in the states. Legislative supremacy was no longer the constitutional norm. Berger simply misleads his readers when he quotes Sherman's claim that the executive was to be nothing more than an "errand boy" for the congressional will as though this claim was representative of the thought of the convention. On the contrary, Sherman's position on the executive was quickly and decisively rejected by the convention. [57]

Dismissing Sherman's whiggish view, the framers attempted to alleviate the problem of legislative abuse by creating an executive independent of and equal to the legislature. This is illustrated by comparing the executive of the United States Constitution with the governorships of the then existing states. Short terms, limitations on reeligibility, election by the legislature, and provisions for acting only in concert with an executive council chosen by the legislature were the overwhelming norms of the day. [58] In each of these respects the office of the president was strikingly different from that of the state governors. Add to these the veto power and a salary insulated from congressional alteration and the framers' desire to promote an independent and separate executive is clearly seen. [59]

Because the new executive was decisively detached from the legislature, the Constitution, unlike the Articles of Confederation, effectively incorporated the principle of separation of powers. Yet it would be wrong to conclude from this that the independent executive was established only as a means of checking the expected excesses of the legislature. Properly constructed, an independent executive was also a prime requisite for the "steady administration of the laws." The history of ministerial incompetence under the Articles moved the framers away from a system of congressional dominance. By 1787 separation of powers was not only a "bulwark against tyranny" but also "the *sine qua non* of governmental efficiency." By isolating the executive function and distributing it to the appropriately designed office, the separate and single president became the fitting repository of "the executive power."[60]

Broadly understood, the execution of the laws depends upon a judicious mixture of equity and force. Because of man's seeming contumacy at some point the former must cease and the latter must begin. However, to deny the executive the right to keep certain matters private is to invite (and, in practice, ensure) congressional inspection and discussion beyond those points which are productive for timely and energetic execution:[61]

> In planning, forming and arranging laws, deliberation is always becoming, and always useful. But in the active schemes of government, there are emergencies, in which the man, as, in other cases, the woman, who deliberates, is lost. Secrecy may be equally necessary as despatch. But, can either secrecy or despatch be expected, when, to every enterprise, and to every step in the progress of every enterprise, mutual communication, mutual consultation, and mutual agreement among men, perhaps of discordant views, of discordant tempers and of discordant interests, are indispensably necessary? How much time will be consumed! and when it is consumed how little business will be done![62]

James Wilson reminds us that the failure to act may often be as dangerous as the failure to act wisely. This is true not only in foreign affairs but also in domestic concerns where the rule of law may suffer as much from indecisive administration as bad law. At times, "energy is wisdom."[63] Executive privilege is a constitutional discretion implied in the framers' desire to foster the independence in the executive office necessary to ensure no "want of method and energy in the administration" of the new government.

In addition to fostering an energetic and decisive administration of the laws, executive privilege is necessary to sustain the conditions required for sound presidential decision making. At the very least this will require the mature canvassing of all possible options. Yet congressional control of executive papers, for which Berger argues, would undermine the possibility of such a review. Opening up the presidency must eventuate in the narrowing of the president's perspective in response to the need to close ranks against congressional opposition. What president would allow serious "no holds barred" discussion among his advisors when there hangs over his head the potential use of those same discussions by partisan opponents in the Congress? The healthy goal of a president open to various possibilities is subverted by desires to see an open presidency. The "faithful" execution of the office is a constitutional demand that the president be both responsive and competent. Should the president be denied that tool which seems essential for the latter out of a current desire to dogmatize the former?[64]

To conclude, executive privilege is a necessary and proper discretion without which the president could not responsibly conduct his office and therewith could not fulfill his constitutionally intended executive duties.

THE LIMITS

Separation of Powers. To this point the discussion has focused on the constitutional case for executive privilege. However, in making the case for this prerogative it cannot be overlooked that the exercise of privilege is as liable to abuse as congressional demands for information. Thus, like the latter, it must be subjected to appropriate limits.

Although the framers feared primarily legislative encroachments and usurpations, the common view today is that the main threat to liberty comes from the presidency; for it is the presidency which now seems to draw all power into its own impetuous vortex. Even if this is true, however, it is not obvious that Berger's solution to today's problem is the correct one. Surely a return to congressional supremacy is no more judicious than were earlier unqualified scholarly calls for presidential government. Promoting legislative dominance as Berger does in *Executive Privilege* would result only in trading one imperial crown for another.

Moreover, government continues to need the capacity to act with the decision, speed, and secrecy that the framers recognized as coming only from the single independent executive. Attempts to preserve those qualities by shifting the burden of providing them from the presidency to Congress ignore the lessons drawn from the national experience under the Articles of Confederation. Somewhere in transit those elements are bound to be lost. Thus, a sober attempt to moderate the excesses of the presidency must do so without enervating its capacity to provide those still necessary qualities. While common sense teaches us that power may be abused, foresight warns us that power is nevertheless required if government is to govern. The solution then to the danger inherent in granting power cannot be a simplistic trimming of power. Rather, the prudent solution must lie in how power is arranged.[65]

According to its creators, the Constitution provided such a solution. By its adoption not only of separated powers but principled separation the Constitution more adequately provides for safety, through a division of powers, and competence, by the allocation of powers along functional lines. It is the thesis of this paper that a clear understanding of separation of powers principle is the key to tempering the abuses possible in executive privilege while simultaneously avoiding the pitfalls of an imperial Congress.

The best explication of how a system of separation of powers would aid in preventing abuses or encroachments by any one branch is furnished by Publius in *Federalist*, Number 47–51. There Publius demonstrates that "the great security against a gradual concentration of the several powers in the same department, consists in giving to those who administer each department the necessary constitutional means and personal motives to resist encroachments of the others. The provision for defense must in this . . . be made commensurate to the danger of attack. Ambition must be made to counteract ambition."[66]

In brief, encroachments by one branch will be resisted by members of the other branch, who will have an interest in protecting its threatened prerogatives. Here Congress' interest in checking the president's desire to withhold information is its desire to gather information in pursuit of its own legislative tasks.

To understand the status of executive privilege it must always be balanced against the congressional privilege of inquiry. So balanced, the rather remarkable symmetry of these two implied powers comes to the fore, and with it, the animation of Publius' words: "[To] oblige [government] to control itself [the formula is] by opposite and rival interests . . . where the constant aim is to divide and arrange the several offices in such a manner as that each may be a check on the other." [67]

The checks which give Congress an effective voice in limiting presidential claims of executive privilege are, among others, its control of the purse, its use of advice and consent, and ultimately impeachment. Simply stated, the solution to executive excess is not elimination of the power from which that excess may come but rather the vigorous use by Congress of those tools it has at its disposal. The president cannot deny Congress too lightly or too often since Congress has sufficient powers—and, of late, sufficient will—to compel divulgence. [68] And since the tension between the two branches is based upon legitimate and necessary, if also clearly opposed, prerogatives, *the constitutionally designed solution to the inevitable conflict should and must remain a political resolution.* As a result, the theoretically opposed claims resolve themselves in the political arena in ways that practically moderate the privileges asserted by each of the two branches. Because "neither the executive nor the Congress is very sure of its rights . . . both usually evince a tactful disposition not to push the assertion of their rights to abusive extremes. Of such is the system of checks and balances." [69]

Finally, the historical evidence surrounding relevant events reveals to a remarkable degree the ability of each branch to preserve its independence, and hence, the "administration of its respective powers." Significantly, recent history indicates that the continued use of executive privilege has not, in fact, undermined the constitutional system. [70] To the contrary, not only is executive privilege not a myth, but it is, when understood in its proper context, an essential ingredient in sustaining the constitutional order. [71]

Judicial Review as a Possible Limit. Unfortunately, while political balancing of the kind suggested here does foster a moderating give and take between the branches, it can also be extremely disorderly and give the appearance of arbitrariness. The moderation which results is dependent upon the ironical fact that general governmental willfulness is less probable the more each branch is willful. To a significant extent American constitutionalism seems at times to rest less on its legal or parchment character than on political restraints. Yet, for a people whose civil religion admonishes "a reverence for law" and proclaims that theirs is a "government under law," the vigorous political struggles that may occur between the two branches can be troubling. It is no surprise then that some attempt to relieve this anxiety is made by assigning to the judiciary, the branch which in the public's mind most "embodies the ideal of government under law," the task of resolving impasses between the Congress and the president. This, Berger argues, is constitutional, effective, and wise.[72]

Berger advocates judicial intervention despite the traditional argument that the questions involved in conflicts between the two branches are of a political nature, and therefore, nonjudiciable. He dismisses the long-established "political questions" doctrine as a "misnomer." Citing Marshall in *Marbury* vs. *Madison*, he declares, "It is emphatically the province and duty of the judicial department to say what the law is." The court is to be the final arbiter. This, Berger contends, remains consistent with Publius' declaration in *Federalist*, Number 40, that neither of the two branches "can pretend to an exclusive or superior right of settling the boundaries between their respective powers."[73]

Yet Berger begs the question when he claims it is the task of the court "to say what the law is," for the Court may declare that the law, the Constitution, grants executive discretion. Specifically, the judiciary might interpret "the law" to be such that the president should make the sole determination of the need for protecting his branch's papers. Certainly nothing in *Marbury* v. *Madison* precludes this constitutional interpretation. Indeed, Marshall's opinion appears to support such a judgment:

> By the constitution of the United States, the President is invested with certain important political powers, in the exercise of which he is to use his own discretion, and is accountable only to his country in his political character and to his own conscience. . . . In such cases,

their acts are his acts; and whatever opinion may be entertained of the manner in which executive discretion may be used, still there exists, and can exist, no power to control that discretion. The subjects are political. They respect the nation, not individual rights and being intrusted to the executive, the decision of the executive is conclusive. . . . The acts of such an officer, as an officer, can never be examinable by the courts. . . . The conclusion from this reasoning is, that where the heads of departments are the political or confidential agents of the executive, merely to execute the will of the President, or rather to act in cases in which the executive possesses a constitutional or legal discretion, nothing can be more perfectly clear than that their acts are only politically examinable.

And further,

The province of the court is, solely, to decide on the rights of individuals, not to inquire how the executive, or executive officers, perform duties in which they have a discretion. Questions in their nature political, or which are, by the constitution and laws, submitted to the executive, can never be made in this court.[74]

Berger distorts the opinion in *Marbury* v. *Madison* by implying that Marshall held that the Court should settle all controversies between the president and Congress. It is in fact this judicial opinion which first postulated the doctrine of "political questions." This misuse of Marshall's opinion leads Berger to regard lightly the possibility that there are areas into which it is neither wise nor proper for the courts to enter. For example, in referring to Madison's statement in *Federalist*, Number 49, that none of the "several departments . . . can pretend to an exclusive or superior right of settling the boundaries between their respective powers" Berger fails to notice that the judiciary is not excluded from the statement.[75] More importantly, Berger accepts Madison's statement of the problem but ignores his remedy. That remedy—"contriving the interior structure of the government" so that "its several constituent parts may, by their mutual relations, be the means to keeping each other in their proper places" suggests the political balancing discussed above rather than judicial resolution. According to Madison, then, the designed solution to the kind of impasse possible when executive privilege is invoked is eminently political and not judicial.

In contrast to Madison, Berger expressly prefers what he considers to be a *non*-political resolution of conflicts between president and Congress.

> To avoid adjudication by resort to the leaky doctrine of "political questions" is to throw Congress back on its own resources. . . . When Congress proceeded along that path with President Andrew Johnson, Chief Justice Salmon Chase was of the opinion that the conflicting claims of constitutional power had better have been submitted to the courts. Impartial adjudication promises a better solution than trial of its own cause by a Congress whose temper has been frayed by protracted controversy.[76]

Judicial review is the best method for resolving disputes because according to Berger, it is "impartial."[77] He implies that any remedy devised by the other two branches will be inadequate since these branches are essentially partisan and their solution equally so. Berger's remedy is to remove the conflict from the passionate fray of political infighting to the unprejudiced arms of the judiciary. The Supreme Court is to be trusted because it is separated, removed, and independent of the political departments.

But how is the Court to reach its "impartial" judgment? The Court will begin by considering and balancing the wisdom of each branch's claim.[78] But what then is to be the criterion for that balance? Will it not necessarily be political? The adjudication in fact will turn on a political judgment and not an assessment of the demands of equity or the rights of individuals. Instead, here the Court is asked to discern whose political judgment is better— Congress' or the president's. In effect the Court is asked to have the political wisdom *par excellence*. Is there any reason to expect this of the Court?[79]

At least in regard to evidentiary matters, where a Court might subpoena a president for information relevant to a trial, the Court can claim some degree of competency. Even if it has no expertise in regard to the president's claim, the Court can recognize the degree of relevancy and materiality of the information as evidence in the trial before it. But can the same be said when the Court must weigh the needs and policies of two branches distinct from each other and, more importantly, distinct from the Court? The fact is that the Courts often lack the experience necessary to assess adequately the political conditions and nuances which may infect a dispute. The Court may be nonpartisan, but that hardly means that its political judgment will be astute. While the Court may be truly "impartial," that fact does not make it politically wise.

More pragmatically, it is not obvious that a Court ruling requiring disclosure by the president would be effective. It should not be forgotten that the Court "must ultimately depend upon the aid of the executive arm . . . for the efficacy of its judgments."[80] Does not that circumstance return the final determination of the question back to the president?[81] Perhaps the Court will only act against the president when it is sure that public opinion is with it?[82] Or will the Court act against the president only when it is clear that Congress is willing to support the Court's determination with its "resources," including the impeachment process? And while we may be certain that Congress would have effectively supported a decision by the Court in a confrontation with President Nixon, are we so certain that they would have acted similarly if that president had been Jefferson, Roosevelt, or even Humphrey? These questions lead one to ask just how effective Berger's judicial solution is in escaping those dangers he wishes to avoid. For, in the final analysis, judicial omnipotence does not avoid the ultimate resolution of the impasse by the two political branches.

Moreover, does not Berger's solution of judicial review expose the judiciary to the most hostile of controversies? He would plunge the Court into disputes at their most politically raw state. Rarely do these conditions make for the best decisions.[83] And more importantly, will not these manifestly political decisions undermine that healthy public opinion concerning the "neutrality" of the Court upon which Berger's own idea of "impartial adjudication" and much of our constitutional spirit rests? These considerations should indicate that Berger's solution to the problem of a congressional-presidential impasse on executive privilege is constitutionally suspect, potentially ineffective, and, in the end, most imprudent.

CONCLUSION

We have argued that the framers intended to create an independent and energetic executive branch and that executive privilege is an essential component of that constitutional design. Yet, we also concluded that executive privilege should not be understood to be an unlimited prerogative. In theory, its use is restricted to implementing legitimate presidential tasks and, in practice, it is balanced against Congress' need for information to carry out its legislative task. Hence, while executive privilege may free the president to provide government with the necessary qualities of decision and dispatch, he is by the constitutional fabric of separated powers simultaneously compelled to take seriously the interests of Congress if he is in the long run to be effective. The use of executive privilege is moderated and limited then not by the chimera of judicial omnipotence but by a realistic assessment of congressional political power.

However, there is another limit of executive privilege perhaps as significant as those derived from the constitutional fabric of separation of powers. This other limit is generated by the fact that the Constitution itself rests upon the tacit but ever-present consent of the people. As a result there is a strong inclination to assume that "the people" are capable of deliberating on the most essential matters. Yet there is in the doctrine of executive privilege an implicit judgment that not everything is fit for "public consumption." There is some truth then in Berger's thought that there is a tension between this presidential prerogative and the spirit of the regime.[84]

There is no simple resolution to this tension, but we begin to understand better the function of secrecy in popular government when we recall that the Constitution itself was formulated behind closed doors.[85] The thought that justifies actions of this type is that the interests of the people, the end for which popular government exists, are often best served by seemingly non-popular means.[86] Nevertheless, no matter what the justification, in practice democracies will not readily tolerate the elitism implicit in secrecy.[87] Thus, no matter how necessary a president may believe secrecy to be, he should be sure that his use of such measures does not make the people wary of it.[88] The tension between secrecy and popular government will be decisive in moderating any prolonged, extensive, or suspicious use of executive privilege.

A question that remains today is whether democracy's natural and largely salutary suspicion of secrecy will overwhelm the prudent constitutional design of a vigorous and independent executive. As Hamilton noted, the idea "that a vigorous executive is inconsistent with the genius of republican government" "is not without its advocates."[89]

NOTES TO CHAPTER V

1. Raoul Berger, *Executive Privilege: A Constitutional Myth* (New York: Bantam Books, 1975). Alexander Hamilton, James Madison, and John Jay, *The Federalist*, ed. Edward M. Earle (New York: Modern Library, 1937), No. 51, p. 388; Berger, *Executive Privilege*, 15, 16, 145, 222.

2. Berger states that "our democratic system is bottomed on the legislative process." Rather, it is "bottomed on" a constitution. The presidency receives its grants of power not from the Congress but directly from the Constitution. Compare Berger, *Executive Privilege*, 3, with Madison in Max Farrand (ed.), *The Records of the Federal Convention of 1787* (4 vols.; New Haven: Yale University Press, 1966), I, 67. Berger reflects his own understanding (and its inadequacy) when he repeats Madison's statement that "in a republican form of government the legislative authority necessarily dominates." In contrast to Berger, Madison goes on to argue that this tendency should be resisted.

3. Berger, *Executive Privilege*, 41, 295.

4. Berger leaves his readers with the impression that statements made by Presidents Polk and Buchanan and cited by him can be used as precedents to substantiate his interpretation of the impeachment clause and executive privilege. However, upon investigation these statements do not support the interpretative weight Berger wishes to place on them. For, while each recognized the unlimited power of inquiry which may follow from the impeachment power, both statements can be read to imply that short of impeachment the president would have the right to invoke executive privilege. For instance, Buchanan claimed that "except in this single case [the case of impeachment], the Constitution has invested the House of Representatives with no power, no jurisdiction, no supremacy whatever over the President. In all other respects he is quite as independent of them as they are of him. As a coordinate branch of the Government he is their equal." James D. Richardson (ed.), *A Compilation of the Messages and Papers of the Presidents, 1789–1897* (10 vols.; Washington: U.S. Government Printing Office, 1896–1899), V, 615. See also Richardson (ed.), *A Compilation*, IV, 434. Berger, *Executive Privilege*, 205, 294–95, 39.

5. Berger, *Executive Privilege*, 12 and 39, 17*ff*, 39, 49. In his discussion of the congressional power of inquiry Berger interprets four statements made by founders which refer to the House of Representatives as the "grand inquest of the Nation" to imply that Congress had been granted Parliament's broad inquisitorial powers. However, it may be objected that one House does not make a Congress. And moreover, none of the references he cites when examined in context suggests that the phrase was understood by them to affirm that Congress had on a day-to-day basis a plenary power of inquiry. See Berger, *Executive Privilege*, 39–40; *cf*. Philip B. Kurland, *Watergate and the Constitution* (Chicago: University of Chicago Press, 1978), 18–19.

6. See notes 56 and 57 below.

7. Raoul Berger, *Impeachment: The Constitutional Problems* (Cambridge: Harvard University Press, 1973), 298. See in particular, "The Limits of High Crimes and Misdemeanors," Chap. 2, pp. 86*ff*. Berger says here, among other things, that the "design of the Framers to confer a limited (impeachment) power is confirmed by their rejection of removal by Address which knew no limits," 87–88. Consider also the fate of Mason's proposal in the Constitutional Convention that the executive be removable for "maladministration." The convention rejected that proposal as being in the words of Madison

"so vague" as to be "equivalent to a tenure during pleasure of the Senate." Farrand (ed.), *Records*, II, 550.

8. Abraham Sofaer, *War, Foreign Affairs and Constitutional Power: The Origins* (Cambridge: Ballinger, 1976), 10.

9. Berger, *Executive Privilege*, 41–43.

10. Berger refers to Joseph Story's *Commentaries* to de-majestize these clauses. Berger uses Story's broadened interpretation of this passage to disassociate it from its traditional tie to the State of the Union message. However, Berger's use of Story is somewhat dubious since the justice reads the provision so as to *enhance* not limit the president's power. Story, *Commentaries on the Constitution of the United States* (2 vols.; Boston: Little, Brown, 1905), II, Sec. 1561.

11. Berger, *Executive Privilege*, 42.

12. Charles Thach, *The Creation of the Presidency, 1775–1789* (Baltimore: Johns Hopkins University Press, 1969), 116. Berger's interpretation that the president is to have no discretion as to when or what information he gives to Congress is also suspect since this provision appears in the convention notes as part of a set of powers added to the executive by the Committee of Detail. These powers were added to strengthen the power of the executive not limit him. "The executive which had gone into committee with only the appointing power, the veto power, and the power to execute the laws, came out, not only with additional powers, but with all of them granted in terms which left no loophole for subsequent legislative interference. What have come to be known as the political powers were now the President's and the President's alone." Thach, *Creation*, 116.

13. See Story, "Rules of Interpretation," *Commentaries*, I, Sec. 400.

14. *Annals of Congress*, XVIII, 1641, 1644. See also William Rawle, *A View of the Constitution of the United States of America* (Philadelphia: P. H. Nicklin, 1829), Ch. 16, p. 171. Rawle says that while it is "the duty of the president from time to time to give congress information of the state of the union . . . it has been always understood that he is not required to communicate more than, in his apprehension, may be consistent with the public interests. Either house may at any time apply to him for information" yet these "applications . . . are generally accompanied with a qualification evincing a correct sense of the obligation on his part to avoid or suspend disclosures, by which the public interest . . . might be affected," 171–72.

15. Berger, *Executive Privilege*, 47–48.

16. Farrand (ed.), *Records*, II, 180.

17. Madison in his convention notes comments that "it was thought by others that provision should be made with respect to these when that part came under consideration which proposed to vest those [additional] authorities in the Senate." Farrand (ed.), *Records*, II, 255–56.

18. Farrand (ed.), *Records*, II, 259*ff*.

19. See Locke, *Second Treatise on Government*, para. 146, 147, and Montesquieu, *Spirit of the Laws*, Bk. 11, Ch. 6. See also Farrand (ed.), *Records*, III, 478, Appendix A, CCCLXVII.

20. Berger, *Executive Privilege*, 131.

21. *Ibid.*, 133.

22. *Ibid.*, 157.

23. Arthur Rovine, "Separation of Powers and International Executive Agreements," *Indiana Law Journal*, LII (1977), 412; Louis Fisher, *President and Congress* (New York: Free Press, 1972), 45. Berger does call our attention to the Rush-Bagot Agreement of 1817. This accord was an executive agreement between Monroe's secretary of state and the British minister to the United States that limited naval armaments on the Great Lakes. Monroe submitted the agreement to the Senate the next year and inquired whether it "is such an arrangement as the Executive is competent to enter into, by the powers in it by the Constitution, or is such an one as requires the advice and consent of the Senate." Berger argues that Monroe had concluded that he was required to submit the arrangement to the Senate to ensure its validity since Monroe "did not consider that a shared

power could be unilaterally altered." Yet, note several things: one, Monroe's language here presumes that there is in fact some reserved presidential power in the area of foreign relations to act alone; two, Monroe's actions do indicate that he thought he could "unilaterally alter" this power since Monroe never put this would-be treaty into effect by the customary exchange of ratifications; three, despite the importance of the accord—perhaps comparable today to our own SALT accords—neither President Madison nor Monroe considered it necessary to consult the Senate before implementing it; and finally, even assuming Berger is correct in his interpretation of these events, does either Monroe's actions or the way in which he used the phrase "advice and consent" suggest an understanding of the Senate as the president's substantive partner in the negotiation of treaties? Berger, *Executive Privilege*, 169–70.

24. Berger, *Executive Privilege*, 149–51.

25. *Ibid.*, 151, 150. The phrase "instrument of communication" is Edward Corwin's.

26. The question debated was whether President Adams' extradition—under a provision in the Jay Treaty—of one Thomas Nash to Britain to stand trial for murder was a task that one of the other branches should have done. Marshall argued that it was the president's task but that Congress through law might either "prescribe the mode" for implementing this segment of the treaty or even decide who should execute the extradition. Yet, even after saying this, Marshall clearly states that the president would still be responsible for whatever action this person or branch might take since he alone "is accountable to the nation for the violation of its engagements with foreign nations and for the consequences resulting from such violation." *Annals of Congress*, X, 614.

27. *Annals of Congress*, X, 614–15. Also consider here Marshall's comments in *Marbury*: "By the Constitution of the United States, the President is invested with certain important political powers, in the exercise of which he is to use his own discretion and is accountable only to his country in his political character . . . the decision of the executive is conclusive. The application of this remark will be perceived by adverting to the act of Congress for establishing the department of foreign affairs." *Marbury* v. *Madison*, 1 Cranch 137, 165–66 (1803).

28. Berger claims that the actions of the First Congress are of particular constitutional interest since its members constituted "'almost an adjourned session' of the Constitutional Convention." Berger, *Executive Privilege*, 295.

29. *Annals of Congress*, I, 512.

30. "An Act for establishing an Executive Department, to be denominated the Department of Foreign Affairs," 1 Stat. 28 (1789).

31. "In the act creating the Department of State, Congress placed full control of the Secretary of State in the President, four times repeating his subordination to the Chief Executive." Leonard D. White, *The Federalists* (New York: Macmillan, 1956), 130. See note 27 above.

32. Thach, *Creation*, 160–61. Thach quotes from a speech made during the debate by Roger Sherman who, like Berger, argued that because the "establishment of every treaty requires the voice of the Senate, as does the appointment of every officer for conducting the business . . . [I am led] to believe that the two bodies ought to act jointly in every transaction which respects the business of negotiation with foreign powers." Thach comments that "the majority turned its back on these arguments, and by allowing the President to exercise this discretion alone, indicated again its purpose to pare the executive powers of the Senate to the irreducible minimum." Congress' willingness to pare legislative participation in this area to a minimum is understandable in the light of inefficiency and inconveniences experienced by the government under the Articles of Confederation. Under the Articles Congress directed the country's foreign affairs. For an account of the dissatisfaction with such a system, see Louis Fisher, "The Efficiency Side of Separated Powers," *Journal of American Studies*, V (1971), 113, and J. B. Sanders, *Evolution of Executive Departments of the Continental Congress, 1774–1789* (Chapel Hill: University of North Carolina Press, 1935).

33. "An Act providing the means of intercourse between the United States and foreign nations," 1 Stat., 128–29. The full provision reads: "That the President shall account

specifically for all such expenditures of the said money as in his judgment may be made public, and also for the amount of such expenditures as he may think it advisable not to specify, and cause a regular statement and account thereof to be laid before Congress annually." For other examples of Congress' deference to executive discretion in the withholding of information, see *Annals of Congress*, XV, 67*ff* (1806); and *Annals of Congress*, XVI, 336 (1807).

34. Berger, *Executive Privilege*, 134.

35. *Ibid.*, 136–37. Berger cites an article by Arthur Bestor ("Separation of Powers in the Domain of Foreign Affairs," *Seton Hall Law Review*, V, 527) in which Bestor argues that the phrase "advice and consent," if properly understood, mandates that the president consult the Senate not only after a treaty has been negotiated but also before: "In actual practice, the Senate's constitutional right and duty to offer advice on the terms of treaties about to be negotiated has been allowed to dwindle away, until it is no more than the power to advise the President to ratify or not to ratify a treaty that he has already negotiated at his own discretion" (540). Certainly the early years of Washington's administration do contain instances where the president did consult with the Senate before the negotiation began. Yet whether he thought such practice was constitutionally mandated by the phrase "advice and consent" is another matter. Both Jay and Hamilton agreed that "the President might give the instructions [to those negotiating a treaty] without consulting the Senate." Raylston Hayden, *The Senate and Treaties, 1789–1817* (New York: DaCapo, 1970). Moreover, according to Jefferson, Washington was "in the habit of consulting the Senate previously" because "it would be prudent to consult them" since "their subsequent ratification would be necessary." Jefferson's brief statement seems to suggest that Washington need not have so consulted with the Senate. The comment that it was prudent to do so can perhaps be explained by the suggestion that Washington's brief habit of prior consultation was likely dictated by his attempt to have the newly formed government act in accordance with the existing principles of diplomacy. International law at that time prescribed that a nation was bound, its faith pledged, to ratify any treaty which it had instructed its diplomatic representatives to make. Thus, while the Constitution may not have mandated prior consultation with the Senate it was thought to be "prudent" to do so since a refusal by the Senate to ratify subsequently would have been considered a serious violation of eighteenth-century diplomatic custom. See Jefferson, *Writings*, ed. Paul Ford (10 vols.; Washington: Putnam, 1892–99), 294; J. B. Moore, *International Law Digest* (8 vols.; Washington: Government Printing Office, 1906), V, 184–202. However, it is interesting to note that these prudential concerns which led to prior consultation with the Senate were shelved when the need for secrecy became paramount. See note 41 below.

36. Berger, *Executive Privilege*, 143.

37. Such a limited conception of "advice and consent" was not unfamiliar to the members of the Constitutional Convention. For instance, numerous laws drafted in England for the colony of Virginia had preambles which stated that the laws had been "enacted . . . by and with the advice and consent of the General Assembly." However, acts which originated in the assembly did not use the phrase "advice and consent." Presumably, the assembly's "advice and consent" meant nothing more than mere acceptance and enactment of a previously prepared statute. See Henry M. Wriston, *Executive Agents in American Foreign Relations* (Baltimore: Johns Hopkins University Press, 1929), 63.

38. For statements that support this view of the Senate's role see Farrand (ed.), *Records*, III, 251, 342; II, 348; Jonathan Elliot (ed.), *Debates on the Adoption of the Federal Constitution* (4 vols.; Philadelphia: J. P. Lippincott & Co., 1836), II, 466, 477; III, 499. It should be noted here that the Jay Treaty, the first truly significant treaty completed under the new constitution, was negotiated without prior consultation with the Senate. The first great treaty was, therefore, negotiated upon principles dictated by the executive alone. Moreover, it is worth considering the fact that when the minority who opposed the treaty recorded their final and formal objections to the highly controversial pact they did not mention among their list of seven (three of which were constitutional) the president's failure to be "advised" by the Senate. *Journal of the Executive Proceedings of the Senate of the United States of America* (Washington: Government Printing Office, 1828), I, 185–86.

39. Jefferson, *Writings*, V, 161. On its face, this statement need not mean much more than that the president is the chief clerk in the area of foreign affairs. However, when the statement is placed within its context Jefferson's comments are quite substantive. Jefferson's comments are in answer to a Washington request for an opinion on whether he had acted properly in not asking Senate advice as to where the new nation's chief diplomats should be stationed. This issue was of some consequence since the government had at its disposal only a few first-line ministers yet had numerous potential countries to which they might be advantageously sent. (In passing, both Jay and Madison agreed with Jefferson that the Senate's opinion should not be requested on this matter.) See John C. Fitzpatrick (ed.), *Diaries of Washington* (New York: Houghton-Mifflin, 1925), 122.

40. *Federalist*, No. 75, pp. 486–87.

41. *Ibid.*, No. 64, p. 419. Washington, in connection with what would become the Treaty of Greenville, asked his cabinet for their opinion on whether or not he should consult with the Senate about the terms to be negotiated in the treaty. Their unanimous response was that he should not. Jefferson explains that "all thought if the Senate should be consulted, and consequently appraised of our line, it would become known to Hammond," the British minister to the United States, and that, he goes on to note, would be harmful to the best interests of the nation. Washington followed the advice of his cabinet and secrecy was maintained, the treaty completed, and without objection approved by the Senate. F. B. Sawvel (ed.), *Anas of Thomas Jefferson* (New York: Round Table Press, 1903), 108–11; *Senate Executive Journal*, 193–97. The Senate voted to keep the completed Jay Treaty secret during the ratification debate. Hamilton, writing to Oliver Wolcott, said that the Senate had so acted "because they thought it (the secrecy) the affair of the President to do as he thought fit." Hamilton, *Works*, ed. Henry C. Lodge (12 vols.; New York: Putnam, 1903), X, 107.

42. Hawkins Taylor (comp.), *Compilation of Reports of the Committee on Foreign Relations, U.S. Senate, 1789–1901* (8 vols.; Washington: Government Printing Office, 1901), VIII, 24–25. Berger disparages the report in two ways. First, he suggests that the report is "based upon notions of expediency" and not, it is implied, upon constitutional verities. And second, the report is unfavorably contrasted with comments made by Constitutional Conventionist Rufus King in 1818. King there claims for the Senate a much broader role in foreign affairs than did the report. In reply to the first objection it may be simply stated that expediency and law are not necessarily in tension and that furthermore one man's law is another man's expediency. For instance, it should be pointed out that in two famous instances in which presidents, after Washington, did consult with the Senate before asking for formal ratification of a treaty (Jackson in 1830 and Polk in 1846) both were justified—in Jackson's case explicitly—upon motives of expediency. See Berger, *Executive Privilege*, 155. *Cf. Federalist*, No. 23, and *Senate Executive Journal*, IV, 97–99, and VII, 84–85. As to King, it is far from evident that we should take his comments in 1818 as more of a guide than an earlier statement made by him at the time of the Jay Treaty in which he said that it seemed to him "most suitable that the president should instruct, and that the Treaty should be concluded subject to the approbation of the Senate." *Life and Correspondence of Rufus King*, I, 521, quoted in Hayden, *The Senate and Treaties*, 70.

43. *Federalist*, No. 64, p. 420. Publius in this paper does seem to assume that the president will consult with the Senate before treaty negotiations have been completed. Again, however, it is not clear that such consultation was mandated because of a constitutional prescription or because it was required by the then existing laws of diplomacy. See note 35 above. Yet what is clear is that this practice of prior consultation and the necessity of dispatch and secrecy in negotiations would inevitably collide. See note 41 above. However, as a practical matter this tension between the respective presidential and senatorial prerogatives in the making of treaties has been wisely ameliorated since Washington's administration. It has been ameliorated by giving full scope to the president's capacity as negotiator and at the same time by allowing the Senate to expand its powers to include amending negotiated treaties. Thus, although the historical practice under the treaty provision may have varied somewhat from the expectations of some of the framers, this

variation has effectively retained the essential elements meant to be potentially available to the government by the "joint possession" of the treaty-making power.

44. Washington twice during his first administration exercised his discretion in this area and refused papers asked for first by the Senate and then the House. In the first instance, Washington rejected the Senate's request to see the whole of the diplomatic correspondence between our minister to France, Gouverneur Morris, and Secretary of State Edmund Randolph. Sending some of the letters, Washington deleted those "which, in [his] judgment, for public considerations, ought not to be communicated." *Annals of Congress*, IV, 56. In the second case Washington refused papers called for by the House concerning the negotiation of the Jay Treaty with Great Britain. *Annals of Congress*, V, 760. Madison defended Washington by declaring that "the Executive had a right, under a due responsibility, to withhold information, when of a nature that did not permit a disclosure." *Annals of Congress*, V, 773.

45. Berger, *Executive Privilege*, 77.

46. *Ibid.*, 69ff.

47. *Ibid.*, 70, 73; *Federalist*, No. 69, p. 448. Berger supports this analysis by use of a misleadingly truncated quotation from James Wilson. Wilson is quoted by Berger, p. 69, as saying in effect that "the power to 'declare war' was lodged in Congress as a guard against being 'hurried' into war, so that no 'single man [can] involve us in such distress.'" The suggestion is that this war power was denied to the executive out of fear of a "single man." Yet the full statement by Wilson reads: "This system will not hurry us into war; it is calculated to guard against it. It will not be in the power of a single man, *or a single body of men*, to involve us in such distress" (emphasis added). Elliott (ed.), *Debates*, II, 528.

48. *Federalist*, No. 69, is part of Publius' argument that acts as a preface to the general discussion of the presidency which follows. Both the context and the questions Publius answers there suggest the essay should be read carefully. For example, Publius' concern in these preliminary papers is to allay the fears of some that the convention had created an executive office which seemed too monarchic. To show that this was not the case he compares the powers of the president with the king of Great Britain, on the one hand, and the governor of New York, on the other. In light of this analysis the president does, comparatively speaking, seem to be weaker than the Anti-Federalists were claiming. Yet Publius' argument is somewhat disingenuous since in the end he does consider the president to be at least equal in power to the governor of New York—the unquestionably *strongest* executive of any of the state governments. In comparison to the other chief magistrates the president was indeed quite powerful.

49. *Federalist*, No. 74, p. 482; Berger, *Executive Privilege*, 70. This statement ("creature . . .") is borrowed by Berger from an article by Eugene Rostow. It should be noted, however, that Professor Rostow, unlike Berger, does not suggest that this statement is an adequate depiction of the president's capacities as commander-in-chief under the Constitution. Rostow follows this depiction by commenting that this kind of subordination was thought by the framers to be a "critical weakness" in the Articles and was thought to have been remedied by the Constitution. Eugene Rostow, "Great Cases Make Bad Law: The War Powers Act," *Texas Law Review*, L (1972), 840.

50. Louis Fisher, *President and Congress*, 254; Farrand (ed.), *Records*, II, 318–19; Sofaer, *War*, 118. Berger attempts to support his conception of the president as commander-in-chief by the example of Jefferson's response in 1801 to Tripoli's armed attack on American naval vessels. He cites approvingly Jefferson's speech to Congress in which he claims that the release of a captured and disarmed Tripolitan ship by an American captain was the result of a constitutional understanding that only Congress could authorize measures beyond mere self-defense. Yet, this precedent is hardly as clear as Berger presents it. The value of Jefferson's remarks for supporting presidential deference to Congress is clouded by one important fact: Jefferson and his cabinet, prior to the actual incident, had issued to the American captain orders authorizing not only defensive but also offensive actions against the marauding Barbary vessels. Berger, *Executive Privilege*, 87–88; *Annals of Congress*, XI, 11–12; *Naval Documents Related to U.S. War with Barbary Powers, 1785–1807* (6

vols.; Washington: Naval Records and Library Office, 1939–44), I, 467. See also, Sofaer, *War*, 209, and *Annals of Congress*, XI, 327–28, 432, and Hamilton, *Works*, III, 247*ff*.

51. *Executive Privilege*, 68, 69.

52. It is possible to assume that the commander-in-chief clause was left undefined because it might be expected to "grow" as circumstances and necessity warranted. Berger—reasonably—criticizes the concept of a "living constitution" as finally incompatible with "constitutionalism." While his criticism of this modern judicial thesis is laudable, it should be moderated by and contrasted with the framers' understanding that differing circumstances tend to enhance or diminish the power of the several branches. As originally understood, the Constitution embodies the principle that certain stresses on the nation are better countered by a particular branch. Attempts to prevent such a natural shifting must certainly result in a constitution that would bring about "necessary usurpations." Berger, *Executive Privilege*, 99; *cf. Federalist*, No. 8, p. 43; No. 23, p. 142; no. 74, p. 484; No 41, p. 262; and Tocqueville, *Democracy in America*, Vol. I, Pt. 1, Ch. 8, "Accidental Causes that May Increase the Influence of the Executive Power." For an historical account of the problems fostered by Jefferson's self-imposed constitutional straight-jacketing, see Sofaer, *War*, 226.

53. Montesquieu, *The Spirit of the Laws*, Bk. 11, Ch. 6; Locke, *Second Treatise on Government*, para. 108, 148. See note 50 above.

54. Congress, upon hearing of General St. Clair's ill-fated expedition into the Northwest Territory in 1792, demanded from Washington all the papers relevant to the expedition. Washington did meet those demands, yet did so only after he and his cabinet had concurred that the president could, if he thought it necessary, deny Congress those papers. Jefferson, *Anas*, 71. Berger argues that the fact that Washington did turn over the papers renders the discussion in the cabinet "academic." Academic, perhaps; irrelevant, no. Berger, *Executive Privilege*, 189.

55. Berger, *Executive Privilege*, 55, 66, 59. Berger's first quotation is from Corwin's *The President: Office and Powers*. Corwin is summarizing the general colonial antipathy toward executive power. However, Corwin, unlike Berger, does not suggest that this belief was successfully transferred into the Constitution. In fact, Corwin immediately suggests the opposite is true when he declares that "Sir Henry Maine's dictum that 'the American constitution is the British constitution with the monarch left out' is, from the point of view of 1789, almost the exact reverse of the truth, for the presidency was designed in great measure to reproduce the monarch of George III with the corruption left out, and also of course the hereditary feature." Edward S. Corwin, *The President: Office and Powers* (New York: New York University Press, 1974), 14–15.

56. Thach, *Creation*, 49–52. See also, M. J. C. Vile, *Constitutionalism and Separation of Powers* (New York: Oxford University Press, 1967), 159–60; Gordon S. Wood, *The Creation of the American Republic, 1776–1787* (Chapel Hill: University of North Carolina Press, 1969), 132–61, 435–57; Edward S. Corwin, "The Progress of Constitutional Theory Between the Declaration of Independence and the Meeting of the Philadelphia Convention," *American Historical Review*, XXX (1925), 511–36; Farrand (ed.), *Records*, II, 74, 322–23, and II, 52. Philip Kurland has contested this point by arguing that it "rests largely on the unjustified notion that Madison's voice at the Convention was to be considered the voice of the Convention" and that "the expressions of the fear of legislative democracy that underlay" his motions were not accepted by the rest of the convention. Kurland's specific example is the "repeated attempts of Madison and Wilson to establish a council of revision made up of the executive and judicial branches to control the powers of the legislature." Kurland notes that each time it came to a vote the convention rejected it and concludes from this that "rather than supporting the Madisonian position, the Convention abjured it." However, a review of the debate Kurland cites indicates that Madison's position on the specific proposal for a council of revision was not rejected because the convention had failed to adopt as unwarranted his fears of the first branch. Indeed, "all agree," Ghorum is reported as saying, "that a check on the Legislature is necessary." Rather, Madison's proposal failed primarily, so the debate reveals, because many thought this institution would have significantly violated the principle of separation of powers. In summary, then, Madi-

son's "position" in the deepest sense was here not contested, rather, only his means. See Kurland, *Watergate*, 159; Farrand (ed.), *Records*, II, 73–80. On the prevalency of the "fear of legislative democracy" in general, see Thach, *Creation*, 25ff.

57. Fisher, *President and Congress*, 18; Farrand (ed.), *Records*, I, 65. Sherman's comments occur early in the convention, June 1. His proposal died there. No effort was made to implement his suggestions or even to debate his view.

58. Terms were in most states one year, two in South Carolina, and three in Delaware and New York. As to reeligibility, only New York and New Jersey had no restriction on reeligibility.

59. See *Federalist*, No. 73.

60. *Federalist*, No. 70, p. 454. The "period from 1774 to 1787 demonstrates the degree to which the idea of separation of powers was based on the search for administrative efficiency." Thach, *Creation*, 74. See also Fisher, *President and Congress*, 15. *Cf*. Warren's opinion in *U.S.* v. *Brown*, 381 U.S. 437; and Brandeis' in *Myers* v. *U.S.*, 272 U.S. 52. Berger claims that the framers never intended to create a president who in executing the laws would be substantially independent of Congress. Yet neither the result of the removal debate in the First Congress nor the willingness of the Constitutional Convention to transfer control of the Treasurer—the administrative officer most "naturally" associated with Congress' special power of "the purse"—from Congress to the president seem to support his argument. See, Thach, *Creation*, 159; Farrand (ed.), *Records*, II, 594, 614; and *Federalist*, No. 70, p. 455.

61. Hamilton, reflecting on a congressionally dominated system declared that "Congress have kept the power too much in their own hand and have meddled too much with details of every sort. Congress is, properly, a deliberative corps, and it forgets itself when it attempts to play the executive. It is impossible such a body, numerous as it is, and constantly fluctuating, can ever act with sufficient decision or with system." Alexander Hamilton, *Works*, I, 209.

62. James Wilson, *Works*, ed. R. G. McCloskey (2 vols.; Cambridge: Harvard University Press, 1967), I, 294.

63. Hamilton, *Works*, X, 446.

64. Succinctly stated, the president "cannot efficaciously conduct his office without it." Charles Black, "Mr. Nixon, the Tapes and Common Sense," *New York Times*, August 3, 1973, p. 71. See also *Federalist*, No. 71, p. 464.

65. Elliot, *Debates*, II, 348ff. (Hamilton).

66. *Federalist*, No. 51, p. 337.

67. *Ibid.*

68. Consider, for example, Congress' confrontations with Secretary of Commerce Rogers Morton and Secretary of State Henry Kissinger over their respective failures to provide information requested by the Congress. In both cases Congress was furnished with that material when it was made clear to the executive branch that the Congress was willing to use those powers it had at its disposal to compel compliance. Here, at least, the lesson to be drawn is that congressional failures to control possible past abuses by the executive are not so much the result of a lack of powers but an abdication or lack of resolve on the part of Congress to use those powers it has. See *Contempt Proceedings against Secretary of Commerce, Rogers C. B. Morton*, Hearings before the Subcommittee on Oversight and Investigations of the Committee on Interstate and Foreign Commerce, House of Representatives, 94th Congress, 1st Session (1975).

69. J. W. Bishop, "Executive Right to Privacy: An Unresolved Constitutional Question," *Yale Law Journal*, LXVI (1957), 477. Berger claims that this "system of checks and balances" results in government by crisis, or rather, "government by cliff-hanger." Berger, *Executive Privilege*, 343. Yet, in fact, history reveals that such crises are, in general, few. Perhaps it is because there is at all times the evident potential for paralyzing conflict that the actual interest in interbranch cooperation is enhanced, not lessened. As Montesquieu suggests, such "powers should naturally form a state of . . . inaction. But as there is a necessity for movement in the course of human affairs, they are forced to move, but still in concert." Montesquieu, *The Spirit of the Laws*, Bk. 11, Ch. 6. See also Wilson, *Works*, I,

300. Moreover, it may be the memory of past confrontations which aids in accounting for "responsive" presidents. Was not Nixon's problems with Congress the reason why the Carter Administration has attempted to be so open and why the Ford Administration "sought to avoid confrontation by voluntarily furnishing Congress more information than ever before available on sacrosanct agencies, such as the CIA and FBI?" Robert G. Dixon, "Shared Administration and Executive Privilege," in *Congress Against the President*, ed. Harvey C. Mansfield (New York: Praeger, 1975), 129.

70. Since 1954 executive privilege has been exercised approximately sixty-seven times: Eisenhower (34), Kennedy (4), Johnson (2), Nixon (19), Nixon-Ford (6), Carter— as of May, 1978—(2). Eisenhower's administration accounts for over half the total number. His expansive use of privilege was in reaction to the Army-McCarthy hearings. Beginning with Kennedy the average number of invocations of privilege is less than seven per administration. When one stops to consider the number of congressional requests for information each year, the actual number of times executive privilege has been invoked does not seem large. "In fact, present debate on and the most recent history of executive privilege in American constitutional law are perhaps a measure of how relatively 'uninhibited, robust, and wide-open' the American polity is. From the vantage point of comparative politics, I think, there can be little doubt that governmental *Geheimniskramerei* (petty secretiveness) looms less large in the United States than anywhere else. While this is no reason to belittle the cost of secrecy in American public life, it should alert us to the . . . exaggerated claims . . . on both sides of the issue." Gehard Casper, "American Geheimniskramerei," *Reviews in American History*, III (June 1975), p. 158. However, some have argued that secrecy in the executive branch is a much more serious problem and is, furthermore, not adequately comprehended if confined to actual invocations of executive privilege. For instance, one Senate report suggested that so numerous were the ways in which members of the second branch avoided giving Congress information it had asked for that a whole system of evasion was now available to those wishing to avoid answering congressional requests yet unwilling to claim privilege. If this is true it must be said that such a situation exists with the forbearance of Congress, since Congress, in fact, has sufficient means available, if it wishes, to secure the information that it has been "denied." An example of the means, albeit extreme, Congress has at its disposal to end such circumvention is a bill proposed by Senator Fulbright in 1971. Fulbright's bill required the agencies of the executive branch to produce all information called for by Congress. The only exemption to that mandate was an invocation of executive privilege by the president in writing. Denial of information in any other form would immediately cost the offending office or agencies its operating funds. See "Refusals by the Executive Branch to Provide Information to the Congress, 1964–1973," A Survey Conducted by the Subcommittee on Separation of Powers, Senate Committee on the Judiciary, 93rd Congress, 2nd Session (1974), and *Executive Privilege: The Withholding of Information by the Executive*, Hearings before the Subcommittee on Separation of Powers, Senate Committee on the Judiciary, 92nd Congress, 1st Session (1971).

71. It should be noted here that neither Congress nor the Court has suggested that their own papers should be open to inspection by either of the other two branches. "Few utterances are more confidential than Supreme Court conferences. . . . Congress has not only exempted itself from the Freedom of Information Act in respect to citizen inquiries, but it has also provided that no court subpoena is to be honored without a vote of the house concerned." Dixon, "Shared Administration," 133. "Each of the great powers of government should be independent as well as distinct. . . . The independence of each power consists in this, that the proceedings and the motives, views, and principles, which produce those proceedings, should be free from the remotest influence . . . of either of the other two powers." James Wilson, *Works*, II, 299. "If the Executive conceived that, in relation to his own department, papers could not be safely communicated, he might on that ground, refuse them, because he was the competent though responsible judge within his own department." Madison, *Annals of Congress*, V, 773–74.

72. Kenneth L. Karst and Harold W. Horowitz, "Presidential Prerogative and Judicial Review," *UCLA Law Review*, XXII (1974), 47; Berger, *Executive Privilege*, 341ff.

73. Berger, *Executive Privilege*, 369, 368, 370.

74. *Marbury* v. *Madison*, 1 Cranch 137, 165, 166, 170 (1803).

75. When Berger quotes this passage he omits the phrase "the several departments" and substitutes, in its place, "neither of the two branches." Berger, *Executive Privilege*, 370.

76. Berger, *Executive Privilege*, 381–82. Berger implies that if this issue is not submitted to the courts the president will be better off and Congress enfeebled. Yet, consider the comments by Gerald Gunther on this same point in light of *U.S.* v. *Nixon*: "*U.S. v. Nixon* suggests that the judiciary too has attained new strength. It is this I find troubling. . . . It seems to me that some of the added strength of the Court has been achieved—unnecessarily, unfortunately and unwisely—at the expense of the most emaciated and deserving of the three branches, the legislature." Gerald Gunther, "Judicial Hegemony and Legislative Autonomy: The Nixon Case and the Impeachment Process," *UCLA Law Review*, XXII (1974), 30.

77. Berger, *Executive Privilege*, 382.

78. The "balance test" was essential to the opinion in *U.S.* v. *Nixon*, 418 U.S. 683 (1974), in that the need for the presidential privilege was balanced by the Court against the need for evidence in a criminal justice proceeding (712–13). Of course, the real importance of *U.S.* v. *Nixon* with regard to the topic at hand, congressional requests, is what it could mean for a future litigation brought by Congress to the Court against the president. Justice Burger's opinion seems to leave open that question since he explicitly says that the Court is "not here concerned with . . . congressional demands for information" (712). But Paul Freund suggests that while the "opinion of the Supreme Court was careful to state that it was concerned with executive privilege only in the context of the criminal law, and not in settling of presidential relations with Congress [the balance test there adopted] will doubtless have a radiating effect. Indeed the United States Court of Appeals for the District of Columbia Circuit, in judging the Watergate Committee's suits for presidential tapes (*Senate Select Committee on Presidential Campaign Activities v. Nixon*, 498 F. 2d 725; D. C. Cir., 1974), applied essentially the same standards it had employed in the first Special Prosecutor's suit though with a different outcome." That is, Judge Gesell in district court rejected the Ervin committee's demand for the tapes by applying the balancing criteria first administered by Judge Sirica in *Nixon* v. *Sirica*, 487 F. 2d 700; D. C. Cir. 1973. Paul A. Freund, "Foreword: On Presidential Privilege," *Harvard Law Review*, LXXXVIII (1974), 13.

79. "Routine resort to the courts could . . . expose the courts to the risk of rendering unsatisfactory judgments on matters where the judicial touch is likely to be unsure. Here as elsewhere in our constitutional order, when personal rights are not in jeopardy, it is well to give scope for a 'frank and candid cooperation for the general good.'" Freund, "Foreword," 39. For a more general discussion of this point see Donald L. Horowitz, *The Courts and Social Policy* (Washington, D.C.: Brookings, 1977).

80. *Federalist*, No. 78, p. 504.

81. The opinion in *U.S.* v. *Nixon* seems to have been a compromise (denying executive privilege in the judicial matter at hand while at the same time recognizing that discretion as constitutional) since four justices initially were in favor of an opinion which would totally limit the concept of executive privilege. See Alan Westin, "Foreword" to *U.S. v. Nixon: The President Before the Supreme Court*, ed. Leon Friedman (New York: Chelsea House, 1974). The compromise resulted apparently out of a desire to present a united, that is, unanimous front. Why? Consider the reply of the president's attorney, James St. Clair, when asked if the president would abide by the subpoena for the tapes if the Court issued one: "Yes, in a sense." The Court asked then, "In what sense?" St. Clair replied, "In the sense that this Court has the obligation to determine the law. The president also has an obligation to carry out his constitutional duties." And further, "This is being submitted to this Court for its guidance and judgment with respect to the law. The President, on the other hand, has his obligations, under the Constitution." See "Transcript of Oral Arguments," *U.S.* v. *Nixon*, 94 S. Ct. 3090 (1974).

82. "It seems equally plausible that the Court in [*U.S.* v. *Nixon*] correctly perceived

that public opinion was united only in the limited proposition that the unindicted co-conspirator, who was just coincidentally the President, should turn over the so-called Watergate tapes, and that there was no consensus on the broader question of the nature of presidential authority and the separation of powers in the abstract." D. S. Hobbs, "*U.S. v. Nixon*: An Historical Perspective-Foreword," *Loyola of L.A. Law Review*, IX (1975), 13.

83. For an explication of the political considerations that surrounded *U.S. v. Nixon* see Paul J. Mishkin, "Great Cases and Soft Law: A Comment on *U.S. v. Nixon*," *UCLA Law Review*, XXII (1974), 76. See notes 81 and 82 above.

84. Berger, *Executive Privilege*, 3, 15, 385ff. "Secrecy in a Republican Government wounds the majesty of the sovereign people: that this Government is in the hands of the people; and they have a right to know all the transactions relative to their own affairs; this right ought not to be infringed incautiously, for such secrecy tends to injure the confidence of the people in their own Government." *Annals of Congress*, IV, 150.

85. Negotiations, whether of constitutional or foreign affairs, often require secrecy because the individual agreements they produce may appear markedly different than the whole that finally results. Thus, George Mason could write of the secrecy surrounding the Constitutional Convention that it was "a proper precaution" in that it prevented "mistakes and misrepresentations until the business shall have been completed, when the whole may have a very different complexion from that in which the several parts might in their first shape appear if submitted to the public eye." Farrand (ed.), *Records*, III, 28; 32; Appendix A, XXIII and XXXII.

86. "Because this Government is Republican, it will not be presented that it can have no secrets. The President of the United States is the depository of secret transactions, his duty *may* lead him to delegate those secrets to the members of the House, and the success, safety and energy of the Government may depend on keeping those secrets inviolably. *The people have a right to be well governed*; they have interests as well as rights and it is the duty of the Legislature to take every possible measure to promote those interests." *Annals of Congress*, IV, 150 (emphasis added).

87. This is not to suggest that there is no principled argument for those who would have a weak and open executive. See George Mason's speech of June 4 in the convention. Farrand (ed.), *Records*, I, 110–14. Yet, it is safe to say that Mason's alternative source for 'energy' in republican government is today even less practical than at the founding. See Herbert J. Storing, "Introduction," and Thach, *Creation*, x.

88. Locke, *Second Treatise*, para. 168. See Joseph Lash, *Roosevelt and Churchill* (New York: W. W. Norton, 1976), 150–53.

89. At this time "the enduring problem is to avoid a reactive, institutional overkill by an imperial Congress, which could leave the presidency imperiled in function under the delusive idea that power fragmented is power purified. . . . Congress has an instinctive thrust toward control of the executive. It seeks ever-greater authority over executive personnel and pursues a variety of other devices toward shared administration . . . forms of congressional veto of administration action (e.g., War Powers Act of 1973) . . . attempts to limit the pocket veto, to create independent agencies, such as the new Federal Elections Commission, to perform executive functions, and the aborted plan of Senator Ervin in 1974 to remove the Department of Justice from the executive branch. Many of these congressional forces are enduring. They are not readily amenable to judicial check . . . or to a political check when the presidential faction in Congress is divided and small. Indeed, it could be said that the balance in the separation of powers system between the executive and Congress largely exists at the sufferance of the latter, its disinclination to exercise fully the power it constitutionally possesses." Dixon, "Shared Administration," 139. *Federalist*, No. 70, p. 454.

VI

The Congressional Veto and the Constitutional Separation of Powers[1]

MURRAY DRY

The congressional veto, also known as the legislative veto, permits Congress to (1) disapprove a proposed presidential action; (2) disapprove a regulation proposed by an executive department, a legislative or administrative agency, or a court; or (3) terminate presidential action already underway. The veto may require positive action to authorize a proposed presidential action or may simply permit a resolution of disapproval. It usually requires the action of one house (simple resolution) or both houses (concurrent resolution), although in some cases committees have the power of disapproval. In all cases, the legislation establishing the veto is presented to the president for his signature. We shall call it a congressional, rather than legislative, veto on the grounds that this review and oversight mechanism is not in itself an act of legislation, although it does derive its authority from previous legislation.

The generally recognized starting point for the congressional veto is 1932, when it was attached to that part of the legislative appropriations of 1933 that concerned executive reorganization.[2] It has also been attached to many of the subsequent executive reorganization acts, and it is also a prominent part of the War Powers Act of 1973, the Congressional Budget and Impoundment Control Act of 1974, and the Federal Election Campaign Act of 1974, to name three recent examples. The Congressional Research Service of the Library of Congress (CRS) has compiled a digest of 297 congressional review provisions in 196 statutes during the years 1932 to 1975. To those numbers must be added two statutes, with one resolution each, that were separated out as involving nonexecutive review. In addition, some of the statutes provide only for advance submission to Congress. A recent CRS study, for the period 1976 to May 25, 1978, found an additional 22 statutes.[3] There is no official statistic for the number of current statutes containing congressional veto provisions. However, using the statutes listed in the 1977 Rules of the House of Representatives,[4] and noting the additions from the recent CRS study, we arrive at 61 current statutes with disapproval, or veto, provisions; 52 of them permit one- or two-house disapproval and 9 permit a committee disapproval.

Recent Congresses have been actively involved with the congressional veto. First, as part of their consideration of regulatory reform, both Houses have held hearings on a bill to extend a veto to virtually all proposed agency rules and regulations. In 1976, the House majority was only two votes shy of the necessary two-thirds required to suspend the rules and pass the bill.[5] The same bill has been introduced in subsequent Congresses and will be discussed below. Piecemeal versions of the same proposal, which would apply the veto to all regulations of a given agency, such as the Federal Trade Commission, have also been attempted, so far unsuccessfully. Second, the congressional veto provisions of the Arms Export Control Act of 1976 brought Congress into the recent debate on the Carter Administration's controversial plan to sell $4.8 billion worth of jet fighters to Israel, Saudi Arabia, and Egypt. The congressional disapproval resolution, which required the concurrence of both houses, was defeated in the Senate on May 15, 1978, by a vote of 44–54.[6]

This survey suggests what this essay will confirm: that the congressional veto has been important to Congress in the reclamation of constitutional powers during the post-Watergate era. Its enactment and use have been, in part, a reaction to the "imperial presidency," a phenomenon which has been aptly described in terms of both congressional abdication and presidential usurpation of power.[7] Supporters of the congressional veto also regard it as an efficient means of controlling the bureaucracy. Critics, on the other hand, especially those who oppose the veto of agency regulations, argue that the federal government is now threatened with an "imperial congress," a legislature which encroaches into the executive sphere of government.[8]

Since the congressional veto raises a fundamental constitutional question about the proper relationship between two political branches of our national government, we shall begin with the general inquiry into the separation of powers. Then, we shall consider the particular constitutional issues surrounding the congressional veto. Finally, we shall discuss the different uses of the veto, focusing on the more controversial examples.

THE SEPARATION OF POWERS AND THE FRAMERS' INTENT

Many commentators believe that the congressional veto is contrary to the separation of powers for the simple reason that it appears to give Congress something other than legislative power, *i.e.*, the power to execute the laws or administer government. This objection resembles the one lodged against the Constitution by the Anti-Federalist critics, who saw the mixing of powers as contrary to the separation of powers doctrine. The Constitution does not spell out the precise meaning of the separation of powers. For example, the framers did not include the statement, found in the Massachusetts constitution, that no one branch of government may exercise the powers of another. The clearest statement of the meaning of the separation comes from Article I, section 6: "And no person holding office under the United States, shall be a member of either House during his Continuance in Office." While the first three articles begin with reference to legislative, executive, and judicial power, and there is no reference to any other kind of governmental power, a strict functional interpretation of the separation of powers is not tenable; there are powers that are shared and others that are not clearly identifiable on the three-part scheme. The executive veto, the treaty making power, and the appointment power exemplify a mixing and sharing of powers. The powers of impeachment and removal from office, lodged in the House and Senate respectively, are closer to judicial than legislative powers. Also, the vice president acts as president of the Senate, and is thus at once a member of the executive and legislative branches.[9]

James Madison's response to the Anti-Federalists' charge that the Constitution's mixing of powers violated the separation of powers applies to our current controversy as well as to the earlier one. Noting that Montesquieu was the "oracle who is always consulted and cited on this subject," Madison, after reviewing the English Constitution (Montesquieu's model), concluded:

> From these facts, by which Montesquieu was guided, it may clearly be inferred that in saying "There can be no liberty where the legislative and executive powers are united in the same person, or body of magistrates," or, "if the power of judging be not separated from the legislative and executive powers," he did not mean that these departments ought to have no *partial agency* in, or no *control* over, the acts of each other. His meaning, as his own words import, and still more conclusively as illustrated by the example in his eye, can amount to no more than this, that where the *whole* power of one department is exercised by the same hands which possess the *whole* power of another department the fundamental principles of a free constitution are subverted.[10]

The Federalist's discussion of treaty making is instructive for our understanding of the separation of powers. Alexander Hamilton describes it as partaking "more of the legislative than of the executive character, though it does not seem strictly to fall within the definition of either of them." Hamilton goes on to define legislation as the act of prescribing "rules for the regulation of society," and executive power as the "execution of the laws and the employment of the common strength, either for this purpose or for the common defense." [11]

Foreign affairs complicate the separation of powers doctrine. Following Locke and Montesquieu, Hamilton acknowledges a difference between execution of the laws and foreign affairs. Treaty making involves a power which "seems to form a distinct department, and to belong, properly, neither to the legislative nor to the executive." Then Hamilton goes on to argue on the basis of expediency as well as function. The qualities indispensable in the management of foreign negotiations "point out the executive as the most fit agent in those transactions; while the vast importance of the trust and the operation of treaties as laws plead strongly for the participation of the whole or a part of the legislative body in the office of making them." [12]

The Federalist's treatment of the treaty-making power shows that the separation of powers is not to be understood as a simple "one branch–one function" doctrine of government. The doctrine must take into account the requirements of efficiency, political balance, and consent of the governed in a republican government. So, while efficiency and political balance dictated a single executive with a veto, the republican principle dictated that the veto be qualified; Congress can override it with a two-thirds vote in both houses.

The framers' construction of the presidency reflects the importance of the issue of republican government for the separation of powers in America. This is revealed in the discussion of unity, reeligibility, and, finally, in the limited attempts to define executive power. For example, as soon as the framers took up the resolution to create a single executive, "a considerable pause" ensued, and Benjamin Franklin had to urge discussion of the subject. Eventually, George Mason and Edmund Randolph, two active supporters of a strong national government, vigorously opposed a unitary executive as inconsistent with the republican genius of America. In neither the closed session of the convention nor the widely published *Federalist* did Hamilton flatly deny the charge. He simply responded that the enlightened well-wishers of republican government had better hope they were wrong because "energy in the executive is a leading character in the definition of good government." [13]

The issue of reeligibility was joined to the mode of election; those who wanted a strong executive desired a mode of election that permitted the president to be independent and to be eligible for reelection, while those who desired an independent but limited executive wanted him chosen by Congress and not eligible for reelection. On this point, as on the unity point, the advocates of a strong executive won. Still, there was little discussion of the scope of executive power, and Madison called for a substantive discussion of executive power before deciding on the unity question. All James Wilson could provide was the suggestion that executive power involved executing the laws and appointing officers "not appertaining to and appointed by the legislature." Only later did the Committee of Detail succeed in including important additional, albeit subordinate, powers of administration, such as requiring written opinions of other officers, receiving public ministers, and convening Congress under special circumstances. [14]

The attempt to combine the virtues of energy with republican

government caused Hamilton and Madison, the great constitutional collaborators, to disagree on two substantial aspects of
legislative-executive relations immediately after the new government started. The first point involved administration, which
Hamilton tended to identify with executive power and the presidency. While this position has gained general acceptance, it is
worth recalling why Madison did not agree. In a speech he gave
concerning the location of the capital, Madison warned that
Americans should not take the meaning of terms applied in monarchies as a proper understanding of them in the republican
United States. While the residence of the monarch is the seat of
government, in our government the seat can only be where Congress sits. And, as the American government comprehends both
Congress and the president, "so the term Administration, which
is in other countries is specially appropriated to the Executive
branch of government, is used here for both the Executive and
Legislative branches."[15]

In addition to that general disagreement on administration,
Hamilton and Madison disagreed on whether or not President
Washington had the power to declare neutrality in 1793, after war
broke out in Europe. Hamilton argued that the power to declare
neutrality could be inferred from executive power. He also
claimed that the interpretation of treaties was a form of executing
the laws. Madison replied that the powers to declare war and
make treaties were "substantially of a legislative, not an executive
nature," and he denied that the executive had a concurrent right
to judge the obligation to declare war. He termed such sharing
"as awkward in practice as it is unnatural in theory." In the end,
however, Hamilton did acknowledge that Congress could, by exercising its powers to declare war, revoke the neutrality declaration. Hence, he was not arguing for an exclusive sphere of presidential war power or foreign policy making.[16]

The founders recognized that as foreign affairs became more
prominent the national government would become more important, and so would presidential power. What started with foreign
affairs extended to internal affairs under Presidents Woodrow
Wilson and Franklin Roosevelt. Legislative delegation permitted
the president to become "legislative leader," but this practice con-

tradicted the maxim that the legislature may not delegate its power. As Locke put it, "The Legislative cannot transfer the power of making laws to any other hands. For it being but a delegated power from the people, they, who have it, cannot pass it over to others." [17]

A strict interpretation of the Lockean principle would have produced a rigid separation of powers. Presumably legislation would be self-explanatory, so the subsequent presidential action would be mere "office-boy" execution. Since Locke used the term *transfer*, it is reasonable to assume that he was referring to delegation without any subsequent control, that is, abdication. At any rate, as Edward S. Corwin has pointed out, the Supreme Court first attempted to judge delegation in terms of a strict view of the distinction between legislation and execution and then gave up. In 1904, Justice Edward White, speaking for the Court, said:

> Congress legislated on the subjects as far as was reasonably practicable, and from the necessities of the case was compelled to leave to executive officials the duty of bringing about the result pointed out by the statute. To deny the power of Congress to delegate such a duty would, in effect, amount but to declaring that the plenary power vested in Congress to regulate foreign commerce could not be efficaciously exercised. [18]

Delegation increased with the New Deal, and the Court invalidated two laws on the ground of excessive delegation in 1935. In one case, Justice Benjamin Cardozo described the National Industrial Recovery Act as "delegation run riot," but such hesitancy on the part of the Court was short-lived. Subsequent decisions of 1937 and after upheld extensive regulatory delegation. [19] This broad delegation of legislative power involves a very significant amount of mixing and sharing of governmental powers. Executive departments exercise legislative power when they promulgate rules, and regulatory agencies exercise what has been called quasilegislative and quasijudicial powers when they do.

AN ANSWER TO LEGISLATIVE DELEGATION

By qualifying its delegation of power with provisions for disapproval or termination resolutions, Congress has found a means to benefit from the energy in the executive branch and the expertise of the bureaucracy, while retaining control over the exercise of legislative power. The requirements of big government in the twentieth century do not allow any other alternative that would permit Congress to retain its constitutional vigor. Cutting back significantly on delegation, or relying on full-scale legislation to correct improper regulations, is not satisfactory; the latter is far too time-consuming and the former would necessitate a massive reduction in governmental activity. If such a reduction is desired, it should be considered on its merits, not as a consequence of prohibiting qualified delegation of legislative power. In addition, it is difficult to discipline offending agencies through oversight or reduced budgets.

The general argument for the congressional veto was clearly stated by Corwin long before the device was widely used.

> It is generally agreed that Congress, being free not to delegate, is free to do so on certain stipulated conditions, as, for example, that the delegation shall terminate by a certain date or on the occurrence of a specified event; the end of a war, for instance. Why then, should not one condition be that the delegation shall continue only as long as the two houses are of opinion that it is working beneficially? As we have seen, moreover, it is generally agreed that the maxim that the legislature may not *delegate* its powers signifies at the very least that the legislature may not *abdicate* its power. Yet how, in view of the scope that legislative delegations take nowadays, is the line between *delegation* and *abdication* to be maintained? Only, I urge, by rendering the delegated powers recoverable without the consent of the delegate.[20]

The constitutional authorities who disagree with Corwin adopt either a strict functional view of the separation of powers or a strict view of delegation. An example of the first sort of critic is H. Lee Watson, who begins his argument against the congressional veto as follows:

> The basic function of Congress is to legislate. Normally, Congress has no further role after it considers and passes on a bill or votes whether to override in the event of a presidential veto.
>
> Congress steps outside of the legislative process when it passes and acts according to a statute authorizing later action by resolution or committee vote, thereby retaining jurisdiction over the subject mat-

ter of legislation. Such a statute creates a new role for Congress, ambiguously situated between the legislative and executive functions.[21]

Watson's argument against the congressional veto is based on a strict functional separation of powers. He refers to a new role for Congress, in an area apparently in "no-man's land," and yet he acknowledges that the constitutionally prescribed powers of impeachment, treaty making, and appointment are likewise not strictly legislative. After reviewing the development of congressional resolutions requesting information or reports from the executive branch and congressional adminstration of services necessary to the legislative function, Watson insists that they differ in kind from the congressional veto, because "in each of these cases . . . the purpose of Congress was the facilitation of legislation rather than its execution."[22] We cannot regard this fine line as persuasively drawn, if we recall that the purpose of the congressional veto is to control the legislative power which has been delegated.

An example of the second sort of critic of the congressional veto is Antonin Scalia, formerly an assistant attorney general in the Justice Department, who makes the following argument against the review provision of the Executive Reorganization Act of 1977:

> Congress must either delegate to the president the authority to reorganize the Executive Branch, subject to their undoing his work through the normal process of legislation, or else they must themselves adopt such reorganization through the constitutionally prescribed legislative process. . . . In creating a form of governmental action which lies somewhere between these two acknowledged constitutional forms, the present bill evades the deterrent and the restraint which they contain, and this substantially reduces the people's control over their government.[23]

This argument emphasizes the need to delegate without conditions for the sake of popular control of government. Scalia does not explain how popular control is enhanced by congressional delegation of legislative power which is not subject to effective oversight and control. On the other hand, it is not feasible for Congress to avoid delegation today. The only means of assuring a popular control over administrative rule making is to permit

Congress, which is the most politically responsive branch of government, to scrutinize proposed regulations.

Whereas critics of the congressional veto begin from a position that restricts the powers of Congress, our constitutional founders intended that an expansive approach be taken towards Congress and the new national government. For example, in the classic case on the powers of Congress, *McCulloch* v. *Maryland*, Chief Justice John Marshall reminded us that "it is a constitution we are expounding," as opposed to a prolix legal code, and that it is "intended to endure for ages to come, and consequently to be adapted to the various *crises* of human affairs." While the specific issue in *McCulloch* involved the range of congressional powers vis-à-vis the states, the same principle applies where a new device permits Congress to retain its coordinate status by effectively participating in major governmental policies and overseeing administrative rule making. Marshall's general test for the scope of Congress' powers was:

> Let the end be legitimate, let it be within the scope of the constitution, and all means which are appropriate, which are plainly adapted to that end, which are not prohibited but consist with the letter and spirit of the constitution, are constitutional.[24]

In such a test, the only serious constitutional question is raised by the presentation clause of Article I, section 7, which is not insurmountable and is discussed below. Certainly on the basis of the general purpose of the separation of powers, the congressional veto is a model of adaptation to changing circumstances within the constitutional framework. The *Federalist* was rightly concerned about legislative tyranny, but Madison, Jefferson, and Hamilton knew that the time of executive government would come. Although they did not greet that prospect with the same amount of apprehension or anticipation, their views on the constitutional separation of powers do not lend support to the contention that the congressional veto is an impermissible response to executive government. For, while it is a relatively new device in American constitutionalism, the congressional veto was fashioned to serve the founding aims of efficiency and political balance.

MAJOR CONSTITUTIONAL ISSUES

We turn now to an examination of the major constitutional issues raised by the congressional veto. These include the presentation clause, bicameralism, and the relationship between executive power and administration.

The Constitution's Presentation Clause. The strongest constitutional argument against the congressional veto rests on the last paragraph of Article I, section 7, clause 3:

> Every Order, Resolution, or Vote to which the Concurrence of the Senate and House of Representatives may be necessary (except on a question of adjournment) shall be presented to the President of the United States; and before the same bill shall take effect, shall be approved by him, or being disapproved by him, shall be repassed by two thirds of the Senate and House of Representatives, according to the Rules and Limitations prescribed in the Case of a Bill.

In the Federal Convention Madison argued for the inclusion of this language, "observing that if the negative of the President was confined to bills; it would be evaded by acts under the form and name of Resolutions, votes, etc."[25]

The argument against the congressional veto is that it is substantive legislation by a means which unconstitutionally evades the executive's veto. Congress could, as an alternative, either ask for executive branch proposals, which would be subject to the full legislative process, or delegate legislative power and require a certain waiting period, during which Congress could pass a statute, or a joint resolution (which is presented to the president) disapproving of the proposed action or regulation. My argument is that the Constitution does not require these less efficient devices, because the congressional veto is not independent legislation. Rather, it is qualified delegation, which is a part of previous legislation which was presented to the president. The evidence which will be presented demonstrates that this interpretation is at least as valid as the one which disallows the veto. Given two equally plausible constitutional interpretations, the one which serves the fundamental constitutional requirement of an effective Congress should be favored.

Robert W. Ginnane, in his critical article "The Control of Federal Administration by Congressional Resolutions and Committees," cites Madison's statement on the reach of the presidential veto to support his conclusion that except for adjournment, "policymaking decisions of Congress must be submitted to the President." Therefore he does not think Congress can exercise administrative oversight with concurrent resolutions of disapproval.[26]

Ginnane also cites an 1897 Report of the Senate Judiciary Committee, on the subject of joint and concurrent resolutions and their approval by the president, in support of his contention that "concurrent resolutions were appropriate only in matters which were the exclusive concern of the two Houses—such as printing joint rules, and expressing the sense of Congress upon a given subject."[27]

The action precipitating the Senate report concerned a Rivers and Harbors Appropriations Act of 1892 and subsequent resolutions requesting information on a harbor.[28] The report concluded that requests for information did not require the president's consent. The committee's interpretation of Article I, section 7, which is cited in *Hinds' Precedents of the House of Representatives* as the authoritative statement, was:

> We conclude this branch of the subject by deciding [that] the general question submitted to us, to wit, "whether concurrent resolutions are required to be submitted to the President of the United States," must depend not upon their mere form, but upon the fact whether they contain matter which is properly to be regarded as legislative in its character and effect. If they do they must be presented for his approval; otherwise they need not be. In other words, we hold that the clause in the Constitution which declares that every order, resolution, or vote must be presented to the President to "which the concurrence of the Senate and House of Representatives may be necessary" refers to the necessity occasioned by the requirement of the other provisions of the Constitution, whereby every exercise of the "legislative powers" involves the concurrence of the two Houses; and every resolution not so requiring such concurrent action, to wit, not involving the exercise of legislative powers, need not be presented to the President. In brief, the nature of the substance of the resolution, and not its form, controls the question of its disposition.[29]

Ginnane's interpretation of the limited reach of this precedent rests on a distinction between "legislative mechanics and legislation,"[30] similar to Watson's distinction between the facilitation of legislation and execution. Granted that the congressional veto goes beyond previous examples of concurrent resolutions, such as requests for reports from the executive branch, it is a mode of oversight of administration. That supports my contention that the congressional veto is not separate and independent legislation; it is qualified delegation, which must be in the service of a legislative purpose, of legislation that is presented to the president. On the other hand, it is more than "legislative mechanics." The language of the Senate report refers to matter "which is properly to be regarded as legislative in its character and effect."

A congressional veto, by disapproving a proposed action or regulation, or terminating a specifically authorized executive action, seems to have the effect of legislation. It also, to return to the language of John Marshall, contravenes the letter of Article I, section 7's statement about every order, resolution, or vote requiring the concurrence of both houses, except adjournment. How, then, can the congressional veto be reconciled with the presentation clause?

The argument in favor of the congressional veto as a more efficient and constitutional alternative to the full legislative process goes as follows. Wherever Congress has the power to legislate, it has the power to delegate, and where it can delegate it can delegate subject to a congressional review of the proposed regulation or action. If the requirements of efficiency suggest a delegation to the president or to an agency, then the requirements of consent necessitate a second look at the topic after it has been developed into a specific proposal or course of action.

Applying this argument to the presentation clause, recall that Madison was concerned about semantic justifications for legislative usurpations of the executive veto. It was, of course, not yet known that the executive veto would develop into a fully discretionary political power; that the removal power would be regarded as constitutionally based in the executive alone; that the executive would have control of a centralized bureau of the bud-

get; and that substantial legislative power would have to be delegated. Furthermore, the 1897 Senate's "character and effect" test
is also satisfied as applied to the entire act of qualified delegation
of legislative power. That is, as long as the original legislation is
presented to the president for his signature or veto, and as long as
what is reserved for congressional approval or disapproval is a
power that Congress could have exercised originally, then this
more efficient means of delegation with subsequent review is
constitutional.

We find support for this position from former Attorney General, and later Justice, Robert H. Jackson, who made public an
important presidential legal opinion on the congressional veto, or
termination, provision in the Lend Lease Act of 1941 after the
publication of Ginnane's article in 1953. The law conferred special
authority on the president to sell, transfer, exchange, lease, or
otherwise dispose of certain defense articles for countries deemed
vital to the defense of the United States. The law then set the following limits:

> After June 30, 1943, or after the passage of a concurrent resolution of
> the two Houses before June 30, 1943, which declares that the powers
> conferred by or pursuant to subsection (a) are no longer necessary to
> promote the defense of the United States, neither the President nor
> the head of any department or agency shall exercise any of the
> powers conferred by or pursuant to subsection (a).[31]

Jackson reported that Secretary of State Edward R. Stettinius, Jr.,
regarded the termination provision as "not damaging to the essential principles of the Bill and designed to meet criticism from
the opposition that the Bill gave too much power to the Executive."[32] President Roosevelt regarded the provision as unconstitutional, but he could not say so openly because it would have
undermined his congressional support. Opponents of the bill
agreed with the president on the constitutional question, and for
that reason argued against the entire measure. The president's
supporters argued that the measure was both constitutional and
that it provided a sufficient check on the executive.

President Roosevelt instructed Jackson to have a memorandum
drafted for him to submit to the attorney general expressing his
opinion that the measure was unconstitutional. Jackson recounts

how he had this done, and, also at the president's instruction, how he kept it among his personal papers, making it known only in 1953 after Ginnane's article was published. The memorandum argued that the concurrent resolution terminating the delegated power was a repeal of legislation by unconstitutional means, since it avoided the presidential veto. Jackson regarded this as a "debatable point," formulating the issue as follows:

> The question on which my doubts were not fully satisfied never bothered the President in the least. It seemed to me to depend on whether the provision was to be considered as a reservation or limitation by which granted power would expire or terminate on the contingency of a concurrent resolution or was to be regarded as authorizing a repeal by concurrent resolution.[33]

It is my contention that Congress may regard the congressional veto as a reservation or limitation on granted power, which expires or terminates on the contingency of a concurrent or simple (or in some cases committee) resolution, as long as Congress is delegating part of its legislative power. Hence, the presentation clause is satisfied by the original statute's being presented to the president.

In addition, note that, except for the cases of rule making delegated to regulatory agencies, Congress gives the president, or one of his political appointees, the power to initiate action or propose a rule. Acknowledging this fact, in part, Attorney General Griffin Bell took the position that congressional veto provisions in administrative reorganization statutes were constitutional. In his letter of January 31, 1977, the attorney general took the position that reorganization statutes permit the president to "submit to Congress only those plans which he approves." This differs from congressional review of administrative rule making where "the pressures of an ongoing program with prior commitments force a president to act." The attorney general argues that since urgency of action increases congressional influence "and effectively compromises the President's control over his actions, such statutes frustrate the constitutional check of the presidential veto in violation of Article I and infringe on the doctrine of separation of powers."[34] The attorney general's argument seems to have been based more on political considerations than on constitutional principles, since there is no constitutional basis for his distinction.

Executive branch ambivalence toward the congressional veto is also present in President Carter's June 21, 1978, statement on the subject. He associates himself with every president since Herbert Hoover in his opposition to the congressional veto, but then he accepts it in reorganization statutes, which originally provoked presidential opposition. After threatening to ignore congressional vetoes by treating them as "report and wait" provisions only, the president says Congress responded to the abuses of executive power, associated with President Richard Nixon, by "enacting constructive safeguards in such areas as war powers and the budget process." He goes on to say that "the legislative veto is an overreaction which increases conflict between the branches of government." [35] Yet the veto provisions of the war powers and budget and impoundments control acts were precisely what permitted Congress to reclaim its constitutional powers.

I agree with the attorney general when he says that the true test of the presentation clause dispute turns on the effect of the congressional veto on the constitutional separation of powers. I disagree with his contention that by putting a qualification on its own delegation of legislative power, Congress violates the separation of powers. It is hardly true, as the attorney general implies, that Congress will therefore "dominate the executive." I also agree with the president on the importance of the major legislation of the 93rd, or Watergate Congress. I simply note with surprise his inability to recognize that he was praising statutes containing the very device he condemns.

Except for the existence of regulatory agencies, over which the president has no control after appointing the commissioners, one could fashion a narrower constitutional argument for the congressional veto than the one presented here. One could describe the congressional veto as a form of reverse legislation. As long as the president controls the department or agency that is promulgating the regulations, he has an effective participation in the delegated power. Judge Bell's objection was that the control is illusory with respect to the numerous regulations. The control is certainly potentially there, and the president can direct that certain regulations be proposed or withdrawn. The case for the congressional veto cannot rest on this argument by itself, however, because the review of independent agency regulations is at least as important as the review of executive department regulations. Independence from the president's removal power does not imply independence of Congress, especially not when the agency's powers are described as "quasi-legislative" and "quasi-judicial." This particular argument will be considered more fully in connection with our consideration of executive power and its relation to administration.

Bicameralism. The congressional veto provisions, with some insignificant exceptions, involve one or both houses. The bicameralism principle, if it is used as a guide, would seem to require the approval of both houses for a proposed regulation or action to take effect. While the constitutional requirement of bicameralism is satisfied by the original legislation authorizing the congressional veto, it is worth considering whether disapproval resolutions support the intent of bicameralism, which is a full collective deliberation. In this context, bicameralism would not necessarily favor concurrent over simple resolutions, however. For example, if a regulation is proposed by the president or one of his political appointees, bicameralism would suggest either a concurrent resolution of approval or a simple resolution of disapproval. In those two cases, both houses would have to be in agreement, either actively or passively, for the proposal to take effect. To require a concurrent resolution of disapproval, or a simple resolution of approval, would mean that such an action could go ahead without the agreement of both houses, in apparent violation of the principle of bicameralism. Congressional practice follows the bicameralism analogy only partly. For example, CRS figures on procedures involving the Senate and House as entities show 127 approval or disapproval resolutions, classified as follows:[36]

Concurrent resolutions of disapproval	34
Concurrent resolutions of approval	16

Simple resolutions of disapproval	53
Simple resolutions of approval	0
Concurrent resolutions terminating activity prior to scheduled time	8
Concurrent resolutions approving, contravening, or rescinding executive proposals	6
Miscellaneous resolutions	10

From these figures we may conclude that the principle of bicameralism is followed in most cases, and in the most significant category where it is not followed—the thirty-four cases in which a concurrent resolution of disapproval is provided for—the presumption is with the president to exercise a delegated power and the burden of responsibility is with Congress to disallow the exercise of that delegated power.

A few examples of legislation fitting the different veto devices illustrate the reason for the diversity. Consider the War Powers Act of 1973, the Congressional Budget and Impoundment Control Act of 1974, and the International Security Assistance and Arms Export Control Act of 1976.[37] The War Powers Act directs the president, once he has committed American forces to foreign combat in the absence of a declaration of war or any other specific statute, to report to Congress within forty-eight hours, and to terminate the hostilities within, at most, ninety days in the absence of explicit congressional support. In addition, Congress can, by a concurrent resolution, terminate hostilities immediately. The Congressional Budget and Impoundment Control Act includes two forms of congressional veto for the two different forms of presidential impoundment. For the more drastic rescissions the president reports to Congress and a concurrent resolution of approval must be passed within forty-five days, or the budget authority must be made available for obligation. For deferral, the president makes the same report, and the budget authority must be made available for obligation if either house passes an "impoundment resolution" disapproving the proposed deferral at any time after receipt of the special message. In the case of rescission, the subject matter dictates that the burden of proof lies with the president. The Arms Export Control Act puts the burden on Congress to disallow a proposed sale. Under section 211 of this act, the president transmits to Congress notice of his intention to sell arms to foreign countries. Congress has the power to disapprove the sale by a concurrent resolution, which must be passed within thirty days of formal notification. This provision might be said to violate the bicameralism principle, since one house might disapprove of the sale and be unable to persuade the other house to disapprove, but both houses had to agree to the law initially and the subject matter suggests that Congress rightly intended to place the major responsibility with the president.

Congress' assignment of veto devices to legislation has reflected a sober consideration of the kind of power involved as well as the principle of bicameralism. Where bicameralism is departed from, the departure is due to the importance of the subject matter for presidential consideration. The executive's proposals are given greater weight than they would otherwise have.

Committee vetoes are certainly the most significant examples of departure from bicameralism, since they do not even provide for deliberation by a single legislative chamber. Nine of the sixty-one current statutes with congressional vetoes contain committee disapproval provisions. As noted above, since our constitutional argument does not regard the congressional veto as independent legislation, committee vetoes are not immediately suspect. It would be surprising, even inappropriate, if Congress gave final review authority to committees in matters of prime political importance. Examination of the nine cases of committee vetoes reveals that Congress has applied the division of labor with due regard for its responsibilities. Examples of statutes with committee vetoes include special projects in education, certain public works provisions, the Eisenhower Memorial Bicentennial Civic Art Center, reprogramming of funds for foreign assistance and related programs (appropriations committees), and pilot projects regarding food stamps.

Executive Power and the Administration of Government. We return to an issue that Hamilton and Madison disagreed on as early as 1789:

the relationship between executive power and the administration of government. As applied to the congressional veto, the question becomes: at what point does Congress unconstitutionally infringe either on the president's power as chief executive or on the power of independent administrative agencies? Since Hamilton's position has generally gained acceptance, let us begin with his robust definition of administration:

> The administration of government, in its largest sense, comprehends all the operations of the body politics, whether legislative, executive, or judiciary; but in its most precise signification, it is limited to executive details, and falls peculiarly within the province of the executive department. The actual conduct of foreign negotiations, the preparatory plans of finance, the application and disbursement of the public moneys in conformity to the general appropriations of the legislature, the arrangement of the army and navy, the direction of the operations of war—these, and other matters of a like nature, constitute what seems to be most properly understood by the administration of government.[38]

When we ask what administration is, one source of confusion is the tendency to identify all of government with administration. But even Hamilton's limited definition goes beyond mere executive details to comprehend important governmental activities, such as the management of the budget and foreign affairs. Thus, as governmental activity increases, administration will also increase. For example, a recent Joint Economic Committee study showed that the regulatory budget is increasing more rapidly than the overall federal budget. The 1978 study estimated that spending for the federal regulatory agencies would reach $4.8 billion in 1979, and the cost to the economy, of the regulations they promulgate, would be $97.9 billion in 1979.[39]

Obviously the question "who governs?" is not settled at the level of general legislation, or even with the passage of authorization and appropriation bills. Congress uses the congressional veto as a means of ensuring effective oversight of administrative rules and regulations. Can an argument be made, in the name of executive power, which denies Congress the right to interfere in administration?

We have already considered a general account of executive

power which supports the congressional veto. We shall now examine Supreme Court decisions on the appointment and removal powers to see whether the veto, by giving Congress a negative participation in administration, is invalid.

The Supreme Court decision which has been cited to support the limited view of congressional powers is *Springer* v. *Philippine Islands*.[40] The Court held that the separation of powers provisions of the Philippine constitution, patterned after the American, were violated by a law which gave the legislative officers the power to vote the stock which elected the directors and managing agents of corporations created by the legislature. While the holding was based on the appointment power, here taking the form of voting shares of stock to appoint the officers, this dictum has been cited by opponents of the congressional veto:

> It may be stated, then, as a general rule inherent in the American constitutional system that, unless otherwise expressly provided or incidental to the power conferred, the legislature cannot exercise either executive or judicial power; the executive cannot exercise either legislative or judicial power; the judiciary cannot exercise either legislative or executive power. The existence in the various constitutions of occasional provisions expressly giving to one of the departments powers which by their nature otherwise would fall within the general scope of the authority of another department emphasizes, rather than casts doubt upon, the generally inviolate character of this basic rule.[41]

This rigid interpretation of the separation of powers, which finds no support in the Constitution, drew a dissent from Justices Holmes and Brandeis:

> It does not seem to need argument to show that however we may disguise it by unveiling words we do not and cannot carry out the distinction between legislative and executive action with mathematical precision and divide the branches into watertight compartments, were it ever so desirable to do so, which I am far from believing that it is, or that the Constitution requires.[42]

While it is true, as Ginnane pointed out, that *Springer* "has never been qualified by the Supreme Court or by the lower federal courts,"[43] it applies only to the narrow holding regarding appointments, not to the obiter dicta regarding the separation of powers.[44]

Then in *Humphrey's Executor* v. *United States*, decided in 1935, the Supreme Court upheld the law establishing the Federal Trade Commission, including the part which insulated the commissioners from the president by giving them fixed terms and limiting their prior removal for cause only. In qualifying the earlier *Myers* v. *United States* (1926) decision, which upheld the president's right to remove a postmaster at his discretion, the Court distinguished executive officers from "quasi-legislative, quasi-judicial" officers:

> The commission is to be non-partisan; and it must, from the very nature of its duties, act with entire impartiality. It is charged with the enforcement of no policy except the policy of the law. Its duties are neither political nor executive, but predominantly quasi-judicial and quasi-legislative.[45]

The *Humphrey's* decision sanctioned a significant restriction on executive power, by insulating regulatory commissions from presidential control. Such a decision certainly undermines the general rule articulated in *Springer*, according to which all governmental powers are either legislative, executive, or judicial, and that each power is set off in a separate watertight compartment, to borrow from the Holmes-Brandeis dissent. Even aside from *Humphrey's*, however, the *Springer* decision should not be regarded as having any validity outside the specific context of appointment, because the principle of the separation of powers which Justice Sutherland articulated is wrong: it never carried the day in the debates on the construction of the Constitution and it will simply not work in practice. *Springer* and *Humphrey's*, taken together, suggest a very narrow sphere of exclusive executive action; appointment, removal of officers that are executive (where that determination will have to be made by legislative fiat to be clear), and the specific carrying out of law or policy as applied to individuals.

The only argument against the congressional veto that could be made on the basis of *Humphrey's*, and a subsequent decision which upheld the power of independent agencies to make rules not subject to presidential control,[46] would be made on behalf of a politically independent administration. At this point we should note an odd transformation in the case against the congressional veto. First, a strict view of separation of powers prohibits the veto. Now the alleged necessity of keeping regulatory agencies, with their quasi-judicial and quasi-legislative activities, wholly independent prohibits the veto of their regulations. Or is it that if the president cannot control the agencies, neither can Congress?

Jacob Javits and Gary J. Klein make these arguments in a recent law review article. They take the position that the presentation clause requires that the president not only have the enacting legislation presented to him for his signature, but "also have a role equivalent to his presidential power." This would prohibit congressional vetoes of independent agency regulations. Javits and Klein give two additional reasons for this interpretation:

> First, postenactment congressional control would render any regulations promulgated by the agencies subject only to the influence of Congress. Although no express constitutional injunction against an increase in congressional authority over the rulemaking functions of these agencies exists—at least with respect to matters that Congress could have initially controlled by legislation—the agencies perform administrative functions as well. Postenactment review which in effect converts these bodies into direct agents of Congress thus presents separation of powers problems. Second, to the extent that these agencies exercise congressional influence over policymaking could probe perilously close to the adjudicative area.[47]

On the second point, administrative orders which result from the adjudication of individual claims are not covered by the Administrative Rulemaking Reform Act, which will be discussed more fully below. On the first point, it is interesting that they find no separation of powers problems with administrative agencies existing outside the legislative and executive branches of government. If agency independence from the president is necessary, however, it is also necessary to make sure that the administrative regulations are consistent with legislative intent. Furthermore, the regulations are clearly legislative activities, as the term *rulemaking* implies. Making legislation more precise may be desirable, but it is not always possible. Nor is it sufficient with 7031 final rules published in the Federal Register in 1977.[48] The conflict here is not between Congress and the president, but between the political branches of government and the bureaucracy. Republican government requires that the politically responsible branches of government be in a position to direct and oversee the activities of the civil service. That the president is unable to control independent agencies because Congress judges that certain regulatory activities should be free of presidential control does not imply that Congress also should be prohibited from overseeing those agencies. The power at issue is legislative and the control is different. The power to say "no" to a proposed regulation differs from the power to control agency directors or to propose the regulations.[49] Congress may well become more active in its oversight of administration, but, as I will contend later on, considerations of time and resources preclude its getting overly involved in the administrative process.

We turn now to the Supreme Court's recent opinion in *Buckley* v. *Valeo*,[50] which upheld parts of the Federal Election Campaign Act of 1974 and overturned other parts, including the original mode of appointing the commissioners. While the Court did not explicitly reach the congressional veto provision in the law, Justice Byron White, in a partially concurring and partially dissenting opinion, discussed it favorably:

> Under section 438 (c) the FEC's regulations are subject to disapproval; but for a regulation to become effective, neither House need approve it, pass it, or take any action at all with respect to it. The regulation becomes effective by non-action. This no more invades the President's powers than does a regulation not required to be laid before Congress. Congressional influence over the substantive content of agency regulations may be enhanced, but I would not view the power of either House to disapprove as equivalent to legislation or to an order, resolution or vote requiring the concurrence of both Houses.
>
> I would be much more concerned if Congress purported to usurp the functions of law enforcement, to control the outcome of particular adjudications, or to pre-empt the President's appointment power; but in light of history and modern reality, the provision for congressional disapproval of agency regulations does not appear to transgress the constitutional design, at least where the President has agreed to legislation establishing the disapproval procedure or the legislation has passed over his veto. It would be considerably different if Congress

itself purported to adopt and propound regulations by the actions of both Houses. But here no action of either House is required for the agency rule to go into effect and the veto power of the President does not appear to be implicated.[51]

In addition to the *Buckley* case, the Supreme Court recently let stand a decision of the Court of Claims which upheld the one-house veto provisions of the Federal Salary Act of 1967. The Court of Claims was careful to limit itself to the context in which the one-house veto was attacked. Under the law, a commission proposes salary increases which become effective unless either house vetoes them. This case and the companion cases involved the power of Congress to regulate the pay of members of Congress, judges, and members of the executive branch. The Court said:

> Article I, section 1 endows Congress with the broadest reach of power in this instance, so long as executive functions are not infringed and presidential veto rights not compromised, because the subject of the one House veto, the salaries of judges and congressmen and other government officers, is at the center of the congressional sphere. On this foundation, the necessary and proper clause authorizes Congress to choose, first, to delegate the initial power to make proposals to the President, and, then, to select for itself the appropriate method for checking and monitoring the President's action.[52]

After citing *McCulloch* on the necessary and proper clause, and the district court's decision upholding the one-house veto against the objections of an individual congressman in *Pressler* v. *Simon*, the court stated this general principle: "Where there has been no violation of separation of powers principles or of any specific provisions of the Constitution, the necessary and proper clause can authorize a given method of obtaining a desired result, as well as ground a substantive provision (as in *McCulloch*)."[53]

If, as we have argued, qualified delegation does not violate the presentation clause, no specific provision is violated by the congressional veto, whether it affects salaries or any other subject within Congress' jurisdiction. Furthermore, since the *Buckley* Court said that Congress' power is plenary in all areas in which it has substantive legislative jurisdiction,[54] it undermined any suggestion that the veto, having been upheld in one area, might still be invalidated in another.

USES OF THE CONGRESSIONAL VETO

According to a CRS study, of the 351 approval or disapproval resolutions offered from 1960 to 1975 (85 in the Senate, 266 in the
House), over 300 came from the following five subjects: disposal
of materials from the national stockpile—14; executive reorganization plans presented by the president—59; federal employee
pay levels—109; proposed budget expenditure deferrals and rescissions—106; and foreign assistance—16.[55] That distribution
only partially describes the significance of the veto today. For one
thing, the veto provisions of the War Powers Act of 1973 have not
yet been tested but are of great significance for presidential leadership in foreign affairs. Likewise, the Arms Export Control Act
of 1976, which produced a full-scale debate on the Mideast arms
sale in 1978, is another example of congressional participation in
foreign affairs. Of course, the veto is not the only device for this:
The Clark Amendment to the 1976 Military Aid bill prohibited
direct or indirect aid to Angola for military or paramilitary operations.[56] Despite the number of resolutions offered, and many
were multiple copies of the same measure, the CRS study found
that only 63 were actually passed and became effective during
the years 1960 to 1975. Of that number, 44 were passed in 1975
alone. Furthermore, 40 of the 63 resolutions involved budget
resolutions.[57]

If we classified vetoes by subject matter, from the least to the
most controversial, from either a constitutional or political perspective, it would look like this:

1. Executive reorganization
2. Budget resolutions
3. Federal salary increases
4. Interstate and foreign commerce (Arms Export Act)
5. Immigration law cases involving the suspension of deporta-
    tion orders
6. War powers
7. Comprehensive veto of agency rules and regulations

The veto over executive reorganization acts is the oldest, and
even the Justice Department accepts it now.[58] It is clearly a form
of "reverse legislation" that permits the president to propose

what he wants and have it go into effect unless Congress disapproves. The budget resolutions are part of an act that established a Congressional Budget Office and an orderly congressional budgetary process in order that Congress might assume more responsibility for spending. Congressional control over presidential impoundment, which President Richard Nixon developed to such an art, has not drawn special criticism from critics of the congressional veto. The power of the purse is after all distinctly congressional. The setting of federal salaries involves the same power, and the veto provision was upheld in the courts. The full debate on the Mideast arms sale informed the public and established support for selling F-15 fighter planes to Saudi Arabia. No one objected to the disapproval mechanism, and the congressional power over commerce is clear. The final three examples are more controversial and merit lengthier consideration.

Suspension of Deportation Orders. Congress has the power, under Article I, section 8, clause 4, to pass naturalization laws. With that power, and under the necessary and proper clause, it has taken a special interest in the administration of immigration statutes. The Immigration and Naturalization Act of 1952[59] authorizes the attorney general to suspend deportation of an alien and adjust his status to "lawfully admitted for permanent residence" where the person has been in the country for seven years and proves he is of good moral character and that his deportation would result in extreme hardship to himself or his immediate family, if a member of that family is a citizen or a lawfully admitted alien. Section 244 (c) (1) requires the attorney general to submit a statement of every proposed case for suspension of deportation to Congress. Section 244 (c) (2) permits either house to pass a resolution of disapproval of the proposed suspension, in which case the deportation takes place.

A case challenging this one-house veto is before the Ninth Circuit. Petitioner Chadha was a student in this country under nonimmigrant status. After finishing his studies and after being here for seven years, he petitioned for a suspension of deportation and for permanent residency, alleging that as an Asian he was not welcome in Kenya, where he was born, and that the United

Kingdom could not give him an employment voucher for at least a year. Given these facts, an immigration judge found that Chadha met the requirements for a suspension, and, on his recommendation, the attorney general recommended it. The House Subcommittee on Immigration and Naturalization reviewed 340 cases and reported to the House, recommending disapproval of the proposed suspension in Chadha's case and five others. The subcommittee reported to the House that these six cases did not meet the requirements of "extreme hardship" established in the law, and Congress voted the disapproval resolution. Chadha is suing on the grounds that the one-house veto is unconstitutional. The opposing party, the Immigration and Naturalization Service, agrees with Chadha on the constitutional issue, raising some doubt as to the existence of a true case or controversy. Due to the importance of the issue, Congress has been permitted to file *amicus curiae* briefs.[60]

Since the congressional veto only nullifies the proposed suspension, it is not punishment in the constitutional sense. Congress is simply withdrawing a proposed benefit, or exemption from the law, on the grounds that it was improperly applied by the attorney general. Counsel for the House of Representatives even argues that this is not a true veto case, since the executive action is "limited by statute to the discretionary grant of temporary suspension orders."[61] As with private bills, however, Congress is acting on individuals in particular cases. A remark of Madison's in the Federal Convention lends support to this congressional concern about immigration law. Objecting to a motion to attach a fourteen-year citizenship requirement for election to the Senate, Madison said it was improper not only for its illiberality, but also "because it will put it out of the power of the National legislature even by special acts of naturalization to confer the full rank of citizens on meritorious strangers and because it will discourage the most desirable class of people from emigrating to the United States."[62]

From a strict constitutional perspective, this is the most questionable example of the congressional veto. It appears to violate Justice White's requirement that Congress not control the outcome of particular adjudications. Congress decides which deportation orders may be suspended on a case-by-case basis. On the other hand, Congress can point to the long-established practice of private bills as well as the inference from Madison that it can reach individual naturalization and immigration cases. We cannot conclude, therefore, that this veto is unconstitutional, although it penetrates more deeply into administration, in the strict sense, than any other. Of course, one wonders whether Congress might not be able to assist the Justice Department by providing legislative guidelines for the "extreme hardship" test.

War Powers. The War Powers Act of 1973 exemplifies the disjunction between constitutionality and wisdom. It is easier to conjure up situations in which the restrictions on the president's power to commence and prosecute hostilities may inhibit sound political action than it is to argue that Congress did not have the power to do what it did. The commander-in-chief clause of the Constitution reads: "The President shall be Commander in Chief of the Army and Navy of the United States, and of the Militia of the several states, when called into the actual service of the United States." Until the War Powers Act, presidents could cite treaty obligations, or authorizations such as the Tonkin Gulf Resolution, or appropriations, as authority for prosecuting undeclared wars. Now, the president has ninety days to get an explicit authorization, and Congress may, by concurrent resolution order him to withdraw forces engaged in hostilities. Congress decided that ninety days was long enough for the president to respond to sudden attacks on his authority alone. Do these provisions violate the commander-in-chief clause?

President Abraham Lincoln's emergency actions at the start of the civil war, which included his calling out the militia, paying money out of the treasury from unappropriated funds, blockading the southern ports, and suspending the privilege of the writ of habeas corpus, as well as his later Emancipation Proclamation have been cited as the origin of the development of the executive power and commander-in-chief clauses into the modern presidential war powers.[63] But neither the suspension of the writ of habeas corpus nor the Emancipation Proclamation gives support to an interpretation of the executive's war powers that would render the congressional veto provisions of the war powers act un-constitutional. As for Lincoln's actions at the start of the war, he subsequently sought congressional approval in his Special Message to Congress on July 4, 1861. As for emancipation, Lincoln conceded that as a political rather than a military action it came under congressional jurisdiction, and he recommended legislation for compensated emancipation. Congress passed a resolution offering financial assistance to any state that adopted gradual emancipation. Only after the states did not act, and emancipation became essential to the preservation of the union, did he issue the Proclamation. Furthermore, since it was justified as a military necessity, the Proclamation covered only those states, and parts of states, that were in rebellion. Finally, the president acknowledged that the Proclamation might not be valid as law and urged the passage of a constitutional amendment. And later, in his Message to Congress of December 6, 1864, he said: "If the people should, by whatever mode or means, make it an executive duty to re-enslave such persons, another, and not I, must be their instrument to perform it." [64]

The exclusive sphere of presidential power that President Lincoln claimed is not substantial enough to argue against the War Powers Act on its face. The Union's existence would have to be endangered in a direct and compelling way for President Lincoln's precedents to apply. Only such a threat would justify presidential disobedience of the War Powers Act.

Justice Jackson's well-known formulation of executive power, in his concurring opinion in the *Steel Seizure* case, supports the constitutionality of the War Powers Act also. The justice does not delineate the boundaries of the president's war powers, but he does say that a president can do much less in explicit opposition to Congress than he can do in the absence of legislation. Jackson's reference to "a zone of twilight in which the President and Congress may have concurrent authority, or in which its distribution is uncertain" suggests the constitutionality of both the presidential action in Vietnam and the War Powers Act. [65]

The Administrative Rulemaking Reform Act. The specific issue surrounding the proposed comprehensive veto of agency regulations does not involve constitutionality so much as the desirability of such congressional involvement in administration. The purpose of HR 1776 (96th Congress), the Administrative Rulemaking Reform Act, is to permit Congress to disapprove any proposed regulation without having to go through the full-scale legislative process. Very few of the seven thousand regulations promulgated annually would receive a full review. A Congressional Budget Office cost estimate assumed that one hundred would be reviewed. The one hundred would surely be the controversial or troublesome regulations that might prompt constituents to complain to senators and congressmen.

The review process would begin with each house receiving notification of the proposed rule or regulation. Each house would then have ninety days to pass a concurrent resolution of disapproval. If one house passed a disapproval resolution within sixty days, and the other house did not do anything in the next thirty days, the regulation would also be disapproved. Otherwise, the regulation would take effect, either at the end of ninety days, if a committee had examined the regulation, or after sixty days of congressional inaction. There are special provisions to expedite floor consideration in both houses.

The two major arguments against HR 1776, the main bill before the House, are that it would overburden the members of Congress and that it would involve Congress too deeply in administration. The first argument raises a legitimate concern, and it is difficult to get a precise estimate of the additional work that would be involved. It should be acknowledged that there is more support for this comprehensive agency regulation veto bill in the House than in the Senate, and this is probably due to senators having more committee assignments and more widespread governmental responsibilities than representatives. On the other hand, much of the scrutiny of administrative programs and regulations already takes place in the relevant committee and subcommittee staffs. It seems to this writer, especially after experience in a congressional office for a year, unlikely that members of Congress, individually, in committees, or in legislative bodies, would spend more time reviewing regulations than their legislative and representative responsibilities required. The second ar-

gument, which we previously considered in terms of constitutionality, deserves to be examined on the merits as well.

Two critics of the act, Professors Harold Bruff and Ernest
Gellhorn, who studied five agency programs which were subject
to the congressional veto from 1972 to 1977, had this to say about
its effect on congressional oversight: "The principal difference is
the negotiating process between congressional committee staffs
and agencies, which seldom occurs in the absence of a veto provision." Later, they contrasted the sporadic review that takes place
under authorization renewal and appropriation hearings with review under a congressional veto scheme, which is "specifically
and narrowly focused on the substance of proposed rules." "Thus
the veto, unlike any of the traditional oversight techniques, permits regular and systematic examination of the substantive details of an agency's program." The negotiations between congressional oversight committees and agencies are described as "a
highly efficient review technique in the sense that they resolve
policy differences between the agency and the committee relatively quickly and without destroying the coherence of the resulting rule as an item veto might." Notwithstanding all this, the authors do not approve of it because the congressional committees
and staffs are involved "deeply in the rulemaking process." [66]

To explain what is wrong with such an involvement, the authors ask, rhetorically: "To what extent is rulemaking a normative or political process which is brought closer to the people's
representatives by the legislative veto, and to what extent is it an
expert or rational process that should not be subject to political
influences?" Later, they answer their own question: "Members of
Congress are unaccustomed, and the institution is ill-equipped,
to make a restrained and judicious examination of a rule's subser-
vience to statutory purpose." [67]

The authors apparently regard the administration of government as a science with a method and procedure altogether different from the method and procedure of that part of government
which is responsible for establishing objectives, providing for
means to accomplish those objectives, and facing an electorate. If
we recall Hamilton's statement on administration, it is clear that a
"scientific" approach to administration, with its complementary

view of the rest of government as "politics," in the sense of mere preference seeking and consensus building, does not do justice to Congress or to American government as a whole. Administrators as well as politicians must deal with contending interests and evaluate arguments about what public policies are good. On behalf of Bruff and Gellhorn, it can be said that a public official's sphere of responsibility and range of discretion within a particular area of government varies from branch to branch and within the executive departments and the independent agencies. Certainly a well-trained career civil service is better equipped to administer programs than an elected legislature. However, politically neutral civil servants are not mere technicians who simply apply the legislative mandate. If they were they would not be very helpful, because their work, while guided by broad political objectives, requires sound judgment about the most desirable and plausible political action. Congress must rely on the experience and training of career civil servants, but this reliance does not mean that Congress is incapable of informing itself quickly about the positive and negative aspects of a proposed regulation which may affect millions of people. As long as administrators make decisions which affect our national life in important ways, they can neither claim nor expect an immunity from searching congressional scrutiny. Given all that Americans expect from their national government today, a new device is needed to make that scrutiny effective.

Congress is the branch of government with the most diversified responsibilities. A senator recently described himself and his colleagues as the last of the generalists in government.[68] The same could certainly be said of representatives. Members of Congress are both legislators and representatives. They are the link between a national governmental policy, usually initiated by the executive branch, and the diverse decentralized geographic constituencies composing the nation. That a large national government is consistent with republican government (a fact gravely doubted by the Anti-Federalist critics of the Constitution) is due, in large part, to Congress' collective capacity to consult with individual citizens—to discuss issues and to assist citizens with special problems—and also to deliberate on national policy. National legislation passes through a federal filter as it works its way through Congress. In this way American federalism retains its vitality and bolsters republican government in America. To argue against the congressional veto in the name of a scientific administrative process which cannot be interfered with, even in the form of a power to say "no" to proposed rules, is to ignore Congress' constitutional responsibilities.

CONCLUSION

The purpose of this essay has been to demonstrate that the congressional veto is consistent with the constitutional separation of powers and, moreover, that it is an excellent example of adaptation to changing circumstances within our constitutional framework. We examined three major constitutional arguments against the congressional veto: the first was based on the presentation clause, the second on bicameralism, and the third on executive power and its relation to administration. We argued that the very legitimate question raised by the presentation clause cannot be answered definitively with reference to the language of the Constitution and the limited debate on its meaning in the Federal Convention. Madison was not thinking about a mechanism to control presidential government when he made his remarks about the purpose of the clause. He was thinking of a direct form of legislative avoidance of the presidential veto, and at a time when overbearing legislatures was one of his major concerns. It is true that a literal interpretation of the presentation clause would prohibit all forms of congressional veto, but the alternative interpretation, whereby it is regarded as a condition attached to a previous act of legislation which is presented to the president, is plausible on its face and compelling in light of the necessity for legislative delegation. Put another way, the congressional veto is constitutional because it satisfies the objectives of efficiency and political balance implicit in the separation of powers.

As for bicameralism, we found that principle followed in most cases, either by means of a concurrent resolution of approval or a simple resolution of disapproval. In each of these cases, both houses would have to agree with the executive. The main exception to these cases was a concurrent resolution of disapproval, which reflected a congressional judgment to give the president additional leverage in certain areas of government, such as foreign affairs. The small number of committee vetoes involved minor programs and has reflected a sound use of the division of labor.

On the question of administration, we have seen that the Constitution provides for a strong and independent executive, but that his sphere of exclusive action is narrow. The enumerated powers are significant and, when taken together with unity and independent mode of election, practically guarantee presidential government. For the president to make full use of the powers that he can infer from his office, however, he will have to gain the approval, or at least the acquiescence, of Congress.

The constitutional separation of powers reflects the political wisdom of our founders, but we cannot focus exclusively on the constitutional question in assessing the congressional veto. We must also ask whether it is politically feasible and whether it is ultimately wise. Nonetheless, we have argued that the congressional veto is constitutional in all fields where Congress has the power to legislate. In most cases, especially in the major ones, it has been prudently used. It has permitted Congress to regain a share of the major decisions of government and oversee administration more effectively.

Some questions remain about the immigration law veto, since it involves individual cases. Other questions remain about the War Powers Act, which has not yet hampered a president and has not yet been fully tested. If Congress attempts to control the presidential direction in this latter area in a manner that might be harmful to the country, then it is for the president to persuade Congress and the people that he needs greater freedom of action. As for the veto of all agency regulations, since it has not been enacted yet, no one knows whether the administrative burden would be excessive.

In closing, we should be reminded of Montesquieu's final statement about the separation of powers: "As there are in this state two visible powers—the legislative and executive—and as every citizen has a will of his own, and may at pleasure assert his independence, most men have a greater fondness for one of these powers than for the other, and the multitude have commonly neither equity nor sense enough to show equal affection to both.[69] In an age when the demands on government necessitate an energetic executive and an extensive administration, the congressional veto stands as an effective counterweight to presidential power and bureaucracy.

NOTES TO CHAPTER VI

1. This essay was written while I was on leave from Middlebury College and serving as an American Political Science Association congressional fellow in the office of the Honorable Lee H. Hamilton (D. Ind.). Mr. Hamilton has been an active supporter of the congressional veto of agency regulations, and his comments on how such an oversight device would work have been extremely helpful. I also wish to acknowledge the special assistance of Mr. Vanda McMurty, Congressman Hamilton's legislative director, who gave generously of his time in reading and commenting on earlier drafts of the essay.

2. *Legislative Appropriations for Fiscal Year 1933* (47 Stat. Ch. 314, pp. 413–15; P.L. 72–212; approved June 30, 1932).

3. Clark F. Norton, *Congressional Review, Deferral and Disapproval of Executive Actions: A Summary and Inventory of Statutory Authority*, Congressional Research Service Report No. 76–88 G, April 30, 1976, and *Congressional Acts Authorizing Prior Review Approval or Disapproval of Proposed Executive Actions, 1976–1977*, Report No. 78–117, May 25, 1978. Norton's third study, *1978 Congressional Acts Authorizing Congressional Approval or Disapproval of Proposed Executive Actions*, Report No. 79–46, February 12, 1979, was published after this essay was written and sent to press.

4. William Holmes Brown, *Constitution, Jefferson's Manual and Rules of the House of Representatives of the United States* (Washington: Government Printing Office, 1977), 744–46.

5. *Congressional Quarterly Almanac*, XXXII 1976 (Washington, D.C.: Congressional Quarterly, 1977), Vote 602 at 168H. The suspension procedure was necessary because the House leadership opposed the bill, as it has continued to do.

6. On May 21, 1980, the House succeeded in persuading the Senate to accept a two-house veto of FTC regulations. The FTC's appropriations for fiscal 1980 were finally passed and signed into law on June 4, 1980. See *Congressional Record* (Daily Edition), 95th Cong., 2nd Sess. The debate starts at S7373 and the vote is recorded at S7446.

7. Arthur M. Schlesinger, Jr., *The Imperial Presidency* (Boston: Houghton Mifflin Company, 1973), viii.

8. See editorial of Louisville *Courier-Journal*, June 24, 1978, reprinted, along with the reply of Congressman Lee H. Hamilton in the *Congressional Record* (Daily Edition) of July 12, 1978, at E3707-8.

9. The vice-president's collaboration with the Senate majority leader in October, 1977, to cut off a Senate filibuster on natural gas deregulation indicates that his legislative position is more than ceremonial. See *Congressional Quarterly Weekly Report*, XXXV (October 8, 1977), 2119–27. In addition, of course, the vice-president votes when the Senate is evenly divided.

10. Alexander Hamilton, James Madison, John Jay, *The Federalist Papers*, ed. Clinton Rossiter (New York and Toronto: New American Library, 1961), No. 47, pp. 302–303.

11. *Federalist*, No. 75, p. 450.

12. *Ibid.*, 451.

13. *Ibid.*, No. 70. For an earlier version, see Hamilton's speech in the Federal Convention on June 18, in Max Farrand (ed.), *Records of the Federal Convention* (4 vols.; New Haven: Yale University Press, 1937), I, 289. See Herbert J. Storing, introduction to Charles C. Thach, Jr., *The Creation of the Presidency* (Baltimore: Johns Hopkins, 1969), v–xii.

14. Farrand (ed.), *Records*, I, 156 (June 1). On the action of the Committee of Detail, compare what was referred to the committee on July 26 with its report to the convention of August 6. Farrand (ed.), *Records*, II, 132, 185–86.

15. Speech on the location of the capital, in Gaillard Hunt (ed.), *The Writings of James Madison* (9 vols.; New York: G. P. Putnam's Sons, 1906), V, 423.

16. For the Pacificus letters, see J. C. Hamilton (ed.), *The Works of Alexander Hamilton* (7 vols.; New York: Joint Library Committee of Congress, 1850–51), VII, 84. For the Helvidius letters, see *Letters and Other Writings of James Madison* (4 vols.; Philadelphia: James Lippincott & Company, 1865), I, 616, 622–25.

17. John Locke, *The Second Treatise of Government*, Ch. IX, para. 141.

18. *Butterfield* v. *Stranahan*, 192 U.S. 471, 494 (1904); the passage is quoted in Edward Corwin, *The President: Office and Powers* (4th edition; New York: New York University Press, 1957), 125.

19. The two cases striking down statutes for excessive delegation were *Schecter Bros.* v. *United States*, 295 U.S. 495 (1935) and *Panama Refining Company* v. *Ryan*, 293 U.S. 388 (1934). Justice Cardozo's statement is from his Schecter opinion. The case establishing, or reestablishing, Congress' broad power of delegation was *United States* v. *Rock Royal Co-operative*, 307 U.S. 533 (1939). See Corwin, *The President*, 127. For other cases not cited by Corwin, see Gerald Gunther, *Constitutional Law: Cases and Materials* (9th ed.; Foundation Press, 1975), 177–81.

20. Corwin, *The President*, 130.

21. H. Lee Watson, "Congress Steps Out: A Look at Congressional Control of the Executive," in *California Law Review*, LXIII (July 1975), 983.

22. *Ibid.*, 1002.

23. Antonin Scalia, Written testimony submitted to the House Committee on Government Operations, Subcommittee on Legislation and National Security, March 1, 1977, in connection with hearings on "Providing Reorganization Authority to the President."

24. 4 Wheaton 316, 406, 413, 421 (1819). Compare *Federalist*, No. 23; see also *Federalist*, No. 44, for an expansive view of the necessary and proper clause.

25. Farrand (ed.), *Records*, II, 301 (August 15).

26. Robert W. Ginnane, "The Control of Federal Administration by Congressional Resolutions and Committees," *Harvard Law Review*, LXVI (February, 1953), 569, 573, 595.

27. *Ibid.*, 574.

28. See Watson, "Congress Steps Out," 998*ff.*

29. From *Senate Reports* No. 1335, 54th Congress, 2nd Session (1897), 8; quoted in Asher C. Hinds, *Precedents of the House of Representatives* (5 vols.; Washington: Government Printing Office, 1907), IV, Sect. 3483, p. 331.

30. Ginnane, "The Control of Federal Administration," 573.

31. 55 Stat. 32 (1941); quoted in Robert H. Jackson, "A Presidential Legal Opinion," *Harvard Law Review*, LXVI (June, 1953), 1353.

32. *Ibid.*, 1354.

33. *Ibid.*, 1355.

34. Letter of attorney general to the president, in response to an inquiry on the constitutionality of section 906(a) of the executive reorganization statute, 5 U.S. Code, Sect. 901*ff.*: 43 Opins. A.G. 10 (1977).

35. The full text of President Carter's message to Congress on the congressional veto is in *Congressional Quarterly Weekly Report*, XXXVI (June 24, 1978), 1623–24.

36. Clark F. Norton, *Congressional Review of Executive Actions*, table II, 9–10. The chart is an adaptation from Norton's table.

37. P.L. 93–148, P.L. 93–344, P.L. 94–329.

38. *Federalist*, No. 72.

39. *The Cost of Government Regulation of Business*, a study prepared for the Subcommittee on Economic Growth and Stabilization of the Joint Economic Committee, 95th Cong., 2d Sess., April 1978, 4–5.

40. 277 U.S. 189 (1928).

41. *Ibid.*, 201–202.

42. *Ibid.*, 211.

43. Ginnane, "The Control of Federal Administration," 605.

44. According to Louis Fisher, Justice Sutherland was in error on two counts: "for assuming a doctrinaire separation of powers at the state level, and for failing to admit that Congress, in legislating for the territories, had made no effort to bind these governments to the characteristics of the American system." Louis Fisher, "Funds Impounded by the President: The Constitutional Issue," in *The George Washington Law Review*, XXXVIII (October, 1969), 135. See also Fisher's note 72.

45. 295 U.S. 602, 624 (1935).

46. *Sunshine Coal Co.* v. *Atkins*, 310 U.S. 381 (1940).

47. Jacob K. Javits and Gary J. Klein, "Congressional Oversight and the Legislative Veto: A Constitutional Analysis," *New York University Law Review*, LII (June, 1977), 490.

48. Mrs. Ruth Pontius, acting director of the Executive Agencies and Legislative Division, Office of the Federal Register, supplied the author with this figure in a letter dated June 21, 1978.

49. Perhaps Congress should be urged to give the president more control over some, or all, independent agencies, to strengthen the political control of the bureaucracy. That is a separate issue which does not affect Congress' power to review independent agency regulations. The independence, after all, is primarily from the executive. Congress may transform the agencies or abolish them.

50. 46 L. Ed. 2d 659 (1976).

51. *Ibid.*, 839.

52. *Atkins et al.* v. *United States*, no. 40–76, decided May 18, 1977, p. 54. The Supreme Court denied certiorari on January 9, 1978.

53. *Ibid.*, 55.

54. "But Congress has plenary authority in all areas in which it has substantive legislative jurisdiction, *McCulloch* v. *Maryland*, so long as the exercise of that authority does not offend some other constitutional restriction." *Buckley* v. *Valeo*, 752.

55. Clark F. Norton, "Interim Report on the Exercise of Congressional Review, Deferral and Disapproval Authority Over Proposed Executive Actions, 1960–1975," in *Study on Federal Regulation*, Committee on Government Operations, U.S. Senate, vol. II, Congressional Oversight of Regulatory Agencies, 95th Congress, 1st session, Doc. No. 95–26, pp. 161–64.

56. P. L. 94–329. This and other congressional limitations on military and economic foreign aid are discussed in *Congressional Quarterly Weekly Report*, XXXVI (June 3, 1978), 1409–12.

57. Clark Norton, "Interim Report," 163–64.

58. See note 33.

59. 8 U.S. Code, Sect. 1254(c) (2).

60. I am grateful to Mr. Eugene Gressman, attorney for the House of Representatives in this case, for information on the case.

61. Amicus Curiae Brief on behalf of the U.S. House of Representatives, in *Chadha* v. *Immigration and Naturalization Service*, No. 77–1702, Ninth Circuit, 50 (February 16, 1978).

62. Farrand (ed.), *Records*, II, 236 (August 9).

63. Roy P. Basler (ed.), *The Collected Works of Abraham Lincoln* (9 vols.; New Brunswick: Rutgers University Press, 1959), IV, 421–41; V, 144–45, 530; VI, 28–30, 408; VII,

380; VIII, 152. I am grateful to Valerie Cohen for developing this argument on Lincoln's emancipation policy, which departs from the interpretations of Corwin and Randall, and bringing the citations to my attention in her senior thesis on "Lincoln's Emancipation Policy," Middlebury College, Department of Political Science.

64. *Works of Abraham Lincoln*, VIII, 152.

65. *Youngstown Street and Tube Company* v. *Sawyer*, 343 U.S. 579, 637 (1952).

66. Harold Bruff and Ernest Gellhorn, "Congressional Control of Administrative Regulations: A Study of Legislative Vetoes," in *Harvard Law Review*, XC (May, 1977), 1369, 1420, 1423, 1433.

67. *Ibid.*, 1377, 1419.

68. Senator Daniel Patrick Moynihan on a television interview.

69. Montesquieu, *The Spirit of the Laws*, trans. Thomas Nugent (New York: Hafner Publishing Company, 1949), Bk. 19, Ch. 27, p. 307.

VII
Presidential Selection

JAMES CEASER

According to political scientists of the last generation, party competition was an essential feature of any form of popular government. How dismayed they would be, therefore, to learn from contemporary students of American politics that our parties are "decomposing" and that our national electoral process is increasingly taking on the characteristics of nonpartisan competition.[1] Although the labels of the two traditional parties continue to exist, the institutions bearing these labels have lost many of their previous functions. Parties no longer structure the voting behavior of large numbers of citizens. They have ceased to play a major role in constraining presidential decision making, and presidents now place little reliance on them in their efforts to generate public support for policy initiatives. Perhaps most important of all, party organizations have lost their influence in determining the outcome of presidential nominations. Under the "open" nominating process that has emerged since 1968, the races have for all practical purposes become plebiscitory contests among the individual contenders. Candidates create large personal campaign organizations and devise their own programs and electoral strategies, very much as if they were establishing national parties of their own. These personalistic features of the nomination contests continue into the final election stage, as the parties become the extensions of the organizations of the victorious nominees.

What are the implications of this decline in the role of traditional parties for the presidential selection process and for the presidency itself? Is it a positive development, as many reformers argue, or does it pose a serious threat to moderate republican government, as many of their opponents contend? Addressing these questions today is of more than academic significance. The recent changes in the presidential selection process have resulted not primarily from forces beyond the control of political actors but from the decisions of practicing politicians in party commissions and state legislatures. These decisions have been made under the influence of a theory of the selection process that has yet to win general acceptance, ...i. d even some of its original proponents have now begun to have second thoughts.[2] Any clarification, therefore, ot the basic purposes and functions of the selection process could influence prevailing theoretical views and thereby the direction of future institutional development.

The reform theory of selection on which the current open system is based was introduced to national politics at the 1968 Democratic Convention. In its original formulation, the theory attacked the legitimacy of the influence of the regular party organizations and called for "direct democracy" in the selection of presidential nominees.[3] As the theory evolved within the official reform commissions established by the party in 1968 and 1972, the ideal of "fairness" emerged as the single most important value for the nomination process. By fairness was meant procedural regularity and the replication in the selection of delegates of the expressed candidate preferences of the participants. Although the reform commissions did not expressly call for direct democracy in the form of more primaries, the emphasis reformers placed on popular participation and the individual's right to the expression of a candidate preference certainly encouraged the subsequent adoption of presidential primaries in many states.

The reform view of presidential selection should be compared with the very different perspective of the founders and the originators of permanent party competition. For these statesmen the concern was not so much with the procedural goal of fairness as with the substantive results of how power was sought and exercised. After satisfying themselves of the compatibility of their systems with the basic requirements of popular government, they turned their attention to regulating the behavior of presidential aspirants with a view to preventing dangerous political divisions and leadership styles that might undermine the intended character of the presidency.

To speak of a single perspective on selection that includes the founders with the originators of party competition might seem like a serious misreading of the historical record. The founders, after all, were opponents of national parties and sought to establish a nonpartisan selection system. Yet if one focuses on their objectives rather than on the institutional forms they established, it is plausible to argue that by the 1820s permanent party competition was the solution that was most compatible with their goals. The key to this last argument is an understanding of the theme of presidential ambition in the thought of each group.

For the founders, a major objective in selection was to prevent the creation of factions that form around "different leaders ambitiously contending for pre-eminence and power."[4] By their electoral institutions the founders sought to deflect the great force of presidential ambition from its possible manifestations in demagoguery of "image" appeals and to channel it into conduct that would promote the public good. This also was the goal of Martin Van Buren and his followers in the party school of the 1820s and 1830s. They held that the nonpartisan system that emerged in 1824 encouraged the very kind of leadership appeals that the founders wanted to avoid. Only by instituting party competition between two parties of moderate principle could leadership be circumscribed within safe limits. The answer to personal faction for Van Buren was party, though party of a different sort from that which the founders had feared. Whatever differences exist between the views of the founders and Van Buren—and these, as we shall see, are not insignificant—they both accepted the premise that the electoral process should be considered as an institution that controlled candidate behavior.

This premise went unchallenged until the rise of the Populist and Progressive movements at the turn of the century. According to Woodrow Wilson, the most thoughtful spokesman of the Progressive view, the selection system should be designed to elevate a dynamic leader above the political party and make the party serve his will. In Wilson's thought, party is transformed from an institution that constrains leadership to an instrument that enhances it. "Leadership," the central theme of Wilson's proposed revision of the constitutional system, could best take root in an open nominating process in which each contender presented his program directly to the people. The winners would then earn the right to "own" their parties. Wilson accordingly proposed national primaries, making it clear that contenders might appeal beyond traditional partisan followings to form new constituencies. Wilson was satisfied that the problem of dangerous leadership appeals could be avoided in an open selection process: the wisdom of the people along with the self-restraint of the leaders obviated the need for any institutional guidance.

A balance of sorts existed throughout most of this century between institutional elements representing Van Buren's theory of selection and those representing Wilsonian ideas. This system, known sometimes as the "mixed" system because of the presence of both candidate-oriented primaries and organization-dominated selection procedures, was overthrown after 1968.[5] Although there are some differences between the Progressive and the reform views, the reformers have accepted the crucial Progressive premise about the safety of an open nominating system. The use of institutions to influence the character of what V. O. Key called the "echo chamber" has been abandoned in exchange for the right of the people to hear each aspirant shout what he pleases.[6]

THE FUNCTIONS OF THE PRESIDENTIAL SELECTION
SYSTEM

From the perspective of the legislator or the constitution maker, each institution and political process should be designed to promote certain substantive goals. In the case of the selection system, one can identify five such goals. It should: promote the proper kind of executive leadership and the proper scope of executive power; ensure a legitimate accession; encourage the selection of an able individual; prevent the harmful effects of the pursuit of office by highly ambitious contenders; and allow for the proper degree of innovation or political change. These goals or functions are stated here in normative terms, but they can be reformulated as descriptive categories to refer to the major aspects of the political system influenced by the selection process. Thus, depending on how the selection system is constituted, it will differentially affect the character of the presidential office, the probability that the outcome will be accepted as legitimate, the type of individual who is chosen, the manner in which the contenders will seek the office, and the way in which the electoral process controls the pace of change.

The selection system, as the term is used here, refers to both the nomination and the final election stages. Both are phases of the same general process, and it is merely a convention of political science today that scholars subdivide the field and often treat one aspect of the question in isolation from the other. The true constitutional approach, *i.e.*, the approach that considers the impact of the selection system on the political system as a whole, seeks to overcome this subdivision and uncover the perspective from which the serious legislators in the past viewed the problem.

The first function of the selection system is to promote the proper character of the presidential office in respect both to its powers and to the style of presidential leadership. This implies that, at least up to a certain point, the office should be thought of as the end and the selection process the means. Many today might take exception to this assumption. Two recent defenders of reform theory, John Saloma and Frederick Sontag, argue that the goal of the selection system should be increased participation, which they see as a means of building citizen virtue.[7] Theorists before the Progressive era, though no less concerned about citizen virtue, looked elsewhere for its cultivation. They viewed the problem of virtue in presidential selection as applying to the candidates more than to the citizens. More to the point here, these theorists, unlike so many today, were concerned with the question of how the selection process affected the presidency. The way in which power was sought, they believed, would have a profound influence on the way it was subsequently exercised. Many of the important historical debates on the role of parties in our system focused on this issue rather than on how democratic the process should be. The founders and John Quincy Adams opposed party competition because they thought it would compromise the president's independence, whereas Woodrow Wilson sought to transform parties into candidate-centered organizations in order to increase the president's power.

Second, the selection system should ensure an accession to power that is unproblematic and widely regarded as legitimate. By unproblematic we refer to the "mechanical" aspects of the process, most notably to those that relate to its capacity to determine a winner without confusion or delay.[8] Legitimacy refers to whether the people accept the process as being in accord with their understanding of republican principles. A system that is widely regarded as corrupt or undemocratic imposes a heavy burden on its choice, whether at the nomination stage, as Taft learned in 1912, or for the final election, as John Quincy Adams discovered after 1824. It is important, therefore, for the selection system to conform to a well-established conception of republicanism. This must be distinguished, however, from calls for change in response to emphemeral interpretations of republican principles which may be championed by some particular candidate or faction seeking a temporary advantage. Since the selection system is an important "teacher" of the meaning of republicanism, such changes present a danger that the regime will be altered without sufficient attention to long-term effects. These changes are most likely to occur at the nominating stage which lies outside the sphere of direct Constitutional regulation.

Third, the selection system should help promote the choice of a capable individual. What transforms this concern from a meaningless expression of hope to a legitimate institutional question is the reasonable assumption, backed by comparative research into selection in various liberal democracies, that different systems affect the type of person apt to compete and succeed. A plebiscitary nomination system would seem to place a greater premium on those qualities that appeal to a mass audience, such as vigor, appearance, and the aura of sanctimony; "closed" systems will value to a greater degree those qualities esteemed by the narrower group empowered to select, for example, "keeping one's word" in the case of American politicians or trustworthiness in the case of British parliamentarians.[9]

Of course what constitutes an able and good person is, beyond broad agreement on certain basic qualities such as honesty and intelligence, a matter of great dispute. After a long period of neglect, some political scientists have returned to this kind of nor-

mative issue, especially since Watergate. The predominant contemporary school in the study of presidential character classifies
character according to different "personality types" defined primarily by reference to psychological attributes. Apart from considerations of the adequacy of this approach for assessing qualifications, there is the additional question of how helpful it is in
informing the debate over the *institutions* of presidential selection.
One well-known scholar who recently made use of this approach
seems implicitly to have conceded its irrelevance in this respect.
In an article entitled "What Manner of Man?" Erwin Hargrove
develops a profile of the ideal presidential personality, which he
chooses to call a "democratic character." Persons of this description, among other things, would "give every sign of so loving
themselves in the biblical sense that they are free to have concern
for others." Unfortunately—and, one might add, paradoxically—Hargrove finds that the extremely democratic system
now used to select the president does little to promote democratic
characters. Indeed, the only institutional device by which to encourage this character type would be to establish a board of "elite
gate keepers" to screen the candidates. But Hargrove recoils from
a solution that is so obviously undemocratic, and the best he can
offer is the noninstitutional recommendation that we "emphasize
democratic styles of leadership in all organizations of our society
. . . so that the selection of leaders, including Presidents, will be
implicitly guided by a search for 'democratic characters.'" [10]
From the difficulties Hargrove encounters with this approach, it
seems clear that in a popular regime no single personality type
could ever be mandated by law or institutional arrangement. The
most the selection system can do is to influence character choice
by indirect means—by determining who has the power to select,
and thereby which political and character attributes may be favored, and by certain general injunctions regulating candidate eligibility, such as the Constitution's age requirement.

But for all its problems, the modern concern with the question
of presidential character has at least served to refocus attention on
the importance of judging the selection system by the criterion of
the quality of the individual chosen rather than by that of how
much democracy exists in the process of choosing. When a book

as widely read as James Barber's *Presidential Character* can instruct Americans to "look to character first" in choosing the president, it is apparent that a "nonpartisan" perspective on the problem of selection has reemerged. Shorn of its psychoanalytic gloss, Barber's concern is not after all very different from the founders' attempt to construct a system that would offer "a constant probability of seeing the station filled by characters preeminent for ability and virtue," though the way in which they each understand good character is very different.[11]

Fourth, the selection system should prevent the harmful effects of the pursuit of office by highly ambitious contenders. Almost every major politician will at one time or another fix his attention on becoming president and adjust his behavior to improve his chances of being considered. For those who enter the select circle of legitimate contenders, the tendency will be to adopt whatever strategies are legal and acceptable—and even some that are not—if they promise results. It is reasonable to assume, therefore, that the ambition of contenders, if not properly guided, can lead to strategies and appeals that threaten the public good. Such in fact would seem to be the "natural" tendency of ambition, for the ambitious seek first that which is advantageous for themselves. It is this problem which led some of the past legislators of the selection process to look for institutional arrangements that could create a degree of harmony between personal ambition and behavior that promotes the public good. Every student of American politics recognizes this principle as it applies to office holders, but it is surprising how many ignore it or deny its applicability in the case of office seekers.

The problems that presidential ambition can create may be classified under two broad headings. The first is the disruption of the proper functioning of an office or institution: officeholders, using their positions to further their presidential aspirations, may perform in a way that conflicts with their intended constitutional role. One striking instance of this problem is discussed by James Sterling Young in his account of the effects of the caucus system of nomination in the early nineteenth century. Young shows how that system led cabinet members who were interested in becoming president to court favor with congressmen, with the consequence that the unity and independence of the executive branch were undermined. The failure in this case to structure presidential ambition in accord with the intended character of the Constitution very nearly led to a transformation of the entire political system.[12]

The second problem, by no means exclusive of the first, is the attempt of candidates to build a popular following by the "arts of popularity"—by empty "image" appeals, by flattery, or by the exploitation of dangerous passions.[13] The general term for such appeals is demagoguery, although one often finds the term restricted today to harsh utterances that evoke anger and fear. It is a mistake, however, to fail to recognize the demagogic character of a "soft" flattery that tells the people they can do no wrong or of seductive appeals that hide behind a veil of liberality, making promises that can never be kept or raising hopes that can never be satisfied.

The approach usually relied upon today to control candidate abuses is the imposition of legal restrictions. This approach was used in the campaign finance legislation of 1972 and 1974, which was designed to protect the public interest from candidates' granting special privileges or favors to large contributors. Thus while one arm of the modern reform movement makes the selection process more open, the other attempts to prevent certain excesses, in some cases encouraged by that very openness, by means of new legal limitations and regulatory procedures.[14] But whatever the merits of this legal approach for curbing certain kinds of abuses, it cannot reach those which by their very nature cannot be classified as criminal or proscribed by statute. Into this category fall most of the abuses discussed above.

If ambition in these instances cannot be checked by law, it might nevertheless be controlled by the institutional arrangements of the selection system. Institutional regulation of behavior consists in establishing certain constraints and incentives—not criminal penalties—that promote desired habits and actions and discourage unwanted behavior. The selection system, conceived in this sense, is the institution that structures the conduct of presidential aspirants and their supporters. By marking out a certain path to the presidency, it influences the behavior of the nation's leading politicians and, by their example, the style of politics in the regime as a whole. Regulation of presidential ambition is likely to work most effectively where it relies on the candidate's own strongest impulse: if matters can be arranged such that undesirable behavior will detract from the chance of success, candidates will turn "voluntarily" to other strategies. Properly channeled, ambition can be used to curb its own excesses.

Finally, the selection system should allow for the proper degree of political change in the nation. Prior to the Progressive era, this function was rarely confronted in a direct way in the debates over electoral reform. But since the Progressive era, it has probably been the most widely discussed of all the issues. For the present it is sufficient merely to identify the two major schools of thought on the question. One group of thinkers, which includes Pendleton Herring, Edward Banfield, and V. O. Key, has stressed the need for establishing electoral institutions that promote consensus and erect barriers to disruptive and dangerous movements that may emanate from the electorate. The selection process should not strive to be neutral, but should, in some measure, manage political conflict. Only where a large and persistent force pushes for decisive change should the system be completely responsive.[15] A second school of thought that began with the Progressives and continues with the party government advocates and the modern reformers argues that the selection system should be designed to foster rapid change and open the way quickly to new departures in public policy.[16] The prominence which adherents of this school assign to the selection process—a prominence which often exceeds that accorded to the formal constitutional institutions—is perhaps best explained by their "bias" in favor of change and their belief that the formal institutions left to their own devices cannot accommodate it. What is required in their view is a restructuring of the electoral system to facilitate change, though adherents of this school disagree among themselves about the exact form this restructuring should assume.

THE FOUNDERS

Although the founders addressed directly or indirectly all of the functions identified above, their main concerns were to protect the independence of the presidential office and to control the ambitions of presidential aspirants. The first of these has been carefully examined by a number of scholars of the founders' thought, and it is sufficient merely to remind the reader of their main solution: the president, through the device of the electoral college, was to be given an electoral base independent of the Congress. The founders' attempt to control presidential ambition, by contrast, has been almost entirely neglected in the scholarly literature. One reason, perhaps, is that modern political scientists see no practical reason for consulting the founders' views on this question: in contrast to the presidency and the Congress, where the Constitution still is the most important determinant of political behavior, the presidential campaign as we know it today is a totally extra-Constitutional development, having "escaped" from the regulation intended by the founders. But if this helps explain why the founders' views on ambition have been neglected, it does not totally justify it. While no one would contend that the founders' institutional prescriptions for the selection process are a viable alternative today, their thought on the question may nevertheless be reexamined to help us analyze and even assess contemporary developments.

One of the distinguishing features of constitutional government for the founders was rule based on institutional authority. Office holders, in their view, were to rest their claim to govern on the legally defined rights and prerogatives of their offices. This kind of authority was threatened by claims to rule on informal grounds, such as personal heroic standing or assertions of embodying the will of the people. The latter claim was particularly dangerous to constitutional government in a popular regime. Because the people were recognized as the source of ultimate authority for the system as a whole, the founders believed that it would take but one small step for an enterprising leader to activate the principle of popular sovereignty and transform it into the immediate basis of political rule. Popular authority was accordingly identified as the likeliest ground on which attempts would be made to throw off constitutional restraints and concentrate power in the hands of one person or institution. It was the most probable source for what the founders called "encroachment" or "usurpation" and for what we refer to today as institutional "imperialism."[17]

The founders' analysis of the problem of popular authority appears in *The Federalist* mostly in the context of their discussion of the House of Representatives. Here they warn against the danger that the House, urged on by some of its "leaders," might seek to "draw all power into its impetuous vortex." But it is crucial to observe that it is not the House itself that the founders feared, but the claim to informal popular authority. Any institution asserting power on the basis of "its supposed influence over the people" is properly suspect on the founders' grounds. Although the founders did not emphasize this problem in the case of the executive— probably because their opponents, fearing only the monarchic tendency of the presidency, never made an issue of it—their concern is evident from their discussions of the possibility of an executive "demagogue" at the convention and from their occasional references to the danger of a presidential "favorite" in *The Federalist*. The prospect that the president might emerge as a leader in this sense was especially alarming to the founders, for they were relying on the executive in particular to check any tendency to popular authority and protect the constitutional tone of the government.[18]

The general name we have given to this kind of noninstitutional rule is "popular leadership." "Popular" refers to the source of the authority and "leadership" to its informal character. Although the founders conceded the need for popular leadership in establishing the regime—twice they speak approvingly of "leaders" of the revolution—elsewhere the term is used disparagingly.[19] The founders no doubt thought that the establishment of the Constitution obviated any need for popular leaders—except perhaps in extraordinary circumstances—as authority would henceforth rest on an institutional foundation. This foundation was also understood to protect the possibility for the exercise of statesmanship by providing the president with a margin of discretion free from the immediate constraint of public opinion. Though leadership on rare occasions could be statesmanlike, as at the time of the Revolution, the founders held that admitting it as the normal means of seeking and exercising power would promote demagoguery. Where authority rests on the leader's supposed representation of the popular will, competition for public favor ensues and with it the tendency to cultivate whatever currents of opinion provide a following. Power that is generated in this fashion might well be formidable, but its scope and discretion are apt to be circumscribed. Popular leadership tends to degenerate into rule that follows public opinion rather than directs it.

The terms used above to designate different kinds of political rule call for greater clarification. *Leadership* is being used here not in its general descriptive sense to refer to the exercise of power, but rather in a special sense to designate a form of rule which rests on an informal and noninstitutional basis, even where the leader may occupy a formal office. Leadership may rest, for example, on the awe the people have for a hero, the reverence they feel toward one who is believed to be chosen by God, or—in the particular case with which we have been concerned—on the claim of an individual to represent the popular will.[20] Constitutional rule, by contrast, rests on the authority of the office along with the normal respect that is accorded to its occupant. Statesmanship is the virtue or excellence of ruling, meaning power exercised in accordance with sound judgment or prudence. Both the popular leader and the one who governs by constitutional authority may be statesmen. The question that the Constitution maker must consider is which of these forms of rule is most likely to encourage statesmanship and avoid the other dangers of ruling. The founders' judgment was clear: constitutional rule was a safer and wiser depository of political power than popular leadership.

Besides serving as a claim to authority, popular leadership is a way of soliciting power. The founders refer to it in this context as "the popular arts." Where the popular arts are employed in seeking office, the danger increases that informal authority will be claimed as the basis for governing. The popular arts accustom the people to the style of popular leadership and train aspirants to generate support and power by this means. Thus to protect the constitutional character of the presidency, the founders thought it essential to discourage the use of the popular arts in the selection process.

The founders identified two basic forms of the popular arts. The first was issue arousal. From their experience with elections for state legislatures after the Revolutionary War, the founders became deeply concerned about demagogic issue appeals directed against property and merit.[21] These same prejudices, they feared, could be tapped at the level of national politics, either directly or through attacks on the allegedly undemocratic branches of the government. Contrary to what is commonly believed by scholars today, Madison's pluralist scheme was *not* envisaged by the founders as a foolproof solution to this problem. True, society would be fractionalized into many parts or interest groups. But these would be electorally significant principally in elections for the House, where relatively small districts would enable geographically concentrated groups to secure a voice in particular locations.[22] By this means, Madisonian pluralism worked in the context of the House to diminish the likelihood or the force of a unitary national appeal. In a national constituency, however, the strength of these particular interests was apt to be less, precisely because they were so small and might have to be ignored by any candidate seeking a broader following. Thus the search for a national majority might well take place—supposing issue arousal were permitted—on a more general level, on a plane either "above" or "below" the level of pluralistic interests.[23]

The second form of the popular arts that the founders identified was the use of appeals that played upon certain passions relating to the personal qualities of the leader, what we might call today "image" appeals. Of course the founders wanted the voters to focus on character qualifications, but they drew a distinction between character assessments based on a calm consideration of the candidates' merits and those influenced by strong emotions or flattery. Madison called attention to the danger of factions forming around "persons whose fortunes have been interesting to human passions," while Jay stressed the importance of closing the door to "those brilliant appearances of genius and patriotism, which, like the transient meteors, sometimes mislead as well as dazzle."[24]

The general principle the founders followed in attempting to discourage the use of the popular arts was to make the election

turn on personal reputation, not issue appeals. Personal reputation, the founders believed, could serve as a rough approximation for merit: those who became well-known at the national
level would most likely have had to earn a reputation by distinguished service to the state.[25] The institutional means for
favoring reputation over issue appeals was sought in the first instance by creating large electoral districts, a principle referred to
by Hamilton as "the extension of spheres of election."[26] The
founders reasoned that since all elections pose the problem of
name recognition for the candidates, persons with established
reputations begin with a decided advantage. The larger the size of
the district, the more difficult it becomes for one using issue
arousal to overcome this advantage. (This assessment is one that
probably needs to be reversed today as a result of changes
wrought by modern communications, which allow a newcomer
more easily to challenge established reputations, and by the extended campaign, which gives more time for an outsider to build
a reputation.) As Madison observed in a personal note taken at
the Constitutional Convention: "Large districts are manifestly
favorable to the election of persons of general respectability and
probable attachment to the rights of property over competitors
depending on personal solicitation in a contracted theatre."[27] Applied to the case of the largest possible district, a nationwide constituency, there was all the more reason to expect a safe result.
As Gouverneur Morris argued, "If the people should elect, they
will never fail to prefer some man of distinguished character or
services, some man, if [one] might so speak, of continental
reputation."[28]

The founders were thus not the inveterate foes of direct popular election that some of their democratic critics have charged.
But it is equally important to observe that their qualified approval
of this method was based on the belief that it would normally
produce a "conservative," *i.e.*, nonpopulist, result. Their position can therefore in no way be construed as an endorsement of
the concept of a "people's president" brandishing the sword of a
popular electoral mandate. The selection process, in their view,
was to be neutral with respect to presidential power, neither de-
tracting from the independence of the executive branch nor

providing it with an added source of extra-constitutional authority. In contrast to the "mandate" view of popular elections that
began with Jefferson and Jackson and was fully articulated by
Wilson and the party government school, the founders' theory of
selection promotes a more restrained concept of executive power.
The presidency, according to Hamilton, could be a strong office—as strong as the public would at the time accept—and still
be consistent with republican government because it lacked the
supplementary claim to popular authority. It was Hamilton's
position, which still merits consideration today, that, in certain
respects, the more popular the office, the more it may need to be
controlled by formal institutional restraints.[29]

The proposal for direct election failed to gain the support of
most delegates at the convention. The opposition came from a
number of quarters, including some who objected on the "practical" grounds that there would not normally be a supply of persons having sufficiently powerful national reputations to win the
votes of the people in the face of competition from popular state
or regional candidates. The direct election advocates were thus
forced to search for another plan, and they readily shifted their
support to a proposal of an election by specially chosen electors.
Not only did this plan seem to offer the same guaranty of presidential independence, but it also increased the chance of selecting
a continental figure, as the electors could be expected to be more
knowledgeable about national affairs. These practical reasons for
abandoning the direct election plan also served to allay certain
theoretical reservations held by Hamilton and to some extent by
Madison as well, for while both men believed that a large constituency would enhance the pull of personal reputation, they nonetheless thought that a popular election might still on occasion
leave the door open to demagogic appeals.[30]

To the extent, therefore, that theoretical concerns influenced
their decision, the founders' choice of an indirect system was dictated not by their desire to limit democracy but rather by their
intent to discourage the candidates' use of issue appeals in their
pursuit of the presidency. This may also help explain why the
founders were not overly preoccupied with an issue that modern
scholars have taken to be so important, *viz.*, who should choose

the electors, the people or the state legislators. To the founders the question of "who rules" in this context was not nearly so important as the anticipated effect of the selection system on the character of the presidential contest. By attempting to make the choice of electors a significant event in its own right, no matter whether selected by the people or the legislators, the founders were attempting to enlist the interests of those wishing to be chosen for this role. They hoped thereby to sever, or at least to diminish, the connection between the contest for the electors and the choice of a national candidate. As Hamilton explained in *Federalist* Number 68, "The choice of *several* to form an intermediate body of electors will be much less apt to convulse the community with any violent movements than the choice of the *one* who was himself to be the final object of the public wishes." [31] The electors, it was thought, would be less likely than the people to be swayed by popular appeals by the candidates and might even resent them, even as—to cite an analogy that is only partly apt—delegates to party nominating conventions, most of whom until recently had a certain discretion about their choice, often resented attempts by candidates to go over their heads to the people. By making the use of the popular arts unnecessary and perhaps counterproductive, the founders sought to prevent direct popular appeals and induce the ablest candidates to pursue the office by establishing a record of distinguished public service that might earn them a reputation for virtue. There would be no campaign in the modern sense. [32]

From a cursory reading of the one paper in *The Federalist* that is devoted to presidential selection (Number 68), one might receive the impression that the founders viewed the pursuit of the presidency as a gentlemanly affair conducted among reluctant participants. Yet nothing could be further from the truth. There was a sense, of course, in which they expected that the immediate campaign would *appear* in this light, just as it was formerly the practice in nominating campaigns for aspirants to wait for their party to confer the nomination upon them. But this kind of campaign would conceal, even as it controlled, the powerful ambitions of the candidates. No more "realistic" analysis of political motivation exists in American thought than that which Hamilton provides in *The Federalist*. Hamilton begins with politicians as we find them: high-spirited, ambitious, and in some cases committed to achieving a noble fame. Hamilton's aim is not to make politicians into "democratic characters"—an objective he doubtless would have considered as undesirable as it was utopian—but to make them serve popular government. Ambition, the dominant force that drives most major politicians, is a neutral quality that leads them to seek out the path to success. Properly channeled it can divert politicians from destructive behavior and lead them to act for the public good, even to take risks and incur momentary displeasure for the sake of long-term glory. Hamilton's understanding of virtue admits and allows for the desire for reward: it can best be described as conduct on behalf of the public, even if that conduct is undertaken for self-interested reasons. The office of the presidency was designed by the founders to attract persons of the highest ambition or virtue, and the selection system was meant to point their ambition in the proper direction.

MARTIN VAN BUREN

Martin Van Buren began his national political career as a senator from New York in 1821, during the Era of Good Feelings. Competition between parties had ceased at the national level, and the dominant opinion in Washington was hostile to any manifestations of partisanship. President Monroe called parties the "curse of the country" and his successor, John Quincy Adams, pledged to "break up the [last] remnant of party distinction." Van Buren quickly became the leading opponent of this view, calling immediately on his arrival at the capitol for a "resuscitation of the old Democratic Party" and later, after the election of 1824, for a renewal of two-party competition. To promote his unorthodox position, Van Buren first had to convince others that permanent party competition was not the evil that most believed, but a positive constitutional doctrine that would promote the well-being of the regime. Beyond this, he had to show the way to an actual partisan division in the nation, a step he undertook by reestablishing the Democratic party and forcing its opponents to organize in response. Van Buren was thus acting at one level as a disinterested legislator and at another as a committed partisan.

Despite the appearance of a tension between these two postures, they were in fact perfect complements for effecting the same goal: the doctrine of party competition was necessary to justify a partisan stance, and a partisan stance was necessary to create party competition.[33]

Van Buren's defense of the doctrine of permanent party competition is very different from that which is usually heard today. The contemporary defense, which derives from the responsible-party government school, is based on a theory of democracy which holds that a choice between two, and preferably no more than two, political parties is an essential feature of democratic government. By contrast, Van Buren developed his case for party competition in response to an impending crisis in the presidential selection process. He began from a concrete problem rather than from an abstract theory of democracy, and he subordinated the issue of party competition to the problem of presidential selection. To those trained in modern teaching about parties, this approach might seem to offer little or no theoretical insights. Yet this prejudice is unjustified if, as was suggested earlier, the issues of party competition and presidential selection are inextricably tied to one another.

Van Buren's two main objectives in reforming the presidential selection process were to ensure the legitimacy of the system by keeping the election from being decided in the House and to prevent a dangerous politics of personal factionalism that resulted from nonpartisan competition. To understand his first objective, a word must be said about the inclusion of the House in the original process. The advocates of a strong, independent executive at the Constitutional Convention fought the idea of selection by Congress on the grounds that it would make the president, in Morris' words, "the tool of a faction of some leading demagogue in the Legislature." They won their main point with the adoption of the system of electors, but an auxiliary election by the House, voting by states, was also included for the purpose of breaking a tie or making the choice where no candidate received the required minimum of electoral votes. Madison strongly opposed this plan, fearing that the undemocratic method of voting by states would conflict with the people's understanding of republican legitimacy. Moreover by the end of the convention, he began to have doubts, along with Hamilton, about whether there would continue to be a steady supply of candidates with continental reputations after the founding generation had passed on. Thus while the authors of *The Federalist* went on record as opposing regular selection by the House, they were in fact worried that their plan might produce this very result.[34]

The likelihood of an election by the House increased with the adoption of the Twelfth Amendment in 1804. Designed to eliminate intrigue between the electors of the defeated party and the vice-presidential candidate of the victorious party, the amendment also made it less likely that a final decision could be made at the electoral stage by reducing the number of presidential votes of each elector from two to one while maintaining the same requirement for election. As long as the Republican party continued to coalesce behind one candidate, this tendency of the new amendment was obscured. But with the collapse of the Republican caucus in 1824, it became evident that under nonpartisan competition a House election would be the normal result. The outcome of the election of 1824 demonstrated this at the same time that it confirmed some of the worst fears about the House system, in particular its tendency to promote confusion and intrigue and its inability to win the full confidence of the public.

Van Buren and his followers argued that party competition could ensure that the election was determined at the electoral stage by providing the candidates with broad national followings. If there were no continental figures in the nation, the reputations of the parties would take their place; if there were too many continental figures, the parties would limit the field. Party competition thus offered an institutional solution to a problem that the founders had relied largely on chance to resolve.

The defense of parties on this ground became a major issue in the election campaign of 1836. The Whigs, hoping to defeat the Democrats by running a different candidate in each section of the country, launched an attack against the legitimacy of partisan activity. Their attack was answered by the Democratic party's national campaign committee, which reflected the views of its candidate, Martin Van Buren. "Is it not a thousand times better," the committee asked, "that the evils of a [party] convention . . . should be borne than that we should be exposed to the calamities of an election by the House?" The committee went on to argue that since no constitutional amendment could be agreed upon, party competition was the only practical means to overcome the contradiction between the founders' intention to keep the election from the House and the actual tendency of the existing electoral process.[35]

Van Buren's second defense of party competition was that it was the best device under existing circumstances for controlling preidential ambition. In proposing party competition as the solution to a problem that the founders had wanted to solve by nonpartisanship, Van Buren was not directly challenging the founders' plan, for the nonpartisan competition that developed in the 1820s bore little resemblance to what the founders had intended. Direct popular appeals by the candidates had by then become an accepted part of the campaign, a change that resulted from the precedent of the election of 1800 and from the transformation of the electors from discretionary trustees to bound agents. Given this new circumstance, a different solution to the problem of controlling the popular arts was required. If popular leadership was now legitimate, the challenge was somehow to distinguish its healthy from its unhealthy expressions and to devise some institutional means to admit the former while excluding the latter.

Nonpartisan competition, according to Van Buren, was no longer an answer to this problem. On the contrary, it was the very cause of personal factionalism and dangerous leadership appeals. It allowed a large number of candidates to enter the contest without doing anything to channel the direction of their ambition. In his analysis of the presidential campaign of 1824, Van Buren charged that the contenders treated questions of public policy as mere "shuttle-cocks." Issues were seized by the candidates long before the election year and kept "unsettled . . . as it was expedient to presidential aspirants that they should be." The length of the campaign had no limitation, with the consequence that politics continually interfered with governing. Van Buren summed up his views of the effects of nonpartisan competition as follows:

In the place of two great parties arrayed against each other in a fair and open contest for the establishment of principles in the administration of government [there were] personal factions . . . having few higher motives for the selection of their candidates or stronger incentives to action than individual preference of antipathies. . . . [These] moved the bitter waters of political agitation to their lowest depths.[36]

Van Buren presented his case against nonpartisanship to a large number of his contemporaries, including the influential Thomas Ritchie, editor of the *Virginia Enquirer*. In a letter to Ritchie in 1827, Van Buren identified the two leadership styles that he feared would result from nonpartisan competition: a personalistic image appeal devoid of all principle—he had Jackson specifically in mind—and demagogic issue arousal, particularly as it might play on sectional prejudices. Ritchie had already become an adherent of Van Buren's pro-partisan ideas and had argued the case for restraint on political ambition in a series of editorials in 1824: "Ambitious struggles for power, with the bitter uncontrollable passions which they inevitably engender, are the most formidable evils which threaten free governments." Ritchie hoped he would never see "the spectacle of five or six candidates for the Presidency . . . travelling through the country, courting support . . . and assiduously practicing all the low arts of popularity."[37]

According to Van Buren and Ritchie, party competition would prevent candidates from devising their own appeals and compel them to adhere to the safer principles on which the major parties would be founded. The character of leadership appeals would be controlled by institutions rather than left subject to accident and personal candidate strategies. Nominations would be made by party leaders who were knowledgeable about national politics and who were in a position to deliberate about which candidate could best maintain a delicately balanced party coalition.[38] Issue appeals in the name of one or another of the parties would be admitted, but appeals independent of parties would be discouraged. The system would remain formally open to challenges by new parties, as two-party competition was a doctrine founded on opinion, not law. But the bias of the electoral process was against openness in the modern sense of eliminating all institutional controls designed to discourage certain kinds of appeals. It was the task of those founding the new parties to establish their credibility and enlist public support behind them on a long-term basis. Party in this respect would be made "prior" to political leadership. Leadership would not formulate new principles or create new electoral alignments but articulate the established principles and maintain existing coalitions. If this implied a loss in the dyanamic character of leadership, it also promised a greater degree of safety and moderation.

Having made the theoretical case for renewed party competition, Van Buren turned to his partisan task of creating the Democratic party. Although one should not doubt the sincerity of his frequently expressed commitment to "old republican" principles, there was nevertheless a strong element of pragmatism in his search for a partisan division. To Ritchie he wrote, "It would take longer than our lives (even if this were practicable) to create new party feelings to keep these masses together." The old electoral divisions would do, and Van Buren found in John Quincy Adams' program for national improvements the perfect opportunity for rallying the old forces together against the neo-Federalism of the administration. Van Buren sought to show his fellow partisans that the same doctrine of party competition that promoted the general good also contributed to the advantage of the Democratic party. Disguised Federalists would be denied the luxury of being considered safe Democrats. Moreover, nonpartisan politics, though appearing fair on the surface, in fact benefited those elements in society which could more easily concert their activities without parties—the same criticism one often hears today against primaries and nonpartisan elections. Van Buren argued that it was chiefly the wealthy, and hence the Whigs, who derived the advantage from nonpartisan politics. The people, being easily divided, needed a recognizable label and a trusted organization around which to rally.[39]

While Van Buren wanted to retain the same basic electoral alignment that existed under the first party division, he sought to establish a different kind of partisanship. The contest over first principles of the regime would be replaced by a more moderate division over the question of the use of federal power to promote economic and cultural development. If parties could be devised that would divide on this secondary question, there was no reason why they could not coexist without each feeling the need to destroy a seditious rival. To go along with this more restrained partisanship, Van Buren proposed a new ethic of tolerance. The original partisans, Jefferson once wrote, "cross the streets and turn their heads the other way, lest they should be obliged to touch their hats." Van Buren offered a different model. He proclaimed his pride in not being "rancorous in my party prejudices" and in maintaining friendly personal relations with many political opponents.[40]

From Van Buren's argument about the need for party principles, one might conclude that he favored what some scholars refer to as "Burkean" parties, *i.e.*, parties that are divided by a significant difference of principle but which nevertheless share a commitment to the existing political system. But Van Buren's parties were criticized at the time—as they would be again at the turn of the century—for avoiding real divisions and for promoting the self-interest of their job-seeking members.[41] It must be admitted that there was some basis for this criticism. Van Buren acknowledged that the principles of the parties would be very general, in part so that each party could accommodate a broad coalition of interests. Morever, Van Buren recognized the need for patronage, no doubt in the belief that with a partisan division based on secondary issues, the maintenance of viable party organizations required that the motivation of purposive activity by members would have to be supplemented by that of material interest. Van Buren's position seemed to be that the ideal of pure Burkean parties is not viable for mass electoral institutions: the real choice is between dangerous parties of first principles and those that blend principle and interest. Although the modern "amateur" conception of party finds the slightest touch of interest unacceptable, it remains an unanswered question whether an ideal equilibrium point can be found and maintained at which the division over principle is sufficiently serious to sustain partisan organizations yet not so great as to threaten the underlying consensus in the regime.

The consensual character of Van Buren's parties raises another and more important question. It is clear that Van Buren founded permanent party competition not only to achieve the general goals of preventing demagogic appeals and moderating political conflict, but also to cope with the specific problem of avoiding a sectional division within the nation over the issue of slavery. The parties were in a sense deliberately created artifacts designed to contain or suppress this powerful and dangerous electoral cleavage. If party conflict based on national principles was not instituted, Van Buren told Ritchie, "prejudicies between free and slaveholding states will inevitably take their place [since] party attachment in former times furnished a complete antidote for sectional prejudicies by producing counteracting feelings." [42]

The deliberate attempt to use the party system to moderate or cover over a fundamental political cleavage has been criticized by theorists who contend that it is undemocratic and that it erects barriers to necessary change. [43] Of course these criticisms reflect a standard of democracy that emerged after Van Buren's time. Nearly all scholars of the subject concede that the establishment of permanent parties coincided with, and probably helped stimulate, a profound democratization of American politics. [44] More voters were mobilized and brought into the active electorate, and the system of patronage enabled men from the middle ranks of society to pursue a political career. It cannot be expected, therefore, that Van Buren would have a complete answer to the criticism that his system was undemocratic. Nevertheless, his analysis of the alternative to his plan—the multifactional system— contains a partial response. Fully open competition, he argued, introduces undemocratic aspects of its own, in fact if not in theory. A realistic understanding of voting behavior indicates that the people do not always grasp the nuances of issue politics in each campaign. To Van Buren it was better—and more democratic—for the people to have enduring parties whose positions they could assess over a period of time. [45] Beyond this, nonpartisan (or multifactional) politics would divide and confuse the people and in the end favor the wealthy and the well-organized. There is little, in fact, in Van Buren's position that does not anticipate the findings of V. O. Key and other modern scholars about the character of multifactional politics. [46]

The charge of preventing necessary change is a more serious one to which Van Buren never developed a complete response. As a general matter, Van Buren took the view that the electoral process should be arranged to avoid dangerous divisions. Electoral politics should in some degree be "managed" by institutions that encourage moderation. As to Van Buren's specific position on the slavery question, it should be pointed out that he was not, in the 1820s, proposing a change from the status quo. His defense of the two-party system was premised on the assumption that the parties would continue to regard slavery as a necessary evil. Only if one contends that the nation would have been better served by bringing the slavery issue to a head in the 1820s—a view which few statesmen of the time accepted—can it be argued that Van Buren acted irresponsibly.

But whatever one may think of Van Buren's position in the 1820s, developments within the Democratic party soon undercut the crucial assumption on which it rested. After 1844, the Democratic party fell increasingly under the influence of southerners who sought to use it as an instrument to protect and promote the interests of slavery. With southerners exercising a determining influence over the selection of the party's nominee, northern candidates often fit their views to their presidential aspirations and became the friends, or at least the accomplices, of the slave power. Van Buren had established the party system to channel ambition in a beneficial direction, but ambition was now tempting candidates to proceed along a path that would lead the nation to crisis.[47]

The issue remains, then, whether a consensual party system may not at times prevent necessary change. The doctrine of two-party competition gives the major parties what in effect is a privileged position in the electoral sphere; the parties are long-standing institutions which are able, up to a point, to decide which issues are presented to the nation. As with any "power" or privilege, it is only fair to ask what may happen when it is misused. What recourse exists when the parties avoid change, become stagnant, and lose touch with the vital elements in society that are raising the real issues which politics must confront? Is there no check to the privileged position the parties enjoy?

Van Buren's acceptance of the nomination of the Free Soil party in 1848 points to a partial resolution of this problem: recourse to a third party as a check on the usual two-party competition. Two-party competition, though intended by Van Buren as a constitutional doctrine, was not to be written into the formal constitution. It was a doctrine that would be accepted generally, as a norm, in the realm of opinion and practice. This distinction is not without a difference, and presumably a difference that Van Buren recognized. The absence of a formal constitutional status for the major parties means that they are not official public institutions whose existence is legally guaranteed. However great their reservoir of support, they must continue to win adherents or face the prospect of extinction. Despite their apparent solidity, the major parties operate under the threat that they will be challenged, and perhaps replaced, by a new party.

When the major parties deviated from what Van Buren thought to be the proper stand on slavery, he felt obliged to lead a third-party challenge, even though he realized the danger this action posed to the newly established doctrine of two-party competition. Van Buren felt a certain ambivalence about his decision, though many of his followers never doubted its wisdom.[48] The "resolution" to the problem of political change that their actions suggest may be stated as follows. A consensual two-party system remains the preferred institutional solution for the electoral process. There may be occasions, however, when the major parties resist necessary change. Recourse to a new party then becomes an acceptable way to challenge the major parties. It is an exceptional method, but in no sense an illegitimate one. In the doctrine of permanent two-party competition the third party remains, as it must, at the edge or fringe of general public acceptance. It must not be precluded, but neither should it be encouraged. The third party is a two-edged sword. On the one hand, it may serve as a vehicle for the kind of extremism and demagoguery that the major parties shun. This danger fully justifies the privileged position that the two major parties enjoy. On the other hand, the third party may on occasion serve as a beneficial instrument for "renewing" the political system during periods of political stagnation. This possibility requires that the privileged position of the major parties should never be extended to achieve the status of a legally supported monopoly.

There is much in Van Buren's plan for party competition that is consistent with the intentions of the founders. Each sought to control personal factions and demagogic appeals, and each wanted to moderate or "manage" political conflict. But having said this, it must also be acknowledged that the new doctrine modified the regime in some very important respects. First, party competition recognized and institutionalized a more active role for the voice of the majority in determining national policy. Elections were no longer understood merely as a way of elevating a worthy individual; they were also contests between competing groups in which the victorious party could claim authority for carrying out its program.

Second, party competition implied a different conception of executive leadership. The founders had wanted illustrious "continental figures" whose freedom from control by any electoral group would enable them to stand above the conflict of factions. By recognizing the need for parties of a broad coalitional character under an umbrella of general principle, Van Buren was required to accept a less elevated kind of leader. His model was what we might call the "politician," one skilled at brokering among various groups. Executive leadership would have to be at least partially partisan in character, although the broad principles on which the parties stood would still leave a president with considerable discretion. Because of the pluralist nature of Van Buren's parties, some scholars have argued that the party system is perfectly consistent with—and indeed perfects—the so-called "Madisonian system" of the founders, for in both one finds encouragement for the formation of coalitional majorities. But while the similarities are important, there is one crucial difference that cannot be ignored. Madison intended that the competition of factions and the process of coalition building would take place in the House and that it would be "balanced" by an executive standing above factions. Van Buren, on the other hand, extended the influence of the "Madisonian system" to the executive by introducing a coalitional concept of leadership into the choice of the president.

Finally, in emphasizing the restraint of ambition, Van Buren, in contrast to the founders, may not have given sufficient scope to it. One finds a continual concern in Van Buren's thought with preventing the potential abuse of power, but little appreciation of its positive use. It was the absence of a doctrine of the positive executive power, much more than the self-interested character of the parties, that troubled Woodrow Wilson.

WOODROW WILSON

The Progressives inaugurated the modern idea of presidential selection—a plebiscitory nomination race in which the candidates build their own constituencies within the electorate and in which the victorious candidate "captures" his party label. Along with this idea came a rejection of the view that the electoral process should control presidential ambition. The new purpose of the selection process was to build a base of popular support for the victorious candidate and help establish the concept of leadership as the central feature of the regime.

The Progressives are perhaps best remembered for their efforts to rid the political process of rampant self-interest. The plebiscitory selection process can in this respect be seen as a device to work around the corrupt party organizations and restore a measure of principle to political life. But one underestimates the full scope of the change sought by many Progressives if only these "negative" objectives are cited. A number of Progressive spokesmen articulated a new conception of how to attain the public good that rejected entirely the pluralist concept of adding together various interests to make a coalitional majority. The public good, in the view of these Progressives, could only be known directly and as a whole. The connection between this conception of politics and the new institutional roles for the presidency and presidential selection is most clearly formulated in the thought of Woodrow Wilson.

Wilson began with nothing less than a full-scale attack on the old basis of constitutional government. The public good, in his view, could not be realized through the operation of formal institutions working within the confines of legally delegated and separated powers. It had to be forged in a "life" relationship between a leader and the people. The task for what Wilson called a "popular leader" or a "popular statesman" was to overcome the inertia of institutional rule and "interpret" for the people the truly progressive principles of the era.[49]

The most striking aspect of this concept of leadership is its informal or noninstitutional character. Wilson called for the rule of those who would lead "not by reason of legal authority, but by reason of their contact and amenability to public opinion." In justifying a much greater role for the presidency, which was to be the source of leadership, Wilson claimed that the "greater power lies with that part of the government that is in most direct communication with the nation." This kind of sanction for popular leadership contrasts directly with the founders' idea of executive authority. Wilson argued that this new basis for the presidency was necessary in order to reestablish the possibility of presidential statesmanship, an objective for which he claimed the sanction of Alexander Hamilton. But while Wilson sought to give great scope to executive power—greater, in many respects, than Hamilton might have countenanced—he did so by draining the office of its formal constitutional authority and by transforming the concept of statesmanship from one that was understood to require a substantial degree of freedom from public opinion to one that operated entirely on the plane of public opinion. Statesmanship for Wilson was understood above all as the art of guiding public sentiment. "Policy—where there is no arbitrary ruler to do the choosing for the whole nation—means massed opinion, and the forming of the masses is the whole art and mastery of politics." The seemingly contradictory criticisms of the modern presidency that one finds in contemporary political science—that the executive is an "imperial" institution, and that it is too closely constrained by public opinion—are understandable in light of the Wilsonian underpinning of the modern executive: popular support, which is claimed as the active source of presidential authority, is also the very factor that limits the president's discretion.[50]

While Wilson believed that public opinion should rule, he was well aware that public opinion is not formed in a vacuum. Political leaders have a role to play in shaping opinion, though Wilson was never clear about what that role could or should be. On the one hand, he seemed at times to hold out the prospect of a leader who could completely control public opinion. The power of the leader, in this view, derives from the power of rhetoric, and it is therefore not surprising that Wilson assigned a much higher status to rhetoric than the founders. On the other hand, however, Wilson implied that the leader should follow public opinion. "I hold," he said in a speech during the 1912 campaign, "that government belongs to the people and that they have a right to that intimate access to it which will determine every turn of its policy." Perhaps the closest Wilson came to an attempt at reconciling these two views was through his aforementioned concept of "interpretation." According to this concept, the popular statesman selects from among the possible currents of opinion the ones that are progressive and then transforms these from their latent status to one that is active and dynamic. "The general sense of the community may wait to be aroused . . . and that statesman must formulate and make it explicit. But he cannot, and should not, do more."[51]

Implicit in Wilson's view of the role of the political leader is the undermining of what we have called constitutional authority. Wilson in effect was proposing that constitutional authority be replaced by authority based on the support of public opinion. This understanding of the role of public opinion contrasts directly with the founders' view according to which the deepest level of opinion—which we may call constitutional opinion— would support the forms of the Constitution and its institutions. In the founders' understanding of the executive, this meant that there would be a stratum of opinion that a president could rely on to uphold the rights of his office, even against a current of public opinion on matters of particular policy. For Wilson, there could be no such thing as constitutional opinion, a result that followed in part from his deliberate design to undermine reverence for the Constitution and to replace its law of mechanics with the law of life and in part from his plan to make leadership the basis of authority.[52]

With this understanding of leadership it becomes clear why Wilson objected to the nineteenth-century view of the role of political parties. For Van Buren party was designed to tie down leadership and confine its appeals. Wilson, however, wanted to encourage leaders to introduce new programs and ideas and to develop new electoral bases to support them. His plan for presidential selection, which he outlined before the Congress in 1913, was to hold national party primaries, with the party conventions to meet *after* the nominees had been chosen.[53] This plan was plainly designed to give the widest latitude to popular leadership and to encourage constant "growth" or change in American politics.

Wilson is known today as the father of the party government school in America, but his commitment to party government and in particular to the concrete policies that would sustain parties is tenuous at best. A party for Wilson is a body of people that forms around and serves a particular leader. "No leaders, no principles; no principles, no parties."[54] Yet as Herbert Croly pointed out, the concepts of party and leadership are in tension, and it was only by means of rhetorical legerdemain that Wilson could keep the two together.[55] Wilson makes parties appear strong when they can assist the leader, but transforms them into empty shells when they might restrict the leader's freedom. One finds the same confusion in many treatments of party today—an insistence on the one hand on party strength, yet an unwillingness on the other to interfere with the right of each aspirant to go to the people with his own program and appeal.

The transformation of the American system that Wilson sought can best be understood by contrasting two methods for effecting major change in American politics. One is to set forth a new program and then win the political power to enact it. This may be done by an extraordinary kind of leadership that brings into being a new party or reconstitutes an existing one. By such means, for example, Lincoln was able to reconstitute the American regime in the 1860s. The other method, proposed among others by the party government school, is to change the constitutional system itself, meaning here the way in which power is distributed. The problem is defined as one more of process than substance; particular political crises are seen as recurring manifestations of some underlying structural inadequacy and cannot be solved until the institutional arrangement of power is altered. Wilson defined the existing problem of American politics in the latter sense, arguing that the root of the national crisis that he declared to exist in the 1890s lay with structural defects in our system that produced "leaderless government."[56] Wilson's objective, at least while he was a scholar, was not to delineate the principles of a new partisan division—indeed he was always vague about what programs the parties should adopt—but to alter the traditional relationship between party and leader in order to institutionalize dynamic leadership.

Every regime, it is clear, needs to be "renewed" at moments of crisis by extraordinary acts of political leadership. Given this fact, it might be said that the constraints that the founders and Van Buren imposed on leadership were too severe. Yet one must bear in mind that they were speaking at the level of analysis of institutional structures, and institutions operating "as usual" may not be able to meet every situation or challenge. Seen from this perspective, they might not have wanted to prevent absolutely a recourse to popular leadership, but only to erect a bias against it, such that it would have to "prove" itself in the face of institutional deterrents. A bias of this kind would normally prevent the dangers of popular leadership yet still not preclude change and renewal when needed. Wilson took the opposite view and argued that a bias in favor of change in the electoral process was desirable and that under such a system leaders of high quality would continually emerge. Whereas Madison cautioned that statesmen could not always be at the helm, Wilson seemed to be divising a system in which they had to be, in which the people would constantly look for political and even moral regeneration from a dynamic leader who spoke to the conscience of the nation.

A fundamental question is whether in opening the selection system to continual change Wilson did not also open it to dangerous or demeaning leadership appeals. Wilson himself was aware that his concept of leadership was not easy to separate from demagoguery. Both were popular, both rested on awakening the people's feeling and building new issue constituencies, and both implied a concentration of power in the hands of the leader. How then might one distinguish between them? Wilson answered as follows:

> This function of interpretation, this careful exclusion of individual origination it is that makes it difficult for the impatient original mind to distinguish the popular statesman from the demagogue. The demagogue sees and seeks self-interest in an acquiescent reading of that

part of the public thought upon which he depends for votes; the statesman, also reading the common inclination, also, when he reads aright, obtains the votes that keep him in power. But if you will justly observe the two, you will find the one trimming to the inclinations of the moment, the other obedient to the permanent purposes of the public mind. . . . The one ministers to himself, the other to the race.[57]

Wilson's reliance on the nature of the issue to distinguish between the two kinds of leaders is, to say the least, vague; and his reference to intent can hardly suffice as a practical means of identification. The earlier theorists sought to identify dangerous leadership by a clear external criterion, even if that criterion was only an approximation of the leadership they sought to prevent. For the founders, it had been popular leadership, for Van Buren, personal leadership independent of a party. Only after such a visible standard had been devised could one begin to inculcate an effective norm against demagoguery and build institutional barriers against it. By refusing to adopt any such standard, Wilson cleared the way for the development of the modern plebiscitary system.

MODERN REFORM

The Progressives' call for a plebiscitary selection system met with only partial success. The movement for a system of universal state primaries got off to a promising start between 1911 and 1916, but then stalled with the decline of the Progressive movement after the First World War. In some states primary laws were repealed, while in others the party organizations were able to reassert control over the primary process. What resulted was a "mixed" system that contained elements deriving from the conflicting theories of Martin Van Buren and the Progressives. For the defenders of this system, each of these elements was seen as imposing a check on the potential of its rival. The representation of the party organization served to thwart a demagogue, while the primaries enabled a popular candidate to challenge the insularity of the power brokers.[58] However, the new process was something less than a system in the full sense of the word. Its two constituent elements continued to be reflected in two alternative nomination campaigns: the inside strategy of negotiation with party leaders and the outside strategy of direct appeals to the people. To the extent that the system gave rise to its own distinctive method of presidential solicitation, it was through a blending of these two strategies into what Hugh Heclo called an "entrepreneurial" leadership style.[59]

Even before the recent reform movement in the Democratic party, a slight shift had begun to occur in the direction of a greater reliance on the outside strategy. But it was the reforms, and in particular the increase in primaries which they prompted, that decisively established the plebiscitory character of the current system. Since 1968, fourteen states have added primaries, and the share of delegates selected by this method has increased in both parties from one-half to nearly three-quarters.[60] Though the reformers' intention on the question of increasing the number of primaries remains a matter of dispute, there can be no doubt that their rhetoric encouraged this development.[61] One can see this most clearly in the report of the Democratic party's first reform commission, chaired by Governor Harold Hughes. After accepting a widely held view of the late sixties that a "movement politics" of "issue-oriented individuals" had permanently replaced a politics based on organized groups, the Hughes commission went on to suggest that party organizations had lost all legitimacy: "Whereas bargaining among representatives of party organizations once could be said to represent the interests and views of the mass constituency of the party, the decline of the interest groups behind the bosses has undercut the rationale." The only way in which the new kind of citizen could be represented in the selection process was through the direct expression of a national candidate preference, and ensuring this right became the chief objective of the reforms. History was claimed as an ally of this new principle: "A confluence of historical forces has made the 1968 Democratic National Convention an occasion of great moment in the inexorable movement of Presidential politics in America toward direct democracy."[62]

The reform commissions rested their case on the grounds of reestablishing legitimacy. Without the reforms, it was said, not only the Democratic party but the two-party system itself would be threatened. Yet one might well ask whether the reformers did not concede too much to the populist sentiments of the moment. Reforming the internal rules of a party is one thing; undermining the role of party organizations in the name of direct democracy is something quite different. The reliance on "closed" nominating procedures by parties in other democratic nations seems to belie the claim that direct democracy in candidate selection is a requisite of republican legitimacy. As long as the *electoral* system remains open, meaning that the right of new parties to challenge is not denied or impaired, it would seem that the legitimacy of the system could be defended. Under the modern reform impulse, however, a very different conception of legitimacy has been propagated. The idea of an "open" selection process within the two major parties has in some respects been offered not as a supplement to, but as a substitute for, the idea of an open electoral process. Third parties have been linked by reformers with activity that is outside of the political system; and the recent campaign finance legislation, itself a product of the reform impulse, has placed serious impediments in the way of forming new parties.[63]

Some reformers have pressed for more democracy not only to promote legitimacy but also to foster more citizen participation and thereby, supposedly, to build citizen virtue. Because reformers publicly embraced the movement for more primaries, one can assume that the activity of voting in primaries meets and fulfills their objective of building citizen virtue. But while there is no question that more people take part in primaries than in systems run by the parties, participation cannot be equated with citizen virtue. Qualitative as well as quantitative considerations must be taken into account, and here it appears that there is an amazing disproportion between the reformers' end (building citizen virtue) and the means they espouse (expressing a preference for a party nominee). If there is anything to the idea of building citizen virtue through the selection process, it is doubtful that it could have very much to do with the mere act of voting; rather it would have to involve the activity of citizens' learning and practicing the art of associating, which Tocqueville identified as one of the chief virtues of a free people. For most of the participants in primaries, however, nothing is learned about the art of associating.

In place of the activity of exchanging viewpoints, bargaining, and attending the formal meetings of an association, the "citizen" is asked only to express his opinion privately in silent confrontation with a voting machine. Of course some citizens—the workers in the candidates' organizations—do take a more active part under primary processes. But such organizations are evanescent and are focused on a narrow objective; they are a poor substitute for a genuine party organization which continues over time and has, in most cases, broader objectives than furthering the goals of a single individual. Party reformers certainly had a strong case when they emphasized the importance of opening the party *organization*. Where they erred was in taking the additional step of calling for—or not disavowing—a plebiscitary nominating process. This latter step, born of an unreflective enthusiasm for more democracy, served to undercut the very objective of building a stronger party organization. It has resulted, in Jeane Kirkpatrick's apt phrase, in the "dismantling" of our parties.[64]

Yet even learning the art of associating for political purposes may not be sufficient for the full development of citizen virtue. Tocqueville, for example, argues that the most serious attempt to cultivate virtue must involve activity in which the individual assumes a degree of active responsibility in the performance of a public duty, *e.g.*, holding office or serving on juries. It is for this reason that the cultivation of citizen virtue must take place chiefly at the local level, for only here do the offices and duties exist in sufficient number to allow for widespread participation. (Indeed, this consideration should give pause to the reformers' plan to centralize the rule-making authority for the conduct of party affairs in the hands of the national organization.) It is a testimony to the triumph of the idea of mass democracy that the effort to build civic virtue should now be associated with the act of voting for a party nominee rather than with the activities of ruling and being ruled.

If the plebiscitary system is not required to assure the legitimacy of the selection process or to promote citizen virtue, neither, it seems, can it be justified in terms of its effects on the other functions of presidential selection. Promoting "good character," as we have seen, is a difficult function to assess, but there is no basis in theory and surely none in experience for concluding that a plebiscitary system guarantees candidates of greater competence or superior virtue.

As regards the prevention of the harmful effects of the campaign, a number of serious problems have already become evident. By encouraging more candidates and an earlier start of the campaign, the new system introduces considerations of electoral politics into the process of governing at a much earlier date. Campaigns inevitably tend to drain normal legal authority and force an incumbent who is reeligible to become absorbed, in Tocqueville's words, "in the task of defending himself [rather than] ruling in the interest of the state." Moreover, the "openness" of the campaign to many contestants excites the ambitions of a large number of politicians and influences their conduct in the performance of their official duties. Observers of the Congress have already noted the effect of the new system in contributing to a decline of the Senate as a serious deliberative body. In accord with the need under the current system to build popular constituencies, senators with presidential aspirations have been more apt to emphasize "media coverage over legislative craftmanship."[65]

Understanding how presidential aspirants now seek to build popular constituencies is one of the most important questions facing students of contemporary American politics. In seeking guidance on this question, some scholars have turned to V. O. Key's analysis of candidate-centered politics in the era of one-party dominance in the South. Key, like Van Buren, identified two basic forms of what we have called popular leadership: issue arousal and image appeals. After the Democratic nomination race of 1972, it was widely believed that the issue-based campaign was the most likely result of the new system, with the attendant consequence of bitter factional rivalries within the parties. The triumph of Jimmy Carter in 1976, however, has called this analysis at least partly into question and has indicated that "image" politics may also have a role to play in future politics, at least in quieter times. Carter's campaign, which deliberately played down hard issues and focused on moods and personality, was centrist in its ideological content and managed to hold the Democratic coalition together in a way that would have been the envy of any power broker. Yet there is no reason for believing that a system that replaces negotiation among party leaders with a popular election among a number of candidates will encourage moderate appeals or promote party consensus. Carter, it must be remembered, ran as an outsider attacking established institutions and traditional party leaders. His unique accomplishment was to have been an insurgent of the middle.[66]

The effect of the plebiscitary selection system on presidential leadership and executive power is difficult to isolate, as so many other factors exert a simultaneous influence. But one should at least take seriously the charge that the personalistic campaign tends to encourage executive "imperialism" by removing a former source of direct restraint on the president.[67] The checks on presidential power in the American system have traditionally been formal as well as informal, deriving from the constitutional system of separated powers and from the power brokers within the parties whose support was required by candidates and incumbent presidents seeking reelection. Under the present system, however, the successful candidate "owns" his party label and need not answer to specific persons who can hold him accountable. This ownership, it must be added, has come at a high price, for the decline of parties has taken away from the executive a valuable resource that could buy support from the public and from members of Congress. The president now stands directly before the bar of public opinion, and it therefore should not be surprising if presidents become more assertive in their claims to authority and more "popular" or demagogic in their methods of appeal, if only to compensate for their loss of partisan support. In light of these difficulties, it may be asked whether we should not reconsider the wisdom of the recent reforms, even if this implies resisting "the inexorable movement . . . toward direct democracy."

Finally, whether the new system will promote beneficial change is a matter open to serious doubt. Even reformers themselves have had second thoughts. Initially, in 1968, they were confident that democracy was the ally of progressive change. But their faith in the progressive impulse of the people was shaken first by McGovern's defeat in 1972 and even more so by the triumph of Jimmy Carter *within* the Democratic party in 1976. No one yet knows, of course, what the final outcome of the plebiscitary system will be. But, except during periods in which the public is in the midst of a spasmodic burst of anger over a particular issue, it is quite possible that open parties will be more flacid and will produce less vital divisions than the parties in the past. Moreover, if open parties along with the campaign finance legislation succeed in stifling minor parties, another important source for stimulating periodic renewal may be lost.

The more serious danger, however, may well be if the reformers succeed in their original intention to introduce a strong bias for change. The assumption of many reformers, derived no doubt from their acute frustration with American politics in the late 1960s and the early 1970s is that change is continually needed and that in each election the parties should bring "hard" issues to the attention of the American people. The selection process, in this view, is seen as the principle means for stimulating change. It may be argued in response, however, that not all elections pose the dramatic dilemma of making decisive changes; and not all decisive changes are generated by the electoral process. Elections often turn—and properly so—on judgments of the candidates' competence or on a retrospective assessment of an incumbent's record. Decisive changes are frequently initiated by the formal institutions—sometimes against the immediate inclinations of the majority. Reformers seem to have taken as their standard the exceptional case, the critical election, and have sought to make it into the rule. This enthusiasm for electorally stimulated change represents an ill-conceived, and probably ill-fated, attempt to provide for good government by means of a formless process rather than by institutional forms.

When the responsible party government advocates launched their appeal in the 1940s for an electoral process that promoted change, they normally specified that the parties should divide along the cleavage of liberalism (meaning an expanded welfare state) and conservatism (meaning limited government). To all but the most naïve, it was apparent that this "neutral" reform was in actuality designed to further the cause of liberalism. While one can certainly question the wisdom of seeking a permanent institutional transformation to accomplish a particular policy goal, it was at least possible to know what goal these reformers had in mind. Present-day reformers, by contrast, have no such goal. Liberalism today is a label without a program. To introduce an electoral system designed to force change is thus not, as it once was, a (furtive) appeal to join in the worthwhile cause of establishing the welfare state. It is rather an invitation to open the political system to continual upheaval without any end or purpose. Scarcely any transformation in our political system that Americans would be likely to accept could be further removed from the founders' goal of constitutional government.

POSTSCRIPT ON ELECTORAL COLLEGE REFORM

The modern impulse for reform has not been confined to the nominating process. An attempt is once again underway to abolish the electoral college, this time with the active support of the president. The proposal which has won the most widespread support is the direct popular election plan sponsored by Senator Birch Bayh. The plan has the apparent virtue of great simplicity: the president would be chosen by direct balloting on a nationwide constituency. There is one qualification designed to meet the problem of providing for a sufficiently large plurality. If no candidate receives over 40 percent of the total vote, a runoff election would be held between the two candidates receiving the most votes in the first round.[68]

Because this plan requires a constitutional amendment, it is often thought that it would constitute a more profound change in the selection system than any reform which has yet taken place in the nominating process. This is probably untrue, at least as regards the plan's simple intention to have the final election determined by a popular majority. The plain fact of the matter is that the United States already has what amounts to a direct popular election of the president. Of course the votes under the current system are counted within each of the fifty states, with all the electoral votes of each state going to the plurality winner. But this hardly alters the fact that a candidate who hopes to be elected will almost inevitably have to capture, and plan to capture, a national majority. Proponents of the plan, in fact, usually claim that they have no intention of introducing any new bias into the electoral system. The chief purpose of the new electoral plan, they argue, is to avoid the potential "nightmare" that exists under the current system under which a president might be chosen without winning a plurality of the popular vote. This outcome, proponents claim, would impair the legitimacy of the accession, a charge that most opponents concede but argue is being exacerbated by the very emphasis which direct-election advocates give to the purely democratic argument.[69]

To say that the adoption of a formal, direct popular election would not constitute a decisive change is not to deny that it might have some significant incremental effects. Opponents of the plan have cited some of the following potential consequences: (1) the weight given to minority groups would diminish, as they would no longer be the key swing groups within some of the larger states; (2) the federal structure of our parties—and thus indirectly federalism itself—would be impaired, as the states would no longer be the basic electoral units; (3) a national takeover of registration and election administration would almost inevitably result, because, where each vote counts the same, the federal government could not permit the diversity in registration laws and practices that exists under the current state-operated system. Beyond this, opponents argue that while the direct election plan would solve one of the problems of potential illegitimacy—the "minority" president—it would create a far more serious one. In a close election in which a recount was demanded, every ballot in the nation would have to be counted a second time. This would result in confusion, delay, and quite possibly lingering doubts about the final outcome.

These incremental effects of the direct-election plan may be far outweighed, however, by the unintended consequences of the runoff provision, which is necessitated by the generally accepted requirement that the winner receive a substantial plurality of the popular vote (defined in the Bayh plan as at least 40 percent). This aspect of the plan introduces the possibility of a major transformation in the party system, which could ultimately have profound effects on all of the functions of the selection system. The main issue involved here is how the runoff provision might alter the bias of the electoral system toward minor parties. The litera-

ture on the effect of electoral systems on voting behavior is premised on the assumption that voters will normally not wish to
throw away their votes, but will want to see that they have some
chance to count in a positive sense.[70] Under the current system,
this tendency works to discourage nationally based minor parties, but perhaps to encourage those having a strong regional base
of support. The reason is clear enough. Since a party must obtain
a plurality within a state to receive potential share of the actual
decision-making power (*i.e.*, electoral votes), the voter is "directed" by the current system to vote for a minor party only
where it has the prospect of winning a statewide plurality. Voters
favoring a minor party with what seems like a narrow base in
each state—say around 20 percent—will be discouraged and vote
for one of the major parties. The anticipation of this effect in turn
discourages the formation of nationally based third parties. On
the other hand, where the strength of the party is concentrated in
a particular region, the voters supporting a minor party may be
encouraged to support it in the hope that they can win the full
share of the state's electoral vote. Even if the party cannot win the
election, it can use its strength to gain significant bargaining
power with a major party in the next election. The most the
minor party can hope for in the election in which it participates is
to throw the election into the House, where it is certain to lose
anyhow.[71]

Under a direct plan, the incentives for minor party votes—and
thus for the minor parties—change significantly. Of course if
there were no runoff provision, it could be argued that such a
plan would produce the strongest possible disincentive to the
minor party, regional or national. Like the current system, such a
plan would give the national-based minor party nothing, although the third party voter might not be quite so discouraged as
under the present system; but unlike the present system, it would
also offer no encouragement to the regionally based minor party,
because there would be intermediary reward in the form of the
electoral votes.[72] But where the runoff provision exists, a new set
of factors comes into play. The runoff holds out the prospect of a
tangible and immediate reward to the third party voter: the opportunity to send the election into a second round. The minor

party voter could thereby hope not only to show the strength of his party, but also to win for it some practical concessions from one of the major parties in the second round, *e.g.*, a promise to follow a certain policy or to appoint the party leader to a governmental position. A truly dramatic change might ensue if, after some experience with the system, it came generally to be thought that the election would not be decided until the second round. This could alter profoundly the basic frame of mind of the voter and provide all the more incentive for the creation of minor parties. Unlike today, voters would no longer operate under the assumption that they have but one chance to express their preference. The discipline which this "one chance" assumption imposes would accordingly be lost. The first round would be regarded as a "test" round in which the voter could express his preferred alternative, irrespective of whether his vote is "thrown away." Minor parties would find in this system fertile ground for building permanent bases of support. It is difficult to believe that the major parties would be able to discipline their various factions prior to the first round. A tendency would exist for each faction to take its case directly to the people and demonstrate its appeal in the first round. Even if it were defeated, it would still be in a position to join in the hasty coalition-building process that would take place before the second round.

The case for maintaining the current system cannot plausibly be made to rest on reverence for the founders' institutional prescriptions for presidential selection. Neither the direct-election element of the current system nor the practice of granting all the electors within each state to the plurality winner was intended by the founders. Indeed, in its operation, the current selection system bears little resemblance to the founders' original plan. Yet, if one looks at the founders' objectives for the selection process, it can reasonably be argued that they are better served by the current system, with its general bias in favor of a two-party system, than by a direct-election plan which might open the gates to minor parties and destroy the major parties. At least under the current system, the chance still exists that the parties will decide to embark on another round of reform in which they would reassert the moderating role on presidential ambition which they once performed. It is better to live with the imperfections of the current electoral system than to invite the potentially more serious problems of the proposed direct-election scheme.

NOTES TO CHAPTER VII

1. The thesis of party decomposition or decay has been developed by among others Walter Dean Burnham in "American Politics in the 1970s," in William Chambers and Walter Burnham (eds.), *The American Party System* (New York: Oxford University Press, 1975), 308–57. See also Jeane Jordan Kirkpatrick, *Dismantling the Parties* (Washington, D.C.: American Enterprise Institute, 1978); Norman H. Nie, Sydney Verba, and John R. Petrocik, *The Changing American Voter* (Cambridge: Harvard University Press, 1976), 346–47; and Everett Carl Ladd, Jr., *Transformations of the American Party System* (New York: W. W. Norton, 1975), 14–19. For a catalog of the views of the last generation of political scientists on party competition see Richard Hofstadter, *The Idea of a Party System* (Berkeley: University of California Press, 1972), 7. I have also developed the thesis of party decomposition at greater length in *Presidential Selection: Theory and Development* (Princeton, N.J.: Princeton University Press, 1979).

2. Austin Ranney, *Curing the Mischiefs of Faction* (Berkeley: University of California Press, 1975), 188–210; for the second thoughts of some reformers see Rick Stearns' comments in Allen Otten's column in The *Wall Street Journal*, July 9, 1976, p. 1, and the preliminary report of the Winograd Commission, September 1977 (available from the Democratic National Committee, Washington, D.C.)

3. The preference for direct democracy was evident from the many calls for national presidential primaries that were heard in 1968. See Alexander Bickel, *The New Age of Political Reform* (New York: Harper and Row, 1968), 74–79. The first of the reform commissions, the Hughes Commission, while defending the convention system, also stated its clear preference for "direct democracy" in the selection of delegates. *Report of the Commission on the Democratic Selection of Presidential Nominees*, reprinted in *Congressional Record*, 90th Cong., 2nd sess., 31546.

4. Alexander Hamilton, James Madison, and John Jay, *The Federalist Papers*, ed. Clinton Rossiter (New York: New American Library, 1961), No. 10, p. 79. This definition of a faction is not mentioned specifically in the context of presidential selection, but its applicability to that process becomes clear from the discussions in Numbers 64 and 68.

5. Nelson Polsby and Aaron Wildavsky, *Presidential Elections* (3rd ed.; New York: Charles Scribner's Sons, 1971), 238. James Davis called it a "hybrid system" in *Presidential Primaries* (New York: Thomas Y. Crowell, 1967), 269.

6. V. O. Key, *The Responsible Electorate* (New York: Random House, 1966), 6–7.

7. John S. Saloma III and Federick H. Sontag, *Parties* (New York: Random House, 1973), 7, 374.

8. A frequently cited problem is the inability of our system to guarantee a winner once the election goes to the House. See, for example, Alexis de Tocqueville, *Democracy in America*, trans. George Lawrence (Garden City: Doubleday and Co., 1969), 134, and James Madison's letter to George Hay, August 23, 1823, in *Letters and Other Writings of James Madison* (4 vols.; New York: Worthington, 1884), III, 332–37.

9. Hugh Heclo, "Presidential and Prime Ministerial Selection," in Donald R. Matthews (ed.), *Perspectives on Presidential Selection* (Washington: The Brookings Institution, 1973), 32–37.

10. Erwin C. Hargrove, "What Manner of Man?" in James David Barber (ed.), *Choosing the President* (Englewood Cliffs, N.J.: Prentice-Hall, 1974), 31–33. It should be observed that Hargrove is aware of the difficulties involved in the "personality approach" and that his own work has shown a great emphasis on the role of institutional restraints. See Erwin Hargrove, *The Power of the Modern Presidency* (New York: Alfred A. Knopf, 1974), 295–98 and 308–12.

11. James David Barber, *Presidential Character* (Englewood Cliffs, N.J.: Prentice-Hall, 1977), 445; *Federalist*, No. 68, p. 414.

12. James Sterling Young, *The Washington Community* (New York: Harcourt, Brace and World, 1966), 245–49.

13. *Federalist*, No. 68, p. 414, and No. 10, p. 82.

14. The extremely high costs of campaigns are attributable in large measure to the open nominating process, a fact cited by William J. Crotty in *Political Reform and the American Experiment* (New York: Thomas Y. Crowell, 1977), 106. More importantly, it has been frequently argued that the "dirty tricks" practiced by the Nixon campaign in 1972 were a natural if not inevitable outgrowth of the kind of personal campaign organizations that have now become standard under the open process. For this thesis see especially the Ripon Society and Clifford W. Brown, Jr., *The Jaws of Victory* (Boston: Little, Brown and Company, 1973), 226–42.

15. Pendleton Herring, *The Politics of Democracy* (New York: W. W. Norton, 1965), 100–16; Edward Banfield, "In Defense of the American Party System," in Robert Goldwin (ed.), *Political Parties, U.S.A.* (Chicago: Rand McNally, 1961); V. O. Key, *Politics, Parties and Pressure Groups* (4th edition; New York: Thomas Y. Crowell, 1958), 218–49.

16. Some examples are: James MacGregor Burns, *The Deadlock of Democracy* (Englewood Cliffs, N.J.: Prentice-Hall, 1963); Stephen K. Bailey, "Our National Political Parties" in Goldwin, *Political Parties U.S.A.*; and James Sundquist, *Dynamics of the Party System* (Washington, D.C.: The Brookings Institution, 1973), 306–307.

17. For a discussion in the *Federalist* of what we have called "informal authority" see Numbers 48, 63, 71.

18. *Federalist*, No. 48, p. 309. For a discussion of this problem at the convention see James Madison, *Notes of Debates in the Federal Convention*, ed. Adrienne Koch (New York: W. W. Norton, 1969), debates of June 1, July 12, and July 19. In the *Federalist*, the references to a "favorite" appear at No. 49, p. 317; No. 72, p. 440; and No. 85, p. 521.

19. The positive references come in the *Federalist* at No. 14, p. 104 and No. 49, p. 315. The term "leader" is associated with the "favorite" at No. 85, p. 521. I am indebted to Robert Eden for this general point about the founders' understanding of leadership.

20. For a general treatment of different types of political authority, see Max Weber, *From Max Weber*, ed. H. H. Gerth and C. Wright Mills (New York: Oxford University Press, 1969), 245–52.

21. For a full treatment of the founders' views on this problem, see Gordon Wood, *The Creation of the American Republic, 1776–1787* (New York: W. W. Norton, 1969), 475–83.

22. See *Federalist*, Nos. 10, 35, 57, and 60.

23. For the possibility of this type of appeal see note 18. See also Hamilton's comments in a note made to himself at the convention on June 6, in Max Farrand (ed.), *The Records of the Federal Convention of 1787* (New Haven: Yale University Press, 1937), I, 147.

24. *Federalist*, No. 10, p. 79, and No. 64, p. 391.

25. *Ibid.*, No. 3, p. 43, and No. 68, p. 414.

26. *Ibid.*, No. 27, p. 174. For a full discussion of the understanding of this principle at the time see Wood, *Creation*, 506–18.

27. Gaillard Hunt (ed.), *The Writings of James Madison* (9 vols.; New York: G. P. Putnam's Sons, 1903), IV, 126.

28. James Madison, *Notes*, 306. See also the comments of Madison, 327, and James Wilson, 481.

29. *Federalist*, No. 75, p. 451.

30. See Hamilton's note of June 6 in Farrand (ed.), *Records*, I, 147, and the qualification that Madison adds to his own note on large districts quoted above in note 27.

31. *Federalist*, No. 68, p. 412.

32. As to the practical problem of finding a continental figure, the founders hoped that the electors' greater knowledge of national candidates would facilitate such a choice. Moreover, each elector would be given two votes, only one of which could be given to a candidate from his own state. Although the electors might be "instructed" on one vote, most likely to vote for a favorite son, they would have the other vote to use at their discretion.

33. S. M. Hamilton (ed.), *The Writings of James Monroe* (7 vols.; New York: G. P. Putnam's Sons, 1902), VI, 289; Harry Jaffa, "The Nature and Origin of the American Party System," in Goldwin, *Political Parties U.S.A.*, 65; letter to Charles Dudley, January 10, 1822, in Catherina Bonney, *A Legacy of Historical Gleanings* (Albany: J. Munsell, 1875), 382–84; letter to Thomas Ritchie, January 13, 1827, in Van Buren Papers, Library of Congress.

34. Madison, *Notes*, 324, 589–96.

35. Cited in Arthur Schlesinger, Jr. (ed.), *History of American Presidential Elections* (4 vols; New York: Chelsea House, 1973), I, 618–19.

36. John C. Fitzpatrick (ed.), *The Autobiography of Martin Van Buren*, Annual Report of the American Historical Association of 1918 (Washington, D.C.), 115, 116. Martin Van Buren, *Inquiry into the Origin and Course of Political Parties in the United States* (New York: Hurd and Houghton, 1867), 3–4. Note the distinction Van Buren draws between party and faction, the former referring to a significant body adhering over time to the same principles and the latter to the temporary creation of some one individual.

37. Letter to Ritchie, January 13, 1827; *Virginia Enquirer*, December 23, 1823, January 3, 1824.

38. *Virginia Enquirer*, January 2, 1824.

39. Letter to Ritchie, January 13, 1827; Van Buren, *Inquiry*, 5.

40. Paul L. Ford (ed.), *The Works of Thomas Jefferson* (12 vols.; New York: G. P. Putnam's Sons, 1905), VII, 154–55; Van Buren, *Autobiography*, 125.

41. For a contemporary criticism see John C. Calhoun, *A Disquisition on Government* (Indianapolis: Bobbs Merrill Company, 1953), 32. Other critiques are discussed in Hofstadter, *The Idea of a Party System*, 252–71.

42. Letter to Ritchie, January 13, 1827.

43. See, for example, Sundquist, *Dynamics*, 306–307, and Burns, *Deadlock*, 3–4.

44. See, for example, William Chambers, "Party Development and the American Mainstream," in Chambers and Burnham, *The American Party System*, 21.

45. Van Buren, *Political Parties*, 6.

46. For a discussion of the characteristics of multifactional politics, see V. O. Key, *Southern Politics* (New York: Vintage Books, 1949), 87–105. For a discussion of nonpartisan elections see Eugene Lee, *The Politics of Nonpartisanship* (Berkeley: University of California Press, 1964).

47. For a discussion of the views of Van Buren and his followers during the 1840s see Eric Foner, *Free Soil, Free Labor, Free Men* (New York: Oxford University Press, 1970), 151–55.

48. *Ibid.*

49. For his use of the terms *popular leader* and *popular statesman*, see Woodrow Wilson, *Leaders of Men*, ed. T. H. U. Matter (Princeton University Press, 1952), 42, 45; in the same essay, Wilson comments, "Leadership, for the statesman, is interpretation," 42.

50. Woodrow Wilson, *The New Freedom* (Englewood Cliffs, N.J.: Prentice-Hall, 1966), 81; Woodrow Wilson, *Constitutional Government in the United States* (New York: Columbia University Press, 1908), 108–109, 199–200; Woodrow Wilson, "Leaderless Gov-

ernment," in Ray Stannard Baker and William E. Dodd (eds.), *College and State* (2 vols.; New York: Harper and Bros., 1925), I, 339. For the alternative conceptions of the modern executive, see Arthur Schlesinger, Jr., *The Imperial Presidency* (New York: Popular Library, 1973), and Theodore Lowi, *The End of Liberalism* (New York: W. W. Norton, 1969), 187–93.

51. Wilson, *The New Freedom*, 57; Wilson, *Leaders of Men*, 44.

52. Wilson, *Constitutional Government*, 56.

53. Wilson advocated the national primary in his "First Annual Message to the Congress," in Fred L. Israel (ed.), *The State of the Union Messages of the Presidents* (3 vols.; New York: Chelsea House, 1966), III, 2548. The alternative plan of state primary laws was supported by the Democratic party in its 1912 platform.

54. Wilson, "Cabinet Government in the United States," in *College and State*, I, 36–37.

55. Herbert Croly, *Progressive Democracy* (New York: The Macmillan Company, 1914), 337–46.

56. Wilson, "Leaderless Government," in *College and State*, I, 339.

57. Wilson, *Leaders of Men*, 45–46.

58. James W. Davis, *Presidential Primaries*, 252–70; Nelson Polsby and Aaron Wildavsky, *Presidential Elections*, 234–52.

59. Heclo, "Presidential Selection," 29.

60. All of the new state primaries now allow for the identification of the delegate's candidate preference on the ballot, thus strengthening the plebiscitory element. In addition, the reform of 1976, written by the Mikulski Commission, introduced the novel principle of proportional representation into the Democratic party's caucus proceedings and into many of the primaries. For a fuller treatment of these developments see Paul David and James Ceaser, *Proportional Representation in the Delegate Selection Process* (Charlottesville, Va.: University Press of Virginia, 1980).

61. For a discussion of the intentions of the reformers on the McGovern-Fraser Commission see Austin Ranney, "Changing the Rules of the Nominating Game," in Barber, *Choosing the President*, 73–74.

62. *Report of the Commission on the Democratic Selection of Presidential Nominees*, 31547, 31546.

63. *Mandate for Reform*, a report of the Commission on Party Structure and Delegate Selection, Senator George S. McGovern Commission Chairman (Washington: Democratic National Committee, April 1970), 49. For examples of reform advocates who ignore or disparage third party activity in favor of open parties, see *Mandate for Reform*, 49, and Sundquist, *Dynamics*, 307. For the possible effects of the campaign finance legislation on new parties, see Crotty, *Political Reform*, 185.

64. See Saloma and Sontag, *Parties*, 7, 374; Tocqueville, *Democracy in America*, 520–24; Kirkpatrick, *Dismantling the Parties*.

65. Tocqueville, *Democracy in America*, 135; Norman J. Ornstein, Robert Peabody, and David W. Rhode, "The Changing Senate: From the 1950s to the 1970s," in Lawrence Dodd and Bruce Oppenheimer (eds.), *Congress Reconsidered* (New York: Praeger Publishers, 1977), 17; Daniel P. Moynihan, *The Politics of a Guaranteed Income* (New York: Random House, Vintage Books, 1973), 440.

66. V. O. Key, Jr., *Southern Politics in State and Nation* (New York: Vintage Books, 1949), 302–306. See William R. Keech and Donald R. Matthews, *The Party's Choice* (Washington: The Brookings Institution, 1976), 156, and Nelson W. Polsby, *Congress and the Presidency* (3rd edition; Englewood Cliffs: Prentice-Hall, 1976), 180. William Schneider, "Brown Exposes Democratic Splits," *Los Angeles Times*, May 23, 1976.

67. Schlesinger, *The Imperial Presidency*, 206.

68. For a description of Birch Bayh's plan see "Direct Popular Election of the President," *Senate Reports*, 91st Cong., 2nd Sess., No. 1123.

69. For the pros and cons of electoral reform see U.S. Congress, Senate, Committee

on the Judiciary, Subcommittee on the Constitution, *The Electoral College and Direct Election, Hearings*, 95th Cong., 1st Sess.

70. For an account of the influence of this factor, see Allan P. Sindler, *Political Parties in the United States* (New York: St. Martin's Press, 1966), 51–53.

71. There is one other possibility. The *electors* chosen by the third party might actually attempt to strike a bargain with one of the major parties. In most states, such activity on the part of the elector is illegal, although it is not clear whether this would deter most electors from actually making such a bargain.

72. See Daniel A. Mazmanian, *Third Parties in Presidential Elections* (Washington, D.C.: The Brookings Institution, 1974), 110–14.

VIII
On Presidential Character

JEFFREY TULIS

In 1972 Senator Thomas Eagleton of Missouri withdrew from the race for vice-president of the United States because of public reaction to the fact that he had been previously treated for mental illness. Presidential nominee George McGovern also fared poorly due, in part, to that incident; for while the public worried over Eagleton's medical history, they worried too about McGovern's political judgment and skill in selecting and firing Eagleton. The question of presidential character has loomed large in the public eye since 1972, because of political events like the Eagleton debacle and later the Watergate affair. The Eagleton-McGovern incident illustrates nicely the range of issues that have been conflated into the concept of "character." On the one hand are psychological considerations, and on the other are political or judgmental considerations. In everyday discourse, one often distinguishes between people who are in the grip of syndromes and those who are exercising "poor judgment." The line between the two is sometimes fuzzy, as lawyers will often point out in murder trials, but it is noteworthy that the law itself, like our common parlance, captures the distinction between psychological and judgmental causes.

Our common parlance and our everyday understanding of "character" may be changing, due in large measure to a book which first appeared the year of the Eagleton incident—James David Barber's *The Presidential Character*. After Barber, many Americans may no longer be concerned primarily with presidential judgment as such, but rather with personality "types" that lie behind the judgments. To be more precise, many commentators now see "judgment" as a reflection of a psychological variable rather than as an independent cause. Barber's study is not the first

283

study of political personality, or even of presidential personality, but it is the most important because it may be shaping the way citizens evaluate their presidents and presidential candidates. One may consider the examination of the meaning of Barber's enterprise to be a matter of public policy, since Barber has employed his studies in efforts to support candidates in the last two elections.[1]

In addition to the practical concern, there is a scholarly impetus to seriously examine the Barber study. Barber appears to have avoided several of the significant flaws attributed to earlier studies of political personality. The model typological analysis before Barber was Harold Lasswell's *Psychopathology and Politics*.[2] Lasswell constructed a typology based upon data collected in interviews with men who had held political positions, but who, in most cases, subsequently became mental patients. Most of the political positions that these men had held were as low-level functionaries. Lasswell assumed that all were "political men," each embodying a mix of three types: the agitator, the administrator, and the theorist. He sought to discern these types by employing an avowedly Freudian analysis. Thus, Lasswell attempted to fathom the meaning of a political personality from a vantage point that appeared far removed from politics: the men he examined were not significant politicians; he did not focus upon politicians *within* particular political roles; he employed the psychological approach which probes most deeply into the private aspects of his subject's minds. This brief sketch of noteworthy characteristics certainly does not do justice to the Lasswell study. These characteristics are noteworthy, however, because none of them is present in *The Presidential Character*. To be sure, many of the often praised aspects of Lasswell's work have found their way into the Barber study, and these are noted by some of Barber's reviewers.[3] But one should also note that Barber, building upon his previous work examining state legislators, looks at important politicians in their political settings and he eschews strictly Freudian theory. Barber prefers an eclectic approach which, remaining closer to the surface, takes more seriously the actors' own perceptions.

> The psychological approach is simple; some will find it too simple. With a few quite minor exceptions, included for their wider interest,

psychoanalytic interpretations at the symbolic level are avoided. . . . My approach to understanding Presidents is much closer to the psychology of adaptation, stressing the ways interpersonal experience shapes the person's self-image, his worldview, and his political style, and how, in turn these internalized lessons of experience are turned back to shape interpersonal experience.[4]

Barber's study also represents a departure from previous studies of presidential personality, because it is the first attempt to construct a generalized predictive theory of the presidency. A well-known earlier study, *Woodrow Wilson and Colonel House*, by Alexander and Julliette George, utilized a more sophisticated psychological approach, but its restriction to one case precluded the development of a political theory.[5]

Barber does not limit himself to prediction. As Alexander George noted in his very insightful review of *The Presidential Character*, "Barber's study emerges as the first systematic effort to apply personality theory to the task of *assessing* candidates for the Presidency."[6] Barber attempts to link specific kinds of character to specific kinds of policy making. In the final and most important step of the study Barber hierarchically orders the kinds of policy making in an effort to encourage selection of a particular kind of man.

The Presidential Character is significant not only because it culminates in conscious prescription, but also because the prescription is rhetorical rather than institutional. In other words, Barber suggests criteria to guide citizen deliberation about candidates, rather than laws to affect either the selection process or the conduct of the presidential office. Because the presidency is "so highly personalized" Barber suggests that the office has little to do with presidential behavior. "You can organize [the] office in many different ways, but the person who inhabits the office is going to use those instrumentalities for his own purposes." Barber's key to improving the presidency is not to change the office, but rather to help the citizenry select the right man. "If you can't really control the President effectively by law, if you can't really control him effectively during his term of office by a skeptical attitude of public opinion, then basically what you're left with is the thought that you'd better control him at the time you're picking him."[7]

Although contemporary studies of presidential character show little regard for the constitutional order in explaining presidential behavior, the architects of the constitutional order were very much concerned with presidential character. For the founders, the question of character was a central consideration in their design of a selection system and of the presidential office.

Early in the deliberations of the Federal Convention, Benjamin Franklin reminded his colleagues to concern themselves with the character of their future presidents. Franklin proposed that the president should serve without salary, so that presidential ambition would be unable to unite with avarice. Since Madison indicates that the institutional proposal was not taken seriously by the other delegates, some historians have ignored or minimized the importance of Franklin's suggestion.[8] Although the specific proposal was rejected, there is evidence which indicates that the point behind the suggestion was influential. Franklin reminded the delegates that an office of honor that is at the same time a place of profit will attract a certain kind of man.

> And what kind are the men that will strive for this profitable preeminence, through all the bustle of cabal, the heat of contention, the influential mutual abuse of parties, tearing to pieces the best of characters? It will not be the wise and moderate, the lovers of peace and good order, the men fittest for the trust. It will be the bold and the violent, the men of strong passions and indefatigable activity in their selfish pursuits. These will thrust themselves on your government and be your rulers. And these too will be mistaken in the expected happiness of their situation: For their vanquished competitors of the same spirit, and from the same motives will perpetually be endeavoring to distress their administration, thwart their meaning and render them odious to the people.[9]

Moreover, Franklin argued that avaricious presidents would divide the nation into tumultuous factions because there would always be men on both sides of a continuing proposition to increase the salary of the president, and avaricious chief executives would constantly seek to augment their salary. It is important to note that Franklin's discussion of presidential character occurred in the context of an institutional issue: the salary provision. This was the characteristic way in which presidential character was discussed throughout the formation and ratification of the Constitution.

On the matter of salary, the convention did decide to pay the president, but it stipulated that the salary could not be increased or diminished during the president's term in office. Franklin's reasoning apparently affected the deliberations. According to *The Federalist*, "Judicious attention has been paid to this subject in the proposed Constitution. . . . [The legislature] can neither weaken [the president's] fortitude by operating on his necessities, nor corrupt his integrity by appealing to his avarice. . . . He can, of course, have no pecuniary inducement to renounce or desert the independence intended for him by the Constitution." [10]

As *The Federalist* indicates, the interests and motives of the president were to be attached to the structure and duties of his office. With respect to salary, this meant that the president's baser motives would be contained. However, the founders also attempted to build upon low, or selfish qualities of the incumbent, either by making self-interest coincide with public good, or by elevating and transforming selfishness itself. Self-interest would be made to coincide with the public good, for example, by means of the impeachment provision, because "so far as the fear of punishment and disgrace can operate, that motive to good behavior is amply afforded by the article on the subject of impeachment." The founders' deliberation over the provision for indefinite reeligibility illustrates how they believed self-interest could sometimes be elevated. By holding up the possibility of a long tenure, a president's selfishness, or greed, might be converted into a quest for fame, since the prospect of a lengthy tenure carries with it the prospect of monumental projects. [11]

The founders were not solely concerned with the structure of the office; they considered, too, alternative modes of selection. As in contemporary commentary, the question of presidential selection loomed large at the founding, but it was viewed as an institutional rather than rhetorical problem. The electoral college and the minimum age requirement were structural responses to the founders' fear that unqualified and dangerous men (particularly demagogues) might ascend to the nation's highest office. Presidents must be at least thirty-five, not only because the founders wanted experienced men, but also because they wanted men old enough to have revealed their character and ability. Thus the people would "not be liable to be deceived by those brilliant

appearances of genius and patriotism which, like transient meteors sometimes mislead as well as dazzle." [12]

From this very brief sketch of noteworthy founding views, it
should be clear that the framers of the Constitution considered
institutions to be of more perplexity than character. The "new
science of politics" of that time was less interested in discovering
a new conspectus of human types than in discovering ways to
control or mold commonly known qualities of men. James Barber finds character more perplexing than institutions. His political science is directed to developing a new typology of character
different from that known to the average citizen, albeit intended
to instruct the citizenry. This approach rests on an implicit criticism of the faith the founders had in institutional arrangements.
According to Barber, recent history indicates that men "preeminent for wisdom and virtue" are often not elected president, and
those elected are not always prevented "from steering a course
which ends in tragedy for the nation." And even if the men who
become president are a discrete set of character types filtered and
molded by the founders' design, there is enough diversity in
presidential behavior to push scholars beyond the "office" in their
search for explanations of why presidents behave the way they
do.

Conceding that the principles and structure of the office do not
provide sufficient material for comprehensive explanation of
presidential decision making, we wish to know to what extent
Barber's theory does. After briefly summarizing Barber's theory,
we shall reexamine it by replicating it. The theory will be applied
to Abraham Lincoln and Stephen Douglas (a president and presidential candidate not examined by Barber) in order to illuminate
the limits of Barber's enterprise.

THE PRESIDENTIAL CHARACTER IN BRIEF

Barber's objective is fourfold. He attempts to describe the bearing of presidential character upon presidential performance in the
twentieth century. He attempts to predict presidential behavior in
two ways. On the basis of fundamental characteristics which
constitute a particular type of personality, Barber attempts to
predict associated characteristics of men of that type. On the basis

of study of early life, Barber attempts to predict behavior in later life. Finally, he attempts to assess which kind of personalities become the best (and worst) presidents.

There are four basic types of presidential personality generated from the combination of two "baseline" variables. All men are more or less active in their lives' endeavors and all men more or less enjoy those activities. On the basis of data culled from biographies of presidents, Barber classifies each as predominantly active or passive, and predominantly positive or negative with respect to enjoyment. This produces four cells arrayed below and filled in with respective presidents.

	Active	Passive
Positive	Jefferson FDR Truman Kennedy Ford Carter	Madison Taft Harding
Negative	John Adams Wilson Hoover Johnson Nixon	Washington Coolidge Eisenhower

Barber reconfirms his initial categorization with the aid of five major concepts: style, world view, character, power relations, and climate of expectations. The latter two concepts, "power relations" and "climate of expectations," represent Barber's attempt to depict the historical scene that surrounds each president. Barber finds that the "resonance" (or lack thereof) between man and circumstance illuminates personality.

Given depiction of the constellations of power and climate of expectations, "the burden of this book is [to show] that the crucial differences can be anticipated by an understanding of a potential President's character, world view, and his style." These three major concepts are utilized to discern the "integrated pattern" that constitutes each president's personality.[13] The concepts are delineated as follows:

> Character is the way the President orients himself toward life. . . .
> Character is the person's stance as he confronts experience.
>
> World view consists of [a President's] primary, politically relevant
> beliefs, particularly his conceptions of social causality, human nature,
> and the central conflicts of the time.
>
> Style is the President's habitual way of performing his three political
> roles: rhetoric, personal relations, and homework.[14]

Style is the most salient indicator of presidential personality,
and Barber spends most of his analysis describing the disposition of presidents in their three political roles. However, Barber
concludes that character is the most important factor within
personality.

For purposes of prediction, Barber notes that "in general character has its main development in childhood, world view in ado-
lescense, style in early adulthood." The three themes coalesce,
and are expressed by style. The appearance of style is somewhat
peculiar. Barber maintains that presidential style is most clearly
visible at the point at which a youngster moves from home into a
wider public, similar to the period labeled by others as the time
of "identity crisis." Barber labels this period, "the first independent political success," although it involves running for office in
only a few of the cases. According to Barber, the style surrounding the first independent political success *reappears* (having been
somewhat dormant) upon election to the presidency. Barber does
not know why this happens. "Something in him remembers this
earlier victory."[15]

Barber's attempt to predict adult character on the basis of ado-
lescent personality rests on the adequacy of the concept "first independent political success." However, it is Barber's other sort of
prediction, the attempt to assess the probable texture and direction of policy making in the White House on the basis of the president's adult personality, that is our main concern here. This kind
of prediction rests crucially upon the accuracy of the general description of the several basic presidential personality types. The
following summary indicates the prevailing tendencies that Barber discovered in each:

> The 'active-positive' character is 'adaptive.' He displays a con-
> gruence between much of his activity and his enjoyment of it,

thereby 'indicating relatively high self-esteem and relative success in relating to the environment.' He shows 'an orientation toward productiveness as a value and an ability to use styles flexibly, adaptively. . . . He sees himself as developing over time relatively well defined goals,' and emphasizes 'rational mastery.'

The 'active-negative' character is 'compulsive.' He experiences a 'contradiction . . . between relatively intense effort and relatively low emotional reward for that effort.' His activity has a 'compulsive,' compensatory character; 'he seems ambitious, striving upward, power-seeking. . . . He has a persistent problem in managing his aggressive feelings. His self-image is vague and discontinuous.'

The 'passive-positive' character is 'compliant.' He is 'receptive' and 'other-directed,' a personality 'whose life is a search for affection as a reward for being agreeable and cooperative rather than personally assertive.' He experiences a contradiction . . . between low self-esteem (on grounds of being unlovable, unattractive) and a superficial optimism.'

The 'passive-negative' character is 'withdrawn.' He is oriented 'toward doing dutiful service; this compensates for low self-esteem based on a sense of uselessness.' His tendency is 'to withdraw, to escape from the conflict and uncertainty of politics by emphasizing vague principles (especially prohibitions) and procedural arrangements.'[16]

Barber suggests that the best policy and leadership for the nation comes from an active-positive president. His personality leads him to be flexible, and to avoid irrational decisions, to be open to criticism and advice. "This may get him into trouble; he may fail to take account of the irrational in politics," but on the whole the country is safest if its president is an active-positive type.

The worst kind of president for Barber is the active-negative. The active-negative tends to pursue a tragic "rigidification" of policy which is impervious to criticism, public opinion, or the surrounding power situation. Johnson's escalation of the Vietnam War, Nixon's continuance of the war and his behavior in the Watergate affair, Wilson's self-defeating League of Nations campaign, and Hoover's economic policies are all cited as examples of such rigidification. These policies are all considered "disastrous" or near-disastrous.[17]

Passive-positive and passive-negative presidents may in certain times provide the country with reassurance, and respite from previous tumult. But there is a danger that with a passive president the country may "drift," or be lulled into a false sense of security "which diverts popular attention from the hard realities of politics." "What passive Presidents ignore active Presidents inherit." [18]

All of the analysis and predictions in the first edition of *The Presidential Character* were retrospective, except one: the Nixon "tragedy." In the second edition Barber predicted the presidential characters of Ford and Carter, but due to the short tenure of each, Barber's pre-Watergate predictions of Nixon's second term remain "so far this scheme's main test." [19] Nearly one quarter of Barber's book is devoted to analysis of active-negative Richard Nixon. Of course Barber's study did not, and was not intended to, predict historical events like Watergate. Rather, Barber claims to have been successful in predicting Nixon's manner of dealing with Watergate, and more importantly, he predicted that Nixon would probably seize upon and pursue *some* line of policy in the manner of Watergate. [20] Barber's Nixon prediction has been contested by Alexander George, who suggests that Nixon did not "rigidify" his behavior as did other active-negative presidents, most notably Woodrow Wilson. George calls upon Barber to give greater weight to the differences between presidents within each of Barber's types, and less attention to similar tendencies. He suggests that Barber expand the number of cells, adding "mixed types" to the four original categories. [21] It is important to recognize that this kind of criticism is not fundamental. That is to say, whether correct or not, it remains within an horizon of agreement with Barber regarding the theoretical possibility of his enterprise. Thus, the issue between Barber and his critics appears to be over the adequacy of Barber's individual interpretations and over the relative merits of a simple versus a complex typology, not over the limits inherent to a typological understanding per se.

REPLICATING THE BARBER STUDY

What follows is another "test" of Barber's theory, one which is intended to raise questions about the nature and consequences of his endeavor as a whole. Barber's theory will be partially replicated by applying it to two politicians not examined by him—

Abraham Lincoln and Stephen A. Douglas. Lincoln is a crucial case because his administration and political qualities have been well studied and are so well known. Lincoln is widely regarded as America's greatest president, possessed of qualities so admirable that it is common for scholars, citizens, and pundits to yearn for his uncommon kind of leadership. It is reasonable to expect that a prescriptive thesis like Barber's would square with the considered judgment of Lincoln, or at least not run directly counter to the widely accepted view without explanation. But as will be indicated below, Lincoln does not fare well by Barber's criteria. He appears to have been an active-negative, the worst type of president for Barber, while his opponent Douglas seems to have possessed the praiseworthy active-positive character. It is striking that Lincoln is not mentioned, let alone analyzed in detail, by Barber, not only because the restriction to twentieth-century presidents is "more or less arbitrary" in *The Presidential Character*, but also because Barber examined the style of nineteenth-century Andrew Johnson in an early article.[22]

It should be emphasized that these brief case studies are intended to be faithful replications of the Barber mode of analysis in all details including style of presentation. While interpretations of the sort Barber employs cannot be replicated with the automatic ease of other political studies such as those employing survey techniques, it should not be assumed that no standards or guidelines are available. Barber has been extraordinarily helpful to scholars by making accessible background instructions that he gave to his research assistants as well as by publishing a reflective article that reconstructs the logic and method of his inquiry. To be sure, in *The Presidential Character* itself Barber does not devote much space to his methodology, preferring instead to get right to the business of actual interpretation. The same procedure will be followed here, but the reader is invited to compare these cases with Barber's to test the "faithfulness" of the replication. The best cases for this purpose are Barber's comparison of Nixon and McGovern because there Barber pits an analysis of an actual president against an interpretation of a candidate.[23]

Abraham Lincoln. Throughout his political career Lincoln worked incessantly. He campaigned for many candidates, rarely missed legislative sessions, and undertook his own research and clerical work. Biographer Benjamin P. Thomas gives this account: "Lincoln was diligent in the routine work of the House. He rarely missed a roll call and performed his full share of labor on his two committees—that of the Post Office and Post Roads, and the Committee on Expenditures in the War Department. *Few first term members have been more active*, yet his colleagues generally appraised him as a droll westerner of average talents." [24]

When Lincoln ran against Douglas in the now-famous senatorial battle (which Lincoln lost), he arranged the debates, preparing seven long speeches. The rigorous and long debates, however, represented only a small part of the campaign activity of both men. Thomas reports that "between the debates each man spoke almost everyday for four months to large crowds in the open air, and travelled incessantly between engagements, by railroad, steamboat, or horse and buggy, putting up with the scanty comforts and poor food of country inns and never, so far as the record shows, missing a single engagement." [25]

In the White House, Lincoln pursued the same frenetic pace. He started work early; by breakfast at 8 A.M. he had been at work for an hour. In the early days of the presidency he refused to limit visiting hours. (Later he was convinced to do so by his aides.) In addition to the usual policy preparation, Lincoln personally signed every officer's commission and promotion. He wrote his own speeches, state papers, and wrote many letters, often making copies for his files. Eating little, he would read the newspapers at lunch, visit hospitals at about tea time every day, work through the evening until about midnight. Before he went to bed he would visit the War Department telegraph office for the latest cables from the battlefields. He usually read before sleeping (often *Macbeth* or the *Merry Wives of Windsor*), and would finally doze off, sleeping "light and fitful." Once per week the White House would hold an open house reception; Lincoln's hand was reportedly swollen several times from greeting thousands of visitors each week. (It is claimed by Lincoln himself that such handshaking was the cause of his wavering signature on the Emancipation Proclamation.) The volume of Lincoln's writings is also a measure of his overall activity. It has been tallied that his published words "numbered 1,078,365 in comparison with 1,025,000 for the complete works of Shakespeare, and 926,877 for the entire Bible."[26]

It is clear enough that Lincoln had an active, rather than passive, personality, but where would he fall on the "positive-negative" spectrum? This broad dimension is intended to encompass the president's attitude toward his myriad activities and toward himself. In depicting Lincoln's subjective state, it will be helpful to delineate three predominate themes: his rhetorical style and skills, his world view revealed by his objects of interest (his singleness of purpose), and his character exhibited through expressions of inadequacy and mental torment.

Consistent with the styles of several "negative" presidents, (Wilson and Coolidge) speechmaking served as a release, a burst of exuberance, a surge of good feeling, for Lincoln. He wrote his own speeches, injecting literary allusions and polishing his style. There was a marked contrast between the excitement of his speeches and the ordinary character of his normal discourse. J. C. Randall comments that "no one could call his speeches crude; on the contrary they sometimes rose to the height of literary mastery, though in familiar conversation and in informal utterance he lapsed into colloquialisms." Another scholar notes the difference between Lincoln's prepared and unprepared remarks. "His best ideas and finest phrases did not occur in impromptu speeches. In public he seldom was ready with words."[27]

Lincoln's voice would change as audiences responded to his rhetoric. Beginning in a high pitched "squeaking" voice, Lincoln would gain confidence and mellow a bit in the midst of many of his speeches. When his public speeches were carefully prepared, they served as one of his most effective tools of leadership. "Mastery of language may have been that ultimate factor without which he would have failed."[28]

In his personal relations Lincoln was often reserved; he liked to draw out information without revealing his own thoughts and feelings. He was protective of his self, while inquisitive of others. The blatant contrast between the "prepared" public and the private Lincoln reminds one of Calvin Coolidge's "impenetrable silences."

[Lincoln's] friends were fascinated by his enigmatic silences. Herndon, after sharing a law office with him for more than sixteen years, concluded that he was, when he wanted to be, "the most shut mouthed man who ever lived." David Davis, for many seasons a judge on the circuit court with him and in 1860 his campaign manager wrote: "I know the man so well, he was the most reticent, secretive man I ever saw or expected to see." Leonard Swett, for eleven years a fellow lawyer on the circuit declared, "He always told only enough of his plans and purposes to induce a belief that he had communicated all; yet he reserved enough to have communicated nothing." Ward Hill Lamon, an Illinois crony who served as Lincoln's volunteer bodyguard during the war, stated that Lincoln "made simplicity and candor a mask of deep feelings carefully concealed, and subtle plans studiously veiled."[29]

Lincoln's rhetorical style cannot be completely depicted without mention of the place of humor in his speech. Humor served Lincoln several functions. He used "stories" to avoid discussion of sensitive topics, he told jokes to cheer himself up in times of stress, and he veiled some of his bitterest criticism in cloaks of sarcasm. Sarcasm, carefully planned, replaced a good fight for Lincoln. One Lincoln scholar labeled his humor "merciless satire," but pointed out that Lincoln the president matured to the extent that he suppressed the bite of some of his attacks. (Examples of the early *ad hominem* attacks include Lincoln referring to Douglas as a great man, "a lion in fact, a caged and toothless lion." ("A living dog though is better than a dead lion," he said.) Earlier Lincoln wrote to a friend that his party's strategy would be to ignore Douglas. "Isn't that the best way to treat so small a matter?"[30]

The personal attacking function became more and more suppressed as Lincoln grew into the presidency, but the other functions became more pronounced. At times, Lincoln would engineer his speeches around a joke. For example, Lincoln declared that "the Dred Scott decision made popular sovereignty as thin as homeopathic soup made by boiling the shadow of a pigeon that had starved to death."[31]

Lincoln's ability to joke in times of stress can be cited as a "positive" strand in his personality. As will be apparent later, however, his laughter was not enough to compensate for his feelings of inadequacy, and often his laughter itself might have been a kind of not-so-frivolous self-criticism.

A second "negative" theme is revealed in Lincoln's rhetoric. Two modes of justification were characteristic of Lincoln. One was an emphasis upon duty; the other a constant recourse to the will of God. Both of these justificatory devices remind one of style traits of active-negative Woodrow Wilson. Taken together, these devices reveal a tendency to appeal inflexibly to "principle."

As Lincoln emerged from obscurity and retirement, when the Kansas-Nebraska bill was passed, he affirmed that he was embarking upon a "moral challenge." The Kansas-Nebraska bill repealed the Missouri Compromise, thus allowing determination of the legality of slavery in new states to be left to "popular will." "The news aroused him, 'as he had never been before.' Three months later we shall find him back in politics. But he will emerge as a different Lincoln from the ambitious politician whose hopes were seemingly blighted in 1849. His ambition, reawakened, will become as compelling as before, but it will be restrained by devotion to a cause." [32]

Lincoln often justified his actions by referring to his duty to perform them. Shortly before his second presidential election, for example, Lincoln stashed a note in his desk which promised his opponent cooperation to save the Union between election and inauguration should Lincoln lose the election. After victory, Lincoln read the promise to his cabinet, prompting question as to what he would have done if he had lost the election and if his opponent McClellan had refused to cooperate. Lincoln replied, "At least I should have done my duty and stood clear before my conscience." [33]

Consistent with this adherence to duty was a tendency of Lincoln to "stick to" his decisions. "Those closest to the President had learned that while he came to his decisions slowly, once made he seldom reversed them." [34] As his friend Herndon described, Lincoln's mind was his final standard.

> There was no refraction there, in this man's brain: he was not impulsive, fanciful, or imaginative, but cold, calm, precise and exact: he threw his whole mental light around the objects seen. . . . In his mental view he crushed the unreal . . . the hallow and the sham: he

saw what no man could well dispute, but failed to see what might be seen . . . by other men. . . . His own mind was his exclusive standard.[35]

An often discussed set of incidents which reveals Lincoln's duty-bound inflexibility occurred between his first election and inauguration. At that time Lincoln remained silent on major issues, sticking by his previous statements. He was besieged by newspaper editors for his "latest" views. Lincoln refused to budge.

> I could say nothing which I have not already said, and which is in print and accessible to the public. . . . Please pardon me for suggesting that if the papers like yours which have heretofore persistently garbled, and misrepresented what I have said, will now fully and fairly place it before their readers, there can be no further misunderstanding. I beg you to believe me sincere, when . . . I urge it as the true cure for the uneasiness in the country. . . . The Republican newspapers now, and for some time past, are and have been republishing copious extracts from many published speeches, which would at once reach the whole public if your class of papers would also publish them. I am not at liberty to shift my ground. That is out of the question.[36]

The death of Lincoln's son Willie affected him tremendously. It bolstered his duty-bound notions with a recourse to God. "More and more his official utterances and state papers breathed dependence on a Higher Power, whose existence he may have doubted in his callow years."[37]

Lincoln used the notion of God to justify singleness of purpose in his own mind. If there is a clear difference of opinion, both opinions could not be right, because God would not will a contradiction.[38] Lincoln's notion of duty and increasing recourse to God bolstered his belief that his specific policies were the right ones. Consonant with other active-negatives, Lincoln was often "inflexible." Rhetoric, humor, and other justificatory resources (duty and God) are all ways in which Lincoln made sense of his deeper feelings. That is, he attempted to obliterate, manipulate, or camouflage his feelings with the devices I have discussed. These all are devices that other active-negative presidents have employed.

More fundamentally, Lincoln had negative feelings toward himself. He was self-critical, and often doubted his ability to be president. Lincoln did not harbor bitter feelings over political defeat (as had Richard Nixon, for example). Losing his Senate battle against Douglas, Lincoln recalled thinking at the time that "it's a slip and not a fall." Nevertheless, Lincoln did not have positive feelings toward becoming president. Early in 1860, Lincoln remarked to a newspaper editor, "I must, in candor, say I do not think I am fit for the Presidency." This may have been a political tactic. However, subsequent statements seem to reinforce the sincerity of the claim. When he was "in the running" Lincoln sent an autobiographical sketch to John Fell (to serve as the basis for a campaign biography) with the following note appended. "There is not much of it, for the reason, I suppose, that there is not much of me."[39]

Shortly after the nomination, two fellow Republicans, celebrating with Lincoln in Springfield, noted his reaction to the event.

Lincoln looked much moved, and rather sad . . . feeling the heavy responsibility thrown upon him.[40]

Lincoln's response had been modest and brief, yet not colorless: he almost wished the 'high honor' had fallen to another.[41]

Just before his train departure from Springfield which would, after many victory stops, carry Lincoln to Washington, he said goodbye to his law partner Billy Herndon: "The two men parted with a firm clasp of hands. 'I am sick of office holding already,' Lincoln said, 'and I shudder to think of the tasks ahead.'"[42] Along the train route to Washington, Lincoln delivered thirty-seven "greetings" in five days. "Often Lincoln struck the note of self-depreciation. He referred to himself as an old man; once he had a passage read by 'younger eyes,' at times he confessed he had not the 'voice' nor 'strength' for longer speaking. . . . He declared that 'without a reason why . . . [he] should have a name,' there had fallen upon him, 'a task such as did not rest even upon the Father of our country.'"[43]

During the middle of his first term Lincoln was under a constant barrage of abolitionist criticism for not emancipating slaves.

Lincoln, feeling that the time was not right for a proclamation, also felt the tremendous pressure of his delay: "I know very well that many others might . . . do better than I can; and if I were satisfied that the public confidence was more fully possessed by any one of them than by me, and knew of any Constitutional way in which he could be put in my place, he should have it. I would gladly yield it to him." [44]

Three months later, Lincoln was subjected to yet another shelling of criticism, this time concerning his cabinet. One of the cabinet members recorded Lincoln's statements at the time in his diary: "'They (a Senatorial Committee) wish to get rid of me, and I am sometimes half disposed to gratify them. . . . We are now on the brink of destruction . . . I can hardly see any ray of hope. . . . The Committee is to be up to see me at 7 o'clock. Since I heard last night of the proceedings of the caucus, I have been more distressed than by any event of my life.'" [45]

Lincoln looked forward to a second term (which was contrary to the current presidential practice) but he did not look forward with any semblance of joy: "A second term would be a great honor and a great labor, which together, perhaps I would not decline if tendered." Clearly it was a sense of duty (not of enjoyment) that propelled Lincoln. "The President showed no elation at his renomination." [46]

Lincoln sometimes felt severely betrayed by his "friends." On one occasion, Lincoln supporters sponsored a strong bill (the Wade-Davis bill) which "repudiated the rebels." For example, it denied Confederate officers the right to vote for delegates to state constitutional conventions. Lincoln pocket vetoed the bill, and incurred the wrath of congressional radicals. The radicals published a scathing attack on the president, entitled the Wade-Davis Manifesto. Refusing to read the manifesto, Lincoln claimed, "to be wounded in the house of one's friends is perhaps the most grievous affliction that can befall a man." [47]

Lincoln's self-criticism and self-doubt manifested itself in physical forms. Much evidence suggests that Lincoln was "worn," "tired," and suffered from periodic depression. Herndon observed that "melancholy dripped from him as he walked." Another friend, W. H. L. Wallace, observed in 1860 before Lincoln had been inaugurated (although after the election), "I have seen Mr. Lincoln two or three times since I have been here, but only for a moment and he is continuously surrounded by a crowd of people. He has a world of responsibility and seems to feel it and to be oppressed by it. He looks more care worn and haggard and stooped than I ever saw him." [48]

Lincoln's haggard look increased throughout the presidency as indicated by successive photographs. Although Mary Lincoln also suffered increasing depression throughout her later life, her basic demeanor contrasted with her husband's. "Her qualities were complementary to those of her husband. She was to be a stimulus to him, even if at times that stimulus was somewhat of an irritant. His friends unanimously testify to his sadness, his periods of absent thought when he saw nothing around him." Mary Lincoln's fits of depression led her into irascible states; Abraham's depression manifested itself in melancholic silence—perhaps a response to the pressure of his wife's behavior. [49]

A distinctive development—a note of maturity—in Lincoln's later life, was his increasing ability to control his outward emotions. "So long as I have been here [in the presidency], I have not willingly planted a thorn in any man's bosom," he wrote. [50] Yet his outward control could not obliterate his inner torment. It cannot be said that Lincoln enjoyed being president.

Few of the presidents in *The Presidential Character* fit unambiguously into one of the four cells. Most reveal characteristics of several types, although one emerges as the dominant one. Such is the character of Abraham Lincoln. While his ability to joke reveals an active-positive strain, and his melancholy silence reminds one of the passive-negatives, overall Lincoln was an active-negative president—ambitious, an incessant worker who didn't enjoy his work, but doggedly unwavering in pursuit of objectives he considered to be "right."

Stephen Douglas. In contrast to the despondent Abraham Lincoln, Stephen A. Douglas possessed an active-positive character. The qualities associated with the broad dimension are not in all cases those that we would expect. Several indicators typical of active-negatives can be found in Douglas' life. That Douglas was generally active and enjoyed nearly all facets of his exciting life is apparent even to readers of Lincoln biographies; some of these indicators appear in the Lincoln material analyzed previously. The view is confirmed and enlarged upon examination of the now authoritative biography of Douglas by Robert W. Johannsen.[51]

Douglas was born in 1813 on a farm in Vermont. He never knew his father, who died when Stephen was two years old. His surrogate father was his mother's brother, Edward Fisk, on whose farm Stephen lived until adolescence. "In this environment Douglas developed the physical and personal characteristics which would distinguish him in later years. Quick, alert, and proudly self-reliant, he made friends easily, combining a natural magnetism with a consuming energy." His teachers and classmates report him astute and studious. But Douglas found his situation in Brandon, Vermont, confining and he developed a resentment for his uncle, who, he thought, "held him back."[52]

At fifteen Douglas made the decision to leave home, family, and friends to see "what I could do for myself in the wide world among strangers." In Barber's terms, this was his "first independent political success," although his destination, Middlebury, was but fourteen miles from home.[53]

Douglas signed on as an apprentice cabinet maker. In that role characteristic active-positive style themes emerged: enjoyment of hard work, "an ambitious reading program," and an enthrallment with politics. Due to some disagreements with his employer, Douglas returned home after only three months, but throughout the rest of his adolescence the traits nascent at Middlebury fully emerged and developed. Douglas became active in school debate; he dug deeply into historical accounts of Alexander, Caesar, and Napoleon; he continued to follow contemporary politics avidly. By the time Douglas was twenty, he appeared to fit nicely into the type Barber designates "active-positive."

It is not implausible to argue that Douglas was at least as active as any president examined in *The Presidential Character* and as active as Lincoln. Biographer Johannsen noted that "Douglas was tireless in his congressional role of 1838, when he opposed and eventually lost to Whig John Stuart. Shortly after that campaign, Douglas secured a judgeship. Even Whigs noted the efficiency with which Douglas disposed of cases. Writing to his mother in 1841, Douglas boasted that his clearing of the court docket was the first time it had been done in seven years. "I have thus far led a life of extraordinary activity," he declared.[54]

In his first congressional term, in 1843, he "tackled the responsibilities of his position with characteristic energy." When periodically ill (often considered the result of his activity), Douglas chafed in his sedentary state. His activity is noted by most commentators at each stage of his career. Douglas' energy inspired one correspondent to dub him "a perfect steam engine in breaches." The following description of his activity during the famous 1858 Senate campaign provides a fitting summary example of Douglas' energy.

A *New York Times* correspondent who covered the campaign reported after the election that Douglas delivered 59 set speeches each of two to three hours duration, 17 shorter speeches in response to serenades, and 37 speeches in reply to addresses of welcome. All but two of these were delivered in the open air, and seven were made in downpours of rain. Douglas, in the course of almost four months of strenuous campaigning, traveled over 5,000 miles by railroad, steamboat and horse conveyance. . . . What he lacked in size he made up in energy; square shouldered, broad-chested, tossing his large head "with an air of overbearing superiority," Douglas was, "the very embodiment of force, combativeness and staying power."[55]

Before examining Douglas' developed style, world view, and character, one should note the general bearing of his physical stature upon his disposition. The final sentences of the passage just quoted suggest the possibility that Douglas needed to compensate in some way for his distinctly small physical stature. More mention is made of Douglas' stature in his biographies than of any other element of his countenance or character. It is noteworthy, however, that out of many references in the Johannsen tome, only once is Douglas' response to his physique seen as a problem. At that point Johannsen tells us, "He compensated for his lack of stature by developing a boisterous and exuberant manner and a nervous energy that frequently put people off."[56] While

Douglas' energy was at times considered obsessive, his stature was often described as concealing inner strength rather than calling attention to his compensatory modes.

However, one may plausibly venture beyond the biographer's assessment and suggest another possible reaction by "the Little Giant" to his smallness. Douglas had a temper which erupted over the course of his life into a number of now well-known incidents. He went after a critical newspaper editor with a cane, nearly involved himself in a duel, made several "unseemly" outbursts in the Senate, and once lost his temper when taunted by an unfriendly crowd. These outbursts, which were in all cases short-lived, seemed to follow from Douglas' thorough enjoyment of the larger political fight. These nuisances which provoked Douglas did not preoccupy him; he didn't seem to hold long-term grudges. Indeed, Douglas kept cool when the fight was an important one. This demeanor was particularly noticeable throughout his prolonged battle with the Buchanan Administration.[57]

With respect to "style," the important point is that Douglas thoroughly enjoyed political speaking. His was not the case of an active-negative, who, the more he indulged, the more miserable he felt. With the aid of his second wife, Adele, Douglas began to enjoy social life as well, and his home became a social center in his later years. Earlier, he had not the time or inclination for "frivolity," but as he aged there appeared to be no facet of his life he did not enjoy.[58]

The truly complex themes of Douglas' character concern his world view. In Barber's categories, this found expression in a *mix* of devotion to the principle of popular sovereignty and propensity to compromise. Both of these are consistent with Barber's description of the active-positive world view as "a liquid world in which realities and the opinions which reflect them shift continually."[59] As will be indicated in the concluding section below, a full analysis of the meaning of this "world view" (and of Lincoln's) would shake the framework constructed by Barber. Noteworthy here, from Barber's perspective, is the fact that certain character traits that Barber found in his "dutiful" presidents are not present in Douglas' case. For example, Douglas did not come to despise his enemies. It is well known that Douglas accepted defeat from Lincoln with grace; he did not respond, for example, the way Wilson responded to his several defeats. Also, Douglas' defeats cannot be reasonably construed as due to "dutifulness" or to a "principled" stance per se, however much the defeats may have been due to the particular principles that Douglas embraced. This is quite obvious in the presidential race, since both candidates were dedicated to carefully articulated principles.

From Barber's perspective, Douglas' demeanor is better characterized by the theme of compromise or accommodation than by "dutifulness." Douglas offers us a good depiction of that disposition. "He noted [that] if he wished to gain an object, it was sometimes better to yield to a little that one might desire, in order to get the support of a majority, rather than being impracticable, and insisting upon his own particular views to hazard the whole, and lose the object he had in view." [60]

Douglas enjoyed politics. His career reflects characteristic active-positive themes of flexibility and an orientation toward productiveness. Threats to his self-esteem, expressed through his temper, were transcended; he was not plagued with feelings of inadequacy. He accepted defeat with grace, and did not seem to his contemporaries to conceal bitterness.

Lincoln and Douglas both revealed personality traits that persisted throughout their lives. As in the case of Woodrow Wilson, there was no large change in behavior between the "first independent political success," and later adult life. Thus, there is reason to suggest that Douglas would have continued to be active-positive, had he been elected president.

ON PRESIDENTIAL CHARACTER

If the electorate in 1860 had been guided by Barber's theory, they would have rejected Abraham Lincoln, who as an "active-negative" had the worst type of personality, in favor of Stephen Douglas, whose "active-positive" personality is the type most highly recommended by Barber. Although it is impossible to know how successful a Douglas presidency might have been, the historical judgment of Lincoln's administration, both its sober praise and sometime adulation, contrasts markedly with the dire conclusion reached by applying Barber's theory. [61] Why is there such a disparity between the common assessment of Lincoln's presidency and the "active-negative" conclusion generated by Barber's theory? Perhaps the answer lies in the difference between the starting point of the political understanding of citizens and politicians from that of theoretical perspectives like Barber's. For Lincoln, Douglas, and their contemporary public, issue differences were at the heart of the political crisis. Barber, on the other hand, begins his study by assuming that the content of political issues is of little importance in assessing presidential behavior. Instead of looking through the eyes of the politician under study, Barber encourages his readers to look through the lense of a conceptual apparatus different from that common to political life itself.

By beginning with the assumption that political differences as understood by politicians are unimportant, Barber's theory rules out a myriad of hypotheses which might best explain the Lincoln presidency. Because Barber is attempting to construct a theory, and not simply a set of detailed descriptions of various administrations, he is forced by this theoretical objective to create categories which are formal enough to transcend the exigencies of this or that time, or the infinite variety of political opinions and issues. As a theory, Barber's project requires concepts like "rigidity" and "flexibility" because these are generally applicable, while issues and opinions are not.

Barber is quite aware of the nature of his, or any, typological theory. "What is de-emphasized in this scheme?" he asks. "Everything which does not lend itself to the production of potentially testable generalizations about presidential behavior. Thus we shall be less concerned with the substance or content of particular political issues." Barber is not unconcerned with the content of political issues, but his concern is different from that of the politician. For Barber, political debate covers or partially hides more fundamental aspects of the participants' personalities.

> By moving a step up the ladder of abstraction, from particular issue stands and standardized ideological expressions to the leader's worldview we begin to get at themes at once more persistent and more significant in shaping action. A close review of what he has said over the years may reveal a fairly consistent set of assumptions—about how

history works, what people are like, what the main purposes of politics are (to use the three I have found most useful). The product is a cognitive operational code of sorts, a set of politically relevant perceptual habits, *hardly ever put together in a systematic way by the leader himself* but derivable from his many comments as he experiences practical problems.[62]

The locus of thought relevant to personality is "worldview." The advantage of this concept to the theory builder is that one can focus upon static or at least enduring attachments. Thus, thought is transposed for the purposes of this kind of research into "belief-systems" which are visible to the investigator but not to the investigated.

To be fair, Barber did not adopt this kind of analysis simply because that was what "theory" inherently required. Rather, he turned to constructing a theory because he found issue positions and "ideology" of little help in describing what presidents did.

The straight-out analysis of the content of the reasons the actor offers for his actions is of limited utility. Variations in the actual responses of political leaders to roughly the same circumstances warn against relying too much on the leader's plain spoken explanations. . . . Nor are his expressed intentions much help. . . . Nor have Presidents' ideologies—left or right—helped much in explaining what they did.[63]

Barber's first study of presidential personality was devoted to the political styles of Calvin Coolidge and Herbert Hoover. Barber does not indicate why Hoover's or Coolidge's reasoning can't account for their behavior, but he goes on to make an even more startling claim—that if his theory works with these presidents, it can work with all presidents.

The dull Presidents are a trial for the political analyst, particularly for the student of personality and political leadership. . . . They . . . provide "hard case" tests for the supposition that personality helps shape a President's politics. If a personality approach can work with Coolidge and Hoover, it can work with any chief executive.[64]

But why so? The need for parsimony concomitant with the development of theory *may* be compatible with the characteristics of most presidents. It may be necessary to simplify the "variables," including thought, that impinge upon a weak or common

president in order to discern the determinants of presidential behavior. If this proves true, Barber's kind of approach might be the
most fruitful way to study most presidents. However, Barber is
wrong to suggest that his theory "can work with any chief executive." A theory that explains the behavior of mediocre presidents
cannot be assumed prior to investigation to explain the actions of
great presidents.

Like the view that political issues and political judgment matter, the notion that some presidents are great in terms of political
skill and perspicacity is one common to the citizen perspective.
Scholars frequently denigrate the appellation "great" because it
often betrays unreflective hero-worship rather than sober analysis, but it is hard to deny that some of our political leaders have
had uncommon abilities. Barber might respond that he does not
mean to deny that some presidents are greater than others, but
rather to identify a clearer and more adequate basis for evalua-
tion. Yet Barber's theory precludes one of the important traditional qualities of greatness—uncommon perspicacity. If one
takes seriously the possibility that a politician may be great in this
sense, one must begin by assuming that the politician may have
been able to see and understand things which, without his assistance, remain inaccessible to the inquiring scholar. In short, one
must begin by assuming that one may learn something *from* a
president before, or at least while, one attempts to learn *about* a
president. This procedure by no means prevents one from reach-
ing the conclusion that a particular president had nothing to
teach, but proceeding as Barber does in assuming that he is capable of knowing Lincoln's most important thoughts better than
Lincoln precludes the scholar from discovering that he is mistaken. The "great" presidents pose special difficulties because
they are supposed to have had minds incapable of description according to criteria simple and formal enough to be applied to
most men.

Among Barber's own case studies, one can find some evidence
that this problem plagued Barber. Noteworthy is his admitted
difficulty in describing Franklin Roosevelt. Barber considered
FDR "the most remarkable of all modern Presidents." Not sur-
prisingly, he also proved to be for Barber, "the least self-revealing

President."[65] Although FDR held the longest presidential tenure in history, Barber devotes relatively few pages to discussion of FDR's White House years. In fact, he devotes twice as much space to the discussion of each of the Truman and Kennedy presidencies. Barber spends most of the brief FDR discussion explaining away two incidents that appear to reveal active-negative tendencies. While obviously "active" and obviously "positive," FDR (like Lincoln and the active-negatives) does not unambiguously resemble other presidents of his type, when one proceeds beyond the "baseline" variables.

Does the possibility that presidential understanding molds behavior mean that "thought" is a completely independent variable, attaching itself to the things presidents see? Is it not quite plausible, as a personality theorist might argue, that presidents don't see everything around them, but rather have selective perception, seeing and discussing some things and not others? Certainly this must be true, but the fact that presidents like everyone (even personality theorists) have selective perception should not propel one to the immediate conclusion that the spectacles through which presidents view the world are unknown to them. One of the most striking facts about pre–Civil War politics is the degree to which Lincoln and Douglas chose to view the issues of their day through a constitutional lense. Without going into the merits of their respective arguments—one beginning from the principle of equality, the other from popular sovereignty—it must be emphasized that the agenda of issues that constituted their dispute and framed their arguments was set by the Constitution. The character of the political dispute just prior to the Civil War derived from a widespread deference to "issues." And in this case constitutional issues were the crucial political consideration.[66]

What is the practical consequence of the theoretical deprecation of issues? In considering this question, we move from the adequacy of Barber's theory as explanation to reflection upon the worth of his theory as a pedagogy. Barber is quite explicit in offering his teaching as a guide to the citizenry's selection of future presidents. Implicitly, Barber's theory is also a pedagogy for presidents themselves, because presidents will try to appear to be what their electorate expects. V. O. Key noticed this same political consequence when he criticized the denial of issue voting in seminal studies of voting behavior.

> If leaders believe the route to victory is by projection of images and cultivation of styles rather than by advocacy of policies to cope with the problems of the country, they will project images and cultivate styles to the neglect of the substance of politics. They will abdicate their prime function in a democratic system, which amounts, in essence, to the assumption of the risk of trying to persuade us to lift ourselves by our bootstraps.[67]

To the extent that Barber's vocabulary enters the realm of politics itself, politicians may come to believe that success depends primarily upon appearing to have the right character. This poses difficulty for Barber's future empirical work, because statements which were formerly uttered naïvely by politicians unaware of the use to which they would be put (statements like "I enjoy my work") may now be uttered with the conscious purpose of projecting the right character. While the record is not complete on Carter's personality, for example, he is a president who admired Barber's book and seems to have been influenced by it. How do we know whether Carter's active-positive smiles and repeated claims that he enjoys his work represent his character, or rather his artfulness? (Despite Barber's efforts to "steer clear of obvious puff jobs put out in campaigns" one of the main sources for his data on Carter is *Why Not the Best.*)[68]

The main problem, however, is not the future adequacy of Barber's empirical studies, now that his theory is public, but rather the relative merits of a constitutional pedagogy versus the new personality teaching for the actual conduct of the presidency. Certainly no personality theory, even one wholeheartedly embraced by a president and his public, could obliterate the president's day-to-day concern with issues or with constitutional matters in times of crisis—that is not the danger. Presidents will continue to fashion policies and defend them before Congress and the public. But how sound will these policies be, and how capable will the public be to judge them? Isn't it probable that presidential policy will be better formulated and presidential rhetoric more intelligent if presidents function under the auspices of a public opinion informed by a theory emphasizing policy and reason than by a theory that places a premium on character and style?

NOTES TO CHAPTER VIII

1. James David Barber, *The Presidential Character* (2nd ed.; Englewood, N.J.: Prentice Hall, 1977; orig. pub. 1972). See also Barber's other writings: "The President after Watergate," *World*, July 13, 1973; "Tone-Deaf in the Oval Office," *Saturday Review/World*, January 12, 1974; "Active-Positive Character," *Time*, January 3, 1977; "Comment: Qualls' Nonsensical Analysis of Nonexistent Works," *American Political Science Review*, LXXI (March, 1977); "The Question of Presidential Character," *Saturday Review*, October, 1972. See also Michael Mandelbaum, "Political Science: A Discipline Shaped Not by Accord But by Disagreement," New York *Times*, March 27, 1977.

2. Harold Lasswell, *Psychopathology and Politics*, (Rev. ed.; New York: Viking Press, 1969). For a thorough assessment of Lasswell's work, see Robert Horwitz, "Scientific Propaganda: Harold D. Lasswell," in Herbert J. Storing (ed.), *Essays on the Scientific Study of Politics* (New York: Holt, Rhinehart and Winston, 1962). Some of Barber's conceptual improvements are noted by Alexander George in "Assessing Presidential Character," *World Politics*, XXVII (January, 1974), 2. For a complete survey of previous work in this field, see Fred Greenstein, *Personality and Politics* (Rev. ed.; New York: W. W. Norton, 1975).

3. George, "Assessing Presidential Character," 246; James H. Qualls, "Barber's Typological Analysis of Political Leaders," *American Political Science Review*, LXXI (March, 1977), 185; Erwin Hargrove, "Presidential Personality and Revisionist Views of the Presidency," *American Journal of Political Science*, XVII (November, 1973), 4.

4. Barber, *Presidential Character*, vi.

5. Alexander George and Juliette George, *Woodrow Wilson and Colonel House* (New York: Dover, 1964). There have been many other important single-actor studies (for example Erik Erikson's *Young Man Luther*), but except for George and George, the best of these do not examine American presidents. There has been one atheoretical, and very interesting, study of the personalities of six presidents: Erwin C. Hargrove, *Presidential Leadership, Personality and Political Style* (New York: Macmillan, 1966).

6. George, "Assessing Presidential Character," 278 (my emphasis).

7. "The State of the Presidency," (interview) Chicago *Sunday Sun-Times*, September 23, 1973, Sec. 1A, p. 2.

8. See, for example, George Ticknor Curtis, *Constitutional History of the United States* (New York: Harper & Brothers, 1889), 292.

9. Max Farrand (ed.), *Records of the Federal Convention of 1787* (4 vols.; New Haven: Yale University Press, 1966), I, 82–85.

10. Alexander Hamilton, James Madison, and John Jay, *The Federalist Papers*, ed. Clinton Rossiter (New York: New American Library, 1961), No. 73, p. 441.

11. *Federalist*, No. 64, p. 396. Without reeligibility, "an avaricious man who might happen to fill the office, looking forward to a time when he must at all events yield up the advantages he enjoyed, would feel a propensity not easy to be resisted to such a man to make the best use of his opportunities [and] might not scruple to have recourse to the most corrupt expedients." (*Federalist*, No. 72, p. 437.)

12. *Federalist*, No. 64, p. 391.

13. Barber, *Presidential Character*, 5.

14. *Ibid.*, 7–8.

15. *Ibid.*, 10.

16. This summary of remarks by Barber was compiled by Alexander George. See George, "Assessing Presidential Character," 248–49, and Barber *Presidential Character*, 12–13.

17. Barber, *Presidential Character*, 446–48, 458, 460.

18. *Ibid.*, 145.

19. But see *ibid.*, 445.

20. *Ibid.*, 470.

21. George, "Assessing Presidential Character," 273–75.

22. James David Barber, "Strategies for Understanding Politicians," *American Journal of Political Science*, XVIII (May, 1974), 450; "Adult Identity and Presidential Style: The Rhetorical Emphasis," *Daedalus* (Summer, 1968).

23. Barber, "Strategies for Understanding Politicians"; Barber, "Coding Scheme for Presidential Biographies," mimeo (January, 1960), 39 pp.; Barber, "The Question of Presidential Character."

24. Benjamin P. Thomas, *Abraham Lincoln* (New York: Knopf, 1952), 121.

25. *Ibid.*, 184.

26. *Ibid.*, 456; J. G. Randall, *Lincoln the President* (2 vols.; New York: Dodd Mead & Co., 1945), II, 165; Richard N. Current, *Lincoln Nobody Knows* (New York: Farrar, Straus, 1958).

27. Randall, *Lincoln*, I, 49; Current, *Lincoln Nobody Knows*, 12.

28. Thomas, *Abraham Lincoln*, 500.

29. Barber, *Presidential Character*, 99; Current, *Lincoln Nobody Knows*, 12.

30. Thomas, *Abraham Lincoln*, 70; 181; 93.

31. *Ibid.*, 173.

32. *Ibid.*, 143.

33. *Ibid.*, 454.

34. *Ibid.*, 358.

35. Randall, *Lincoln*, I, 28.

36. Thomas, *Abraham Lincoln*, 226.

37. *Ibid.*, 303.

38. *Ibid.*, 339.

39. *Ibid.*, 195; 200.

40. Randall, *Lincoln*, I, 279.

41. *Ibid.*, II, 243.

42. Thomas, *Abraham Lincoln*, 239.

43. Randall, *Lincoln*, I, 279.

44. *Ibid.*, II, 160.

45. *Ibid.*, 243.

46. Thomas, *Abraham Lincoln*, 409; 425.

47. *Ibid.*, 440.

48. *Ibid.*, 135; 231.

49. *Ibid.*, 267; Randall, *Lincoln*, I, 63.

50. Thomas, *Abraham Lincoln*, 21.

51. Robert W. Johannsen, *Stephen A. Douglas* (New York: Oxford, 1973).

52. *Ibid.*, 8.

53. *Ibid.*

54. *Ibid.*, 67; 598.

55. *Ibid.*, 123*ff*, 658.

56. "When sitting he appeared of medium height, but 'his legs were very short.' His massive and 'intellectual' head was crowned with thick black hair, his light blue or gray eyes sparkled and his mouth and chin were firm." *Ibid.*, 92; 204; 4; 92.

57. *Ibid.*, 501, 342, 453; 551*ff*.

58. *Ibid.*, see especially 256, 45, 236, 491, 79, 291.

59. Barber, *Presidential Character*, 242.

60. *Ibid.*, 177.

61. See, for example, Arthur M. Schlesinger, "Our Presidents: A Rating by 75 Historians," *New York Times Magazine*, July 29, 1962, p. 12, and Erwin Hargrove, *The Power of the Modern Presidency*, (Philadelphia: Temple University Press, 1974), 4–6.

62. Barber, "Coding Scheme," 3; and "Strategies for Understanding," 464 (my emphasis).

63. *Ibid.*, 463.

64. James David Barber, "Classifying and Predicting Presidential Styles: Two Weak Presidents," *Journal of Social Issues*, XXIV (1968).

65. Barber, *Presidential Character*, 211.

66. See Harry Jaffa, *Crisis of the House Divided* (2nd ed.; Seattle, Washington: University of Washington, 1971). For a discussion of Lincoln's character in light of his understanding of the political issues, see Lord Charnwood, *Abraham Lincoln* (New York: Henry Holt, 1916).

67. V. O. Key, Jr., *The Responsible Electorate* (New York: Vintage Books, 1966), 6.

68. Barber, *Presidential Character*, preface to the first edition.

The Ambivalence of Executive Power

HARVEY C. MANSFIELD, JR.

There has long been a party of men who reluctantly admit that all government arises from force and accident rather than reflection and choice. In our day it has been joined by others of a reforming bent who assert this truth (as they suppose it) because they find it hopeful and forget that it is humiliating. This distinction regarding the origin of government is borrowed from the opening page of *The Federalist*, and it states clearly and comprehensively what the American founders claimed to have done. My purpose is to examine one topic of their supposed reflection and choice, the executive power, which is the very power most responsive and most subject to force and accident. Could the executive power have been formed from reflection and choice?

In this essay I shall attempt to approach the nature of executive power by considering whether the modern executive could have been the consequence of a modern doctrine of executive power. Whether the American president was in fact formed from that doctrine or instead fashioned more pragmatically from existing materials left ready to hand by historical circumstances, I shall not determine,[1] but I hope to provide information necessary, if not sufficient, to answer this question. For we cannot know the importance of the doctrine of executive power until we learn what it is, and that is not an easy task. The deepest questions and the best hopes of modern political philosophy are involved in the working of the kingly office with the modest title of executive which has become so familiar to us. These questions and hopes may be introduced through reflection on the current literature in political science on the executive, even though that literature is for the most part unaware of any modern doctrine of executive power.

But is there such a doctrine? It may come as a disagreeable surprise that executive power should be presented as a modern doctrine, when it is universally agreed to be a modern necessity. No modern state is considered viable unless it is equipped with a strong executive, and any state without one is held to be courting disaster and is regarded with pity and contempt by others more fortunate and more virtuous. Nor can the necessity be dismissed as an unconscious assumption which is unchallenged because it is universal. Even though the assumption is universal, but precisely because it extends to free and unfree governments alike, there are always some and sometimes many living under free governments who murmur at strong executive actions they find distasteful. They deplore and oppose them as the practices of tyranny, cursing them with one of the many contemporary equivalents for that term which our prudery requires and our experience makes very familiar. Yet the protesters subside soon enough as if in recognition of necessity, unless indeed they change their tune and begin to clamor for strong executive actions they find beneficial. The necessity of a strong executive has, therefore, been tested by those to whom it has not been obvious. Then to present executive power as a modern doctrine, implying discovery of something previously hidden and choice among the new and the old possibilities thus revealed, is to speak in the face of a need that seems obvious and compelling. Why was it necessary to teach us the institution that seems to be inflicted on us?

If we were at the end of a long inquiry into the nature and history of executive power, it would be sufficient to reply that the early teachers of executive power intended to secure the difference between free and unfree governments by giving the former the power of the latter: in fact, they may have helped to efface that difference. But for now, we can see an ambivalence in executive power which does not arise from straightforward, ineluctable necessity, and calls for some kind of clarification—perhaps a doctrine. For the "executive" has two meanings as used in politics today.

One meaning is the dictionary definition, he who "carries out," as in the American Constitution the president is given the duty to "take care that the laws be faithfully executed." (Article II, section 3). *Execute* derived from the Latin *exsequor*, meaning "follow out" and used by both classical authors and the Roman law in the extended and particular sense of following out a law to the end: to vindicate or to punish.[2] The Greek equivalents λαμβάνειν τελός and ἐκβιβάζειν are also used so. In this primary meaning, the American president would serve merely to carry out the intention of the law, that is, the will of others—of the legislature; and if any actual president confined himself to this, he would be referred to contemptuously as an "errand boy." He would be nothing in himself, a mere agent whose duty is to command actions according to the law. With his usual extremism, the philosopher Kant has represented this meaning of the executive in the form of a syllogism, where the major premise is the legislative will, the minor premise or "the principle of subsumption" is the executive, and the conclusion is the judicial application to particulars.[3] By the syllogistic form the executive function is separated rather artificially from the judicial, but it is definitely made subordinate to the legislative.

Yet it would be unwise for any legislature, willing the major premise, to speak openly of its executive as an errand boy, for fear of diminishing his utility by hurting his pride. Executive pride transcends the primary dictionary definition of "executive." It is expressed in the phrase "law enforcement," in which it is implied that carrying out the law does not come about as a matter of course. "Law enforcement" implies a recalcitrance to law in the human beings who are subject to it, making necessary a claim by the executive to some of the authority and majesty of the law itself. To execute the law it is sometimes not enough for a policeman to ask politely; he must drop the attitude of an errand boy and do something impressive to make himself respected. And, arguing from the clearer case, we may say that if a policeman must be more than an errand boy, so must a president.

Perhaps the authority of law is more evident in "law enforcement" than its majesty. The end of law as stated or implied in the law (the final cause) is a noble thought which we respect, to which we are dedicated, and for which government would execute the law in the primary, instrumental sense; but execution as law enforcement puts us in fear and reminds us of the reason why laws are made (the efficient cause): to dispel fear and provide security. It makes use of legalized lawlessness, that is, of actions which would be illegal if they were not done by the police. These are punitive actions, sometimes done so impressively as to suggest that the purpose of law is to punish. This execution also allows or even requires the executive to gather in his person the power which enabled the first lawgiver to awe his unsettled subjects, and to exude the fearfulness of a being who makes and executes his own law, as if he were an angry god. It would not be too much to say that executive pride smacks of tyranny, so radically does it enlarge upon the instrumental executive.

It is all very well to speak sententiously of a government of laws, not of men, but the executive may reply that this is an unsupported assertion of legislative pride. Laws that are mere demonstrations to the intellect are like prayers to the deaf. Because the government of laws rules over recalcitrant men, the laws are nothing in fact unless they are executed, and to get them executed, the executive must be given some or most or all of the legislative pride. In this view, a government of laws addressed to men is reducible to a government of men.

Thus, in recognition of executive pride, we find in the Constitution that taking care to execute the laws faithfully is only one of the duties imposed on the president, for the performance of which he is given several enumerated powers. Among these are powers neither executive in nature (the veto of legislation) nor subordinate (commander-in-chief of the army and navy). Moreover, he is vested with "the executive power," which according to Hamilton's famous argument,[4] has a nature of its own, bounded only by necessity, which is not exhausted by the enumerated powers; and he takes an oath not to faithfully execute the laws but to faithfully execute his *office*. In Kant (to pursue our previous reference), not only is the executive represented as a minor premise, but we also find, with the covert, corrective realism that is as usual with Kant as his theoretical extremism, that the executive is later described as a moral person of coordinate power with the other two powers.[5] If not a tyrant, the real, practical, informal executive is far more powerful than the supposed, theoretical, formal executive.

He is also quicker and more masterful. In today's political science the term "decision making" is applied indiscriminately to all governmental actions or to all actions whatever, for the sake of the marvelous revelation that all decisions are similar and none of them particularly "executive." It is admitted, however, that decisions sometimes follow one another in a series, and so one hears of "the legislative process," "the judicial process," and "the administrative process." But Chester Barnard's phrase, "the executive process," has not caught on.[6] In the actual usage of this political science, as distinguished from its intent, an aroma of "decisive" issues from the workaday, reassuring notion of "decision making."

In the literature of political science on the presidency, the ambivalence of the executive is reflected more obviously. The two works that have led the field in the recent past, Richard E. Neustadt's *Presidential Power* and Edward S. Corwin's *The President: Offices and Powers*, represent the real, informal presidency and the limited formal presidency, respectively. Neustadt defines two conceptions of the office as clerkship and leadership, and clearly prefers the president who builds his own position out of his own initiatives, using the formal powers of his office and making himself from a clerk into a leader. Corwin, for his part, does not deny the reality of personal power in the president; but he deplores it. Instead of studying examples of executive power like Neustadt, he divides it into powers or functions or roles, thereby defining and delimiting it. He is not ashamed to study the "literary theory"[7] of the presidency partly in the intention of the framers of the Constitution and at length in cases of constitutional law. His understanding is legal and prescriptive rather than realistic, and if Corwin does not reduce the president to a clerk, he asks us to recall Dunning's resolution on the influence of the crown in the eighteenth century and revise it thus: "The power of the President has increased, is increasing, and ought to be diminished."[8]

Corwin's opinion, expressed as minority comment on Franklin Roosevelt and Harry Truman, and almost forgotten in the lauding of the presidency that accompanied John F. Kennedy's accession, has recently gained favor among observers having Richard Nixon in view.[9] A cynic might have said that no theory of a strong republican executive could survive the appearance of a strong Republican executive—until Nixon made this sayable by a partisan. But it would be a mistake to suppose that our minds are always narrowed, never broadened, by partisanship. We should take the opportunity to observe that the realistic school of interpretation, even with the advantage of long periods of domination, has never succeeded in destroying the formal school, just as the formal school has never quite succeeded in defining the reality of executive power. One school serves justice, the other necessity; and both serve partisans according as they claim justice in opposition and necessity in power.

When examined, moreover, each of the schools reveals something of the other in itself. Corwin admits that the Constitution itself reflects a struggle between two conceptions of executive power which may be identified with the two discussed here: a weak executive resulting from the notion that the people are *represented* in the legislature, a strong executive from the notion that they are *embodied* in the executive.[10] Though Corwin would seem to prefer the former conception, he never questions the need for both conceptions; and it is hard to see why the people should be embodied in one man if not to secure the unity of executive powers despite their separate definitions through the unity of one human body. He proposes to control presidential power, to make it more regular and less personal, and to establish a cabinet council including legislative leaders, but not to remove executive power from one man. As the reality of that one man is quite personal, so must be the reality of the power formally conferred on him.

Or does the reality of the president's power depend on the form? It is always curious, if not always gratifying, to observe the power of innocence in this world; and one interesting expression of it is to be found in the way that those who in theory reject the influence of constitutional forms in reality take them for granted. For instance, Neustadt's main argument is that the president must acquire and use personal power in order to secure the formal power promised, but not guaranteed, by the "literary theory," the constitutional forms, and the developed expectations of the office. He holds that the president is formally a strong executive, and in reality either weak or strong according to his personal strength. But with this view one takes for granted the opportunity for strength afforded by the Constitution, since it is the Constitution that gives the president "his unique place in our political system" and enables or requires him to sit where he sits—a favorite phrase of Neustadt's borrowed from Harry Truman to denote the base of operations rather than formal occupancy. Neustadt distinguishes between formal power and "effective influence," thus making it clear that for him formal power is ineffectual. Formal power is the power to compel, and Neustadt's book is devoted to the proposition that the power to compel is worthless by itself. It is actually harmful if a president believes that he can rely on it, and it is useful only if it is recognized to be a subordinate factor in the work of persuasion or among the "incidents in a persuasive process." [11]

But is it not more reasonable and realistic to suppose, on the contrary, that persuasion is incidental or instrumental to compulsion? Although the power to compel must often or even always be supplemented by the power to persuade, a president's power to persuade would be much less without his power to compel, his appeal to interest much weaker without his ability to raise fear. Moreover, to the extent that he must persuade (which is admittedly considerable), is this not by command of the Constitution? Persuading others (or bargaining with them) is made a regular necessity for the president, and generally in American politics, by the peculiar separation and sharing of powers ordained by the Constitution. As Neustadt says, "the limits on command suggest the structure of our government"; and he traces the structure to the Constitution. It would seem that "effective influence" is thereby grounded in formal power. But he does not appreciate the force of his concession, for he concludes shortly afterward that "the probabilities of power do not derive from the literary theory of the Constitution." [12] Neustadt, then, takes for granted the potential strength of the presidential office, which might become active in the most self-effacing personality with or even without the tutelage of Neustadt's "literary theory." [13] There is a kind of teaching in the constitutional powers themselves discernible or at least presentable to political men.

Besides taking for granted the formal strength of the executive, Neustadt overlooks its formal weakness and thus its ambivalence. "The limits on command" suggesting the structure of our government thereby also suggest that formal restraints impose real restraints compelling presidents to bargain rather than command. Moreover, although convinced of the need for a strong executive, he pays no heed to the dictionary definition of *executive* and takes no account of the modest pretense, required of even the strongest presidents and perhaps especially of them, to be executing the will of someone else. He identifies the formal executive with the constitutional presidency, but the latter includes, as we have seen, powers that go beyond the merely formal executive power. It is perhaps by constitutional design that the president must achieve his leadership and that the alternative of clerkship is open to him either as a refuge from responsibility or a cloak for his aggrandizement. Neustadt rightly lays emphasis on the truth that persuading others means persuading them that something is in their interest. But to succeed in such persuasion, it is useful to have the instrumental conception of the office by which it can be made to appear that the president in himself is so to speak nothing, a mere representative of stronger forces. Thus he need not demand obedience to his will but only implore that his listener take pity on him for what he must do, and adjust his own conduct accordingly. The very notion of "interest" is a disguise for assertiveness, as it implies something abstract and objective to be followed, distinct from will or caprice. What I must do in my interest is, as it were, imposed on me. Too bad for you, but surely you understand?

As for the president's personal power, one can sometimes get more from a broker's commission than from a direct payment. Neustadt knows this and affirms that "persuasion becomes bargaining," [14] but he does not note that the president's formal weakness is suited to the character of his personal power. And when this has been said, one must wonder what his personal power is. Neustadt leaves it ambiguous whether it is the power of the presidential (or any other) office, with which the president identifies himself, or the pursuit of his private interest to which his official power is merely an instrument. Given this ambiguity, the president's "unique place in our political system" cannot guarantee that his is the only concern for the whole. Does the rule of law necessarily reduce to executive pride served by executive connivance? If so, the executive would be more than the leader who can be compared to a clerk.

Recently a more psychological theory of the informal executive has gained new expression. It offers to explain the personality of the president, which is assumed to be the critical factor in his behavior as opposed to the political situation or his constitutional office. One might expect therefore, that the fearsome aspect of the executive, which is the more personal, would be stressed and its lawful character made light of. This expectation is neither entirely frustrated nor happily fulfilled. Personality is divided into personalities, and these are defined as types or roles with much of the formalism used by constitution makers to define offices. James Barber, in his influential book, fixes on the "active-positive" personality as the preferred type of president, an active president who enjoys his activity free of the compulsive drive for power for its own sake. Such a personality is very fortunately composed: he is, as we expect, active, and so escapes the mean compliance of the "passive-positive" executive as well as the dutiful propriety of the "passive-negative" type; but since he is also positive, he avoids the temptations to violence to which the active-negative executive yields, in his silly heroism and braggart masculinity. The active-positive executive is permitted and even encouraged by Barber to indulge his love of fun and his belief that politics is fun.[15]

The sunny democratic optimism of this character and his maker is quite remarkable. Barber apparently assumes, contrary to his premise that personality is more important than institutions, that the modern executive cannot be passive or weak. He may mean to imply that the weak executive serves the compulsiveness of legislators in meekly executing the laws they pass, and thus becomes strong by servility to strength; but the modern executive must be strong somehow. In any case Franklin D. Roosevelt cannot be described as weak, and he clearly loved politics. But did he love all the sterner deeds that strength sometimes requires, such as ordering his country to war; and did he love the deceptions[16] suggested by his political skill, not all of which could be considered practical jokes? Is not Lincoln's melancholy irony, though negative, appropriate to these negative necessities? [17] If a strong executive is necessary, it is not to lead the nation at play, unless the game is understood as a competition; and then it is too much to believe that a politician's desire to win will rouse him from passivity without ever carrying him past the threshold of a dangerous desire for mastery. The active-positive character is nothing but a wish, a political hope displaced upon psychological theory. Such a character could not check his own desire for mastery without having the diffident "civic virtue" of the passive-negative character, and if he were checked by others with institutional restraints in the spirit of *The Federalist*'s maxim, "Ambition must be made to counteract ambition," [18] he would be one active-negative character among others.

Barber's work has prospered in the current fashion of psychohistory, and also because he can claim to have called the turn on active-negative Richard Nixon. But his proximate intellectual antecedent is Harold Lasswell, whose *Power and Personality* (1948) also reflects the problem of a not-so-playful desire for mastery, and more sharply.[19] Lasswell is never loath to grasp the far-off and far-out consequences of the fashionable ideas he promotes, and his chief merit is the zeal with which he promotes them to an unfashionable degree: he reveals them for what they are and may, perhaps, unwittingly sound an alarm with the piercing shriek of his trumpet of progress. When he describes the traits of the power seeker, he does not hesitate to draw the necessary conclusion that they are completely satisfied only in a world ruler.[20] And he is not embarrassed to assert that the long-run aim of his policy sciences is to "get rid of power," [21] that is, to get rid of politics, because politics includes—or rather centers on—what he clinically entitles "severe deprivations." [22]

In the short run, however, Lasswell is interested in curbing and chastening power by promoting the democratic personality which is free of social anxiety and accompanying unhealthy negativism. In government Lasswell would in general favor the type "agitator," responsive to change, flexible in crisis, and tolerant of diversity, over the type "bureaucrat," whose compulsive desire for uniformity expresses the wish to avoid responsibility.[23]

These agitators, like Barber's active-passive presidents, are intended to be strong executives, but not too strong. Again, the
notion of executing another's will which is essential to the institution of executive awkwardly and noticeably limits the psychological role which has been arbitrarily constructed to replace
it—as if nature had undertaken to provide the souls suitable for
leaders of the Democratic party.[24]

Leaving the American presidency, we remark two notable
works by M. J. C. Vile and W. B. Gwyn that have recently appeared, in which we again observe the ambivalence of executive
power. Both authors insist that the doctrine of separation of
powers must be understood in connection or, as they say, confusion with the notion of the mixed or balanced constitution.[25]
The cause of this confusion, although they do not say so, would
seem to be the problem of executive power. Since the separation
of powers is argued on the basis of an analysis of functions, it
must result in a weak executive subordinate to the legislative
function. Yet the powers do not remain separate in operation unless they are powerful against each other, and thus independent;
for this a strong executive is required. As no formal definition of
"executive" power based on the dictionary or functional meaning
can elevate it to equality with legislative power, a supplement of
informal reality must be found and justified with the doctrine of
the mixed or balanced constitution. To secure actually separate
powers, the doctrine of separation of powers must reach outside
its justification for separation and grasp some notion of executive
power in the expanded sense. The supposed confusion of the separation of powers and the mixed constitution arises from a recognition, more or less profound, of this necessity; and the history of
the doctrine of separation of powers needs to be considered in relation to executive power.

If the weak and strong executives are admitted to be both persistent and pervasive, it may be advanced next that they depend
on one another.[26] For executive power is typical of modern government, in which form and reality are consistently to be found
at a certain distance from each other. Modern government claims
to be representative of the people as a whole, but in reality some
people are better represented than others; it claims to be demo-

cratic, but is actually oligarchic or elitist; it claims to be constitutional, but extra-constitutional forces, such as parties, actually run it; it claims to be merely instrumental to the "pursuit of happiness," but in reality fosters a certain notion of happiness; its peoples claim to be citizens, but are in fact no more than voters, if that; and its leaders claim to be executives, but are actually rulers. The pattern is sufficiently distinct to make one suspect the presence of a deliberate intention to separate the form from the reality.

As regards the executive, we have suggested that the weak, formal executive is an aid to the strong, informal executive. When explaining the policy laid down by the Emperor Augustus, Gibbon says, on the first page of his history, that "the Roman Senate appeared to possess the sovereign authority, and devolved on the emperors all the executive powers of governments."[27] He meant that the real government was supposedly executive for the supposed government; and from its origin the notion of executive seems to have held, not weakness but the semblance of weakness, a disguise of its own strength in the strength of another, the bashful and retiring habit, together with the efficient activity, of the *éminence grise*. For it is an addition of power to conceal it or deprecate it, and the regular pretense of "executing" another's wishes, however easily penetrated, is so far from disgusting to those who think they cannot be fooled that they come to value the courtesies of their "executives" as much as they would enjoy the exercise of their own power. Modern citizens in the more jaded liberal democracies even take a perverse pleasure in figuring out the tricks by which they are, not deceived to be sure, but merely governed; and our modern political science offers its superfluous findings in aid of this dubious contemplation.

Yet it is also necessary to look in the reverse direction at the strong executive as an aid to the weak, and to make another obvious observation. For if the weak executive is bashful and retiring, the strong executive is, on the contrary, bold and impressive. Instead of a cloak to wear, he has an image to create and to cultivate; and it is an image of bursting masculine energy impressively controlled because just barely under control. The regularity of his execution is interrupted by unpredictable shifts which can later be seen (by the sophisticated courtiers of modern democracies: journalists, columnists, and political scientists) to have been calculated. He may well be suspected of a disconcerting taste for the sensational, so eagerly does he seize upon an accident of politics to magnify it for his own use. He may even create accidents; he is a master of what Neustadt calls "initiatives," which are motions toward something new—designs for him, surprises to others. He surely does not shrink from raising alarms, or from making forceful reminders of what is what and who is who. His indulgences are sweetened by his punishments, and the effect of his active-positive smile is enhanced by the occasional appearance of his active-negative frown. The purpose of all this, however, may not be merely to boost the ego of the weak executive (who is a character of comedy), but also to make his lawful executions easier and less oppressive. A snarl or a bite every once in a while, if carefully chosen, will quiet the brave and satisfy the multitude by venting pent-up humors and releasing a wholesome, wondering fear. The result is more useful to free governments than to tyrannies, because the necessary exactions of any government bring more danger and dishonor to the former; and every lessening of the inevitable hatreds of a free people reduces those necessary exactions upon it. A single, quick stroke is always impressive and almost painless. When thoughts such as these have been elaborated to explain "the economy of violence"[28]—one might also say, the humanity of violence—the strong executive can be seen to make possible the weak.

Economical government might not seem weak, but government that confines itself to limited ends, such as peace and security, is not ambitious, however energetic it may be. While the strong executive may raise the fear of punishment, he does so for the purpose of quieting the fear of insecurity. His strength serves the government's preoccupation with the necessities that cause men to fear. From the point of view of government by "reflection and choice," such preoccupation could be seen as a surrender to "force and accident," and in that way a sign of weakness in the purposes proposed for government. Thus an energetic executive gives effect to a government of limited purpose that is not energetic as a whole in the service of human nobility.

The ambivalence of the executive, therefore, must be understood not only as two rival, contrary conceptions but more as the same thing in two phases or aspects.[29] One must look beyond the differences between Presidents Coolidge and Roosevelt to the notion of the executive that unites them, which is reflected in the simple and obvious fact that both held the same office. What is the office that can survive, and satisfy, these two men? As for the psychological theory we have reviewed, it does not realize that the matrix of personalities it so proudly displays is not its own discovery but the creation of the office. For the psychological realists have made up their reality out of someone else's creations. If an executive can be active or passive, positive or negative, it is because the office permits it or suggests it; and it is only by previous arrangement of the founders of the office that it corresponds, if it does, to human nature or human natures. The unity of the office implies the possibility, though unlikely, of one man who would be the perfect executive, combining the ambivalence in himself, ducking out of sight and leaping into view when necessary and appropriate. The knowledge this man would have, when combined with the knowledge of how to tolerate the lack of that knowledge in others—for ordinarily executives excel in being weak or strong or whatever, not in being both or anything—would be the doctrine of executive power, uniting its two phases while justifying their separation.

That a doctrine is needed to combine them is as evident for the constitutional executive as for the party executive. Keeping our eyes solely on the free and civilized world so as to avoid complication, we can discern two kinds of chief executives in practice (not to mention intermediate varieties): the constitutional executive like the American, who draws his powers from a formal document, and the party executive like the British, especially under the Labor party, who has them from an informal source, his party. The constitutional executive, having powers stated in the constitution, does not rely on strict party discipline in the legislature when he exercises them; but he does require, it would seem, the aid of some general understanding in favor of strong executive power in order to resist legislative usurpation and its eager partner, overbearing bureaucracy. He needs a doctrine, a "literary theory," to protect himself against the partisan application of the dictionary definition of *executive* by the legislature, reducing him to its instrument.

In such a case, necessity might recommend strong executive action, but necessity is a teacher only to those compelled to recognize it, and that is often too late. Moreover, necessity cannot teach successfully if the actions it requires leave a bad conscience in the strong executive and in those who acquiesced in his strong actions. Even the constitution would not be enough to defend him if there were no public reasoning available to tell men why the executive should have access to powers which are not strictly executive. The American president is not sufficiently fortified by his constitutional powers, for in practice they might be denied to him. Some justification, such as Hamilton's argument in *The Federalist*, Numbers 70–77, to show why a strong executive is compatible with republican government, is also needed. And the party executive, who is the beneficiary of party discipline more than formal constitutional powers, needs the same protection against party dictation that the constitutional executive needs against legislative usurpation. Here even the legislature is sustained against party dictation through the justification for the strong executive, for legislative independence is greatly restricted by party discipline but can be sustained by the task of calling to account the strong executive, a task which parties cannot perform so well.

If a doctrine is needed to explain and support the ambivalence of executive power, what might it be? What advantages are expected from an office that expands and contracts, that reveals itself and hides? A general hypothesis may now be suggested. From the superficial observation with which we began, it seems evident that the executive cannot merely "execute" in the dictionary sense; yet if he must therefore acquire and exercise a "personal power,"[30] the danger that it will swell into tyranny (for we find it convenient to speak of tyranny by its name) is equally obvious and just as much to be averted. Why the executive cannot merely "execute" should now be clearly stated, beyond what was said above in the executive's partisan argument, so that the necessary risk of tyranny may be fairly estimated.

An executive could execute the law dutifully and faithfully, without an insubordinate exercise of his own power, if the law were reasonable, that is, if it made all necessary distinctions and if its provisions did not omit anything that might make its intention impossible. For a reasonable law must be first exact and then self-sufficient or perfect. But in fact a law can be neither. It cannot be exact because it is addressed to human beings, who are recalcitrant to reason; and their recalcitrance, though by no means simply to be deplored, takes the form of a stubborn insistence that no matter how reasonable the law or how wise the lawgiver, *I* want to be able to say "no." Also, the right to say "no" is exercised often enough to prevent anyone from believing that the very human insistence on it is abstract or whimsical, no matter how abstract or whimsical any particular "no" may be. This insistence is responsible for the need to punish offenders against the law. Both needs compel the legislator to depart from exactness in making the law. In seeking consent for the law he must make it conform to what most men like, which is to some extent different from what is good for them; and in punishing offenders, he must make the punishments seem reasonable to most men, which is to some extent different from what is reasonable. For consent, he must define privileges according to what men like; and for punishment, he must define offenses according to what men will accept. Both needs, therefore, compel the legislator to depart from exactness in the direction of generality, either with a welcome to the undeserving claimant or with a denial to the deserving exception. Even the best law is always too general to be reasonable because it must defer to the human nay-sayer.

Human nay-saying arises from the brute fact that every human being has a separate body which constitutes his unshareable self-interest and his own care to a degree that can never be anyone else's. Someone else may be wiser than you, but since he cannot care for your body as much as you, and also must look out for his own, there is always the suspicion that his wisdom is not for your own good, and hence the insistence on a right of veto. To the nay-sayer, the generality of law will usually appear a more useful protection than the exactness of wisdom, and his suspicion is received as, or transformed into, prudence by the legislator. Now the separateness of human bodies, which makes the law inexact, also shows us its imperfection. For it would not matter that human bodies are separate if they were not mortal. Only the imminent return to ashes and dust makes us aware that we are not only surrounded by alien matter but actually encased in it. This material fact causes us to fear, and to regard the law's provisions for us, which to our vision reach only from cradle to grave, as quite inadequate. The claim of the law on our obedience because it takes care of us may seem nothing but a human boast,[31] and we are disposed to disobey when it seems necessary to us.

That the law cannot control nature is the fundamental cause of its injustice—for its generality is injustice when compared to exactness, and is justice only when compared to mere favoritism—and of its inability to remove fear. Since injustice and fear necessarily accompany law, law can be executed only with injustice and fear, with the injustice that institutes executive pride and majesty and with the fear that overcomes our recalcitrance. It must be said, then, that since some taint of tyranny necessarily accompanies law, law can be executed only with tyranny: for injustice and fear are the bases of tyranny.

It is only natural, and somewhat reasonable, to recoil from the extremism of this conclusion in shock or amusement as we contemplate, for instance, the necessary tyranny of Calvin Coolidge. From the American and other modern executives, the power to punish (originally considered an executive power even in the weak sense) has been substracted and given over in good part to an independent judiciary. There its tyrannizing is effectually concealed as "neither force nor will, but merely judgment" by judges who are checked by a jury so that punishment seems to come from one's peers.[32] And it might be urged that although naysaying to reasonable law is not reasonable, it is a not unreasonable response to the fact that men cannot help being unreasonable; and so too are the generality of the law and the (occasional) fearfulness of the executive. But this argument does not impugn the conclusion. It only gives us reason's reasons for coming to terms with unreason, whose human name is tyranny.

It is important to recognize that reason must come to terms with tyranny because there is more than one way to do it. To conclude this essay, two ways may be suggested by which political science, being unable to avoid tyranny, attempts to tame it and use it. The first is the way of Aristotelian political science, in which the political scientist takes the place of the tyrant and, so far as he can, transforms him from the destroyer of law into a king, the guardian of law. He does this as unobtrusively as he can, without making a public office of his task and without openly proclaiming the inadequacy of the law. The second remedy is originally Machiavelli's, though it had been substantially modified by the time that the American founders made use of it. This is to give open recognition to the necessity of tyranny in the character of the prince, who initiates and innovates, and at the same time to seek democratic sanction for his actions so that he may seem merely to execute the people's will. Later, chiefly by John Locke, the Machiavellian prince was regularized as an office, named the executive, and juxtaposed to the legislative power, in the ambivalence we recognize: now subordinate, now independent. In the deliberate construction of this ambivalence may be found the modern doctrine of executive power.

NOTES TO CHAPTER IX

1. See Charles C. Thach, *The Creation of the Presidency 1775–1789* (Baltimore: Johns Hopkins Press, 1923, reprinted 1969 with an introduction by Herbert J. Storing), which details the American experience available to the founders and concludes that neither British experience nor political philosophy had much to do with the "creation" of the American presidency.

2. I am grateful to Clifford W. Brown for help on this point.

3. Kant, *Metaphysik der Sitten, Rechtslehre*, II, 45.

4. J. C. Hamilton (ed.), *Works of Alexander Hamilton* (8 vols.; New York: C. S. Francis & Co., 1851), VII, 76–81; *Federalist*, No. 70.

5. Kant, *Metaphysik*, II, 48: the executive in the syllogism is a "person"; as coordinate, he is a "moral person." The question of executive power provides a useful vignette of Kant's political and moral philosophy.

6. Chester I. Barnard, *The Functions of the Executive* (Cambridge, Mass.: Harvard University Press, 1938), Ch. 16. For Barnard, "executive process" is the only way to speak of the executive's sense of the whole organization, but it is "non-logical." Similarly, one might find "the executive process" in Hobbes's definition of deliberation as an alternation of appetite and aversion; but the last appetite is called the will. Thomas Hobbes, *Leviathan*, ed. W. G. Pogson Smith (Oxford: Clarendon Press, 1909), Ch. 6, pp. 46–47.

7. Nor is C. Herman Pritchett, "The President's Constitutional Position," in Thomas E. Cronin and Rexford G. Tugwell (eds.), *The Presidency Reappraised* (2d ed.; New York: Praeger, 1977), 3–23. See also Richard M. Pious, *The American Presidency*

(New York: Basic Books, 1979), Ch. 1; this recent book deserves treatment among outstanding studies of the presidency. The phrase "literary theory" is from Walter Bagehot, quoted by Woodrow Wilson in *Congressional Government* (New York: World Publishing Co., 1956), 30, and used by Richard Neustadt, *Presidential Power* (New York: John Wiley & Sons, 1962), 43; see note 12 below.

8. Edward Corwin, *The President: Office and Powers 1787–1957* (4th ed., New York: New York University Press, 1957), 291.

9. Arthur M. Schlesinger, Jr., *The Imperial Presidency* (New York: Popular Library, 1973), 169.

10. Corwin, *The President*, 307.

11. Neustadt, *Presidential Power*, 7, 9–10, 179, 183; 198*n*; 31.

12. *Ibid.*, 33, 43. Perhaps the "literary theory" is not adequate to the forms of the Constitution if it means that the president should be a mere dictionary executive. But see the literary theory in *Federalist*, No. 47.

13. For Neustadt's book, first published in 1960, was recognized to be the most formative in the creation of what Thomas E. Cronin has called "the textbook presidency," which shows that even realism may be, indeed must be, formalized in a doctrine. Cronin, *The State of the Presidency* (Boston: Little, Brown & Co., 1975), Ch. 2.

14. Neustadt, *Presidential Power*, 38, 46.

15. James D. Barber, *The Presidential Character: Predicting Performance in the White House* (Englewood Cliffs, N.J.: Prentice Hall, 1972), 11; Erwin C. Hargrove, *Presidential Leadership: Personality and Political Style* (New York: Macmillan, 1966), 3. This active-positive executive, with characteristic executive ambivalence, frequently pops out of the matrix in which he is merely one among four possibilities to become the standard by which all executives are judged. *Cf.* James H. Qualls, "Barber's Typological Analysis of Political Leaders," *American Political Science Review*, LXXI (March, 1977), 192.

16. Hargrove, *Presidential Leadership*, 72.

17. Barber's book (published in 1972) is greatly influenced by his revulsion against American involvement in the Vietnam War, which helps him to equate political power with the power to persuade (447). This is an illusion that none of his "active-positive" presidents has shared. But besides this, his psychological method exerts a logical compulsion on him to find a psychological compulsion in his subjects that can be explained by his psychology. He must transform errors or dubieties of judgment into obsessions, and he must do this so stealthily that we do not suspect he is calling all American presidents crazy, even the active-positive ones. The assurance of his historical and biographical remarks is imposed on him by his method, which cannot explain a wrong choice if it was a mistake. See Alexander L. George, "Assessing Presidential Character," *World Politics*, XXVI (January, 1974), 275.

18. *Federalist*, No. 51.

19. See the account of Erwin C. Hargrove, "What Manner of Man?" in James D. Barber (ed.), *Choosing the President* (Englewood Cliffs, N.J.: Prentice Hall, 1974), 18.

20. Harold D. Lasswell, *Power and Personality* (New York: Viking, 1948), 54. See Aristotle, *Politics*, 1325a34–37.

21. Lasswell, *Power and Personality*, 108.

22. *Ibid.*, 9–16, 174, 181. Note how the discussion of power moves from the giving and taking of cues to something rather more punitive. *Cf.* Barber, note 17 above.

23. Lasswell, *Power and Personality*, 59–89. One should not miss his celebrated lively portraits of Judges X, Y, and Z, 64–87.

24. Hargrove, *Presidential Leadership*, 153.

25. M. J. C. Vile, *Constitutionalism and the Separation of Powers* (Oxford: Clarendon Press, 1967), 2, 17, 33–34, 101, 135, 143; W. B. Gwyn, *The Meaning of the Separation of Powers*, Tulane Studies in Political Science, IX (New Orleans: Tulane University, 1965), 26, 37, 108.

26. As Herbert J. Storing has said, "the administrative principle, while calling for the

executive's independence, implies executive subordination to the legislature; the political principle, on the other hand, implies an equality (if not, indeed, a superiority) of the executive in the constitutional scheme. The beginning of wisdom about the American Presidency is to see that it contains both principles and to reflect on their complex and subtle relation." Introduction to Thach, *The Creation of the Presidency*, vii. Also Doris Kearns: "The analytical problem is to understand not only where the president is too strong but also where he is too weak; to delineate what is meant by strong and weak and to describe the curious relationship between the two." "Lyndon Johnson's Political Personality," in Cronin and Tugwell, *The Presidency Reappraised*, 131. And see Edward S. Corwin, "Some Aspects of the Presidency," *Annals of the American Academy of Political and Social Science*, CCXVIII (November, 1941), 122–31.

27. *History of the Decline and Fall of the Roman Empire* (6 vols.; Everyman edition; New York: E. P. Dutton & Co., 1911), I, 1; *cf.* I, 370; IV, 131.

28. Sheldon S. Wolin, *Politics and Vision* (Boston: Little Brown, 1960), 221–24.

29. This is implied in Thomas E. Cronin, "The Presidency and Its Paradoxes," in Cronin and Tugwell, *The Presidency Reappraised*, 69–85; but one should consider whether the Constitution is indeed "of little help in explaining any of this" (69).

30. Neustadt, *Presidential Power*, vii.

31. Plato, *Crito*, 50d–51c.

32. *Federalist*, No. 78. For judicial power as "executive," see John Locke, *Two Treatises of Government*, Second Treatise, para. 130, Montesquieu, *De l'Esprit des Lois*, Bk. 11, Ch. 6 (beginning), and Niccolò Machiavelli, *The Prince*, Ch. 17 (beginning).

Appendix

CONSTITUTIONAL PROVISIONS RELATING
TO THE PRESIDENCY

ARTICLE I

Section 3

6. The Senate shall have the sole power to try all impeachments. When sitting for that purpose, they shall be on oath or affirmation. When the President of the United States is tried, the Chief Justice shall preside; and no person shall be convicted without the concurrence of two-thirds of the members present.

7. Judgment in cases of impeachment shall not extend further than to removal from office, and disqualification to hold and enjoy any office of honor, trust, or profit under the United States; but the party convicted shall, nevertheless, be liable and subject to indictment, trial, judgment, and punishment, according to law.

Section 7

2. Every bill which shall have passed the House of Representatives and the Senate shall, before it becomes a law, be presented to the President of the United States; if he approve he shall sign it, but if not he shall return it, with his objections, to that house in which it shall have originated, who shall enter the objections at large on their journal and proceed to reconsider it. If after such reconsideration two-thirds of that house shall agree to pass the bill, it shall be sent together with the objections, to the other house, by which it shall likewise be reconsidered and if approved by two-thirds of that house it shall become a law. But in all such cases the votes of both houses shall be determined by yeas and nays, and the names of the persons voting for and against the bill shall be entered on the journal of each house respectively. If any bill shall not be returned by the President within ten days (Sundays excepted) after it shall have been presented to him, the same shall be a law, in like manner as if he had signed it unless the Congress by their adjournment prevent its return, in which case it shall not be a law.

3. Every order, resolution, or vote to which the concurrence of the Senate and the House of Representatives may be necessary (except on a question of adjournment) shall be presented to the President of the United States; and before the same shall take effect, shall be approved by him, or being disapproved by him shall be repassed by two-thirds of

the Senate and House of Representatives, according to the rules and limitations prescribed in the case of a bill.

ARTICLE II

Section 1

1. The executive power shall be vested in a President of the United States of America. He shall hold his office during the term of four years, and, together with the Vice President, chosen for the same term, be elected as follows:

2. Each state shall appoint, in such manner as the legislature thereof may direct, a number of electors, equal to the whole number of Senators and Representatives to which the State may be entitled in the Congress; but no Senator or Representative, or person holding an office of trust or profit under the United States, shall be appointed an elector.

3* The electors shall meet in their respective states and vote by ballot for two persons, of whom one at least shall not be an inhabitant of the same state with themselves. And they shall make a list of all the persons voted for, and of the number of votes for each; which list they shall sign and certify, and transmit sealed to the seat of the government of the United States, directed to the President of the Senate. The President of the Senate shall, in the presence of the Senate and House of Representatives, open all the certificates, and the votes shall then be counted. The person having the greatest number of votes shall be the President, if such a number be a majority of the whole number of electors appointed; and if there be more than one who have such majority, and have an equal number of votes, then the House of Representatives shall immediately choose by ballot one of them for President; and if no person have a majority, then from the five highest on the list the said House shall in like manner choose the President. But in choosing the President the votes shall be taken by states, the representation from each state having one vote; a quorum for this purpose shall consist of a member or members from two-thirds of the states, and a majority of all the states shall be necessary to a choice. In every case, after the choice of the President, the person having the greatest number of votes of the electors shall be the Vice President. But if there should remain two or more who have equal votes, the Senate shall choose from them by ballot the Vice President.

4. The Congress may determine the time of choosing the electors and the day on which they shall give their votes, which day shall be the same throughout the United States.

5. No person except a natural born citizen, or a citizen of the United States at the time of the adoption of this Constitution, shall be eligible

---

* This paragraph was superseded by the Twelfth Amendment

to the office of President; neither shall any person be eligible to that office who shall not have attained to the age of thirty-five years, and been fourteen years a resident within the United States.

6* In case of the removal of the President from office, or of his death, resignation, or inability to discharge the powers and duties of the said office, the same shall devolve on the Vice President, and the Congress may by law provide for the case of removal, death, resignation, or inability, both of the President and Vice President, declaring what officer shall then act as President, and such officer shall act accordingly until the disability be removed or a President shall be elected.

7. The President shall, at stated times, receive for his services a compensation, which shall neither be increased nor diminished during the period for which he shall have been elected, and he shall not receive within that period any other emolument from the United States or any of them.

8. Before he enter on the execution of his office he shall take the following oath or affirmation:

I do solemnly swear (or affirm) that I will faithfully execute the office of President of the United States, and will to the best of my ability preserve, protect, and defend the Constitution of the United States.

Section 2

1. The President shall be Commander-in-Chief of the Army and Navy of the United States, and of the militia of the several states when called into the actual service of the United States; he may require the opinion, in writing, of the principal officer in each of the executive departments, upon any subject relating to the duties of their respective offices, and he shall have power to grant reprieves and pardons for offenses against the United States, except in cases of impeachment.

2. He shall have power, by and with the advice and consent of the Senate, to make treaties, provided two-thirds of the Senators present concur; and he shall nominate, and, by and with the advice and consent of the Senate, shall appoint ambassadors, other public ministers and consuls, judges of the Supreme Court, and all other officers of the United States, whose appointments are not herein otherwise provided for, and which shall be established by law; but the Congress may by law vest the appointment of such inferior officers, as they think proper, in the President alone, in the courts of law, or in the heads of departments.

3. The President shall have power to fill up all vacancies that may happen during the recess of the Senate, by granting commissions which shall expire at the end of their next session.

---

* This paragraph was modified by the Twenty-fifth Amendment

Section 3

He shall from time to time give to the Congress information of the state of the union, and recommend to their consideration such measures as he shall judge necessary and expedient; he may, on extraordinary occasions, convene both houses, or either of them, and in case of disagreement between them with respect to the time of adjournment, he may adjourn them to such time as he shall think proper; he shall receive ambassadors and other public ministers; he shall take care that the laws be faithfully executed, and shall commission all the officers of the United States.

Section 4

The President, Vice President, and all civil officers of the United States shall be removed from office on impeachment for and conviction of treason, bribery, or other high crimes and misdemeanors.

AMENDMENT XII

The electors shall meet in their respective states and vote by ballot for President and Vice President, one of whom, at least, shall not be an inhabitant of the same state with themselves; they shall name in their ballots the person voted for as President, and in distinct ballots the person voted for as Vice President, and they shall make distinct lists of all persons voted for as President and of all persons voted for as Vice President, and of the number of votes for each; which lists they shall sign and certify, and transmit sealed to the seat of the government of the United States, directed to the President of the Senate. The President of the Senate shall, in the presence of the Senate and House of Representatives, open all the certificates and the votes shall then be counted. The person having the greatest number of votes for President shall be the President, if such number be a majority of the whole number of electors appointed; and if no person have such majority, then from the persons having the highest numbers not exceeding three on the list of those voted for as President, the House of Representatives shall choose immediately, by ballot, the President. But in choosing the President the votes shall be taken by states, the representation from each state having one vote; a quorum for this purpose shall consist of a member or members from two-thirds of the states, and a majority of all states shall be necessary to a choice. And if the House of Representatives shall not choose a President whenever the right of choice shall devolve upon them, before the fourth day of March next following, then the Vice President shall act as President, as in the case of the death or other constitutional disability of the President.

The person having the greatest number of votes as Vice President shall be the Vice President, if such number be a majority of the whole number of electors appointed; and if no person have a majority, then from the two highest numbers on the list the Senate shall choose the Vice President; a quorum for the purpose shall consist of two-thirds of the whole number of Senators, and a majority of the whole number shall be necessary to a choice. But no person constitutionally ineligible to the office of President shall be eligible to that of Vice President of the United States.

AMENDMENT XX

Section 1

The terms of the President and Vice President shall end at noon on the 20th day of January, and the terms of Senators and Representatives at noon on the 3rd day of January, of the years in which such terms would have ended if this article had not been ratified; and the terms of their successors shall then begin.

Section 2

The Congres₃ shall assemble at least once in every year, and such meeting shall begin at noon on the 3rd day of January, unless they shall by law appoint a different day.

Section 3

If, at the time fixed for the beginning of the term of the President, the President elect shall have died, the Vice President elect shall become President. If a President shall not have been chosen before the time fixed for the beginning of his term, or if the President elect shall have failed to qualify, then the Vice President elect shall act as President until a President shall have qualified; and the Congress may by law provide for the case wherein neither a President elect nor a Vice President elect shall have qualified, declaring who shall then act as President, or the manner in which one who is to act shall be selected, and such person shall act accordingly until a President or Vice President shall have qualified.

Section 4

The Congress may by law provide for the case of the death of any of the persons from whom the House of Representatives may choose a President whenever the right of choice shall have devolved upon them, and for the case of the death of any of the persons from whom the Senate may choose a Vice President whenever the right of choice shall have devolved upon them.

AMENDMENT XXII

No person shall be elected to the office of the President more than twice, and no person who has held the office of President, or acted as President, for more than two years of a term to which some other person was elected President shall be elected to the office of the President more than once. But this article shall not apply to any person holding the office of President when this article was proposed by the Congress, and shall not prevent any person who may be holding the office of President, or acting as President, during the term within which this article becomes operative from holding the office of President or acting as President during the remainder of such term.

AMENDMENT XXIII

Section 1

The District constituting the seat of Government of the United States shall appoint in such manner as the Congress may direct:

A number of electors of President and Vice President equal to the whole number of Senators and Representatives in Congress to which the District would be entitled if it were a State, but in no event more than the least populous State; they shall be in addition to those appointed by the States but they shall be considered, for the purposes of the election of President and Vice President, to be electors appointed by a State; and they shall meet in the District and perform such duties as provided by the twelfth article of amendment.

Section 2

The Congress shall have power to enforce this article by appropriate legislation.

AMENDMENT XXIV

Section 1

The right of citizens of the United States to vote in any primary or other election for President or Vice-President, or for Senator or Representative in Congress, shall not be denied or abridged by the United States or any State by reason of failure to pay any poll tax or other tax.

Section 2

The Congress shall have the power to enforce this article by appropriate legislation.

AMENDMENT XXV

Section 1

In case of a removal of the President from office or of his death or resignation, the Vice President shall become President.

Section 2

Whenever there is a vacancy in the office of the Vice President, the President shall nominate a Vice President who shall take office upon confirmation by a majority vote of both Houses of Congress.

Section 3

Whenever the President transmits to the President pro tempore of the Senate and the Speaker of the House of Representatives his written declaration that he is unable to discharge the powers and duties of his office, and until he transmits to them a written declaration to the contrary, such powers and duties shall be discharged by the Vice President as Acting President.

Section 4

Whenever the Vice President and a majority of either the principal officers of the executive department or of such other body as Congress may by law provide, transmit to the President pro tempore of the Senate and the Speaker of the House of Representatives their written declaration that the President is unable to discharge the powers and duties of his office, the Vice President shall immediately assume the powers and duties of the office as Acting President.

Thereafter, when the President transmits to the President pro tempore of the Senate and the Speaker of the House of Representatives his written declaration that no inability exists, he shall resume the powers and duties of his office unless the Vice President and a majority of either the principal officers of the executive department or of such other body as Congress may by law provide, transmit within four days to the President pro tempore of the Senate and the Speaker of the House of Representatives their written declaration that the President is unable to discharge the power and duties of his office. Thereupon Congress shall decide the issue, assembling within forty-eight hours for that purpose if not in session. If the Congress, within twenty-one days after receipt of the latter written declaration, or, if Congress is not in session, within twenty-one days after Congress is required to assemble, determines by two-thirds vote of both Houses that the President is unable to discharge the powers and duties of his office, the Vice President shall continue to discharge the same as Acting President; otherwise, the President shall resume the powers and duties of his office.

Contributors

JOSEPH M. BESSETTE is assistant professor of political science, Catholic University of America. At the time he co-edited this book, Mr. Bessette was acting director of the Program on the Presidency and research associate at the White Burkett Miller Center of Public Affairs, University of Virginia.

JAMES CEASER is associate professor of government and foreign affairs, University of Virginia.

MURRAY DRY is professor of political science, Middlebury College.

HARVEY FLAUMENHAFT is a tutor on the faculty of St. Johns College, Annapolis, Maryland.

RUTH WEISSBOURD GRANT and STEPHEN GRANT are Ph.D. candidates in the Department of Political Science, University of Chicago.

HARVEY C. MANSFIELD, JR., is professor of government at Harvard University.

GARY J. SCHMITT prepared his study while serving as a research associate at the White Burkett Miller Center of Public Affairs. He is currently on the staff of the Senate Select Committee on Intelligence.

ROBERT SCIGLIANO is professor of political science at Boston College. While preparing his study for this volume he was senior scholar in residence at the White Burkett Miller Center of Public Affairs.

JEFFREY TULIS co-edited this volume while serving as research associate at the White Burkett Miller Center of Public Affairs, University of Virginia. He is currently an assistant professor of politics at Princeton University.

Index

345